Sir Thomas More

by E. E. REYNOLDS

Published for The British Council
and the National Book League
by Longmans, Green & Co.

Two shillings and sixpence net

This essay is concerned not with Sir Thomas More's political ideas or his religious convictions, but with his considerable literary achievement. More's lifelong friendship with the great Dutch humanist, Erasmus, brought him into the mainstream of continental scholarship, and *Utopia* —which was not, Mr. Reynolds shows, a picture of an ideal state, but a dramatic criticism of contemporary society—brought him European fame. Others of More's writings repay study: the unfinished *History of King Richard III*, for example, was a notable innovation. It was an attempt without precedent in the English language at a historical narrative, marked by a high standard of dramatic evocation. More's love of learning was matched by his longing for the cloister, and the meditations he wrote were widely known and used for long after his death. They reflect More's profound religious faith, infused with their author's gentle compassion, intelligence and wit.

E. E. Reynolds is President of the Amici Thomae Mori, and also a member of the Advisory Committee for the Yale edition of More's works. He is author of *Saint Thomas More* (1953), *Margaret Roper* (1960), and *Trial of St. Thomas More* (1964).

Bibliographical Series
of Supplements to 'British Book News'
on Writers and Their Work

★

GENERAL EDITOR
Geoffrey Bullough

Tho: Moor L.ᵉ Chancelour

SIR THOMAS MORE

from a drawing of 1526 by Hans Holbein *in the Windsor Castle Collection
reproduced by gracious permission of H.M. the Queen*

SIR THOMAS MORE

by

E. E. REYNOLDS

PUBLISHED FOR
THE BRITISH COUNCIL
AND THE NATIONAL BOOK LEAGUE
BY LONGMANS, GREEN & CO.

LONGMANS, GREEN & CO. LTD.
48 Grosvenor Street, London, W.1

*Associated companies, branches and
representatives throughout the world*

First published 1965
© E. E. Reynolds, 1965

*Printed in Great Britain by
F. Mildner & Sons, London, E.C.1*

CONTENTS

CONTENTS

SIR THOMAS MORE

SIR Thomas More's political ideas, his religious convictions and the crisis of conscience that led to his martyrdom in 1535, are not the concern of this essay; they cannot be completely separated from a consideration of his work for they were the essence of his life, but the emphasis in these pages will be placed on his literary achievement.

I. LIFE

Thomas More, the son of a lawyer, was born in London in 1478. He was educated at St. Anthony's School and in Cardinal Morton's household, followed by two years at Oxford. His legal training began in 1494 and he was called to the Bar at Lincoln's Inn in 1501. For a time he felt drawn to the contemplative life in the Charterhouse, but found that he had no vocation. He was learned in Latin and Greek and in the works of the Early Fathers; he gave public lectures on St. Augustine. Among his close friends were John Colet, William Grocin, William Lily, William Latimer and Thomas Linacre, all of whom had studied in Italy. In 1499 he met Erasmus and they became lifelong friends. More was elected to Parliament in 1504 and in the following year he married Jane Colt. They made their home in Bucklersbury. There were four children: Margaret, Elizabeth, Cecily and John. More became an Under-Sheriff of London in 1510 and was again returned to Parliament. Jane More died in 1511, and he then married a widow, Alice Middleton; her daughter Alice, Margaret More's foster-sister Margaret Giggs, and a ward Anne Cresacre became members of the family and were educated with More's children under his direction. Others joined them to form what has been called More's School. No distinction was made between boys and girls.

More soon gained a reputation with the City Companies for his legal ability and for his skill in negotiations; he was also in demand as a Latin orator at official receptions. His services were used on a commercial embassy to Flanders in 1516, and again to Calais a year later. So successful was he that, reluctantly, he became a member of the King's Council in 1517. The king and queen enjoyed his conversation so much that he accompanied them to their various manors and, for a time, acted as the king's secretary. His learning and wit made him a delightful companion. He was present at the Field of Cloth of Gold in 1520, and, in the following year, was made Under-Treasurer and was knighted. His daughter Margaret married William Roper in 1521, and they, with her sisters and brother when they married, all formed what was a patriarchal household.

Thomas More became Speaker of the House of Commons in 1523; other honours that came to him at this period were his appointment as Chancellor of the Duchy of Lancaster and as High Steward of both Universities. By 1524 his household had outgrown the home in Bucklersbury, so he built a new house at Chelsea. On two occasions he accompanied Wolsey on important embassies, in 1521 to Calais and in 1527 to Amiens. His last embassy was in 1529 when, with his friend Cuthbert Tunstal, he shared in the negotiations that resulted in the Peace of Cambrai. Meanwhile, the king had asked his support in his divorce proceedings, but More felt unable to agree with the king's opinion. In spite of this, he succeeded Wolsey as Lord Chancellor on 23 October 1529. The divorce proceedings made the office burdensome and he resigned on 16 May 1532. When the Act of Succession was passed early in 1534, he refused to take the oath, as it implied a repudiation of papal authority. He was sent to the Tower on 17 April 1534. During his fifteen months' imprisonment, the king assumed the title of Supreme Head of the Church of England. As More could not accept this break from the Roman See, he was indicted under a new Act of Treason for refusing to the king one of his titles. He was tried on 1 July 1535 and was executed five days later. The Roman Catholic Church canonized him in 1935.

II. EARLY WRITINGS

In his character sketch of his friend Thomas More, Erasmus tells us that, 'as a young man he wrote and acted in some little comedies. He rejoices in brilliant sallies, seasoned with true wit, and a clever retort delights him, even when against himself. Hence it was that in youth he amused himself composing epigrams and took special pleasure in Lucian. His first years were given to poetry. Then for a long time he worked hard to acquire a flexible prose style, making experiments of all kinds.' Those 'little comedies' have not survived, but when he was a boy in Cardinal Morton's household he was noted for his ready improvisations in Interludes; this characteristic was preserved in London legend in the unacted Elizabethan play, *The Booke of Sir Thomas Moore*.

The epigrams were translated from Greek into Latin and in these he vied with his friend and fellow-student, William Lily, the first high-master of St. Paul's School. More and Erasmus were both attracted to Lucian and they translated into Latin several of the dialogues. The satire, the mockery and fantastic humour of Lucian were congenial to them, and his influence can be traced in much of their work, notably in *The Praise of Folly*, and *Utopia*. This devotion to classical studies places More in the group of Christian humanists who were his friends.

Some of More's English verses have been preserved but they rarely rise above mediocrity. The best poem is *A ruful lamentacion* on the death of Henry VII's Queen in 1503. It takes the form of a monologue by the dying woman:

Adew myne owne dere spouse, my worthy lorde,
The faithfull love, that dyd us both combyne,
In mariage and peasable concorde,
Into your handes here I cleane resyne,
To be bestowed uppon your children and myne,
Erst wer you father, & now, must ye supply,
The mothers part also, for lo now here I ly.

In this poem and in a number of others, More used Chaucer's seven line stanza (later known as rime royal), but frequently with six instead of five accented syllables in the last line. In the *English Works* of 1557 his verses are described as having been written 'in his youth for his pastime', but I suspect his hand in *Twelve Merry Jests of one called Edyth* printed in 1525 by his brother-in-law, John Rastell, and ascribed to Walter Smyth, More's personal servant.

It is interesting to recall that Dr. Johnson, in the 'History of the English Language' prefaced to his Dictionary, gave over eight folio pages out of twenty-seven to extracts from More; a long passage from *Richard III* filled three pages, but no fewer than five were from these early poems. Johnson's concern was with the vocabulary, not the quality, of the verses. Such a selection seems strange to us, but it points to what may be called their Englishness. They show no classical influences. More's liking for the Chaucerian stanza has been noted; there are a number of references in his books to Chaucer and there are echoes of Chaucerian phrases. This stanza was also favoured by John Skelton, and More's *Merry Jest* is written in a verse form more regular than the Skeltonic but with the same lively movement:

> It happed so,
> Not long a go,
> A thrifty man there dyed,
> An hundred pounde,
> Of nobles rounde,
> That had he layd a side:
> His sonne he wolde,
> Should have this golde,
> For to beginne with all:
> But to suffise
> His chylde, well thrise,
> That money was to smal.

To what extent More and Skelton were acquainted is not known; the only record of their meeting also brings Erasmus and More together for the first time; this was in the summer of 1499. Skelton was then tutor to Henry, Duke of York, and More took Erasmus to Eltham to present him to the Duke.

When Erasmus heard of the execution of Thomas More thirty-five years later, he exclaimed, 'I feel as if I had died with More so closely were our two souls united'. It was a fruitful friendship. There was not only the stimulus of contact between two men of keen intelligence and quick wit, but More was brought into the main stream of European scholarship, and his circle of friends was extended. It was during Erasmus' second visit to England in 1505 that the two friends made their translations from Lucian. A collection of these was published in Paris in 1506; they were reprinted nine times during More's lifetime. Another translation, this time into English, had probably been made a few years earlier, but it was not published until about 1510. This was a free adaptation of a Latin life of Pico della Mirandola (1463-1494). More was attracted to this young Italian humanist because they shared a love of learning and a longing for the cloister which neither was able to satisfy. The book also included translations of some of Pico's letters, and some verses, again in Chaucerian stanzas, composed by More on themes suggested by Pico's writings. More's prose had not yet freed itself from the influence of classical rhetoric, and, while the verses have lost some of the early raciness, they had a more serious intention.

Among More's 'experiments' mentioned by Erasmus, may be included the unfinished *History of King Richard the Third*, written about 1513. The first reliable text was published in the *English Works* in 1557, with this note, 'which worke hath bene before this tyme printed in Hardynges Chronicle and in Hallys Chronicle: but very muche corrupte in many places'. In the Hardynge-Grafton Chronicle (1543) *Richard III* appeared anonymously; in Hall's Chronicle (1548) the author's name was given, as it was also in Holinshed's Chronicle (1577) which followed the text of 1557. More also wrote a Latin version, and the indications are that he worked on both concurrently. The 'experiment' here was in historical narrative with perhaps Sallust in mind. For such a purpose More had excellent material in hand. As a boy he had lived through the reign of Richard III and he could recall stories told by Cardinal Morton; best of all, he could draw upon the recollections of his own father and those of his contemporaries, some of whom had held office under Richard. The influence of classical rhetoric is early shown in the invented declamation 'The Oration of the King in his Death-bed', but as the writer gets into the swing of his narrative and begins to enjoy the story he is telling, so the classical pattern becomes less discernable. Much has been written on the derivation of More's prose, but any discussion must be largely speculative as we know so little about his reading in English. We know more of his classical and patristic studies, but there are few references in his books to native prose literature. We know that he had read the works of such spiritual writers as Richard Rolle and Walter Hilton, but had he read Caxton's translations, or Malory? The question cannot be answered, nor perhaps does it matter very much since he was attempting an historical narrative for which there was no close precedent in English. The Chronicles were pedestrian records and there was no vernacular tradition of historical biography. English prose was still in its formative stage and More had therefore to follow his own genius both in form and expression. The result was a notable innovation. It was a great loss that he did not complete his book; indeed he had something more ambitious in mind, for he hinted that he might write of 'the time of the late noble Prince of famous memory King Henry the Seventh, or percase that history of Perkin [Warbeck]'.

This is not the place to discuss the value of *Richard III* as history; there are some errors of fact but More used to the full his chance of talking with those who had played their parts in those dangerous times, and he could therefore record the oral tradition while it was still forming. His view of Richard was the popularly accepted one, and it was adopted and perpetuated by Shakespeare, and no amount of research seems able to destroy it.

The narrative moves easily but an occasional unevenness comes when a long and involved sentence is used in explaining policy or the significance of events. It soon becomes clear that More is happiest when he is recording action or writing dialogue, when, that is, he is writing dramatically. This is apparent in many scenes. There is, for instance, the account of the meeting between Queen Elizabeth and Cardinal Bourchier when she resisted as long as she could the request that she should allow her younger son to leave sanctuary at Westminster to join his brother. At last she gave way:

And therewithal she said unto the child: 'Farewell, my own sweet son, God send you good keeping. Let me kiss you once yet ere you go, for God knoweth when we shall kiss together again.' And therewith she kissed him and blessed him, turned her back and wept and went her way, leaving the child weeping as fast.

When the Lord Cardinal and these other lords with him had received this young Duke, they brought him into the Star Chamber, where the Protector took him in his arms and kissed him, with these words: 'Now welcome, my lord, even with all my very heart.' And he said in that of likelihood as he thought. Thereupon forthwith they brought him to the King, his brother, unto the Bishop's Palace at Paul's, and from thence through the city honourably into the Tower—out of which after that day they never came abroad.

More's sense of the comic is uppermost in such an incident as Dr. Shaw's sermon at St. Paul's Cross. This had been planned to lead up to the appearance of Richard, but Shaw misjudged the timing and when he gave the cue, 'This is the father's own figure', Richard failed to answer it; so Shaw had to carry on as best he could, and when the Protector at last arrived, the preacher repeated the cue.

But the people were so far from crying 'King Richard!' that they stood as they had been turned into stones, for wonder of this shameful sermon. After which once ended, the preacher got him home and never after durst look out for shame but keep him out of sight like an owl.

A sense of pity is shown in the account of Jane Shore, Edward IV's last mistress:

I doubt not some shall think this woman too slight a thing to be written of and set among the remembrances of great matters: which they shall specially think, that haply shall esteem her only by that they now see her. But meseemeth the chance so much the more worthy to be remembered, in how much she is now in more beggarly condition, unfriended and worn out of acquaintance, after good substance, after as great favour with the Prince, after as great suit and seeking to with all those that those days had business to speed, as many other men were in their times, which be now famous only by the infamy of their ill deeds. Her doings were not much less, albeit they be much less remembered because they were not so evil. For men use, if they have an evil turn, to write it in marble; and who so doth us a good turn, we write it in dust: which is not worst proved by her, for at this day she beggeth of many at this day living, that at this day had begged if she had not been.

More had gone some way towards forming a personal style. His liking for alliteration may be noted. 'Men mused what the matter meant.' 'People diversely divining upon this dealing.' 'Wise ways to win favours.' At times he achieved epigrammatic quality and he could use antithetic phrasing:

Every man answered him fair, as though no man mistrusted the matter which, of truth, no man believed.

Very faithful and trusty enough, trusting too much.

George, Duke of Clarence, was a goodly noble prince, and at all points fortunate, if either his own ambition had not set him against his brother, or the envy of his enemies, his brother against him.

Richard III should be regarded not so much as an historical inquiry as a dramatic evocation.

III.   *UTOPIA* AND *THE FOUR LAST THINGS*

Between 1513 and 1529 More's writings, apart from official letters, were in Latin, with the exception of another unfinished manuscript, *A Treatise on the Four Last Things*. He leapt into European fame by the publication of *Utopia* at the end of 1516. The third edition (Basle, 1518) also contained More's *Epigrams*. *Utopia* was in Latin, but as his name and the title of the book have become almost synonymous, it is impossible to ignore *Utopia* in a consideration of his position as an English author. Moreover the book drew the attention of the learned world to the fact that there were scholars even in England! Books written by Englishmen and circulating in Europe were rare, and one of the services More did for his country was to make it more widely known. *Utopia* was not translated into English until 1551, sixteen years after More's death, by Ralph Robinson. His work cannot be included among the outstanding Tudor translations, but it has held its own, and most people know the book in this version. The only rival is the more accurate rendering by Bishop Gilbert Burnet, first published in 1684 and frequently reprinted. The book was written in Latin because More was addressing himself to the learned world and in his day a knowledge of English was a rare accomplishment. It is to our loss that he did not produce a parallel version in English as he had done for *Richard III*.

The book has proved a stimulus to political thought but some queer ideas have been fathered on More that would have astonished and amused him. Some of those who have found what they were seeking in *Utopia*, have ignored its form and intention. Erasmus, who was staying with More when the First Book was being written, had no doubt of the author's purpose. He urged a friend to read the book 'if you ever want to see the sources from which almost all the ills of the body politic arise'. *Utopia* is not a Utopia! The word has come to mean an ideal state, but we must not read that meaning into More's intention. In describing an imagined state, he was criticizing contemporary society. The form is dramatic. The First Book is a dialogue, and the Second a monologue or discourse by the fictional Hythlodaye; it is therefore as hazardous to deduce More's own opinions from *Utopia* as it is to deduce those of Shakespeare from his plays. We must make allowance for the dramatic irony and for More's love of fun. Those who ignore these Lucianic elements soon get into difficulties and some over-solemn interpreters have been more amusing than convincing. An instance of the danger of taking seriously everything More wrote is worth giving. *Utopia* is prefaced by a dedicatory letter to Peter Gilles of Antwerp, who was the friend of More and Erasmus. He figures in the dialogue. In his letter More asked if his friend could recall what Hythlodaye said about the position of Utopia, as a learned divine wished to go there as a missionary. Gilles entered into the spirit of More's letter and replied that unfortunately he could not help as he had had a fit of coughing just when Hythlodaye was telling them the situation of the island. Ralph Robinson solemnly added a note that the divine was Rowland Philips, the Vicar of Croydon. Robinson shows no trace of a sense of humour and he failed to see the joke, and he was not the last to do so.

Utopia was an island where everything was owned in common under an elected magistracy. Great care was given to the education of the children and of their parents, no distinction being made between the sexes. Each man was taught a trade, but life was divided between town and country so that all shared in work on the land. The houses had gardens and the towns were well planned and sanitary. Hospitals were provided for the sick and aged. They had no use for money and despised personal adornment. The Utopians were deists who believed in immortality; their few priests were carefully chosen and could marry. All forms of religion were respected, but if anyone caused civil disturbance by the violence of his advocacy, he was banished or made a slave. Games and sports, but not hunting, were encouraged, and all were trained in military exercises, but they preferred to employ mercenaries in their wars, which were defensive only.

This bare outline of the polity of Utopia is sufficient to indicate the problems that arise as soon as the details are studied; these problems have been discussed by many commentators, but cannot be adequately considered here.

Those who are bored with descriptions of imaginary disciplined states will find that the First Book of *Utopia* has qualities of its own. The greater part is devoted to two topics: why do men become thieves, and, should a philosopher take service under a prince? The first reflects More's experience as an Under-Sheriff, or magistrate, in London during the previous five years when he had to deal summarily with the rogues and vagabonds of the City. The second was an immediate problem, as, following More's success in an embassy to the Low Countries, during which he had written the Second Book of *Utopia*, Wolsey suggested that he should become a King's Counsel, which would mean putting himself at the service of the Crown. The discussions in the First Book of *Utopia* probably reflected conversations with Erasmus, who was strongly opposed to More concerning himself with 'the busy trifles of princes', as this would prevent him from contributing to the advance of 'bonae litterae'. For the time being More refused the invitation, but, after another successful embassy in 1517, he agreed to become a King's Counsel. As Erasmus predicted, this meant that More had little leisure for scholarship. In 1520 he published a long letter in Latin to a monk who had attacked Erasmus, after which there was a silence of nine years, save for the unfinished *Four Last Things* written in 1522 but not printed until after his death.

This meditation, as it may be described, on Death, Judgement, Heaven and Hell was written for his children and other young people who formed his 'school'; they were now growing up and Margaret had just married William Roper. She also wrote on the same theme but her work is not extant. *The Four Last Things* is the most sombre of More's writings and, though there are passing references to Cicero and Plutarch, it shows little trace of classical influence. We think of More as a Christian humanist, but he cannot be confined to a pigeon-hole. This work is as mediaeval as the Dance of Death painted on the cloister walls of St. Paul's. As we read, we are reminded of the hellfire sermons of the friars. The nearest contemporary parallel was the series of sermons on *The Penitential Psalms* preached by his friend Bishop John Fisher and one of the popular devotional books of the day.

More did not complete his consideration of even the first subject, Death; he discussed the sins of pride, envy, covetousness, gluttony, and, in part, sloth, and then broke off. Had he carried out his intention on the same scale, he would have produced a substantial volume. The text was taken from Ecclesiastes, 'Remember the last things, and thou shalt never sin', but for the portion that was finished the appropriate text would have been, *Sic transit gloria mundi*. Grim as it is, the meditation abounds, as all More's work does, with images drawn from common life:

If thou shouldst perceive that one were earnestly proud of the wearing of the gay golden gown, while the lorel [rogue] playeth the lord in a stage play, wouldst thou not laugh at his folly, considering that thou art very sure that when the play is done he shall go walk a knave in his old coat? Now thou thinkest thyself wise enough while thou art proud in thy player's garment, and forgettest that when thy play is done, though shalt go forth as poor as he. Nor thou rememberest not that thy pageant may happen to be done as soon as his.

We shall leave the example of plays and players which be too merry for this matter. I shall put thee a more earnest image of our condition, and that not feigned similitude but a very true fashion and figure of our worshipful state. Mark this well, for of this thing we be very sure, that old and young, man and woman, rich and poor, prince and page, all the while we live in this world we be but prisoners, and be within a sure prison, out of which there can no man escape. And in worse case be we than those that be taken and imprisoned for theft. For they, albeit their heart heavily harkeneth after the sessions, yet have they some hope either to break prison the while, or to escape there by favour, or after condemnation some hope of pardon. But we stand all in other plight: we be very sure that we be already condemned to death, some one, some other, none of us can tell what death we be doomed to, but surely can we all tell that die we shall.

Even the humour can be grim:

Think ye not now that it will be a gentle pleasure, when we lie dying, all our body in pain, all our mind in trouble, our soul in sorrow, our heart all in dread while our life walketh awayward, while our death draweth toward, while the devil is busy about us, while we lack stomach and strength to bear any one of so manifold heinous troubles, will it not be, as I was about to say, a pleasant thing to see before thine eyes and hear at thine ear a rabble of fleshly friends or rather of flesh flies, skipping about thy bed and thy sick body, like ravens about thy corpse, now almost carrion, crying to thee on every side, 'What shall I have? What shall I have?' Then shall come thy children and cry for their parts; then shall come thy sweet wife, and where in thine health haply she spake thee not one sweet word in six weeks, now shall she call thee sweet husband and weep with much work and ask thee what she shall have; then shall thine executors ask for the keys, and ask what money is owing thee, ask what substance thou hast, and ask where thy money lieth. And while thou liest in that case, their words shall be so tedious that thou wilt wish all that they ask for upon a red fire, so thou mightest lie one half hour in rest.

The Four Last Things reminds us that the mainspring of Thomas More's life was a profound religious faith; it explains his thoughts of becoming a Carthusian monk, the chapel he built at Chelsea, his service at the altar, the hair-shirt he wore, and his death.

IV.   CONTROVERSIAL WRITINGS

More may have left this meditation unfinished because he was called upon to defend Henry VIII against Luther, who in 1520 had finally broken from Rome by, among other writings, his pamphlet entitled *The Babylonish Captivity of the Church*, in which he argued that contrary to Catholic teaching there were three, not seven, sacraments. Henry VIII decided to reply to Luther; his book *Assertio Septem Sacramentorum* was published in 1521; it was for this that the Pope conferred on the royal author the title of Defender of the Faith. It was not a recondite argument but a statement that a well-instructed layman, as the king was, could write. After the theologians had read the manuscript, the king asked Thomas More to edit the book and see it through the press. Luther replied in terms that were unusually scurrilous even for those days. It was beneath the dignity of the king to notice such an attack, so More answered it under the pseudonym of Gulielmus Rosseus; his reply was published in 1523. We need not here discuss the controversy, but it has its importance because it marked the opening of a new phase in More's writings. From that date until he went to the Tower in 1534, his writings were controversial, all, happily, written in English. He was not, however, closely involved until 1528 when his old friend Cuthbert Tunstal, Bishop of London, urged him to undertake the defence of the Church against Lutheranism. William Tyndale's translation of the New Testament was smuggled into England in 1526, to be followed two years later by his *Obedience of a Christian Man*. So Tunstal wrote to Thomas More:

Because, dear brother, you are able to rival Demosthenes in our vernacular tongue no less than in Latin, you cannot spend your leisure hours, if you can steal any from your official duties, better than in writing in our own language such books as may show simple and unlearned men the cunning malice of these heretics.

The first fruit of this labour was *A Dialogue of Sir Thomas More . . . Wherein be treated divers matters . . . with many things touching the pestilent sect of Luther and Tyndale*. This was printed by his brother-in-law, John Rastell, and published in June 1529, six months before Sir Thomas More became

Lord Chancellor. The original title was shortened in the *English Works* of 1557 to *A Dialogue concerning heresies and matters of religion.*

This *Dialogue* is the most readable of More's controversial works and the nearest to Tunstal's suggestion that it should be addressed to the 'simple and unlearned'. He was able to write it in the comparative leisure of the period before he was burdened by the duties of high office and was not yet oppressed by the problems created by the king's desire to break his marriage and to control the Church in England.

More imagines that a friend has sent him an inquirer, the tutor of his sons, who is perturbed by the teaching of Luther and wishes to discuss the doubts that have come into his mind. So the book takes the form of a dialogue between More and this Messenger, carried on partly in More's study and partly in his garden. A fortnight elapsed between Book Two and Book Three; during this interval the Messenger discussed his problems with an old university friend. There is no problem here, as in *Utopia*, of distinguishing More's views for he speaks in his own person. It is a true dialogue since the Messenger is allowed to put his points fully; he is not invented simply to put up a series of Aunt Sallies to be knocked down, though, inevitably, in the end he is persuaded that Luther and Tyndale were heretics. Indeed, anyone who wishes to understand the opening phases of the Catholic-Protestant dispute cannot do better than read this contemporary record written before the atmosphere became too warm for calm discussion. The tone is genial and the argument is persuasive. The following passage illustrates the freedom allowed to the Messenger, and will serve also as an example of More's style:

Surely the thing that maketh in this matter the clergy most suspect, and wherein, as it seemeth, it would be full hard to excuse them is this, that they not only damn Tyndale's translation (wherein there is good cause) but over that do damn all other, and as though a layman were no Christian man, will suffer no layman to have any at all. But when they find any in his keeping, they lay heresy to him therefore. And thereupon they burn up the book, and sometime the good man withal, alleging for the defence of their doing a law of their own making and constitution provincial, whereby they have prohibited that any man shall have any upon pain of heresy. And this is a law very provincial, for it holdeth but here. For in all other countries of Christendom the people have the scripture translated into their own tongue, and the clergy there findeth no such fault therein. Wherefore either our people be worst of all people, or else our clergy is worst of all clergies. But, by my troth, for ought I can see here, or perceive by them that have been elsewhere, our lay people be as good and as honest as be anywhere. And if any be otherwise, the occasion and example cometh of the clergy, among whom we see much more vice than among ourself. Whereas they should give us an example of virtue and the light of learning, now their examples, what they be, we see. And as for learning, they neither will teach us but seldom and that shall be but such things as pleaseth them, some glosses of their own making, nor suffer us to learn by ourself, but by their constitution pull Christ's gospel out of Christian people's hands, I cannot well see why, but lest we should see the truth.

More's style is uneven; he can get involved in long sentences that need close reading. At the end of this *Dialogue*, for instance, there is a sentence of seven hundred and fifty words that leaves the reader breathless. This may be paralleled with a six hundred word sentence in Latin to be found in *Utopia*. Both are exceptionally long but they show the irregular quality of More's prose. One who wrote Latin with ease, as More did, was inevitably influenced by its syntax when turning to the vernacular. It was when he was writing narrative that More was able to use his native language most effectively. An example of this occurs early in this *Dialogue*. The Messenger alleged that some miracles were fraudulent. More agreed, and in illustration told the story of a blind beggar who went to St. Alban's Abbey during a visit of Henry VI. The man declared that St. Alban had restored his sight:

So happened it, then, that Duke Humfrey of Gloucester, a great wise man and very well learned, having great joy to see such a miracle called that poor man unto him. And first shewing himself joyous of God's glory, so shewed in the getting of his sight, and exhorting him to meekness, and to none ascribing of any part the worship to himself nor to be proud of the people's praise which would call him a good and godly man thereby. At last he looked well upon his eyen, and asked him whether he could never see nothing at all in all his life before. And when as well his wife as himself affirmed fastly no, then he looked advisedly upon his eyen again, and said, I believe you very well, for me thinketh that ye cannot see well yet.

Yes, Sir, quod he, I thank God and his holy martyr, I can see now as well as any man.

Ye can, quod the Duke. What colour is my gown? Then anon the beggar told him.

What colour, quod he, is this man's gown? He told him also, and so forth without sticking, he told him the names of all the colours that could be shewed him. And when my lord saw that, he bade him walk faytoure [imposter], and made him be set openly in the stocks. For though he could have seen suddenly by miracle the difference between divers colours, yet could he not by sight so suddenly tell the names of all these colours but if he had known them before, no more than the names of all the men that he should suddenly see.

Soon after he had finished this *Dialogue*, More must have begun his second controversial work; this was a reply to *A Supplication of the Beggars*, a savage attack on the clergy by a lawyer, Simon Fish, in the form of a petition to the king from the beggars of England; this short pamphlet was in circulation by the end of 1528. More's book, entitled *The Supplication of Souls*, was published in September 1529. In this he adopted the form of Erasmus' *Praise of Folly*, which is a discourse by Folly herself. More's book is a declamation on behalf of the souls in purgatory in which they plead that they should not be deprived of the prayers of the living. The charges made by Fish against the clergy are examined, but the emphasis is put on the teaching of the Church, especially on the doctrine of purgatory. Within this framework, More was able to give play to his dramatic sense, and his humour lightens what could have been a pedestrian theological exposition. So the Souls see their widows, 'waxen wanton and forgetting us their old husbands':

Yet we hear sometimes our wives pray for us warmly; for in chiding with her second husband, to spite him withal, 'God have mercy', saith she, 'on my first husband's soul, for he was a wise and honest man, far unlike you'. And then marvel we much when we hear them say so well of us, for they were ever wont to tell us far otherwise.

More did not limit himself to Fish's complaints but used the opportunity for some ironical comments of his own. He represented the Souls as regretting the lavish funerals they had ordered:

For some hath there of us, while we were in health, not so much studied how we might die penitent and in good Christian plight, as how we might be solemnly borne out to burying, have gay and goodly funerals, with heralds at our hearses, and offering of our helmets, setting up our escutcheon and coat armours on the walls, though there never came harness on our backs, nor never ancestor of ours ever bare arms before.

In *Utopia*, by contrast, where the dead were cremated,

when any die cheerfully and full of hope, they do not mourn for them, but sing hymns when they carry out their bodies, commending their souls very earnestly to God.

The controversialist seems doomed to follow a path that gets dustier and dustier. At first he steps out with a light step, but he soon discovers that whatever he says, his opponent can always find something further to say. This was the course to which More found himself committed. He had a formidable opponent in William Tyndale, who, at his best, could put his arguments into clear English. His *Answer unto Sir Thomas More's Dialogue* was published in the spring of 1531. To this More replied with a *Confutation of Tyndale's Answer;* Books I-III were published in 1532, and Books

IV-VIII in 1533. A ninth book, unfinished, was published after his death. The first volume was issued about the time More resigned the Chancellorship (16 May 1532). He was now freed from public duties, and 1533 saw the publication, in addition to the second volume of the *Confutation*, of *The Apology*, *The Debellation of Salem and Bizance*, and the *Letter impugning John Frith;* in 1534 came his last controversial work, *Answer to the First Part of the Poisoned Book*. These works fill eight hundred pages of the folio edition of 1557, in all, about eight hundred thousand words. Allowance must be made for his practice of quoting his opponent's statements, always with scrupulous accuracy, but, even so, this vast output is astonishing. It is not surprising that at the end of a letter to Thomas Cromwell in March 1534, he wrote: 'I pray you pardon me, that I write not unto you with my own hand, for verily, I am compelled to forbear writing for a while by reason of this disease of mine, whereof the chief occasion is grown, as it is thought, by the stooping and leaning on my breast, that I used in writing.'

It would be out of place here to review this group of writings, but some characteristics may be noted. More's prolixity weakened the effect of his arguments; he let his pen run on as the thoughts poured from his mind; at times the impression is given that he had not planned his books, nor could he have had time for revision and pruning. By contrast the argument of his *Dialogue against Heresies* had clearly been thought out, with the result that the book has a unity that is lacking in others. The dialogue form imposed some restraint on the writer. More was criticized for his longwindedness in his lifetime. In his *Apology* he defended himself:

Howbeit, glad would I have been if it might have been much more short for then should my labour have been so much the less. But they will, if they be reasonable men, consider in themselves that it is a shorter thing and sooner done to write heresies than to answer them. For the most foolish heretic in a town, may write more false heresies in one leaf, than the wisest man in the world can well and conveniently by reason and authority soyle [answer] and confute in forty.

By contrast Tyndale showed skill in marshalling his ideas at reasonable length. His books were therefore easier to read and did not demand the same staying power that More expected from his readers. The 'simple and unlearned men' of whom Tunstal wrote, must have been deterred from tackling a book of the length of the *Confutation*. More's shorter books made a wider appeal, though even *The Supplication of Souls* was ten times the length of Simon Fish's *A Supplication of the Beggars*. The reader with some experience of More's work would be encouraged to persevere in the certainty that the author's love of an anecdote or of a homely illustration, and his quick sense of humour, would be some compensation for the heavier pages, and it is in these passages that More's English becomes lively and nearer the spoken language. At times he even attempted dialect. Here from the *Dialogue*, for instance, is a Kentish labourer speaking:

Nay, by our Lady, masters, yche [I] cannot tell you well, why, but chote [I wote] well it hath. For, by God, I knew it a good haven till that steeple was builded, and by the Mary mass, cha [I have] marked it well, it never throve since.

These stories were often short and pithily told, as for example the following taken from *The Supplication* about 'a lewd gallant and a friar':

Whom when the gallant saw going barefoot in a great frost and snow, he asked him why he did take so much pain. And he answered that it was very little pain if a man would remember hell. 'Yea, friar', quoth the gallant, 'but what an there be none hell, then art thou a great fool'. 'Yea, master', quoth the friar, 'but what an there be hell, then is your mastership a much more fool.'

This use of the anecdote was not unusual at that period. Moral tales had long been a recognized part of the preacher's equipment, and collections, such as the *Gesta Romanorum*, were in common use. More's stories were always apposite, but they were not too pointedly edifying in the preacher's sense. Here is another example, taken this time from the *Debellation*:

And as for the railing fashion—if I durst tell so sad a man a merry tale, I would tell him of the friar that, as he was preaching in the country, spied a poor wife of the parish whispering with her pewfellow; and he, falling angry thereto, cried out unto her aloud, 'Hold thy babble, I bid thee, thou wife in the red hood'. Which when the housewife heard, she waxed as angry again, and suddenly she start up and cried out unto the friar again, that all the church rang thereon, 'Marry, sir, I beshrew his heart that babbleth most of us both. For I do but whisper a word with my neighbour, and thou hast babbled there all this hour.'

V. DEVOTIONAL WRITINGS

There are signs of weariness as the *Confutation* 'drags its slow length along'. At the end of his Preface, More advised his readers to ignore both the books of the heretics and his own, and to read 'such English books as most nourish and increase devotion'. He suggested the *Imitation of Christ* and Walter Hilton's *Scale of Perfection*. His controversial writing ended when, on 17 April 1534, he was committed to the Tower where he was to remain for fifteen months without trial. For the greater part of that time he was allowed his books, pen, ink and paper; he used them not for belabouring heretics but for works that are primarily devotional. 'Calm of mind, all passion spent', he produced his finest and most typical work, *A Dialogue of Comfort Against Tribulation*, with the whimsical explanation that it was 'made by an Hungarian in Latin, and translated out of Latin into French, and out of French into English'. The speakers were the aged Anthony and his nephew Vincent; the background of their conversation was the danger threatening Christendom by the advance of the Turks into Hungary. This figured the spread of heresy in Europe, but the parallel is not unduly pressed. The main part of the work is a disquisition on one of the Compline Psalms, 'He that dwelleth in the secret place of the most High shall abide under the shadow of the Almighty'.

The book has all the attractive qualities of More's works: he calls up pictures of the past with glimpses of his family and of his experiences in state affairs; there are anecdotes from many sources; references to the Fathers and to classical authors show his wide reading, and, above all, his frequent scriptural quotations are evidence of his close knowledge of the Bible. Though he gives no names, it is not difficult to identify some of the characters. For instance, it is Wolsey who is described in this sentence: 'But glorious [vain-glorious] was he very far above all measure, and that was great pity, for it did harm, and made him abuse many great gifts that God had given him.' Then follows an ironical account of a competition among guests at the Cardinal's table to see who could give him the most lavish praise.

Some of More's shortcomings as a writer are not so noticeable in this serene book; there are few involved sentences, and his love of alliteration is kept under control, though it has its fling occasionally. 'Yet are there some fools so fed with this fond fantasy of fame', and, 'peevish pastimes of purpose to put . . . ' We may note too his liking for a triad of terms:

Captivity, bondage or thraldom, what is it but the violent restraint of a man, being so subdued under the dominion, rule and power of another.

The whole book is the expression of a mind and spirit that had come to terms with life. He even hinted at the possibility of reaching an understanding with the Lutherans and their doctrine of justification by faith:

As we, I say, grant unto them these things, so this one thing or twain do they grant us again, that men are bound to work good works if they have time and power, and that whoso worketh in true faith most, shall be most rewarded.

So he declared: 'Therefore will I let God work and leave off contention; and nothing shall I now say, but that with which they that are themself of the contrary mind shall in reason have no cause to be discontented.'

This book was not the only fruit of More's solitude in the Tower, a solitude that brought him back, as it were, to his earlier longing for the life of the cloister. He wrote a *Treatise to receive the Blessed Body of our Lord*. This, short as it is, contains a recollection of the king's visit to him at Chelsea:

For if we will but consider, if there were a great worldly prince which for special favour that he bare us would come visit us in our own house, what a business we would then make, and what a work it would be for us, to see that our house were trimmed up to every point, to the best of our possible power, and everything so provided and ordered, that he should by his honourable receiving perceive what affection we bear him, and in what high estimation we have him.

Another work, a *Treatise upon the Passion of Christ*, was unfinished; shortly before his trial (1 July 1535), his books and writing materials were removed from his cell. He began to write this treatise in English and then continued it in Latin, an interesting return to his love of that language. At his first interrogation in the Tower by members of the Council, he declared that he had 'fully determined with myself neither to study nor to meddle with any matter of this world, but that my whole study should be upon the passion of Christ and mine own passage out of the world'. That this was indeed his intention is shown by this treatise which is of some length. The first group of meditations was on the Fall and the Redemption; he then commented on the Gospel story of the Passion, going into great detail and supporting his exposition by quotations from the Greek and Latin Fathers. A passage on martyrdom has a poignant interest in view of his own perilous situation:

For many of truth have there been that at the first brunt have fearfully shrunk and fainted, and yet afterward valiantly passed through all the pain that was put upon them. Now albeit, I cannot deny but that the example of them that suffer death with a bold and hardy courage is a right expedient for a great many to hearten them to do the like; yet, on the other side, forasmuch as all the sort of us in effect be timorous at the coming of death, who can tell how many take good by these folk too, which though they come to it, as we see, with much anguish and dread, do yet in conclusion manfully pass through those horrible strong stops of weariness, fear, and heaviness, and so, stoutly breaking through all those violent lets [hindrances], do gloriously conquer death, and mightily get up into heaven.

A Dialogue of Comfort was first published in 1553. The other Tower writings in English were first printed in the collected *English Works* of 1557, the Latin ones in 1563.

VI. LETTERS

No account of Thomas More's writings would be complete without some notice of his letters. Most of these were in Latin but there is an important group in English belonging to the last two years of his life. These concern the troubles that were gathering around him. First there was the attempt to implicate him in the prosecution of the Nun of Kent; then followed the king's anger at More's refusal to approve of the annulment of the king's marriage. On both these subjects he wrote to the king and to Thomas Cromwell; the two long letters to the latter are of primary biographical importance, but they do not make easy reading. The involved sentences call for close attention if the full meaning is to be extracted. More, in fact, was not a ready letter-writer and in those that are extant he shows little of the facility and humour of Erasmus. The letters he wrote from the Tower, especially those to his daughter Margaret, are charged with an emotion that gives them a place apart. So we come to 'the last thing that he ever wrote'. It was the eve of his execution. 'Our Lord bless you good daughter and

your good husband and your little boy and all yours and all
my children and all my godchildren and all my friends.'

VII. MORE AND ENGLISH PROSE

It is impossible to assess the influence of Thomas More's
English works on the development of our prose. Only one
book, the *Dialogue against Heresies*, went into a second
edition during his lifetime. The size of each edition is not
known, but the total number could probably be reckoned in
hundreds, not thousands. His execution in 1535 followed by
sermons up and down the country denouncing him and
John Fisher for sedition, effectively stopped further publication. It was not until Mary Tudor's reign that his nephew
William Rastell was able to publish in one volume in 1557
*The Works of Sir Thomas More, Knight, Written by Him in
the English Tongue.* As this did not appear until the end of the
Queen's reign, it had small chance of becoming known.
Queen Elizabeth, daughter of Anne Boleyn, was not likely
to favour the dissemination of the writings of Thomas More.
It was almost by chance that one of his works, *Richard III*,
continued to be printed. As we have seen, it was included
anonymously, in the Hardynge-Grafton Chronicle and so
passed into chronicle literature. Appearing as it did amid a
hotch-potch of indifferent material, it could not fail to
impress the reader with its vivid writing and dramatic
appeal. Dr. Tillyard expressed the opinion that

the effect of More's history was very great and largely incalculable.
Through being incorporated in later chronicles it escaped the anti-
Catholic feeling that might have prejudiced its popularity if it had been
lumped with the rest of his work. I should guess that it not only set the
pattern of Shakespeare's *Richard III* but was a direct incitement to him to
write dramatically rather than anecdotally. Anyhow there it was, one of
the two pieces of original English historical writing apt actively to
incite an Elizabethan dramatist to get close to his matter and to treat it
primarily as human happenings and only secondarily as a repertory of
morals or a mere series of events. (*Shakespeare's History Plays*, p. 39.)

The second piece referred to is the *Life of Cardinal Wolsey* by George Cavendish, who married a niece of Sir Thomas More.

High claims have been put forward for More's prose and its place in the development of the written language. As we have seen, it varied in quality; that is not surprising, for English prose had yet to take shape, and it was to go through several phases before a standard was achieved. More undoubtedly made his contribution, and an important one, to this movement, but it is hard to define the nature of that contribution. It may have been his genius for telling a story in a direct and dramatic manner that had most influence on his readers; the incidents were vividly narrated, and the characters, even if sketched with but a few bold lines, were alive. Nor is it fanciful to suggest that had he been an Elizabethan, he would have been a dramatist.

There is another form of influence that should be noted since it was the fruit of that religious conviction for which he died. The meditations and prayers he composed in the Tower were widely known and used for long after his death. They were printed again and again in Catholic manuals of devotion and repeated by many who were unaware of their origin. Their language places them beside some of the great collects in the Anglican Book of Common Prayer:

Good Lord, give me the grace so to spend my life, that when the day of my death shall come, though I feel pain in my body, I may feel comfort in my soul; and with faithful hope of thy mercy, in due love towards thee and charity towards the world, I may, through thy grace, part hence into thy glory.

SIR THOMAS MORE

A Select Bibliography

(Place of publication London, unless stated otherwise)

Bibliography:

MOREANA, by F. & M. P. Sullivan. Part A-F, Los Angeles (1964) in progress.

A PRELIMINARY BIBLIOGRAPHY, by R. W. Gibson (1961).

Collected Editions:

THE WORKES OF SIR THOMAS MORE WRYTTEN BY HIM IN THE ENGLYSH TONGE (1557)
—edited by More's nephew, W. Rastell.

LUCUBRATIONES. Basel (1563)
—the first collection of More's Latin writings.

THE ENGLISH WORKS, ed. W. E. Campbell, R. W. Chambers, and A. W. Reed.

    I.   Early Poems; Life of Pico; Richard III; Four Last Things (1931).

    II.   The Dialogue Concerning Tyndale (1931)

—a facsimile reproduction from the 1557 folio is given in each volume, followed by a modern transcript; no further volumes issued.

YALE EDITION OF THE COMPLETE WORKS, ed. R. Sylvester and others.

    I.   English and Latin Poems. 2. Richard III (1964). 3. Life of Pico; Four Last Things. 4. Utopia (1964). 5. Responsio ad Lutherum. 6. Dialogue Concerning Heresies; Supplication of Souls; Letter vs. Frith. 7. & 8. Confutation. 9. Apology; Debellation. 10. Answer to a Poisoned Book: Dialogue of Comfort. 11. Treatise on the Passion: On the Blessed Body; Devout Instructions. 12. & 13. Correspondence

—in progress. A shorter series, based on the above, will be issued in modern spelling. Proposed volumes: *Selected Letters* (1961); *Utopia* (1964); *Richard III*, etc.; *Polemical Works*; *Dialogue of Comfort*; *Devotional Works*.

Selections:

SIR THOMAS MORE: SELECTIONS FROM HIS ENGLISH WORKS, ed. P. S. and H. M. Allen. Oxford (1924).

Letters:

THE CORRESPONDENCE OF SIR THOMAS MORE, ed. E. F. Rogers. Princeton and Oxford (1947)

—this does not include More's letters (in Latin) to Erasmus, which are to be found in *Opus Epistolarum Des. Erasmi Roterodami*, ed. P. S. and H. M. Allen, 11 vols., Oxford (1906-1947).

Separate Works:

LIBELLOS VERE AUREUS DE OPTIMO REIP. STATU, DEQUE NOVA INSULA UTOPIAE. . . [Louvain, 1516]

—the first edition of *Utopia:* the original Latin text. Latin and English texts, Yale Edition, 1964.

A FRUTEFUL AND PLEASAUNT WORK OF THE NEWE YLE CALLED UTOPIA (1551)

—the first English version; translated by R. Robinson. The standard edition to date of *Utopia* (Robinson's translation, with the Latin text) is that of J. H. Lupton, Oxford, 1895.

A DIALOGUE OF COMFORT AGAINST TRIBULATION (1553)

—included in the Everyman edition of *Utopia,* 1910. Also edited separately by P. E. Hallett, 1937.

UTOPIA, translated by G. Burnet (1684)

—edited (with English poems) by S. Lee. 1906.

HISTORY OF KING RICHARD III

—early versions of More's *History of King Richard III* are to be found in the Chronicles of Hardyng and Hall. It was edited by J. R. Lumby, Cambridge, 1883. See Yale edition, 1964.

THE APOLOGYE (1533)

—ed. A. I. Taft, Early English Text Society, 1929.

THE FOUR LAST THINGS, ed. D. O'Connor (1935).

ENGLISH PRAYERS, ed. P. E. Hallett (1938).

HISTORY OF THE PASSION, ed. P. E. Hallett (1941).

LATIN EPIGRAMS, ed. L. Bradner and C. A. Lynch. Chicago (1943).

Some Biographical and Critical Studies:

LIFE AND DEATH OF SIR THOMAS MORE, by Cresacre More [1626]

—ed. J. Hunter, 1828.

THE OXFORD REFORMERS OF 1498, by F. Seebohm (1867)

—Colet, More, Erasmus.

LIFE AND WRITINGS OF BLESSED THOMAS MORE, by T. E. Bridgett (1891).

SIR THOMAS MORE, by H. Brémond, trs. H. Child (1904).

EARLY TUDOR DRAMA, by A. W. Reed (1926).

THE SAGA AND MYTH OF SIR THOMAS MORE, by R. W. Chambers (1927)
—British Academy lecture.

SIR THOMAS MORE, by T. Stapleton, translated by P. E. Hallett (1928).

LIFE AND DEATH OF SIR THOMAS MORE, by N. Harpsfield, ed. E. V.
Hitchcock. E.E.T.S. (1932).

THOMAS MORE AND HIS FRIENDS, by E. M. G. Routh. Oxford (1934).

SIR THOMAS MORE, by C. Hollis (1934).

LIFE OF SIR THOMAS MORE, by W. Roper, ed. E. V. Hitchcock.
E.E.T.S. (1935).

THOMAS MORE, by R. W. Chambers (1935).

A PORTRAIT OF SIR THOMAS MORE, by A. Cecil (1937).

ACTA THOMAE MORI, ed. H. de Vocht. Louvain (1947).

INTRODUCTION TO UTOPIA, by H. W. Donner (1947).

ERASMUS, TYNDALE AND MORE, by W. E. Campbell (1949).

THE TRAGEDY OF THE LOLLARD'S TOWER, by A. Ogle. Oxford (1949).

UNDER GOD AND THE LAW, ed. R. O'Sullivan. Oxford (1949)
—studies of More by various hands.

LIFE OF SIR THOMAS MORE, by Ro. Ba., ed. E. V. Hitchcock. E.E.T.S.
(1950).

MORE'S UTOPIA, by J. H. Hexter. Princeton (1952).

SAINT THOMAS MORE, by E. E. Reynolds (1953).

HUMANISM AND POETRY IN THE EARLY TUDOR PERIOD, by H. A. Mason
(1959).

MARGARET ROPER, by E. E. Reynolds (1960).

LIVES OF SAINT THOMAS MORE, by W. Roper and N. Harpsfield (1963)
—Everyman's Library.

THE LIKENESS OF THOMAS MORE, by S. Morison (1963).

THE TRIAL OF ST. THOMAS MORE, by E. E. Reynolds (1964).

Note: The Amici Thomae Mori (29 rue Volney, Angers, France),
publish a Journal, *Moreana*, devoted to More Studies.

William Wycherley

by P. F. VERNON

Published for The British Council
and the National Book League
by Longmans, Green & Co.

Two shillings and sixpence net

In his own lifetime, Wycherley was considered to be the greatest English comic writer since Jonson. Prudish Victorian critics regarded his plays as scandalous; the present age is able to recognize and appreciate his fundamentally serious intent. He can be firmly placed in the mainstream of English satirists: 'he had a clear incisive mind', writes Mr. Vernon, 'which enabled him to seek out the false premises underlying various social habits.' Wycherley was particularly concerned with the effects of the mercenary competition he saw about him in sexual relationships, and his masterpiece, *The Country-Wife*, underlines with splendid out-spokenness the degradation of both sexes when each regards the other as a property, something to be used—nowhere more common than in the marriage of convenience. In this perceptive and sympathetic study, Wycherley's career as a dramatist is examined against the background of his life and contemporary society, and Mr. Vernon concludes that his appeal is especially strong to the modern playgoer, whom he sets laughing 'in the same critical spirit that he intended'.

P. F. Vernon has made special studies of Restoration drama. He has taught in India, and is now a lecturer in the Department of English, King's College, London.

Bibliographical Series
of Supplements to 'British Book News'
on Writers and Their Work

GENERAL EDITOR
Geoffrey Bullough

WILLIAM WYCHERLEY

from a portrait after LELY *in the*
National Portrait Gallery

WILLIAM WYCHERLEY

by

P. F. VERNON

PUBLISHED FOR
THE BRITISH COUNCIL
AND THE NATIONAL BOOK LEAGUE
BY LONGMANS, GREEN & CO.

LONGMANS, GREEN & CO. LTD.
48 Grosvenor Street, London W.1

*Associated companies, branches and
representatives throughout the world*

First published 1965
© P. F. Vernon 1965

*Printed in Great Britain by
F. Mildner & Sons, London, E.C.1*

CONTENTS

¶William Wycherley was born in Hampshire, probably on 28 May 1641, and died in London on 31 December 1716, he was buried in St. Paul's Church, Covent Garden.

WILLIAM WYCHERLEY

I. LIFE

'WILLIAM WYCHERLEY A Shropshire Gentleman, who has excell'd all Writers in all Languages, in Comedy'—a partial view undoubtedly, yet by no means extraordinary in the dramatist's lifetime, when he was generally considered to be the greatest English comic writer since Ben Jonson. He lived in turbulent times, however, when social and moral attitudes were shifting rapidly; and after his death these changes began to undermine his reputation. In the second half of the eighteenth century the theatres would accept only tame adaptations of his comedies which had cut out their satiric bite. His work then disappeared completely from the stage. By the middle of the nineteenth century Restoration comedy was commonly regarded as a scandalous and barely mentionable chapter in the history of English literature. Wycherley was singled out as the most obnoxious offender. Macaulay compared his work to a skunk, protected from the critics because too filthy to handle. In the early part of the present century critics began to take a new and sympathetic interest in Restoration drama, but Wycherley's status remained somewhat ambiguous. The typical comedy of manners was now felt to be cynical, detached and amoral, a view which probably helped to widen the popularity of Restoration comedy after the first world war. But Wycherley, with his obvious fondness for moralizing, seemed something of a misfit; he had now become too moral. His comedies did not catch on as readily as those of William Congreve, the other major comic dramatist of the period. They are still rarely performed and relatively little known. This is a pity, for of all the Restoration and eighteenth-century dramatists Wycherley comes closest in temper to the theatre of the present day, while regular performance of his work would do much to dispel

the widespread rumour that Restoration comedy is trivial
and irresponsible.

Although greatly admired by his contemporaries,
Wycherley did not lead a particularly happy life. His
father, Daniel, was born in the town of Clive, near Shrews-
bury in Shropshire, where members of the family had lived
comfortably for over two centuries. He became High
Steward in the Marquess of Winchester's household at
Basing House in Hampshire and there married Bethia
Shrimpton, lady-of-honour to the Marchioness. William,
the first of six children, was probably born on 28 May
1641; the date is not absolutely certain. Less than two years
later civil war broke out. In 1645 Basing House was
destroyed by parliamentary forces under Cromwell, the
Marquess was imprisoned, his estates confiscated. Daniel
acted as his deputy until the Restoration of the monarchy in
1660 and during this time managed to set aside for himself a
large sum of money with which he later bought substantial
property in his native county. He eventually became a
barrister, spending much of his time and the greater part of
his fortune on lengthy law suits; a fact which helps to
explain his son's lifelong contempt for the legal profession.
When about fifteen years old William was sent to study in
France. While living in the Charente district he seems to
have been deeply impressed by the conversation of the
Marchioness de Montausier, daughter and disciple of the
celebrated Madame de Rambouillet, whose salons had
fostered the cult of refined manners and 'Platonic' love
known as *préciosité*. Thus at an early age he came into direct
contact with a literary movement which deeply influenced
English drama both before and after the Restoration. He
became a Roman Catholic; but on his return to England in
1660 he was sent to Oxford for a short while and there
reconverted to Protestantism. Towards the end of the same
year he took up legal studies at the Inner Temple in London.

Nothing much is known of his activities during his
twenties. He may well have spent some time in Madrid in

the household of the poet-ambassador, Sir Richard Fanshawe, and he probably took part in the naval battle of 1665 against the Dutch. In 1669 his first work was published anonymously, an irreverent verse burlesque of the Hero and Leander story. Feeble as they seem now, burlesques of this kind were popular when the Greek and Roman classics had almost the status of sacred texts in the educational syllabus. Two years later his first comedy, *Love in a Wood, or, St James's Park*, was performed by the actors known as the King's Men at the Theatre Royal in Bridges Street. The London theatres at this time catered for an intimate and privileged social circle; so the success of Wycherley's first play did more than spread his name. It also secured his position among the select group of leading writers and wits who moved within the court circle; gained him the friendship of such important figures as the Earl of Rochester and the Duke of Buckingham; and eventually led to the favour and patronage of King Charles II himself. His next work, *The Gentleman Dancing-Master*, was put on in 1672 by the rival company of actors at the new and splendid Dorset Garden Theatre, as the Theatre Royal had been burnt down earlier in the year. It was a comparative failure. But early in 1675 at the new Theatre Royal in Drury Lane Wycherley scored a triumph with *The Country-Wife*, one of the most influential plays of the century. At the end of the following year *The Plain-Dealer* was produced at the same theatre. The play apparently puzzled the first-night audience and its fate seemed uncertain until the balance was tilted in its favour by the enthusiastic applause of Buckingham and his friends. It soon became the most admired of Wycherley's works and earned him the nickname of 'plain dealer' or 'Manly' from the name of the principal character. But those who knew him always insisted that the dramatist resembled the rude and surly Manly only in his truthfulness and courage, his own manner being courteous and charming.

Wycherley was to live some forty years longer, but he wrote nothing further for the theatre. Already he was suffering from the ill-health which was to trouble him for the rest of his life, and soon other problems were to occupy his mind. He had by now whole-heartedly adopted the habits and outlook of the wealthy gentlemen whose lives centred on the theatres, the coffee-houses and the other places of wit and entertainment to be found in the capital. He despised the mercenary values of the business world and the unsophisticated life of the country, even though these had provided the means for his education. Yet the life led by a London gentleman demanded money, and Wycherley had no secure source of income. In an age when it was considered undignified to write for profit he never escaped from the endless struggle to make ends meet. The King helped him to spend the winter of 1678-9 in the healthier climate of France, and on his return proposed that he should become tutor to the young Duke of Richmond. This plan, which would have brought a permanent pension, came to nothing when it was discovered that in the autumn of 1679 Wycherley had secretly married the recently widowed Countess of Drogheda. It was an unfortunate marriage from every point of view. His wife not only made him miserable by her violent jealousy while she lived; she even failed to leave him, when she died, the fortune for which he had married her. At her death a mere two years after the marriage the legal disputes over her first husband's will, which were to last for more than fifteen years, had only just entered the preliminary stages. Meanwhile Wycherley's debts overwhelmed him, and in 1682 he found himself in a debtors' prison, where he remained until early in 1686 when the new King, James II, helped to clear his debts and promised him a pension after influential friends had arranged a performance of *The Plain-Dealer* at court. When James fled the country less than three years later the dramatist was again left penniless.

After this he lived modestly, partly in London, partly in Shropshire, with occasional visits to Bath to improve his health. He did not lose contact with the literary world, however. When in London he was the accepted leader of the men of letters who gathered at Will's Coffee House. He had many friends and admirers among the younger writers, including the dramatist William Congreve and the critic John Dennis. He had been writing poems off and on throughout his life, and some time before 1696 he decided to bring out a collection consisting mainly of new verse. The volume was ready by 1699, but, owing to difficulties with the publisher, did not appear until 1704. It was poorly received. Wycherley's memory was now failing, and many of the poems suffer from repetitiveness and appalling metrical lapses. At about this time Wycherley met Alexander Pope, then only sixteen years old, and, impressed by the elegance of the young poet's early pieces, asked him to polish up some of his own poems. Pope at first welcomed the task as an honour, but, finding it more and more troublesome, eventually told the dramatist to continue his revision himself. For a while the warm friendship between the two cooled, though Pope kept in touch with the dramatist until the latter's death.

At the age of seventy-four Wycherley married again. The whole affair reads like the plot of one of his own comedies. In 1715 a cousin, Captain Thomas Shrimpton, suggested that Wycherley might marry a young woman who could offer a cash dowry large enough to pay off his debts. She would benefit in turn from the jointure provided by old Daniel's will, should his eldest son remarry. The woman proposed by Shrimpton was, in fact, his own mistress. According to the servants, this unscrupulous fortune-hunter used every possible kind of pressure to force the old dramatist's consent, from getting him drunk to threatening him with the debtors' prison. Seriously ill, Wycherley protested that he needed a panel of doctors rather than a wife. Some time before this he had been reconverted to Catholicism and, his condition worsening, he received the last sacrament. Shrimpton intensified his efforts. Worn out and indifferent, if fully conscious of what was happening, the old man eventually put his signature to the marriage contract. 'Matrimony is plac'd after Extreme Unction in our Cate-chism, as a kind of Hint of the Order of Time in which they are to be taken'—Wycherley would have appreciated Pope's dry comment. Eleven days after the marriage on 31 Decem-ber 1715, he died. He was buried in St. Paul's Church, Covent Garden. Shortly afterwards Shrimpton married the now wealthy widow.

II. SATIRE AND SOCIAL CRITICISM

A first glance at Wycherley's comedies reveals one strik-ing characteristic: his fondness for maxims. The dialogue, particularly in his later comedies, is often made up entirely of an exchange of these terse moral generalizations. This suggests something of his whole approach to comedy. In the first place he set out quite openly to teach his audience. On the titlepage of *The Gentleman Dancing-Master* he placed a motto from Horace which begins, 'It is not enough to make the listener laugh aloud'. He took it for granted that the highest function of comedy was to instruct. Secondly, he shared the common concern of his age for the simple, general truths of experience. Like Descartes, Hobbes and the other influential philosophers of his time, like the scientists and artists who founded the Royal Society after the Restoration, he felt confident that the universe contained an underlying order, a strictly determined pattern of cause and effect. His comedies try to reveal something of this order, to make clear some of the basic principles of human behaviour. In their very structure they give the impression of careful design rather than of spontaneous, accidental growth. Most European comedy displays a 'classical' regularity of this kind, but readers brought up on some of the less disciplined Elizabethan plays often feel that formal symmetry is bound to curb the imagination and lead to superficiality. In fact the art of establishing connections offers plenty of scope for subtlety and imaginative depth.

As a satirist, for instance, Wycherley could not be content simply to judge the things he disliked according to some accepted moral standard. Anti-social behaviour, he assumed, must arise from some confusion in thinking, from some simple inconsistency which people would avoid if only they could be made to think logically. Like Ben Jonson, a dramatist with whom he had a great deal in common, he had a clear, incisive mind which enabled him to seek out the false premises underlying various social habits and to pursue them relentlessly in his comedies to an extreme conclusion where everyone could see how absurd they were.

Wycherley differs from other Restoration dramatists both in his seriousness and in his artistic consistency. Sharp, pointed, bold, masculine, strong—these were the words his contemporaries chose when describing his work. They suggest both sound judgement and acute penetration. His dramatic method is exceptionally purposeful. He begins with a clear end in view and rarely loses sight of it. Consider these opening sentences: 'Not a Husband to be had for money' (*Love in a Wood*); 'To confine a Woman just in her rambling Age! take away her liberty at the very time she shou'd use it!' (*The Gentleman Dancing-Master*). These plunge the audience straight into the problems the plays are about to consider. Everything then turns upon the central themes. The characters are not rounded individuals: once introduced, they do not reveal new and suprising facets of personality. They are rather illustrations in an argument, pruned of all irrelevant features. The audience knows exactly how they will behave; yet they do not seem to be mere puppets manipulated by their creator. This is because their actions follow logically from the attitudes they hold. In this sense the plots are plausible and 'natural', even though they would often be impossible in real life. The dialogue, though it suggests colloquial speech, is quite unlike ordinary conversation. Crammed with imagery, witty aphorisms, similes and double meanings, it is designed as an indirect commentary for the benefit of the audience, rather than as an imitation of the way people really talk.

Despite their neatness and order, Wycherley's comedies retain something of the crowded vigour of earlier English comedy. He will combine in a single play incidents which his older French contemporary, Molière, found sufficient for two or even three separate comedies. But he always succeeded in fusing the separate strands of an action, so that they seemed only related aspects of a single problem. His young friend, John Dennis, one of the most perceptive commentators on his work, noted that he was 'almost the only Man alive who has made Comedy instructive in its Fable; almost all the rest, being contented to instruct by their Characters'. Indeed, although he borrowed the rough outlines of nearly all his plots from other writers, one of his chief excellences lay in his ability to construct a plot in which even the smallest detail had some significance.

Recent studies have abstracted from his work a body of ideas similar to much of the naturalistic and sceptical thinking of the period; but his comedies actually deal with particular social problems rather than with philosophy in the narrow sense. Their themes, generally speaking, concern the preservation of traditional ideals in a changing society. Capitalism, at this time, continued to develop at a rapid pace, despite the apparent set-back of the Restoration. Wycherley regarded the loosening of rigid class divisions, the growing influence of the business community and the spread of acquisitive values as a serious threat to the humane and civilized level of personal relationships achieved, or at least aimed at, by the most intelligent among the upper-class group for whom he wrote. What particularly worried him was the effect of mercenary competition on friendship and sexual relations. The breakdown of family ties, which disturbed the Elizabethan dramatists so much, left him unmoved. 'FRIENDSHIP', he wrote, 'is a greater Tye on Faith than Blood, and free Love than Marriage-Bonds.'

Marriage was a favourite topic with the Restoration dramatists, and it is the main butt of Wycherley's satire.

To understand why, it is necessary to remember what marriage involved in seventeenth-century England. Marriage was not then a private and wholly voluntary contract between two individuals. As in many parts of the world today, it was felt to be the concern of the family group. Matches were generally arranged by the heads of families, by fathers or by elder brothers. An entry in Samuel Pepys's diary concerning his brother's marriage illustrates the typical attitude fairly well:

My chiefest thought is now to get a good wife for Tom, there being one offered by the Joyces, a cozen of theirs, worth £200 in ready money.
(31 December 1661)

Among the wealthy classes such matters as fixing a dowry and jointure and preserving or enlarging family estates took priority. The wishes of those about to be married were not entirely ignored, but normally had to take second place. Women seldom had much say in the choice of their partners. Traditionally they were conceded the right to refuse a proposed husband, but, as Richardson's novel *Clarissa* in the mid-eighteenth century shows so vividly, refusal might well involve a more than average degree of heroism. Men were allowed greater freedom of choice, but would rarely risk offending relatives on whom they depended financially. Parents still sometimes arranged marriages between young children in this period; young women were often coupled with middle-aged men, and Wycherley's personal experiences of marriage show that there were many other ways in which money could destroy the faintest chance of a happy married relationship.

This was, of course, no new state of affairs. For centuries European writers had been expressing their frustrated desire for a love free from the social ties of arranged marriage; nowhere more intensely than in the imaginary 'Platonic' world of the French aristocratic romances and the closely related English court drama under Charles I. But after the

Restoration, plaintive escapism of this kind was stiffened with a good measure of down-to-earth thinking. The traditional code of family conduct had always been intimately linked with political theory and practice. The revolution and the execution of Charles I had forced all thinking men to make a thorough re-assessment of the relations between ruler and subject, and now some of them felt the need to re-examine the bonds which held the miniature state of the family together. They began to question the right of a father to dictate to his adult sons and daughters; began to challenge the absolute sovereignty of husband over wife, and even to doubt the binding force of marriage vows which were not freely contracted. Reasoning of this kind lies behind many of the comic situations in Restoration drama; it is the very fabric of Wycherley's work. His attack on the contemporary marriage of convenience does not, therefore, necessarily imply a criticism of all marriage. For him 'free love' did not have its modern meaning; it meant rather a freely chosen partnership based on mutual attraction and respect. In his comedies he always implied that this partnership could work within the framework of marriage.

Wycherley's emphasis on free choice in personal relationships is clearly related to the new individualism of the century. But he saw himself as a conservative, defending what he believed to be traditional values against the economic effects of individualism. Forced marriage, fortune hunting, jealousy, indifference and inconstancy—all these he considered to be the evil results of treating people as if they were property, and he blamed them, not always fairly, on the rise of the middle class. But he was also interested in other aspects of social climbing. His comedies are crowded with fops and would-be wits, men who have bought titles or try in other ways to edge themselves into the highest social circles. At first sight it may seem as though he is breaking butterflies upon a wheel, that his affected fools are too insignificant to deserve the ridicule he heaps upon them. But

Wycherley sensed danger in their feeble and superficial attempts to imitate the culture of true gentlemen. It was not just that they lacked correct manners; Wycherley always connected their emphasis on display, on external accomplishments, with a crippling moral deficiency which led to selfishness and treachery in their relations with others. His defence of social and literary decorum forms part of that long tradition of satiric writings which includes Dryden's 'MacFlecknoe' and reaches its highest point in Pope's 'Dunciad' where it appears most clearly as a struggle for the survival of an entire way of life and thought.

Wycherley's comedies are also concerned with changes which were taking place in the lives of upper-class women. With the spread of capitalist methods of business organization, the longer periods spent by noblemen in London away from their country estates, and the greater number of servants, women who would formerly have held important responsibilities in the family were leading a life of increasing idleness. In London and the big spas an exclusive feminine social life was developing, trivial, affected and inward-looking. Wycherley attacked this world of card games and scandal with its false veneer of prudery as yet another obstacle in the way of intelligent, open and equal relationships between men and women.

These interests place Wycherley firmly in the main stream of English satirists from Ben Jonson to Swift and Pope. Like all Restoration comedy, however, his work differs from the masterpieces of these great satirists in its narrower scope. It expresses the interests and the limited vision of a small social group. One soon becomes aware of an inability to reach out imaginatively to the motives and needs of other classes, even to see far beyond the limits of the court at Westminster and the fashionable districts of the capital. Wycherley was deeply affected by the major political and social changes of his time, but was able to judge them only by their effect on the personal lives of a privileged group. Yet the class he represented was in many respects enlightened, and its way of life contained qualities worth preserving: qualities which allowed him to see serious limitations in the forces which were altering society. One may miss in his work the breadth of vision revealed in any one of Jonson's finest comedies, or in the total output of Molière, but his analysis of a smaller field is remarkably acute.

III. *LOVE IN A WOOD*

When the public theatres reopened at the Restoration after a long period of enforced silence, it almost seems as though the dramatists consciously set out to search for some fruitful comic tradition they could build upon. As the taste for spiteful satires on the Puritans dwindled, they turned for inspiration to Molière in France, to the Spanish comedy of intrigue, to Beaumont and Fletcher, to Ben Jonson and to other earlier English writers. Almost everything they handled was reduced to undistinguished farce. John Dryden and Sir George Etherege obtained the most promising results by developing elements in the comedies of Brome and Shirley, written before the civil wars. They combined in various ways satire on fops and false wits, the intrigues of cunning cheats, the trials and adventures of romantic heroes and heroines and, most important, witty quarrels between upper-class lovers who, like Beatrice and Benedick in Shakespeare's *Much Ado About Nothing*, after a show of reluctance finally join together in marriage. Wycherley in his first play, *Love in a Wood*, grafted on to this loose comic form an adaptation of a Spanish cloak and sword drama[1] to produce a comedy which, though complicated, had greater unity and more serious meaning than any recent work for the stage.

It is fascinating to see Wycherley's clear mind forcing order out of apparent chaos. The play contains two quite distinct worlds. The first, presented satirically, contains fortune hunters, social climbers and bawds who cheat one

[1] Calderón's *Mañanas de abril y mayo (April and May Mornings)*.

another in a series of intrigues and counter-intrigues which reminds one of Jonson's *Volpone* or *The Alchemist*. The second, more benevolent and urbane in manner, following the Spanish play, consists of true lovers from a higher social class. These two separate strands have at first sight so little in common that, despite the skilful weaving of the plot, they seem doomed to fall apart. But Wycherley cleverly turned this apparent weakness to advantage by making a moral contrast between the two a central part of his play's meaning. Every incident, every joke indeed, has some bearing on the main theme, which is the importance of trust and esteem in love, courtship and marriage.

All the characters in the satiric intrigues are linked by a common weakness; they have all, in some way or another, allowed money to sully their approach to love. Unknown to one another they are all manipulated by a cunning bawd and matchmaker, a fitting representative of the forces which poison love by mixing it with greed for money. She alone prospers as interests clash, plots become entangled and the biters themselves are bit.

The dialogue in these scenes, though vigorous and collo-quial, is stuffed with meaningful images which form a continuous, indirect commentary. A succession of references to card-sharpers and confidence tricksters, for example, creates the atmosphere of an underworld of crooks. When-ever the Puritan miser, Gripe, appears, witty play with religious phrases underlines his hypocrisy. In the following episode he is visiting a mistress in her poor lodgings. The bawd, Mrs. Joyner, tries to force him to spend freely, while he invents pious excuses not to do so. Notice how, in his last speech, images connected with food suggest the coarseness of his real emotions:

Joyn. What do you look for, Sir?

Gripe. Walls have ears, Walls have ears; besides, I look for a private place to retire to, in time of need; oh here's one convenient.

[*Turns up a Hanging, and discovers the slender provisions of the Family*]

Joyn. But you see poor innocent Souls, to what use they put it, not to hide Gallants.

Gripe. Temperance is the nurse of Chastity.

Joyn. But your Worship may please to mend their fare; and when you come, may make them entertain you, better than, you see, they do themselves.

Gripe. No, I am not dainty, as I told you; I abominate Entertainments; no Entertainments, pray, Mrs. *Joyner.*

Joyn. No! [*Aside.*

Gripe. There can be no entertainment to me, more Luscious and Savoury, than the communion with that little Gentlewoman; will you call her out, I fast till I see her.[1] (III.iii)

The two pairs of upper-class lovers, who put genuine feeling before financial interests, provide a decent alternative to fortune-hunting and prostitution. But this is true only at the end of the play. At the start their relationships suffer from serious flaws which plunge them temporarily into the atmosphere of mistrust which surrounds the inferior group. One of the gentlemen is a libertine, the other is absurdly jealous. Wycherley relates both faults to a lack of faith in the intelligence and integrity of their mistresses which comes close to the view held by the other characters, that women can be treated as a form of property. An entertaining sequence of comic disasters finally purges them of their mistaken attitudes.

It is in his use of the stage setting to bind the action together that Wycherley shows most originality.[2] St. James's Park, which gives the play its sub-title and where many of the incidents take place, looms over the whole action. The main

[1] Here the words 'communion' and 'fast' have both religious overtones and associations with food. Quotations from Wycherley's works follow the first editions, with slight alterations in spelling and punctuation where the originals might present difficulty. The figures in brackets refer to the acts and scenes in which quotations occur, according to the divisions in the Mermaid edition.

[2] The Restoration stages, unlike those on which Shakespeare's plays were first acted, used painted scenery which could be changed during performance.

title is itself a pun, for the phrase 'in a wood' at this time meant 'in confusion', and in the play the wooded park at night becomes a symbol of the confusion caused by the various intrigues which take place within it. Wycherley makes the new fashion of rambling in the park stand for the latest patterns of sexual behaviour. St. James's Park had only recently been opened to the public; previously it had been a royal game preserve. How typical of modern life, Wycherley suggests. Gone are the old deer hunts, and instead men and women are now chasing one another in the park. It is a racy idea, handled with wit and subtlety. Wycherley made excellent dramatic use of darkness in his three finest comedies; and here a group of words such as 'see' and 'blind', in the metaphorical senses of 'realize' and 'deceived', give added meaning to the imaginary blackness of the stage. The various characters, muttering about the lack of light, keep mistaking one another in the dark, and in this way the stage scene gradually comes to represent a deeper misunderstanding. The park thus links up all the different forms of deception in the play, including the self-deception of the true lovers. The final confusion in the darkness unravels their mistakes, leading them 'out of the dark' and away from the winding alleys between the trees, the by-paths of love 'where we are still way-lay'd, with Surprizes, Trapans,[1] Dangers, and Murdering disappointments'; leaving the rest to grope their way through the gloomy wood of mistrust.

As one might expect, the play shows signs of inexperience. The dialogue is stiff in places; there are too many set pieces which have not been worked smoothly into the action. Above all, the plot contains unnecessary duplication. Wycherley had a great deal to say and had not yet learnt the importance of sacrificing detail for the sake of clarity. Yet *Love in a Wood* was a break-through: a fully integrated comedy with a consistent, serious purpose.

[1] *Trapans:* traps, tricks.

IV. *THE GENTLEMAN DANCING-MASTER*

The Gentleman Dancing-Master did not fulfil this early
promise. A gayer work, more full of laughter, it is also more
superficial. Were it not for the attack on 'senseless Plays' in
the *Prologue*, one might be tempted to dismiss it merely as
pleasant farce. The basic ingredients of the simple plot come
from the common Restoration stockpot; some of the
flavouring again comes from Spain.[1] The daughter of a
wealthy merchant thwarts his scheme to marry her to a rich
fool and wins a gentleman of her own choosing. It is not
hard to see why the familiar story appealed to Wycherley.
He hammers the implied message home:

> When Children marry, Parents shou'd obey,
> Since Love claims more Obedience far than they.   (V.i)

Though there is plenty of farce, the action does have point:
the incidents bring out effectively the connection between
the father's sternness, the proposed bridegroom's unworthiness and the daughter's rebellion. Whenever he can,
Wycherley darts in with a sharp satiric thrust, such as this
reply by the heroine, Hippolita, to her guardian aunt,
Mrs. Caution:

Mrs. Caut. Well, Malapert! I know you hate me, because I have been
the Guardian of your Reputation. But your Husband may thank me one
day.

Hipp. If he be not a Fool, he would rather be oblig'd to me for my
vertue than to you, since, at long run he must whether he will or no. (I.i)

The richest comedy springs from the supposed naïvety of
Hippolita, who is underestimated by every other character,
including her lover, Gerrard. The love scenes show
Wycherley at his most charming; the mood of tenderness is
enchanced by gentle humour and good sense:

[1] Wycherley developed a hint he found in Calderón's *El maestro de
danzar* (*The Dancing Master*).

Ger. How's this? you surprise me as much as when first I found so much Beauty and Wit in Company with so much Innocency. But, Dearest, I would be assur'd of what you say, and yet dare not ask the question. You h—— do not abuse me again, you h—— will fool me no more sure.

Hipp. Yes, but I will sure.

Ger. How! nay, I was afraid on't.

Hipp. For I say you are to be my Husband, and you say Husbands must be Wittols[1] and some strange things to boot.

Ger. Well, I will take my Fortune.

Hipp. But have a care, rash man.

Ger. I will venture.

Hipp. At your peril, remember I wish'd you to have a care, fore-warn'd, fore-arm'd.

Pru. Indeed now that's fair; for most men are fore-arm'd before they are warn'd.

Hipp. Plain dealing is some kind of honesty however, and few women wou'd have said so much.

Ger. None but those who wou'd delight in a Husband's jealousie, as the proof of his love and her honour.

Hipp. Hold, Sir, let us have a good understanding betwixt one another at first, that we may be long Friends; I differ from you in the point, for a Husband's jealousie, which cunning men wou'd pass upon their Wives for a Compliment, is the worst can be made 'em, for indeed it is a Compliment to their Beauty, but an affront to their Honour.

Ger. But, madam ———

Hipp. So that upon the whole matter I conclude, jealousie in a Gallant is humble true Love, and the height of respect, and only an under-valuing of himself to overvalue her; but in a Husband 'tis arrant sawci-ness, cowardise, and ill-breeding, and not to be suffer'd.

Ger. I stand corrected gracious Miss.   (V.i)

Hippolita's sophisticated wit may seem unlikely in a middle-class girl of fourteen, but Wycherley needed her youth to emphasize the naturalness of her disobedience, and in his eyes no woman could be really desirable without a mature intelligence.

[1] *Wittol:* a contented cuckold, a man who willingly accepts his wife's infidelity.

Paris, the proposed bridegroom, is among the best of the many Frenchified fops in Restoration comedy. With less malice than most of Wycherley's fools, he gives plenty of scope for the pathetic brand of clowning. Colley Cibber, the actor-dramatist immortalized in Pope's 'Dunciad' has given a lively description of James Nokes, the actor who almost certainly played the part on the first night:

In the ludicrous distresses, which by the laws of comedy, folly is often involv'd in; he sunk into such a mixture of piteous pusillanimity, and a consternation so rufully ridiculous and inconsolable, that when he had shook you, to a fatigue of laughter, it became a moot point whether you ought not to have pity'd him. When he debated any matter by himself, he would shut up his mouth with a dumb studious powt, and roll his full eye into such a vacant amazement, such a palpable ignorance of what to think of it, that his silent perplexity (which would sometimes hold him several minutes) gave your imagination as full content as the most absurd thing he could say upon it.

Given this style of acting, one can imagine the effect of the scene where Paris, who has been ordered to change into Spanish clothes, enters wearing a fantastic mixture of French and Spanish costumes and then, struggling to stop himself swearing in French, pleads to be allowed to keep just his favourite French cravat.

Wycherley learnt some useful lessons in writing this play. He now knew how to keep his action clear and uncluttered. The dialogue with its quick exchange of short speeches shows a new lightness of touch. There is none of the stiffness which marred his first play. But the thinness of the plot gave little scope for the rich exposition of ideas at which he excelled.

V.   THE COUNTRY-WIFE

In *The Country-Wife* Wycherley succeeded in combining the thoughtfulness of his first play with the high spirits of his second. He had now turned to comedies by Molière for his plot material, and the example of the great French dramatist seems to have helped him to clarify his own aims. Certainly in *The Country-Wife* he has absolute control over his medium. Built partly out of incidents in *L'Ecole des Maris* (*The School for Husbands*) and *L'Ecole des Femmes* (*The School for Wives*), it is a masterpiece of dramatic design. The plot is planned as a detailed demonstration of the play's main thesis: the failure of contemporary marriage arrangements. Wycherley begins by supposing two typical arranged marriages. These are, as it were, the agreed premises necessary before any argument can take place. Pinchwife, a middle-aged rake, has deliberately picked out for his wife a naïve country girl, on the assumption that ignorance will keep a woman submissive and faithful. Sir Jaspar Fidget, an old businessman, too occupied with business affairs to spend any time on his young wife, imagines he can prevent her thinking about other men by confining her to a trivial social life among safe companions of his own choosing. Blown up into the exaggerated form usual in comedy, these two marriages represent assumptions commonly held by men at the time. Wycherley sets out to show that they contain the seeds of their own destruction, contradictions which can only lead to unhappiness and infidelity. It only needs the appearance on the scene of a determined libertine, Horner, to spark off the inevitable explosion. Having spread the rumour that an attack of venereal disease has left him impotent, Horner becomes in Sir Jaspar's eyes tame enough to join the circle of friends he allows Lady Fidget. Once the opportunity presents itself, she and other women of the town, similarly starved of love, come rushing into the welcoming arms of Horner. The hypocritical mask of prudery, demanded of women by husbands and parents, drops, while the simple country wife develops all the brilliant cunning of a sophisticated townswoman in her efforts to tear a way through to her lover. A third marriage is being arranged. Pinchwife plans to give his sister Alithea to the affected Sparkish, a fool who thinks of her only as a means of making money and as a beautiful possession to show off to his friends. Here again an agent appears, Horner's companion, Harcourt, who opens Alithea's eyes to Sparkish's real motives and himself offers the genuine respect and affection on which they can build together a sound alternative to the diseased marriages all about them.

The action illustrates perfectly Horner's maxim that 'a foolish Rival and a jealous Husband assist their Rival's Designs; for they are sure to make their Women hate them, which is the first step to their love, for another Man'. Once the catalyzing agents are introduced, the process of change sets in quite automatically; to use Wycherley's own image, the disease spreads like an epidemic. Sir Jaspar actually forces Horner on to his wife, so that he can get away to his business; just as Sparkish forces Harcourt on Alithea, so that he can run off to the playhouse. As for Pinchwife, every effort he makes to keep his wife in ignorance only helps to teach her what he wishes to conceal. The situation is rich in irony. The very simplicity of his wife, the quality for which he married her, leaves him completely helpless. Here he is explaining why he has forbidden her to go to the theatre:

> *Mr. Pin.* First, you like the Actors, and the Gallants may like you.
> *Mrs. Pin.* What, a homely Country Girl? no, Bud, no body will like me.
> *Mr. Pin.* I tell you, yes, they may.
> *Mrs. Pin.* No, no, you jest—I won't believe you, I will go.
> *Mr. Pin.* I tell you then, that one of the lewdest Fellows in Town, who saw you there, told me he was in love with you.
> *Mrs. Pin.* Indeed! who, who, pray who wast?   (II.i)

Every step Pinchwife takes to protect his wife brings her closer to her lover. As his treatment grows more cruel, she grows correspondingly more cunning. The humour involves continuous use of dramatic irony. The audience has been shown the logical fallacy in Pinchwife's method and knows that his disappointment is quite unavoidable, that all his efforts are as futile as King Lear's shouts against the wind and rain. No hint of tragedy creeps in, however, since Pinchwife has only himself to blame for his suffering. The country wife does not need our pity, since she remains imperturbable even with a knife thrust in her face. Here Pinchwife is forcing her to write a rude letter to Horner:

Mrs. Pin. Indeed, and indeed, but I won't, so I won't.

Mr. Pin. Why?

Mrs. Pin. Because he's in Town, you may send for him if you will.

Mr. Pin. Very well, you wou'd have him brought to you; is it come to this? I say take the pen and write, or you'll provoke me.

Mrs. Pin. Lord, what d'ye make a fool of me for? Don't I know that Letters are never writ, but from the Countrey to *London*, and from *London* into the Countrey; now he's in Town, and I am in Town too; therefore I can't write to him you know.

Mr. Pin. So I am glad it is no worse, she is innocent enough yet.

                  [Aside

 Yes you may when your Husband bids you write Letters to people that are in Town.

Mrs. Pin. O may I so! Then I'm satisfied.

Mr. Pin. Come begin — Sir —   *[Dictates*

Mrs. Pin. Shan't I say, Dear Sir? You know one says always something more than bare Sir.

Mr. Pin. Write as I bid you, or I will write Whore with this Penknife in your Face.

Mrs. Pin. Nay good Bud — Sir —   *[She writes*

Mr. Pin. Though I suffer'd last night your nauseous, loath'd Kisses and Embraces — Write.

Mrs. Pin. Nay, why shou'd I say so, you know I told you, he had a sweet breath.

Mr. Pin. Write.

Mrs. Pin. Let me but put out, loath'd.

Mr. Pin. Write I say!

Mrs. Pin. Well then.   *[Writes*

Mr. Pin. Let's see what have you writ? — *[Takes the paper and reads]* Though I suffer'd last night your kisses and embraces — Thou impudent creature, where is nauseous and loath'd?

Mrs. Pin. I can't abide to write such filthy words.   (IV.ii)

But having learnt the use of the words, she is ready enough to apply them to her husband when the occasion arises.

This splendid action leads up to a forceful dramatic symbol. His wife being heavily disguised, Pinchwife unwittingly takes her by the hand and leads her into the arms of her lover.

How fresh and unforced Wycherley's wit seems in these scenes! Yet all the time he is building up connections, searching out the root causes of the folly he is satirizing. Sir Jaspar, Sparkish and Pinchwife seem, on the face of it, completely unlike one another. One is a businessman; one a dilettante; one a rake turned countryman. Pinchwife guards his wife like a jailer; Sir Jaspar and Sparkish cannot escape from their women quickly enough. Wycherley finds a common connection: a refusal to recognize that women have an intelligence equal to that of men. That 'sweet, soft, gentle, tame, noble Creature Woman, made for Man's Companion'—Sir Jaspar's phrase captures exactly that mixture of reverence and contempt which, for more than two centuries, reduced women to the position of idolized slaves. Wycherley understood that there was really nothing to choose between the praise of a Sir Jaspar and the contempt of a Pinchwife who saw women as 'dough-bak'd, senseless, indocile animals', or the scorn of a Sparkish who felt that 'virtue makes a Woman as troublesome, as a little reading or learning'. They all contained the assumption expressed so crudely in Pinchwife's description of his wife as 'my own Free-hold'; and they all led to tyranny, whether the physical imprisonment of Mrs. Pinchwife or the intellectual imprisonment of Lady Fidget.

Wycherley's satire on the affectation of Lady Fidget and her companions is a real tour de force. Words like *honour, innocent, virtue, reputation, noble* and *breeding* appear over and over again in situations which undercut their ordinary meaning, until Wycherley only has to introduce one of them to get a laugh. Watch the sly way he attacks the word *honour* in the scene where Lady Fidget discovers Horner's virility. It becomes almost obscene. Lady Fidget has, as Wycherley puts it, so much honour in her mouth, that she has none elsewhere:

Lady Fid. But, poor Gentleman, cou'd you be so generous? so truly a Man of honour, as for the sakes of us Women of honour, to cause your self to be reported no Man? No Man! and to suffer your self the greatest shame that cou'd fall upon a Man, that none might fall upon us Women by your conversation; but indeed, Sir, as perfectly, perfectly, the same Man as before your going into *France*, Sir; as perfectly, perfectly, Sir.

Hor. As perfectly, perfectly, Madam; nay, I scorn you shou'd take my word; I desire to be try'd only, Madam.

Lady Fid. Well, that's spoken again like a Man of honour, all Men of honour desire to come to the test: But indeed, generally you Men report such things of your selves, one does not know how, or whom to believe; and it is come to that pass, we dare not take your words, no more than your Taylors, without some staid Servant of yours be bound with you; but I have so strong a faith in your honour, dear, dear, noble Sir, that I'd forfeit mine for yours at any time, dear Sir.

Hor. No, Madam, you shou'd not need to forfeit it for me, I have given you security already to save you harmless, my late reputation being so well known in the World, Madam.

Lady Fid. But if upon any future falling out, or upon a suspicion of my taking the trust out of your hands, to employ some other, you your self should betray your trust, dear Sir; I mean, if you'l give me leave to speak obscenely, you might tell, dear Sir.

Hor. If I did, nobody wou'd believe me; the reputation of impotency is as hardly recover'd again in the World, as that of cowardise, dear Madam.

Lady Fid. Nay then, as one may say, you may do your worst, dear, dear, Sir.

Sir Jas. Come, is your Ladyship reconciled to him yet? have you agreed on matters? for I must be gone to *Whitehall.*   (II.i)

Although he ridicules the pretended virtue of society ladies like Lady Fidget, Wycherley looks on them quite sympathetically. He shows that their deceitfulness develops naturally as a reaction to the cruelty and indifference of men. The progress of the country wife demonstrates exactly how craft grows in response to tyranny. The women are not ultimately responsible for their behaviour, and so they are left unpunished at the end of the play. But they are not rewarded with the happiness which the true lovers, Alithea and Harcourt, arrive at. 'Love', as Alithea remarks, 'proceeds from esteem'; and esteem cannot exist side by side with hypocrisy.

Though he obviously believed passionately in what he was saying, Wycherley in this play never gives the impression that he is preaching. Mainly, of course, this is owing to his perpetual delight in the absurd; but another important reason is the remarkable fluency of his dialogue. In one sense the language is more artificial than anything he had written before. We have already seen something of his ingenious use of double meanings, and images of every kind abound. There can hardly be another comedy in English which contains so many similes. Nevertheless, the speeches seem tailored to fit the different characters. Take one of the many passages where Wycherley builds up the idea that sexual desire is spreading like a disease. Spoken by Margery Pinchwife, it involves extremely elaborate play on words associated with illness. The organization of the sentence is actually highly sophisticated. Yet, with its simple words, mostly of one syllable only, and its tiny clauses, it has the very ring of a naïve, childlike person talking to herself:

Well, 'tis e'en so, I have got the *London* disease, they call Love, I am sick of my Husband, and for my Gallant; I have heard this distemper, call'd a Feaver, but methinks 'tis liker an Ague, for when I think of my Husband, I tremble and am in a cold sweat, and have inclinations to vomit, but when I think of my Gallant, dear Mr. *Horner*, my hot fit comes, and I am all in a Feaver, indeed, & as in other Feavers my own Chamber is tedious to me, and I would fain be remov'd to his, and then methinks I shou'd be well.   (IV.iv)

Compare this with the conversation between Pinchwife and Sparkish a little further on. They are carrying on with the same analogy, but Sparkish appears foolish and affected, Pinchwife grave and pompous:

Spar. Lord, how shy you are of your Wife, but let me tell you Brother, we men of wit have amongst us a saying, that Cuckolding like the small Pox comes with a fear, and you may keep your Wife as much as you will out of danger of infection, but if her constitution incline her to't, she'l have it sooner or later by the world, say they.

Pin. What a thing is a Cuckold, that every fool can make him ridiculous —   [*Aside*

   Well Sir — But let me advise you, now you are come to be concern'd, because you suspect the danger, not to neglect the means to prevent it, especially when the greatest share of the Malady will light upon your own head . . .   (IV.iv)

In *The Country-Wife* Wycherley brought to perfection his system of writing in maxims. Here a warning may be necessary. One tends to assume that any finely expressed idea in a play carries with it the author's approval. Wycherley's maxims, however, take their place in the normal course of the dialogue. Each character is given witty sentiments appropriate to his special situation and peculiar cast of thought. These may well be the exact opposite of Wycherley's own beliefs. The main advantage of the method is that it allows the dramatist to draw out the general significance of a situation without interrupting the flow of the action. Examined closely, some scenes in *The Country-Wife* seem perilously near to formal and static debate, but, in fact, they are moving the plot forward at the same time. Consider the remarkable scene where Horner worms out of Pinchwife his real reasons for marrying a country wife. On the story level Pinchwife is being teased about his marriage and his past life by the three young men, Horner, Harcourt and Dorilant. It is part of the torture he has inflicted on himself, and the audience enjoys watching him squirm. But the teasing, an ingenious analogy with gambling spread over several speeches, takes the form of a series of general maxims. These raise the particular scene to a more abstract level where Pinchwife becomes only one of thousands, and where Wycherley is able to establish a wider connection between licentiousness and jealousy:

Hor. But tell me, has Marriage cured thee of whoring, which it seldom does.

Har. 'Tis more than age can do.

Hor. No, the word is, I'll marry and live honest; but a Marriage vow is like a penitent Gamester's Oath, and entring into Bonds, and penalties to stint himself to such a particular small sum at play for the future, which makes him but the more eager, and not being able to hold out, loses his Money again, and his forfeit to boot.

Dor. Ay, ay, a Gamester will be a Gamester, whilst his Money lasts; and a Whoremaster, whilst his vigour.

Har. Nay, I have known 'em, when they are broke and can lose no more, keep a fumbling with the Box in their hands to fool with only, and hinder other Gamesters.

Dor. That had wherewithall to make lusty stakes.

Pin. Well, Gentlemen, you may laugh at me, but you shall never lye with my Wife, I know the Town.

Hor. But prithee, was not the way you were in better, is not keeping better than Marriage?

Pin. A Pox on't, the Jades wou'd jilt me, I cou'd never keep a Whore to my self.

Hor. So then you only marry'd to keep a Whore to your self; well, but let me tell you, Women, as you say, are like Souldiers made constant and loyal by good pay, rather than by Oaths and Covenants, therefore I'd advise my Friends to keep rather than marry; since too I find by your example, it does not serve one's turn, for I saw you yesterday in the eighteen penny place with a pretty Country-wench.

Pin. How the Divel, did he see my wife then? I sate there that she might not be seen; but she shall never go to a play again.   [*Aside*

Notice here how Horner's generalization slides perfectly easily into the particular information that he has seen Mrs. Pinchwife. Pinchwife's embarrassment now leads back quite naturally to a further generalization:

Hor. What dost thou blush at nine-and-forty, for having been seen with a Wench?

Dor. No Faith, I warrant 'twas his Wife, which he seated there out of sight, for he's a cunning Rogue, and understands the Town.

Har. He blushes, then 'twas his Wife; for Men are now more ashamed to be seen with them in publick, than with a Wench.   (I.i)

It is difficult to imagine a finer medium for dramatic satire. Packed with meaning, the speeches can carry as much imagery as verse; yet they have all the speed and vigour of colloquial prose.

The Country-Wife is certainly one of the great English comedies. It has gusto, abundant wit and perfect form. Moreover, its shapely structure is no mere embellishment of style; it is the instrument with which Wycherley probes social behaviour to achieve that 'studied insight into the springs of character' which Hazlitt admired so much.

VI.   *THE PLAIN-DEALER*

It was *The Plain-Dealer* and not *The Country-Wife* which made the deepest impression on fellow writers and critics, however. Wycherley's last comedy had a new earnestness: that unmistakeable note of moral seriousness which critical theory insisted the best literature ought to have. It struck the literary world as the grandest, most worthy comedy of the age. But the general public does not always take the favourite of the critics to its heart. *The Plain-Dealer* did not arouse the spontaneous enthusiasm which had greeted *The Country-Wife*. The first night audience had to be prodded into applauding by its betters, and, though the play remained in the repertory for a century, it was less popular than many other Restoration comedies. The instinct of the ordinary theatre-goer in this instance proved sounder than the considered verdict of the critics. *The Plain-Dealer* is an interesting, in many ways an admirable play, but it is less than a masterpiece.

For the first time Wycherley had difficulty in adapting his source material to his own purposes. The play is based on Molière's great comedy *Le Misanthrope*, which deals with an embittered man who, shocked at the hypocrisy and corruption around him, deliberately sets out to make a martyr of himself. The French play contains some satire on affectation and injustice, but its main purpose is to plead for compromise, for a sense of proportion; and its ridicule falls mostly on the central figure of the misanthropist. Wycherley had no more of the man-hater about him than Molière, but he was here more intent on satirizing society. He decided that the figure of the misanthropist could be turned into an excellent satiric spokesman. Being a balanced and urbane man himself, however, he could not resist keeping something of Molière's ridicule of extremism. The result is confusing. Sometimes one is looking at society through the eyes of the misanthropist, Manly; sometimes one is looking at him critically from the outside.

But the failure of the play goes deeper. Wycherley was finally moving away from the analysis of a particular social problem to a more general indictment of society. This in itself deserves praise, for it is unique on the Restoration stage. Yet one is forced to ask whether Wycherley was really equipped to make a sweeping comment of this kind. Moving only in a small social circle, how could he be? He did what he could. He put more stress than ever before on treachery among friends and on the flattery of courtiers. He also brought in the one other field he knew well, the law. But he was unable to invent incidents strong enough to support the ambitious generalizations he wanted to make. He relied, instead, on the long tirades of his plain dealer, Manly:

. . . here you see a *Bishop* bowing low to a gaudy *Atheist;* a Judge to a Door-keeper; a great Lord, to a Fishmonger, or a Scrivener with a Jack-chain about his neck; a Lawyer, to a Serjeant at Arms; a velvet *Physician*, to a threadbare Chymist: and a supple Gentleman Usher, to a surly Beef-eater: and so tread round in a preposterous huddle of Ceremony to each other, whil'st they can hardly hold their solemn false countenances. (I.i)

. . . here thou wilt live to be cherish'd by Fortune and the great ones; for thou may'st easily come to out-flatter a dull Poet, out-lie a Coffeehouse or Gazette-writer, out-swear a Knight of the Post,[1] out-watch a Pimp, out-fawn a Rook,[2] out-promise a Lover, out-rail a Wit, and outbrag a Sea-Captain.

                                                                          (I.i)

Forceful all this may be, but it cries out for a plot of great range, the kind of plot Jonson could offer, sweeping through every corner of society from the palace to the gutter. In fact *The Plain-Dealer* only tells the story of a man who is betrayed by his friend and jilted by his mistress. It is too flimsy to bear the weight of Wycherley's wholesale indictment.

This weakness helps to explain the unsatisfactory figure of Fidelia, a woman dressed in boy's clothes who follows Manly through all his dangers and distresses with dog-like devotion. Wycherley was an optimist at heart. He always included in his comedies characters who stood for the right way of doing things. In the earlier plays the true lovers who join in an intelligent equal partnership provide an effective and convincing contrast to the particular evil of mercenary marriage. Now Wycherley obviously needed a more comprehensive good alternative. Fidelia was his answer, a character representing faithfulness, whose symbolic quality is suggested by the fact that she lapses into blank verse whenever she is left on her own. As an answer to social corruption she seems totally ineffective. One feels that Wycherley is asking decent personal relationships to solve weaknesses in the structure of society. Moreover, the solemnity with which he handles Fidelia strikes an utterly false note in the comedy.

'In Works of Wit and Fancy', Wycherley wrote, 'everything that is not perfectly excellent displeases.' Fortunately this is only a half truth, and there is much to please in *The Plain-Dealer*. On familiar ground he is as entertaining as ever. Manly's outspokenness gives rise to plenty of amusing satire. His effect on the polite world is rather like

[1] *Knight of the post:* a man hired to give false evidence in court.
[2] *Rook:* a swindler.

that of a nasty smell. This is how he receives the genteel
Lord Plausible:

L. Plaus. What, will you be singular then, like no Body? follow, love,
and esteem no Body?

Man. Rather than be general, like you; follow every Body, court and
kiss every Body; though, perhaps at the same time, you hate every
Body.

L. Plaus. Why, seriously with your pardon, my dear Friend —

Man. With your pardon, my no Friend, I will not, as you do whisper
my hatred, or my scorn, call a man Fool or Knave, by signs, or mouths
over his shoulder, whil'st you have him in your arms: for such as you,
like common Whores and Pickpockets, are only dangerous to those you
embrace.

L. Plaus. Such as I! Heavens defend me! — upon my Honour —

Man. Upon your Title, my Lord, if you'd have me believe you. (I.i)

When the marriage of Vernish and Olivia, Manly's false
friend and mistress, falls apart, the results are riotously
funny, with both husband and wife chasing lustfully after
the epicene Fidelia. 'Did you not hear my Husband say, he
found me with a Woman in Man's clothes?' asks Olivia,
'And d'ye think he does not know a Man from a Woman.'
'Not so well, I'm sure, as you do', her cousin replies. When
Olivia receives her lover in the dark only to discover that the
man in her arms is her husband, her reaction is unforgettable: 'Ha! my Husband returned! and have I been
throwing away so many kind Kisses on my Husband, and
wrong'd my Lover already?'

The play also succeeds in capturing something of the
robust spirit of earlier English comedy. With its sailors and
lawyers and bailiffs, it shows a wider, rougher world than
his other plays. Towering above the rest stands the forbid-
ding figure of the Widow Blackacre, a woman eaten up by a
passion for legal brawling, a mother who has crushed all
the independence out of her miserable son, Jerry:

Go, save thy breath for the Cause; talk at the Bar, Mr. *Quaint:* You are so
copiously fluent, you can weary any one's ears, sooner than your own

tongue. Go, weary our Adversaries Counsel, and the Court: Go, thou art a fine-spoken person: Adad, I shall make thy wife jealous of me: if you can but court the Court into a Decree for us. Go, get you gone, and remember — [*Whispers*]   [*Exit* Quaint]

Come, Mr. *Blunder*, pray bawl soundly for me, at the *Kings-Bench;* bluster, sputter, question, cavil; but be sure your Argument be intricate enough, to confound the Court; And then you do my business Talk what you will, but be sure your tongue never stand still; for your own noise will secure your Sense from Censure: 'tis like coughing or heming when one has got the Belly-ake, which stifles the unmannerly noise. Go, dear Rogue, and succeed; and I'll invite thee, ere it be long, to more souz'd Venison.   (III.i)

The Widow Blackacre has all that vigorous abusive speech the Elizabethans delighted in, a gift for the absurdly mundane image. She is derived from characters like Ursula, the pig woman, in Jonson's *Bartholomew Fair*, and she looks forward to Congreve's Lady Wishfort. She is essentially English, with a coarseness French audiences would not have tolerated, but full of life. This is her reply to an old fellow who proposes marriage:

Wid. Thou sensless, impertinent, quibling, driveling, feeble, paralytic, impotent, fumbling, frigid Nincompoop!

Jerr. Hey, brave Mother, for calling of names, ifac!

Wid. Wou'dst thou make a Caudlemaker,[1] a Nurse of me? Can't you be Bed-rid without a Bed-fellow? Won't your Swan-skins, Furs, Flannels, and the scorch'd Trencher[2] keep you warm there? Wou'd you have me your Scotch warming-Pan,[3] with a Pox to you? Me! — (II.i)

If the liveliness of *The Plain-Dealer* needs any further testimony, what more impressive than the enthusiasm of the great French satirist, Voltaire, who declared that he did not know a single comedy, ancient or modern, which contained so much wit.

---

[1] *Caudle:* gruel mixed with wine and spices.

[2] *Scorched trencher:* a wooden dish heated to warm a bed.

[3] *Scotch warming pan:* a slang phrase for a prostitute.

VII. POEMS AND MAXIMS

Some twenty years later Wycherley began to turn out verse in enormous quantities. His debts had forced him to pocket his pride, and he was now making a business of writing. He was no poet, and he knew it. In the errata list to the collection published during his lifetime, 'that Damnd Miscellany of Madrigals of mine' as he called it, he disarmingly included 'the Whole BOOK'. The wits, who had long looked forward to a new work by their leader, had to agree. Wycherley had relied on his good sense and his genius for paradox to carry him through. But his readers demanded a certain minimum of grace and elegance.This Wycherley could not provide. His satires were rambling and shapeless, and even his songs could not be scanned. Senile decay must have been partly responsible, as he had once been able to write competent lyrics for his plays.

The satires shed further light on his beliefs, but there is little that cannot be deduced from the comedies. Once again he attacks misers, poor wits, fortune hunters and flatterers. One poem proves that priests are worse than pimps, because marriage is more mercenary than prostitution; another that business is really idleness because the results of its activity are futile. Some of the light-hearted, risqué love songs might amuse the casual reader, though the titles are often as witty as the poems themselves, and sometimes almost as long: 'To a *Fine Singer*, who had gotten a *Cold;* and, whose *Lover* endeavour'd to stop Her *Tongue* in Her *Mouth* with His, to save her *Honour* (as He call'd it.)'; 'To a fine Young *Woman*, who being ask'd by her Lover, *Why she kept so filthy a thing as a Snake in her Bosom;* answer'd, *'Twas to keep a filthier thing out of it, his Hand;* and, *that her Snake was to play with, and cool her in hot Weather;* which was his Aversion.' One or two of the drinking songs come near to the gracious ease one expects from a good Restoration lyric:

> Reason our Foe, let us destroy,
>   Which still disturbs us, when we drink;
> Which lets us not our selves enjoy,
>   But puts us to the pains to think.

But even here the clumsiness of the third line intrudes.

When looking over the poems Pope kept making the sensible suggestion that Wycherley should turn some of the wittier paradoxes into prose maxims after the manner of La Rochefoucauld and other French writers. Wycherley evidently took the proposal to heart, for the papers published after his death include a collection of over three hundred such maxims. With these he was far more at home:

MAY we not fairly say Marriage makes more Sinners than free Love, since it forces most of its Disciples, first or last, to Repentance?

Anyone who has enjoyed the maxims George Bernard Shaw published with *Man and Superman* would appreciate Wycherley's collection. Not all are original, however. He kept a volume of maxims by various French writers in front of him, and half way through he began translating, carefully taking one from each author in turn so that no one would notice the extent of his borrowing. One feels almost ashamed that modern scholarship should have caught him out. But he had an excellent defence, for, as he insisted in the Preface to his *Miscellany Poems*, necessity 'is always an Excuse for all Thefts'.

Wycherley would not have wanted to be remembered for his dotages, for works created in need. He had been the great dramatist of the seventies, writing then for pleasure, not for business. He had seen his plays direct the course of English drama for thirty years. The best of the younger dramatists had all followed in his footsteps. Congreve had refined upon his wit, Vanbrugh had inherited something of his seriousness. But neither had launched out in strikingly new directions. Until the arrival of sentimental comedy at the turn of the century, his own *Plain-Dealer* had remained the most significant attempt to move away from the pattern set by *The Country-Wife*.

He can hardly affect us now as deeply as he did his contemporaries. The social problems in which he was most interested have lost their urgency, in England at least; though there are many countries where his satire on arranged marriage would still seem relevant and challenging. But he has survived remarkably well the hazards which befall any writer who concentrates on the social scene. We do not have to learn outdated jargon to understand him. There are few of those topical details which make performance of Ben Jonson's comedies so difficult. If we have to rebuild in our imagination the conditions in which he lived, little effort is needed to understand his beliefs. Even in the Victorian era some critics, like Charles Cowden Clarke, could see that 'Wycherley had by nature a generous and an honourable heart, and his real nature shone through his writings'. Today, the deep-rooted faith in the intellectual equality of women which runs through all his work and the importance he attached to sound personal relationships in a world crippled by self-interest compel our sympathy. Despite the cries that he is obscene, or morbid, or trivial, on his rare appearances in the theatre he is still able to set audiences laughing in the same critical spirit that he intended.

WILLIAM WYCHERLEY

A Select Bibliography

(Place of publication London unless stated otherwise)

Collected Works:

MISCELLANY POEMS (1704)
—a folio, with a fine mezzotint portrait-frontispiece.

THE WORKS (1713)
—contains the four comedies. Reprinted in 1720; 1731; 1733, Dublin; 1735; and subsequently.

THE POSTHUMOUS WORKS, ed. L. Theobald (1728)
—contains poems, a collection of maxims, and a memoir by R. Pack.

THE POSTHUMOUS WORKS . . . Vol. II, ed. A. Pope (1729)
—not a continuation of the previous work, but an attempt to prove Theobald's unreliability as an editor. It contains different texts of some poems and the Wycherley-Pope correspondence.

THE DRAMATIC WORKS OF WYCHERLEY, CONGREVE, VANBRUGH, AND FARQUHAR, ed. L. Hunt (1840).

PLAYS, ed. W. C. Ward (1888)
—in the original Mermaid Series.

THE COMPLETE WORKS, ed. M. Summers. 4 vols. (1924)
—the limited Nonesuch Press edition. Amply annotated but textually unreliable.

Separate Works:

HERO AND LEANDER, IN BURLESQUE (1669). *Verse*
—published anonymously.

LOVE IN A WOOD, OR, ST JAMES'S PARK (1672). *Drama*

THE GENTLEMAN DANCING-MASTER (1673). *Drama*

THE COUNTRY-WIFE (1675). *Drama*
—edited with *The Plain Dealer* by G. B. Churchill, *The Belles-Lettres Series*, Boston, 1924. Adaptations by J. Lee, 1765; by D. Garrick (as *The Country Girl*), 1766; by B. C. d'Arien (as *Das Landmaedchen oder Weiberlist geht über Alles*), Schwerin and Weimar, 1794.

THE PLAIN-DEALER (1677). *Drama*
—edited by A. Beljame and H. S. Symmes in *Representative English Comedies*, Vol. IV, New York, 1936. Adaptations by F. M. A. de Voltaire (as *La Prude ou la Gardeuse de Cassette*) in *Œuvres de M. de Voltaire*, Vol. VIII, Dresden, 1748; by I. Bickerstaffe, 1766 (further revised in 1796 by J. P. Kemble).

EPISTLES TO THE KING AND DUKE (1682). *Verse*
—published anonymously.

THE FOLLY OF INDUSTRY (1704). *Verse*
—reissued in 1705 as *The Idleness of Business: A Satyr*.

ON HIS GRACE THE DUKE OF MARLBOROUGH (1707). *Verse*
—published anonymously.

Note:

Three short poems were first published in miscellaneous collections of verse by various authors: 'The Answer' to 'A Letter from Mr. *Shadwell*, to Mr. *Wicherly*' in *Poems on Affairs of State. Part III*, 1698; 'To my Friend, Mr. *Pope*, on his Pastorals' in *Poetical Miscellanies: The Sixth Part*, 1709; 'An Epistle to Mr. *Dryden*, from Mr. *Wycherley*. Occasion'd by his Proposal to write a Comedy together' in *Poems on Several Occasions*, 1717.

Correspondence:

LETTERS UPON SEVERAL OCCASIONS, by J. Dennis, Wycherley and others (1696).

THE CORRESPONDENCE OF ALEXANDER POPE, ed. G. Sherburn. 5 vols. Oxford (1956)
—vol. I contains the Pope-Wycherley correspondence.

Some Biographical and Critical Studies:

LETTERS OF WIT, POLITICKS AND MORALITY, ed. A. Boyer (1701)
—includes a memoir by G. Granville, Lord Lansdowne.

THE TATLER, No. 3, by Sir R. Steele (1709).

MEMOIRS OF THE LIFE OF WILLIAM WYCHERLEY, ESQ., by C. Gildon (1718)
—published anonymously. It includes Lansdowne's memoir.

'Letters on Milton and Wycherley', by J. Dennis (1722)
—reprinted with other works containing critical and biographical remarks on Wycherley in *The Critical Works of John Dennis*, 2 vols., edited by E. N. Hooker, Baltimore, 1939-1943.

LETTERS CONCERNING THE ENGLISH NATION, by F. M. A. de Voltaire (1733).

'On Wycherley, Congreve, Vanbrugh, and Farquhar', by W. Hazlitt. In *Lectures on the English Comic Writers*, 1819.

ANECDOTES, OBSERVATIONS, AND CHARACTERS, OF BOOKS AND MEN, by J. Spence (1820)
—contains Pope's reported comments on Wycherley.

'On the Artificial Comedy of the Last Century', by C. Lamb. In *Elia*, 1823.

'The Dramatic Works of Wycherley, Congreve, Vanbrugh, and Farquhar', a review of Hunt's edition by T. B. Macaulay in *The Edinburgh Review*, xxii, 1841.

'Wycherley and Congreve', by C. Cowden Clarke. In *The Gentleman's Magazine*, vii, 1871.

THE COMEDY OF MANNERS, by J. Palmer (1913).

ENGLISH DRAMA OF THE RESTORATION AND EIGHTEENTH CENTURY, by G. H. Nettleton. New York (1914).

WILLIAM WYCHERLEY. SA VIE—SON OEUVRE, par C. Perromat. Paris (1921).

A HISTORY OF RESTORATION DRAMA, 1660-1700, by A. Nicoll. Cambridge (1923)
—revised edition as *A History of English Drama 1660-1900*, vol. i, Cambridge, 1952.

RESTORATION COMEDY, by B. Dobrée. Oxford (1924).

COMEDY AND CONSCIENCE AFTER THE RESTORATION, by J. W. Krutch. New York (1924).

THE COMIC SPIRIT IN RESTORATION DRAMA, by H. T. E. Perry. New York (1925).

THE SOCIAL MODE OF RESTORATION COMEDY, by K. M. Lynch. New York (1926).

THE OLD DRAMA AND THE NEW, by W. Archer (1929).

BRAWNY WYCHERLEY: FIRST MASTER IN ENGLISH MODERN COMEDY, by W. Connely (1930).

'Wycherley and Dryden', by H. Granville-Barker. In *On Dramatic Method*, 1931.

THE EARLY CAREER OF ALEXANDER POPE, by G. Sherburn. Oxford (1934
—this gives the best account of Wycherley's relations with Pope.

THE RELATION OF MOLIÈRE TO RESTORATION COMEDY, by J. Wilcox
New York (1938).

'Restoration Comedy: the Reality and the Myth', by L. C. Knights
In *Explorations*, 1946.

THE GAY COUPLE IN RESTORATION COMEDY, by J. H. Smith. Cambridge
Mass. (1948).

THE COURT WITS OF THE RESTORATION, by J. H. Wilson. Princeton
(1948).

THE THREAD OF LAUGHTER, by L. Kronenberger. New York (1952).

THE RESTORATION COMEDY OF WIT, by T. H. Fujimura. Princeton
(1952).

THE FIRST MODERN COMEDIES, by N. N. Holland. Cambridge, Mass.
(1959).

George Moore

A. NORMAN JEFFARES

Published for the British Council
and the National Book League
by Longmans, Green & Co.

Three shillings and sixpence net

George Moore (1852-1933) was born on his father's estate in the West of Ireland, went to school in England and spent his early twenties in Paris as an art student: he knew and admired the Impressionists, Manet, Degas, Renoir, and he was deeply impressed by Zola and by Huysmans. He turned from painting to writing, and out of a period of comparative poverty in London came his first novels, *A Modern Lover* (1883), *A Mummer's Wife* (1885) and *A Drama in Muslin* (1886). There followed *Esther Waters* (1894), a triumph of naturalism.

He returned to Ireland and, during his stay of ten years there, style became as important to him as story. *The Untilled Field* (1903) and *The Lake* (1905) showed his brilliance in observation and in prose. He turned his imagination to historical themes, to an imaginative life of Jesus in *The Brook Kerith* (1916), and followed this with *Héloïse and Abélard* (1921), *Ulick and Soracha* (1926) and *Aphrodite in Aulis* (1930).

But Moore's conversational powers and capacity for immediate response found their proper place in autobiography, in his *Confessions of a Young Man* (1888), *Memoirs of my Dead Life* (1906), and the magnificent mixture of malice and memory, of praise and fantasy, contained in the three volumes of *Hail and Farewell* (1911-14).

In this study the Professor of English Literature at the University of Leeds discusses Moore's main works, the stories he made in his auto-biographies out of his preoccupation with writing, with painting, with human life and love, and with the continuous development of his own creative and reflective powers.

Bibliographical Series
of Supplements to 'British Book News'
on Writers and Their Work

★

GENERAL EDITOR
Geoffrey Bullough

GEORGE MOORE

Detail from a pastel drawing by HENRY TONKS *in the*
National Portrait Gallery

GEORGE MOORE

by

A. NORMAN JEFFARES

Humour, irony, indignation, anecdote passed from him. We were his guests; he exhausted himself to entertain and hold us, having then—as always except when Amico Moorini showed his head—an ancient and elaborate courtesy.

Charles Morgan

PUBLISHED FOR
THE BRITISH COUNCIL
AND THE NATIONAL BOOK LEAGUE
BY LONGMANS, GREEN & CO.

LONGMANS, GREEN & CO. LTD.
48 Grosvenor Street, London W.1

*Associated companies, branches and
representatives throughout the world*

First published 1965
©A. Norman Jeffares, 1965

*Printed in Great Britain by
F. Mildner & Sons, London, E.C.1*

CONTENTS

Acknowledgement: Our grateful thanks are due to Messrs. Macmillan & Co. Ltd. for permission to quote from *An Epitaph on George Moore* by Charles Morgan; and to J. C. and R. G. Medley, owners of the copyright in George Moore's literary works, for permission to quote from the works and letters of George Moore.

¶ GEORGE AUGUSTUS MOORE was born on 24 February 1852 at Moore Hall, Muckloon, Lough Carra, Co. Mayo, Ireland. He died on 18 January 1933 in London, and his ashes were buried on Castle Island, Lough Carra.

GEORGE MOORE

I

THE LIFE

GEORGE AUGUSTUS MOORE was born on 24 February, 1852 at Moore Hall, a Georgian house overlooking Lough Carra, in Co. Mayo in the west of Ireland. Another George Moore, his great-grandfather, had built the house out of the large fortune with which he had returned to Ireland from Alicante, after a successful period as a merchant in Spain. While there he had drawn up a pedigree which traced the family back to Sir Thomas More; the document was certainly accurate as far back as the author's own great-grandfather, Captain George Moore, the Vice-Admiral of Connaught, and the connection with Sir Thomas More may well have been genuine. The family was originally Protestant; the first marriage into a Catholic family occurred early in the eighteenth century. George Moore the merchant was a son of this marriage and passed as a Catholic in Spain. His third son was an author, who wrote a Whiggish *History of the British Revolution* and a liberal and rational treatise attacking Kant. His son George Henry returned from Cambridge and subsequent travels in the East to occupy himself with racing and hunting. But at the time of the Irish famine of 1846-48 he sold his stable and turned to politics, heading the poll as an Independent in 1847, a seat he retained for ten years. In 1859, however, he returned to racing and won large sums of money, some of which he spent on his sons' education, sending them to Oscott, the Catholic college where he had himself been educated in England.

His eldest son, George, went to Oscott in the winter of 1861. An attack of bronchitis in 1863 gave him a happy spell at home, fishing on the lake with his brother Maurice, shooting, and joining in the life of his father's racing stables. Both he and Maurice, who joined him at Oscott in 1865, did

7

badly at the school, and the headmaster wrote many letters to their father about George's lack of progress. Eventually he left the school, where a younger brother, Augustus, joined Maurice; he spent a year at home, and then moved to London when his father abandoned racing for a second time and was re-elected to the House of Commons in 1868.

In London George Moore was influenced by the artist Jim Browne and began to attempt to paint; he was, however, sent by his father to work with an army crammer. When his father died he inherited an income of three to four thousand pounds a year from the property in Ireland, but only an income of about five hundred pounds of this was left after the payment of mortgages. He still wanted to become a painter and study in Paris, but, not being of age and as his guardians disagreed with his plans, he had to spend three years in London. He had financial scrapes, he lived a gay life, he made friends, but as soon as he was twenty-one he went to Paris.

In Paris he tried at first to obtain private tuition, but became a pupil in Jullian's Academy. Lewis Weldon Hawkins—the Lewis Ponsonby Marshall of the *Confessions* and *Hail and Farewell*—became his friend. There was a brief return to London where he painted, and lived beyond his income, but, back in Paris in 1875, he made the difficult decision to give up painting. He thought of marrying for money, also of becoming a writer, and he collaborated with Bernard Lopez in *Luther*, a verse drama which he had printed in 1878, a year after his poems, *Flowers of Passion*, were printed, reviewed savagely and later withdrawn. His friendship with Lewis diminished and Hawkins left the luxurious rooms in the Rue de la Tour des Dames, so richly described in the *Confessions*:

... our salon was a pretty resort—English cretonne of a very happy design —vine leaves, dark green and golden, broken up by many fluttering jays. The walls were stretched with this colourful cloth, and the arm-chairs and the couches were to match. The drawing-room was in cardinal red, hung from the middle of the ceiling and looped up to give the appearance of a tent; a faun, in terra-cotta, laughed in the red gloom, and there were Turkish couches and lamps. In another room you faced an altar, a Buddhist temple, a statue of Apollo, and a bust of Shelley. The bedrooms were made unconventional with cushioned seats and rich canopies; and in picturesque corners there were censers, great church candlesticks, and palms; then think of the smell of burning wax and you will have imagined the sentiment of our apartement in Rue de la Tour des Dames. I bought a Persian cat, and a python that made a monthly meal off guinea-pigs; Marshall, who did not care for pets, filled his room with flowers—he used to sleep beneath a tree of gardenias in full bloom.

Moore was moving in French society now, and the period from 1877 to 1880 was also the time of his 'café education', when he got to know Manet and Degas and their circle of friends, whom he met frequently in the Nouvelles Athènes in Montmartre. Yeats described him as 'sitting among art students, young writers about to become famous, in some café; a man carved out of a turnip, looking out of astonished eyes'. His appearance was indeed unusual. He had a receding chin, a long neck, a full if straggling moustache and sloping shoulders; his hair was pale yellow, his prominent eyes a pale grey-green, his complexion delicately pink; in Yeats's phrase again, his body was 'insinuating, upflowing, circulative, curvicular, pop-eyed'.

In 1880 Moore had to face the effects of the Land War in Ireland. His tenants refused to pay their rents, agricultural prices were down, and his uncle, Joe Blake, honest but chaotic, handed over the agency, to be replaced by Tom Ruttledge, young, untried but efficient. After a winter in Ireland, Moore settled down in London to write, living a very frugal and thrifty life, undertaking journalism—he wrote on the naturalistic novel, striving to bring Zola's work before British readers.

Moore's first novel, *A Modern Lover*, was published in 1883, to reappear in rewritten form as *Lewis Seymour and Some Women* in 1917. This was a study of an artist who is

helped throughout his life by women. Shaw remembered
Moore at this time as

always telling stories about himself and women. In every story there was
a room full of mirrors and chandeliers and the story usually ended with
some woman throwing a lamp at George and driving him out of the
house. Everybody used to laugh at George and no one believed him, but
he had an imperturbable good humour and if you said: 'But, George,
don't talk such nonsense, you are making it all up', he was not in the
least put out or angry but just said: 'Don't interrupt me', and went on as
before.

Moore realized later that his ability to write prose was
questionable (as much so as were his earlier attempts to paint
and to become a poet) but the story, he said, enthralled him.
His novel received favourable notice, but the circulating
libraries thought it unsuitable for their readers, so his next
venture was a one-volume novel published cheaply by
Vizetelly. This was *A Mummer's Wife*, a study of a touring
company, which he wrote in Ireland in the winter of 1883-
84, first at Moore Hall and later in Dublin, where he went to
observe and take part in the season at the Viceregal Court,
the Levee, the State Ball, and other social events, thus laying
the foundations of *A Drama in Muslin*.

He moved to chambers in London and there completed *A
Mummer's Wife*, his active answer to the sentimental school,
a novel in which he deepened his portrayal of character and
successfully applied the method of the French naturalistic
writers to English life. The winter of 1884-5 he spent in
Ireland where he finished *A Drama in Muslin*. He launched
an attack on the Viceregal Court in nationalist newspapers,
as he had not been invited, despite his requests, to a State
dinner party. He read Pater with great delight, then transferred himself to London and made a telling attack on the
circulating libraries. He made friends with the English
artists Sickert and Steer; a neighbouring landlord from
Galway, Edward Martyn, recently down from Oxford,

became another close friend. Martyn was portrayed in *A Mere Accident*, a novel written in and about Sussex, which marks the end of Zola's influence on Moore. (This reached its zenith in *Parnell and his Island*, but its waning is perhaps best captured in his 1894 account of a visit to Medan in 1888.) The effect of Huysmans and Flaubert on his writings now became apparent.

Moore had come to Sussex as the guest of old friends, the Bridgers, and in 1887 he joined with Collyer Bridger in a rabbit-farming venture there. He enjoyed what he called the Protestantism of Sussex, and *Spring Days* records this liking, captured in a Balzacian way. Dujardin's writings had a noticeable effect upon Moore, as is shown by his *Confessions of a Young Man* (1888); this rich and full account of his life in Paris led to his alienation from Degas and Zola. Though his next novel *Mike Fletcher* proved a failure, he was already engaged upon *Esther Waters* in 1890; he laid it aside, however, to write *Impressions and Opinions*, a successful collection of essays. *Vain Fortune* was a serial for the *Lady's Pictorial*, but did not do well. The winter of 1891-92 he spent writing *Esther Waters*.

Moore's criticism flourished, and his articles in *The Speaker* were collected as *Modern Painting* (1893). He had extended his friendships among the artists, and now knew William Rothenstein, Henry Tonks and D. S. MacColl, who was currently art critic of the *Spectator* and an equally enthusiastic supporter of the French Impressionists.

During the 'nineties Moore enjoyed a wider social life in London and even joined Boodles, the exclusive Tory club. Though he talked much about his love affairs, sentimental or promiscuous, and though he had set his mind against marriage, he seems to have fallen deeply in love with Mrs. Craigie, an American heiress, who wrote novels under the *nom de plume* John Oliver Hobbes. He collaborated with her in several plays. But she dismissed him savagely, probably because she had hopes of marrying Lord Curzon.

Esther Waters (1894) proved a popular success, and Moore

followed it with the short stories of *Celibate Lives* (1895), in which Mrs. Craigie appears as 'Mildred Lawson'—she is also depicted in 'Lui et Elles' in *Memoirs of my Dead Life* (1921), and in 'Henrietta Marr' in *In Single Strictness* (1922). Hone relates in his biography the story of the third quarrel with Mrs. Craigie which took place in 1904 after Moore and she had agreed to collaborate again in writing a play. Moore told his friend Dujardin what had happened:

'I was walking in the Green Park', he said, 'and I saw her in front of me. I was blind with rage and I ran up behind her and kicked her.' At first he related this story with some embarrassment, but when he grew accustomed to his invention, with relish. The scene in the Green Park was afterwards used in the sketch 'Lui et Elles' . . . where a heartless woman on whose face he detected a mocking smile, receives the assault 'nearly in the centre of the backside, a little to the right', and seems highly gratified to find that she has aroused such a display of feeling. 'It was inevitable, I said, part of the world's history, and I lost sight of all things but the track of my boot on the black crêpe de Chine.'

Mildred Lawson was incapable of love, her sensibility warped by her revulsion from sexuality; she turned to religion, but this was as unsatifactory as the independent life she had sought earlier in her pursuit of art. *Evelyn Innes* (1898) also owed something to Mrs. Craigie's life, though Moore had to learn a lot about music and convents to write it, a thing he did with 'pure joy'. The novel seemed at the time to be very successful indeed, but its sequel, *Sister Teresa* (1901), was less so. Yeats remarked that Moore was jealous of his own creation, Sir Owen Asher, a man about town and materialist; adding that Moore was all self and yet had so little self that he would destroy his reputation, or that of some friend, to make his audience believe that the story running in his head at the moment had happened, and only just happened. He was indeed a master of indiscretion.

By the time *Sister Teresa* was published Moore had left London for Dublin. He was deeply disturbed by the Boer

War, by Kiplingesque Imperialism, and found life in England distasteful. But there were also positive reasons for his move. The formation of the Gaelic League in 1893 had stirred his imagination. As a child he had grown up in a Gaelic-speaking area. He admired Yeats; Edward Martyn was his friend; and so he sympathized with their plans for an Irish literary theatre. He loathed the conventional English theatre; he despised the state of English dramatic criticism; he disliked the power of the great actors and actor-managers; and, as the third Director of the Irish Literary Theatre, he joined eagerly in the early work of getting Martyn's *Heather Field* and Yeats's *The Countess Cathleen* on to the stage in Dublin in 1899. Indeed Yeats wrote that the Irish theatre could not have been founded without his help and his knowledge of the stage. He felt that great art could coincide with national revival and he brought to Dublin his own cosmopolitan concept of art, literature and music.

He hurled himself into the movement to create a culture for Ireland. He spoke at meetings; he wrote art criticism; he wrote *The Bending of the Bough*, a patriotic play begun by Martyn which he took over, and this was produced in Dublin in February 1900. With Yeats he collaborated in the writing of *Diarmuid and Grania;* it was performed in Dublin in 1901. He developed a strong if short-lived enthusiasm for Irish. He settled in a house in Ely Place and, though he lived a laborious life, became part of the Dublin scene. He did not lack company, for a woman friend of his, the 'Stella' of *Hail and Farewell*, came to live in Rathfarnham, near Dublin, and he formed a friendship with AE (George Russell) and with John Eglinton (W. K. Magee, a librarian in the National Library).

The Irish Literary Theatre was replaced by the Irish National Dramatic Company in 1902; this year marked Moore's quarrel with Yeats over further collaboration and, in Yeats's phrase, he 'dropped out of the movement'. Then he wrote *The Untilled Field* (1903), a collection of stories which developed an earlier anti-clericalism and were also

brilliant Turgenev-like pieces of observation. He demon-
strated his anti-catholicism in a letter to the *Irish Times*,
declaring his conversion to the Church of Ireland, an action
which led, ultimately, to his estrangement from his brother
Maurice, whom he had invited to live in Moore Hall with
his family from 1905 onwards. But though he became
disillusioned with Irish life, with what he saw there as an
eternal conflict between literature and dogma, his return to
the Irish scene gave him fresh material. *The Lake* (1905)
seemed to him a triumph over the difficulty of preserving
unity of scene. It also represented a new phase in his art, a
continuous weaving of memories, of highly imaginative
reverie, which reached its peak in the mischievous, malicious
and yet deeply appreciative vignettes of his friends and
acquaintances in *Hail and Farewell* (1911, 1912, 1914) for
which *Memoirs of my Dead Life* (1906) with its memories of
various love affairs had been a lively rehearsal. His biographer, Joseph Hone, remarked that in later life Moore
when mentioning an episode with a woman would usually
say that he was now coming home 'to write an account of it
for his new book'. His brother, Colonel Maurice Moore,
said his adventures were 'half imagination, half reality'.

With the first volume of *Hail and Farewell* about to be
published it was time to leave Dublin for London. Moore
sold his estate to the Land Commission, and, after repaying
mortgages, received between twenty-five and thirty
thousand pounds; he retained Moore Hall and about five
hundred acres around it. He had in the 'nineties broken the
original settlement of the property upon his brother Maurice,
the second son, though they were then on good terms. But
their estrangement had increased steadily until, in 1911,
Colonel Maurice Moore and his family left Moore Hall.
(The house was never again occupied. It was burnt down in
'the Troubles' in 1923, and Moore eventually received
£7,000 in compensation.) A house in Belgravia, 121 Ebury
Street, seemed suitable, and Moore lived here from 1911
until his death in 1933. He made a few trips to Ireland, and a

visit to France was virtually an annual event, with Dujardin often acting as his host. He also visited the Holy Land in 1913. Having written *The Apostle* (1911), a melodramatic play about St. Paul's finding Jesus still alive, he wanted to deal again with the biblical past, and to get the background right. He spent fourteen months writing *The Brook Kerith*, concentrating now on the character of Jesus rather than that of Paul, keeping the stream of his ideas and narrative flowing continuously and melodiously.

This style of his animates *A Storyteller's Holiday* (1918), but in these somewhat contrived tales Moore had to rely upon James Stephens's help with the dialogue. This was the first of his works to be issued in the limited and expensive editions in which the rest of his writings continued to be published in the first instance, before going into cheaper editions. By this means of publication he generally earned at least two thousand pounds on each book.

In 1918 he began to think up *Héloïse and Abélard* (1921), spending three years on it, travelling in France to absorb atmosphere, consulting many friends on points of detail, and developing for the first time his method of dictating about 1,500 or 2,000 words a day, then later revising the whole book. This was a laborious method of writing which, as a letter to a friend put it, made his life pass 'in loneliness and composition'. He saw his friends by appointment only, but he enjoyed regular meetings at Tonks's house, and at Sir Edmund Gosse's. Nancy Cunard, Charles Morgan, David Garnett, Mrs. Belloc Lowndes were added to his friends; there were his older friends, John Eglinton, Richard Best, Oliver Gogarty, Mr. and Mrs. St. John Hutchinson, whom he saw from time to time. There were houses he visited; he had many correspondents; the routine of his own house was watched over by his housekeeper, Clara Warville. It was an agreeable life, darkened only by kidney and prostate troubles from 1927 onwards. He was not strong enough for a major operation, and his friends often found him difficult. Sir John Thomson-Walker, the surgeon, helped him a great deal, became a close friend, and Moore's last completed book, *Aphrodite in Aulis* (1930), was dedicated to him.

The last years of Moore's life were filled with work. He revised his writings constantly, always polishing, removing obstacles and obscurities that might hinder the progress of the tale. He told Geraint Goodwin that if he had a tombstone he would like this written on it: 'Here lies George Moore, who looked upon corrections as the one morality.' He followed *Héloïse and Abélard* with *Ulick and Soracha* (1926), a story of thirteenth-century Ireland. He made a delightful translation of *Daphnis and Chloë* (1924) which gave scope to his skill in story-telling; he wrote more essays, the *Conversations in Ebury Street* (1924) and *A Communication to My Friends* (1933), as well as plays and short stories. At eighty he was an impressive figure in the world of letters. Though he himself sometimes thought his merits had been overlooked by that world of letters, of scholarship, and of politics, he was praised generously in a message in *The Times*, signed by many distinguished writers, which recognized his single-mindedness, his toiling in the perfection of his craft, his effect upon the users of the language and his revival of the art of narrative.

He died, regretting the fact that he seemed unable to accomplish *A Communication to My Friends*, 'telling the story of how writing was forced upon me and the persecution I have undergone for forty years and which is just ended, leaving me a wreck'. He was fundamentally a serious artist, a conscious writer, who through his forty years of work managed to create his own style and to make it the flexible expression of his own personality. He wrote in his *Confessions* that he came into the world

apparently with a nature like a smooth sheet of wax, bearing no impress, but capable of receiving any; of being moulded into all shapes. Nor am I exaggerating when I say I think that I might equally have been a Pharaoh, an ostler, a pimp, an archbishop, and that in the fulfilment of the duties of each a certain measure of success would have been mine.

The result of his experience of life was to make him a mixture of naivety and shrewdness, of mischievousness and an acute awareness of his own limitations. He became a personality filled with apprehensions of beauty and ecstasy, as well as of the absurd, a writer always sharply and persistently aware of the mystery and terrifying speed and shortness of human life.

II

THE NOVELS AND STORIES

Moore has his secure place in the history of the English novel. Most readers, for instance, will have read or know of *Esther Waters*, with the new dimension of naturalism it brought into English writing; they will also know how he developed after 1903 a new kind of prose, a blend of the written and spoken word peculiarly his own achievement. But how many realize how much more there is to Moore, the novelist, than the achievement of his best-known novel or to Moore the raconteur than the apparently artless gossip of *Hail and Farewell?* Of the early works, for example, there is the unusual felicity of *A Drama in Muslin*, foreshadowing the limpidity and brilliance of *The Lake*. The maturity of *The Brook Kerith* and the virtuosity of *Héloïse and Abélard* round off a quintet of novels extremely varied in subject-matter, imaginatively rich and supremely readable. These are his outstanding novels: but there is much to be enjoyed in the others, and this survey will mention them briefly as well as concentrating on Moore's major work.

When Moore looked back at his first novel *A Modern Lover* (1883) in 1917, he thought it the book of a young man who 'in a moment of inspiration, hit upon an excellent anecdote, and being without literary skill to unfold it, devised an uncouth text out of his memories of Balzac, Zola and Goncourt'. He summarized the book neatly:

Three women undertake to work for a young man's welfare: a work-girl, a rich woman, and a lady of high degree. All contribute something, and the young man is put on a high pedestal. One worshipper retains her faith, one loses hers partially, and one altogether.

Filled with revulsion as he re-read the book he finally decided that a new book could be moulded around it, and the Preface to the new version, *Lewis Seymour and Some Women* (1917), tells us engagingly how joyously he dictated and completed the work in three months.

His early desire was to observe and record accurately: the wish to tell a story was, perhaps, a later rationalization. This novel broke new ground in its first version and allowed Moore to portray his knowledge of art and a somewhat flashy view of fashionable life. He was writing an often clumsy English, not to be compared with that of the later version, which has some urbane satire on the relations of the sexes and is more efficiently told as a story: neither version, however, is fully satisfactory.

A Mummer's Wife (1885) was begun with the hope of being, as he wrote to the French novelist, 'Zola's ricochet in England'. He was applying the French Naturalistic method to English material, to the lives of actors in a provincial setting: he spent several weeks with a touring company, and he listened to many stories of the lives of actors and actresses. Out of this came a much more lively interplay of characters than he had achieved in his first novel. Kate Ede, who is seduced by Dick Lennox, is drawn with great sensitivity as well as realism, for Moore had developed and deepened his understanding of personality, of the effect of one sex upon the other, of the human heart; and the treatment of the scenery and the action, despite the mediocre, plain prose style, was sharper than before, more effective and indeed much more frank than anything Moore's contemporaries dared give the public. His desire to escape the bondage of the libraries (evinced in *Literature at Nurse, or Circulating Morals*) had no doubt sharpened his powers of shocking their particular audience. The realism of the early part of the book gives credence to the developing hysteria and violence of the heroine, who is always measured against the stolid matter-of-factness of Dick Lennox.

With *A Drama in Muslin* (1886), however, Moore developed a much more complex theme and treatment of it, and this novel is still most rewarding to read. In it he describes the two Irelands, of gentry and peasantry, during the tensions of the period of the Land League which was set up in 1879. The peasants, exasperated by evictions and bad agricultural seasons, were using weapons of boycott, and their 'No-Rent' campaign was very effective. There were shootings of landlords and their agents until the 1881 Act at last gave the tenants a right in the land without destroying the right of the landlord; it also reduced rents by twenty per cent. Further Land Acts of 1887, 1891 and 1903 were to make Ireland a country of peasant proprietors, and Moore had read the writing on the wall. He was a humane man, who, though he liked the social standing of being a landlord, realized instinctively that the era of the ascendancy was virtually over. The novel, therefore, draws a contrast between the social glitter and tinsel of the Viceregal Court in Dublin and the uneasiness, even boredom, of life in the big houses and lesser Georgian mansions, whose occupants were perpetually conscious of 'the disturbed state of the country'. Chapter Thirteen, for instance, is one of the scenes dissimilar yet interdependent, which are still technically interesting; it is a piece of *montage* which gives an alternating account of the arguments taking place in front of the house between peasants and their landlord and his agent, and of those occurring inside the house between the landlord's wife and an army captain, an unsuccessful suitor for her daughter. The human relationship of the girl and her lover is affected by the general situation:

From the drawing-room window Mrs. Barton watched the conflict. On one side she saw her daughter's beautiful white face becoming the prize of a penniless officer; on the other she saw the pretty furniture, the luxurious idleness, the very silk dress on her back being torn from them, and distributed among a crowd of Irish-speaking, pig-keeping peasants.

The girl, Olive Barton, is one of several well-born (and some not quite so well-born) girls who have grown up together in Galway, and who are presented and dine and dance during the Dublin season. Moore hated this marriage market: he was, like Ibsen, convinced that woman was more than a domestic animal. He had read *A Doll's House* when half-way through his own story, but remarked, so he says in the Preface to the 1915 edition of *A Drama in Muslin*, that he was himself writing of a puritan heroine, 'but not a sexless puritan, and if women cannot win their freedom without leaving their sex behind they had better remain slaves, for a slave with his sex is better than a free eunuch'. He thought that Olive's sister, Alice Barton, was a more objective portrayal than Ibsen's Nora, and this girl is drawn with dignity. She thinks for herself; she begins to write professionally because she does not regard the capture of a husband as the prime aim of her life. She is no prig, however, and supports the harum-scarum May, who has an illegitimate child; eventually she marries a dispensary doctor. To realize herself she has to resist the activities of her mother, who is drawn ruthlessly in all her vulgarity and energy.

The novel has some unevenness in style. It matches the richness, the bustle and crowding, the hectic excitements and the ensuing enervations of its social scenes with a voluptuous prose. Here is a portion of the famous description of the dressmaker's shop:

Lengths of white silk clear as the notes of violins playing in a minor key; white poplin falling into folds statuesque as the bass of a fugue by Bach; yards of ruby velvet, rich as an air from Verdi played on the piano; tender green velvet, pastoral as hautboys heard beneath trees in a fair Arcadian vale; blue turquoise faille francaise fanciful as the twinkling of a guitar twanged by a Watteau shepherd; gold brocade, sumptuous as

organ tones swelling through the jewelled twilight of a nave; scarves and
trains of midnight blue profound as the harmonic snoring of a bassoon.

The Misses Robinson, whom he used to visit, read him out a
passage which they had added in the margin of their copy:
'Everything was represented there, from the light clarinette
of the embroidered lace handkerchief to the profound
trombone of the red flannel pantaloons.' How could he
write such a thing, they asked, and he fell into their trap and
defended the phrase he had never used. He later saw himself
like 'a hound yelping at every trace of scent' in this book.
He records the serious conversations and the gossip with
skill; he catches the crippled Cecilia's religious attacks on
sensuous life in suitably matching tortuous prose. He contrasts the life of wretched cabin and glittering salon effectively; he describes the scenery with economical sensitivity;
he analyzes the situation of women. And the story holds us
with its mixture of satire, objectivity, and insight. It is an
unreasonably neglected novel, and it is also a piece of highly
significant social history.

When did the author of *A Drama in Muslin* change,
Moore asked himself in 1915, and answered himself with
1888, the year of the *Confessions* and *Spring Days*. He wrote
four novels which he did not include in his collected works.
In *A Mere Accident* (1887) he had attempted to capture both
the monastic spirit and its opposite, the 'sleepy smug
material' of Sussex. The model for the hero of the novel was
Edward Martyn, and Moore drew in him a somewhat
paradoxical aesthetic ascetic who ran his estates efficiently,
collected Monets and Renoirs, read mediaeval Latin authors
as well as Pater and Schopenhauer, and liked Wagner and
Palestrina. His mother tried to get him to marry and
eventually he fell in love with a young girl, who was,
however, assaulted by a tramp and died melodramatically
after a fall from a window. The novel shows Moore's
ability to make use of his friends' characters and to get his
material in order, for he drew heavily upon his friends'

knowledge, in this case of mediaeval Latin and music. The story appeared again as 'John Norton' in *Celibates* (1895), and a comparison of the two versions shows the great speed with which Moore's technique was advancing.

Spring Days (1888) was intended as a prelude to a trilogy, which would give a large sweeping survey of human nature. It told the story of three English girls in Sussex who fail to marry, but the narrative wandered a little and the hero, Frank Escott, heir to an Irish peerage, is not an interesting enough dreamer. The trilogy was to deal, first with young men in London, next with a servant's view of servants and finally with the attitudes of old people to their children. *Mike Fletcher* (1889) mainly describes an Irish journalist, a second-rate cad about town, and a complete failure; the other characters were Frank Escott and John Norton. The idea of a serious novel about servants occurred to him shortly after *A Drama in Muslin* was published; it promised to be more human than *Mike Fletcher*. (Mention of this novel irritated him intensely in later life, so much had he come to dislike its lack of order and development.) He told Madame Lanza that he intended to bathe himself in 'the simplest and most naïve emotions, the daily bread of humanity'. But before completing this story of servants he spent the winter of 1890-91 writing *Vain Fortune* (1892) for the *Lady's Pictorial*, where it was published serially under a *nom de plume* and illustrated by Maurice Greiffenhagen. This novel, not as bad as has sometimes been alleged, nor yet, as Moore wrote in a letter, a pot-boiler, has a plot dealing with the frustrations of an unsuccessful author and the girl whom he disinherits. She falls in love with him and commits suicide when he marries her companion.

By 1893 he had completed *Esther Waters:* his plan he announced to Madame Lanza in a letter:

. . it is all about servants—servants devoured by betting. It begins in a house in the country where there are race horses. Towards the end of the book—past the middle—the servants set up a public house. They cannot get custom unless they have betting. Then come the various tragedies of the bar—the hairdresser who cuts his throat—the servant who loses thirty years' character for six shillings—the woman who pledges the plate to give her lover money to bet with. The human drama is the story of the servant girl with an illegitimate child, how she saves the child from the baby farmers, her endless temptations to get rid of it and to steal for it. She succeeds in bringing up her boy, and the last scene is when she is living with her first mistress in the old place, ruined and deserted. The race horses have ruined masters as well as the servants.

The book was very well received; it sold well, and the circulating libraries gave way, Mudie at first, but Smith's after an argument in which Moore proved that they had lost £1,500 by not taking *Esther Waters*. The novel was his tribute to England, 'Pecksniff done seriously, and if the feat does not seem impossible, with love'.

Esther Waters contains Moore's knowledge of horse racing and of betting, and their effects upon human life. There are the great kaleidoscopic scenes of Derby day, the boom of the 'great mob', the cockney crowd; there is Mr. Leopold in his pantry, a picture of the butler of Moore Hall; there are the scenes, too, of the lying-in hospital, and there is the baby-farmer. Balzac inspired this work, and in it Moore achieves a story of commonplace heroism. He begins with the description of the receding train as it appeared to the girl of twenty, and Chapter 44 begins in exactly similar words; but the train is seen now by a woman of seven or eight and thirty; and we realize now with a jolt how much has happened to her in the eighteen years since she first arrived to be a kitchenmaid. His picture of how Esther is deserted and how she wrestles with life to bring up her son is realistic, but it is also written with an innate if unobtrusive compassion. It is a humane book, matching its acute observation with sensitive understanding.

In *Evelyn Innes* (1898) Moore described the battle within an opera singer's heart between her religious feelings and her delight in the pleasures of the world. She is torn between love for Sir Owen Asher (probably modelled on a mixture of Arthur Symons's intellectualism and Sir William Eden's aristocratic sophistication), and for Ulick the Celtic musician (modelled in the first edition upon Yeats, and later upon AE). The novel reflects Moore's own development: he drew upon Arnold Dolmetsch for the character of Evelyn's father, the musician; he attended some of the informal concerts held in the Dolmetschs' house in Dulwich where he set part of the novel, and he learned much from Dolmetsch and from Arthur Symons about Renaissance and baroque music. This novel is one of the first to make use of music as a background. It reflects, as well as Moore's own interest in Wagner, a good deal of fashionable aestheticism. Factual information gives solidity to the story, which is also based upon Moore's own progress in the fashionable world and his financial success. The furniture and the Aubusson carpet in this novel are described with the loving attention that his own similar possessions were receiving in his new flat in Victoria Street, into which he had moved from the Temple.

Evelyn Innes is one of the novels in which he was con- ducting his education publicly but the sequel, *Sister Teresa*, has less of this interest, for in it Moore, possibly stimulated by Mrs. Craigie's conversion to Roman Catholicism, was writing an account of life in a convent which allowed him to explore the religious impulse more fully, but with less certainty of touch, as though he were himself affected by Evelyn's hesitation between life in the convent or outside it. Finally, however, the novel ends with her at peace, but with the reader probably sharing the view of the priest quoted by Yeats, who remarked of the novel, 'everything is there of the convent, except the religious life'. In this novel Moore was echoing the current interest in the opposition of art and reality, spirit and flesh; and the heroine withdraws to the convent's ritual, disappointed by her bid for individual artistic freedom.

A reversal of this progress takes place in *The Lake* (1905), the first of Moore's fully symbolist novels. Some of the hints for it exist in *A Drama in Muslin*, where the influence of Huysmans was clear. In that novel Moore had explored the complications of character, and had shown signs of matching it with a less drab style. Now he was to explore the complexities of style also and, in so doing, to create his own contribution to English prose, the melodic line. The story of *The Lake* is relatively simple. A priest drives a pregnant but unmarried schoolteacher from his parish; he later corresponds with her, and falls in love with her, without ever seeing her again. His desire for the world increases, his belief diminishes, until finally he leaves his clothes beside the lake and swims across it, to leave his parish and Ireland, and begin another life. Father Oliver Gogarty (the name was chosen in mockery of that unpriest-like figure Oliver St. John Gogarty, who appears as Buck Mulligan in Joyce's *Ulysses*) walks by the lakeside, and the story slowly unfolds itself with a convincing, compellingly persuasive development. The technical achievement is superb; the movement from *Esther Waters* to *The Lake* is parallel to that of Joyce from *Dubliners* to *A Portrait of the Artist* (and *Hail and Farewell* captures another aspect—Moore's life in Ely Place—of that Dublin which is also so brilliantly immortalised in Joyce's Eccles Street in *Ulysses*). The change was brought about after he had completed the stories of *The Untilled Field*, in which he had examined some of the sterility and sadness he saw in Irish life, where he attributed poverty and emigration to the work of a puritanical, priestly church. These earlier stories, especially 'The Wedding Gown', 'The Widow' and 'So on he fares' are masterly pieces of story-telling, spare, economical but highly emotive.

The Lake opens with a passage that shows us the kind of association Moore is to evoke throughout the novel between scene and mood; he was writing about the place in which he himself grew up and he wrote with deep feeling:

It was one of those enticing days at the beginning of May when white clouds are drawn about the earth like curtains. The lake lay like a mirror that someone had breathed upon, the brown islands showing through the mist faintly, with gray shadows falling into the water, blurred at the edges. The ducks were talking softly in the reeds, the reeds themselves were talking; and the water lapped softly about the smooth limestone shores. But there was an impulse in the gentle day, and, turning from the sandy spit, Father Oliver walked to and fro along the disused cart-track about the edge of the wood, asking himself if he were going home, knowing quite well that he could not bring himself to interview his parishioners that morning. On a sudden resolve to escape from anyone that might be seeking him, he went into the wood and lay down on the warm grass, and admired the thickly-tasselled branches of the tall larches swinging above him.

After the priest has reached his decision to leave his parish, the lake is still there, its serenity matching the excitement with which he contemplates the oneness of Nature. 'Every man', he says, 'has a lake in his heart', and Moore carries the symbolism forward through the novel, building up his suggestions with subtlety through the apparent simplicity of the famous melodic line:

He walked along the shore feeling like an instrument that had been tuned. His perception seemed to have been indefinitely increased, and it seemed to him as if he were in communion with the stones in the earth and the clouds in heaven; it seemed to him as if the past and the future had become one.

The moment was one of extraordinary sweetness, never might such a moment happen in his life again. The earth and sky were enfolding in one tender harmony of rose and blue, the blue shading down to grey, and the lake floated amid vague shores, vaguely as a dream floats through sleep. The swallows were flying high, quivering overhead in the blue air. There was a sense of security and persuasion and loveliness in the evening.

The Brook Kerith (1916) is often described as a prose epic and fully deserves the name. It is constructed with skill, and its conversational style has a directness, freshness and spontaneity which gives it warmth and colour. In it Moore retells the story of the New Testament with the difference that in the account which he puts in the mouth of Joseph of

Arimathea, Jesus has not died on the cross, but has been rescued by Joseph. He is later discovered by Paul, who seeks refuge among the community of Essenes among whom Jesus has lived as a shepherd in the wilderness for twenty years. Paul at first believes that Jesus is a madman, then fears he may return to Jerusalem to destroy his own work. But Jesus tells him that we must learn to live for ourselves and to suffer our fellows to do likewise; all learning, he says, 'comes out of ourselves, and no one may communicate his thought; for his thought was given to him for himself alone'. The Biblical imagery and rhythms add to the epic quality of the story: it is simple and the narrative unfolds effectively, action, description, thought and speech blending in a pattern which provides variation and tension as well as information and reflection. It is easy to read, and it reads aloud superbly; it is spacious, dignified and captivating, an example of the supreme flexibility of the art of a great story-teller whose essential seriousness of artistic purpose is enlivened by the subtle humour and by the inconsequential trivia which give to the novel its feeling of concrete detail:

Hast slept well, Paul, and hath sleep refreshed thee and given thee strength to pursue thy journey? Paul answered that he was very weary, but however weary must struggle on to Caesarea. Thy strength will not suffer thee to get farther than Bethennabrio, and thy sandals will need mending even to reach the village. And seating himself on a smooth stone Paul watched Jesus's hand tying new thongs, wondering if the madman's mind was still set on Jerusalem and if he would go thither as soon as he (Paul) was safely out of the ways of the Jews. Each shut himself within the circle of his own mind, and the silence was not broken till Paul began to fear that Jesus was plotting against him; and to distract Jesus's mind from his plots, if he were weaving any, he began to compare the country they were passing through with Galilee, and forthright Jesus began to talk to Paul of Peter and John and James, sons of Zebedee, mentioning their appearances, voices, manner of speech, telling of their boats, their fishing tackle, the fish-salting factory of Magdala, Dan, and Joseph his son. He spoke a winning story of the fishing life round the lake, without mention of miracles, for it was not to his purpose to convince Paul of any spiritual power he might have enjoyed, but rather of his own simple humanity. And Paul listened, still believing his guide to be a madman. If thou hadst not run away crying: He is mad! he is mad! thou wouldst have heard how my crucifixion was brought about; how my eyes opened in the tomb and—Interrupting Jesus, Paul hastened to assure him that if he cried out: He is mad! he is mad! he had spoken unwittingly, the words being put into his mouth by the sickness in which Jesus had discovered him. And the sickness, he admitted, might have been brought about by the shock of hearing thee speak of thyself as the Messiah. But, Paul, I did not speak of myself as the Messiah, but as an Essene who during some frenzied months believed himself to be the Messiah. But shepherd, Paul answered, the Messiah promised to the Jews was Jesus of Nazareth, who was raised by his Father from the dead, and thou sayest that thou art the same. If thou didst once believe thyself to be the Messiah thou hast repented thy blasphemy. In the desert these twenty years, Jesus answered. But not till now did I know my folly had borne fruit, and that Joseph knew a story had been set going; or it may be that the story was not set going till after his death. Now it seems too late to go into the field thou hast sown with tares instead of corn. To which Paul answered: It is my knowledge of thy life among rocks that prompts me to listen to thee. The field I have sown like every other field has some tares in it, but it is full of corn ripening fast which will be ready for the reaping when it shall please the Lord to descend with his own son, Jesus of Nazareth, from the skies. As soon as the words: Jesus of Nazareth, had left his lips Paul regretted them, and upon a sudden resolve not to utter another word that might offend the madman's beliefs, he began to tell that he had brought hope to the beggar, to the outcast, to the slave; though this world was but a den of misery to them, another world was coming to which they might look forward in full surety. And many, he said, that led vile lives are now God-fearing men and women who, when the daily work is done, go forth in the evening to beseech the multitude to give some time to God. In every field there are tares, but there are fewer in my field than in any other, and that I hold to be the truth; and seeing that Jesus was listening to his story he began to relate his theology, perplexing Jesus with his doctrines, but interesting him with the glad tidings that the burden of the law had been lifted from all. If he had stopped there all would have been well, so it seemed to Jesus, whose mind was not able to grasp why a miracle should be necessary to prove to men that the love of God was in the heart rather than in observances, and the miracle that Paul continued to relate with much unction seemed to him crude; yet he once believed that God was pleased to send his only begotten son to redeem the world by his death on a cross. A strange conception truly. And while he was thinking these things Paul felling to tell his dogma concerning predestination, and he was anxious that Jesus should digest his reply to Mathias, who had said that predestination conflicted with the doctrine of salvation for all. But Jesus, who was of Mathias's opinion, refrained from expressing himself definitely on the point, preferring to forget Paul, so that he might better consider if he would be able to make plain to Paul that miracles bring no real knowledge of God to man, and that our conscience is the source of our knowledge of God and that perhaps a providence flourishes beyond the world. (ch. XLI)

Héloïse and Abélard (1921) has a rich content: in this philosophical romance Moore mixes thought and tragedy, description and story. Tension begins in Canon Fulbert's house overlooking the Seine; the lovers, the Canon's niece and the brilliant academic, travel through the forests to Britanny with a background of spring sights and sounds; there is always a background unobtrusive yet atmospheric; there is both movement and contemplation:

But to reach Chécy before nightfall they would have to hasten, and the innkeeper told them that the road through the forest looped so that the village of Lorris might be taken into the circuit; but there was no need for him to follow this winding, he would find a by-path across certain low hills which he could not miss. Abélard did not feel sure that the by-path might not be missed, but to hear the road explained out again would be merely a waste of time, and so they hastened towards the forest in a sort of half-knowledge of the way, allowing the horses to trot a little, thinking that they might draw rein when they passed through the fringe of birch-trees that encircled with their pallor the great district of pines that showed in black masses over against Etampes. Now we are well within the forest, Abélard said, as much in the forest as if we were in the middle of it; and he asked Héloïse to peep over the undergrowth that lined the rutted path down which they were riding, so that she might see the pines rising up naked and bare some fifty or sixty feet, some straight, some leaning, in endless aisles. Like the spears, Héloïse said, of Crusaders going into battle; and how penetrating is the smell of the resin. But the pines were in patches only, and the forest passed quickly into rocky hillsides overgrown with oak and beech; and so faint was the path they followed that Abélard often asked Héloïse and Madelon to draw rein while he went forward in search of the path. For if we all went forward together, he said, we should not be able to go back to where the path ends: a tree is no sure landmark; one forgets which tree, and wanders in a circle. I've got it, he cried to them, and they came forward, the forest getting lonelier as they proceeded into it.

All bird cries have ceased, and we hear only the sighing of the boughs, Héloïse said, and the smell of the forest is different from all other smells; a more mysterious smell is about, a smell of earth and moss. There is also a warm smell, said Madelon, that reminds me of our Brittany forests, the great forest about Clisson, where we shall be—Héloïse, myself and my boy—before the month's end, should we catch a fast-sailing barge from Orléans. Did he not say that a little over three leagues from Etampes we should find the by-path that would save us several leagues' journey? Abélard asked, and some hundreds of feet after he told them to rein in while he went on ahead in search of the path. Here it is, he cried, from a clearing; we have but to follow the path that leads through the hollows younder up to the rising ground that the innkeeper spoke of. He spoke to me of oak-trees, and here they are. And they rode beneath the boughs not yet in full leaf, following the path as it wound through hollows, losing it and finding it amid rocks, pushing their way through thickets that seemed impenetrable at a distance but did not prove so hard to force through as they had appeared. There is a rutted way under the brambles, Abélard said; cattle and horses have been through here; and stooping low in their saddles, they broke through somehow, losing bits of clothing in the passage. Soon after the path led them up hills, through thorn and hazel mingled with inter-spaces, till it brought them to a heath, and Abélard said: those pines standing so solitary at the end of the lake embedded in rocks are the trees the inn-keeper told me I was to look out for. We have not missed the way, he continued; look back and see the forest that we have come through. And he pointed to a dark ragged line of pines flowing down the northern sky. But is our way to the right or to the left? Madelon asked. To the left, he answered; we have to ride southward, keeping the setting sun on our right. (ch. XVI)

Abélard's arrogant ambition, Héloïse's agonized love, their joint readiness to lie in pursuance and defence of love, are part of the whole life of the book. Moore's sensualism, and his occasional mischievousness underlie the simplicity of the story; his attitude is consistent. The peasant driving his cart, and Madelon, the Canon's servingwoman, are two examples of an earthy contrast opposed to the intellectualism of the lovers. The romance gains in depth because the conversations and thoughts of Héloïse and Abélard are sharply focussed against a very crowded background of cities and convents, of trouvéres, of classical culture, even of the contentions between nominalists and realists. Moore took immense trouble to get his picture of eleventh century life right. Its complexity is gained through digressions and repetitions in the talk and the learning; the liveliness comes from its picture of the ceaseless sifting of the human mind on earth; the resolution rests upon a human will to believe in heaven and immortal happiness.

Ulick and Soracha (1926) deals with mediaeval Ireland, but it lacks the sheer beauty of *Héloïse and Abélard;* and *Aphrodite in Aulis* (1930) runs the risk of appearing disjointed, for its author's habit of digression and complication is not under the fine architectonic control he had earlier displayed.

It is perhaps fitting to conclude a brief account of Moore's fiction with some comment on the five stories—'a single narrative divided into five chapters'—of *Celibate Lives* (1927) which were based on earlier work in *Celibates* (1895), *A Story-Teller's Holiday* (1918) and *In Single Strictness* (1922). They show Moore's developed artistry in illustrating, in smooth narrative, with calm detachment, the finer points of character, indeed his never ceasing fascination with human motive and behaviour. That the stories were about women reminds us that he had remarked in the *Confessions* that he was enthralled by 'the mystery of petticoats' and confessed in the *Memoirs* that his thoughts ran upon women as the legitimate object of men's thoughts. His own thoughts he translated into an objective portrayal of women's role in a society within which they were moving to greater freedom; his apparently detached portraits were drawn not only with skill but with deep sympathy.

III

THE PLAYS

In all Moore wrote eleven plays, the first two of which, *Worldliness* (1874) and *Martin Luther* (1879), were not performed. Several managers, including Hare and Beerbohm Tree, refused his next play, *The Strike at Arlingford* (1893), but after a few years Moore turned its five acts into three, and it was performed in February 1893. He was greatly attracted by the Ibsen-like qualities of Martyn's *The Heather Field*, and when Martyn's next play, *The Tale of a Town*, was disappointing, he took it over and it was produced, under Moore's name, as *The Bending of the Bough* (1900). He explained the situation thus:

> I am afraid Martyn suffered a good deal. He says I spoil[ed] his play but that is an illusion. I recast the play, but not enough. I should have written a new play on the subject . . . Then Edward said he could not sign it, and he refused to let it be played anonymously, so I had to sign it.

The play revolves around nationalist and unionist attitudes. The potential leader gives up the struggle because of his love for a girl, and his backsliding is received with philosophical serenity by the nationalist *eminence grise*. It is a dull play, but in the politically charged atmosphere of the Dublin of that time it was well received.

Moore's next collaboration was with Yeats, and their work on *Diarmuid and Grania* led to much disagreement between them. The play was put on in Dublin in 1901, but the critics there regarded the treatment of the heroic legend as unsatisfactory. The susceptibilities of nationalists could be easily upset. Moore wrote to his brother that 'they first of all enjoyed the play, and having enjoyed it they repented in sackcloth and ashes, and I really believe that the repentance was much greater than their enjoyment of the play'.

His next adventure into drama was *The Apostle* (1911)

which dealt with a meeting between Jesus and Paul after the crucifixion: it was hastily published, but contains his fascinating *Prefatory Letter on Reading the Bible for the First Time*. In 1906 Moore had begun work on a dramatic version of *Esther Waters* and Lennox Robinson was called in to help with the dialogue—Moore's old weakness—in the second act. The play was performed twice, but unsuccessfully, at the Apollo Theatre. Moore, however, was not put off by its reception, and resumed work on *Elizabeth Cooper* (1913), which was produced by the Stage Society in 1913. Moore had enlisted the aid of Mrs. Craigie in this play in 1904, and five years later was helped by Dujardin (who produced the French version, *Clara Florise*, at the Comedie Royale). Moore's correspondence with a foreign lady of title, begun some ten years earlier, formed the basis of the plot. In the play the foreign countess mistakes the young secretary of the author for his employer and, in one version, marries him. Another rewriting appeared as *The Coming of Gabrielle* (1921) which was rehearsed in 1921 but finally abandoned. It was a near-miss.

The Brook Kerith led to a second play entitled *The Apostle* (1923); this added a scene to the novel, but was also lacking in good dialogue. Moore followed it with *The Making of an Immortal* (1928), an amusing Shakespearean conceit, with clever character sketches; this was well received after its production at the Arts Theatre in 1928.

The Passing of the Essenes (1930) was yet another handling of the theme of *The Brook Kerith*, and the relationship of Jesus and Paul. This time the reception was warm, the play's run extended, and Moore even went to see it himself. He came back as critical of actors as ever, since the

poor play did not come out as it should have come out, and what pleasure is it to me that other people liked it? I wanted to like it and I didn't. The uninspired actors were between me and it all the time.

Moore was his own best actor, and his best writing self-dramatization. His weakness was inability to write good dialogue; his strength was in duologue, provided he was inventing both parts of the conversation.

IV

AUTOBIOGRAPHIES AND ESSAYS

Moore's *Confessions of a Young Man* (1888) were written when he was thirty-six; they describe his life in Paris; they record his impressions of Manet, Degas, and Renoir, of Zola, and of Verlaine and Mallarmé. The book gives us an excellent impression of aestheticism, and of Moore's youthful desire to shock and astonish people. It was certainly original, and the self-portrait is one of Moore as he seemed to Theodore Dorret, 'a golden-haired fop, an aesthete before the days of Wilde . . . his manners were amusing and his French very funny'. Always, Dorret remarked, he remained a gentleman and would never associate with those he thought to be below his rank as an Irish landlord. As a result he describes his early life with satiric detachment. The *Memoirs of my Dead Life* (1906) contained more material likely to astonish, if taken seriously, rather than to shock. 'The Lovers of Orelay' became famous as an account of an elderly man's adventure with a young woman in France, told with comic relish, as well as some naivety, as in the account of the purchase of the silk nightshirt. The volume contained memories of Mayo, London, Paris and Sussex (a moving account of Mrs. Bridger's death). The love stories reflected his comment that his thoughts ran on women: 'On what would you have them run? On coppermines? Woman is the legitimate subject of all men's thoughts.' When he wrote the *Memoirs* he was fifty-four; his energies were increasingly occupied by his writing and rewriting, and this gave him a reputation for cold detachment. It is true that he used his friends as material for his writing, but he used himself even more. During his stay in Ireland at the beginning of the century his style had developed from the flowing narrative of the stories of *The Untilled Field* into the complexities, the repetitions, linkages and cadences of *The Lake*. There he became the raconteur, there he changed from his livelier youth into a search for and a discovery of himself. The *Memoirs* show his flair for maintaining the fluidity of his tales, his mixture of speech and reflection, his blending of past and present thought.

Throughout the superb comedy of *Hail and Farewell*, which is his masterpiece, there runs the ground swell of his preoccupation with Protestantism as he imagined it, with the issues of life as he experienced them, emotionally and instinctively, often wilfully and impatiently. He was not concerned with the reputation of Moore the man; he cared deeply for the reputation of Moore the writer. And so *Hail and Farewell* is a devastating book: ironic, witty, provocative, even at times profound in its accounts of the men and women he observed around him in Dublin. His brilliant evocation of Edward Martyn, his delicate appreciation of AE, his caustic commentary on Yeats, contribute to our sense of human comedy.

The forthrightness of Moore's comments stemmed from his belief that once the veracity of a biographer (or autobiographer) is impugned the book becomes discredited and its value depreciated. And so he gives us magnificent scenes —the dinner in the Shelbourne Hotel, the bicycling around Tara, New Grange and Dowth with AE, as well as the account (which disturbed so many of his contemporaries) of the end of his affair with Stella. This is the artist at work— with the disciple he called Amico Moorini emerging at intervals to nudge his comic work into the risk of seeming farce—for flippancy and wilfulness have never appealed greatly to critics, however much they were an almost inevitable minor part of such an unusual talent as Moore's, committed to both the artistic and the ruthless rendering of a situation, a nuance, an anecdote, which would convey his own attitude of curiosity, of almost innocent interest, to the reader. He recreates yet again but with entirely new memories his days in the Temple, in Paris, in Mayo, in Sussex. With Whelan he avoids mass when staying with Edward Martyn, with whom he visits Bayreuth for *The Ring*. The flow of his mind is strong; he observes Lady Gregory and Yeats in the west of Ireland; he gives us vignettes of Dublin as he walks by the Liffey or the Dodder; he recounts conversations, and retells Dublin gossip: of how, for instance, Sir Thornley Stoker the surgeon collected his antiques:

... on the trail of a Sheraton sideboard and Naylor has been asked to keep it till an appendix should turn up. The Chinese Chippendale mirror over the drawing-room chimney-piece originated in an unsuccessful operation for cancer; the Aubusson carpet in the back drawing-room represents a hernia; the Renaissance bronze on the landing a set of gall-stones; the King Cloisonnee a floating kidney; the Buhl cabinet his opinion on an enlarged liver; and Lady Stoker's jewels a series of small operations performed over a term of years.

All of this is recounted with limpidity; the transitions from speech to thought, to memory, to speech again invite us to tour with him through reveries of rich reminiscence and ideas which are lively, stamped always with a zest and appreciation of living, with shrewdness and naivety.

These qualities permeate his critical prose also. *Avowals* (1919), for instance, contains opinions on literary works 'discovered' by Moore over the years. These are delivered with some panache, for, as Moore reminds us in Chapter XVI, his only affectation was complete naturalness, and on the subject of writing he held strong views. The English eighteenth-century novelists, Jane Austen and Pater, Tolstoi and Turgenev are discussed with vigour and delight. Moore did not read a great deal, but he had listened and discussed; he had formed his opinions and he gave them a curiously personal flavour:

In the fifties was the Word and it was with Flaubert, I said, and began to trace the origin of his reputation to a reaction against Byron, his going to Greece to die for an idea, to Chateaubriand's tomb, to pirates and brigands who had become so intolerable in literature that everybody welcomed the idea that a writer need not dine in a baronial hall among retainers, nor keep for pets pythons, eagles, wolves or jaguars, and of all it was pleasant to hear that Monsieur Flaubert spent much time at his window watching the Seine flowing by, thinking of the inevitable Word, which he never found till late in the evening. Everybody was delighted; fellow-feeling makes wondrous bed-fellows, and when it became known for certain that *Madame Bovary* was written in a dressing-gown, the reaction against romanticism carried the book along with it, and if this explanation prove inacceptable, we shall have to fall back on the depressing belief, for which, indeed, much can be said, that the masterpiece is but our mood, and that as soon as the mood passes—all moods except the Bible, Shakespeare and Sterne pass—the inspired and the uninspired are live as twins.

Conversations in Ebury Street (1924) ranges widely. Balzac, George Eliot and Hardy are discussed with zest. Then the artists Tonks, Steer, and Sickert are given life, and there follow further literary comments and speculations, among them enlightened praise of Anne Brontë's work. There is not, however, so much concentration as in the essays of *Avowals* which represented the flowering of Moore's literary views in the mid-summer of his career, with *Esther Waters, The Lake, The Brook Kerith, Héloïse and Abélard* and *Hail and Farewell* already achieved.

V

THE ACHIEVEMENT

Moore's achievement needs reconsideration. His works have been allowed to drop out of print—one hopes only temporarily—but his merits should not be ignored. For he is a writer of great skill, a serious writer who can give much pleasure to his readers. He affected the course of English fiction and the style of English prose; he developed his own literary personality; he was a man in whom imagination and narrative skill, capacity for industrious work and artistic conscience so fused that he produced fiction and fictionalized autobiography which has the timeless quality of all great art. He carries us on when we read him, and that is perhaps the secret of the enjoyment he can give: it is the art of the story-teller he develops and he appeals to our common delight in and enjoyment of a story well told.

GEORGE MOORE

A Select Bibliography

(Place of publication London, unless stated otherwise)

Bibliography:

BIBLIOGRAPHIES OF MODERN AUTHORS: NO. 3, GEORGE MOORE, by
I. A. Williams (1921).

'George Moore: A Bibliography, 1878-1921', by H. Danielson, in
J. Freeman, *A Portrait of George Moore* (1922).

'George Moore: An Annotated Bibliography of Writings About Him',
by H. E. Gerber, in *English Fiction in Transition (1880-1920)*, vol. ii,
no. 2 (parts i and ii), 1959, and Supplements; vol. III, no. ii, 1960;
vol. iv, no. 2, 1961

—the fullest and most accurate bibliography of Moore yet published.
The information (and sensible comments) are essential for any serious
study of Moore's work.

Collected Works:

THE WORKS OF GEORGE MOORE. 20 vols. (1933)
—the uniform edition.

THE WORKS OF GEORGE MOORE. 20 vols. (1937)
—the Ebury edition.

Separate Works:

WORLDLINESS. A COMEDY IN THREE ACTS (c. 1874)
—'The author believes, and hopes, that no copy of this, his first
published work, now exists.'—I. A. Williams.

FLOWERS OF PASSION (1878). *Verse*

MARTIN LUTHER. A TRAGEDY IN FIVE ACTS (1879). *Verse Drama*
—in collaboration with Bernard Lopez.

PAGAN POEMS (1881).

A MODERN LOVER. 3 vols. (1883). *Novel*
—re-written as *Lewis Seymour and Some Women*, 1917.

A MUMMER'S WIFE (1885). *Novel*
—French translation, Paris, 1888.

LITERATURE AT NURSE, OR CIRCULATING MORALS (1885). *Polemic*
—pamphlet on the selection of books at Mudie's Library.

A DRAMA IN MUSLIN. A REALISTIC NOVEL (1886)
—largely re-written as *Muslin*, 1915.

A MERE ACCIDENT (1887). *Novel*
—'John Norton' in *Celibates*, 1895, is a re-writing of this.

PARNELL AND HIS ISLAND (1887). *Sketches*

CONFESSIONS OF A YOUNG MAN (1888). *Autobiography*
—edited and annotated by Moore, 1904, 1917; revised edition, 1926; in Uniform edition, 1933.

SPRING DAYS. A REALISTIC NOVEL. A PRELUDE TO 'DON JUAN' (1888)
—with preface, 1912.

MIKE FLETCHER (1889). *Novel*

IMPRESSIONS AND OPINIONS (1891). *Criticism*

VAIN FORTUNE (1891). *Novel*
—revised 1895.

MODERN PAINTING (1893). *Criticism*
—enlarged, 1898.

THE STRIKE AT ARLINGFORD. A PLAY IN THREE ACTS (1893).

ESTHER WATERS (1894). *Novel*
—revised and privately printed, 1920; in Uniform edition, 1932; dramatic version, 1913.

CELIBATES (1895). *Stories*
—contains three tales: 'Mildred Lawson', 'John Norton', and 'Agnes Lahens'.

THE ROYAL ACADEMY, 1895 (1895). *Criticism*
—New Budget Extra, No. 1.

EVELYN INNES (1898). *Novel*

THE BENDING OF THE BOUGH. A COMEDY IN FIVE ACTS (1900).

'Literature and the Irish Language' (1901). *Criticism*
—in *Ideals in Ireland*, edited by Lady Gregory.

SISTER TERESA (1901). *Novel*
—continuation of *Evelyn Innes;* entirely re-written, 1928.

THE UNTILLED FIELD (1903). *Short Stories*
—part of the book was first published in Gaelic, Dublin, 1902; revised edition, 1926; in Uniform edition, 1932.

THE LAKE (1905). *Novel*
—revised edition, 1921; in Uniform edition, 1932.

MEMOIRS OF MY DEAD LIFE (1906). *Fictional autobiography*
—revised and enlarged 'Moore Hall' edition, 1921; revised for Uniform edition, 1928.

REMINISCENCES OF THE IMPRESSIONIST PAINTERS. Dublin (1906). *Memoirs.*

HAIL AND FAREWELL: A TRILOGY. 3 vols. (1911-14). *Autobiography*
—*Ave* 1911; *Salve* 1912; *Vale* 1914. Limited edition in two volumes, 1925; in Uniform edition, three volumes, 1933.

THE APOSTLE. A DRAMA IN THREE ACTS. Dublin (1911)
—revised, limited edition, 1923.

ELIZABETH COOPER. A COMEDY IN THREE ACTS. Dublin (1913).

MUSLIN (1915). *Novel*
—revision of *A Drama in Muslin;* in Uniform edition, 1932.

THE BROOK KERITH: A SYRIAN STORY (1916). *Novella*
—5th edition revised, 1921; revised for Uniform edition, 1927; limited edition with engravings by Stephen Gooden, 1929.

LEWIS SEYMOUR AND SOME WOMEN (1917). *Novel*
—revision of *A Modern Lover.*

A STORY-TELLER'S HOLIDAY (1918, limited edition). *Short Stories*
—revised edition in two volumes, including *Ulick and Soracha,* Uniform edition, 1928.

AVOWALS (1919, limited edition). *Criticism*
—in Uniform edition, 1924.

THE COMING OF GABRIELLE. A COMEDY IN THREE ACTS (1920, limited edition).

HÉLOISE AND ABÉLARD. 2 vols. (1921, limited edition). *Historical Romance*
—in Uniform edition, 1925.

FRAGMENTS FROM HÉLOISE AND ABÉLARD: ADDITIONS AND CORRECTIONS (1921).

IN SINGLE STRICTNESS (1922, limited edition). *Short Stories*
—revised as *Celibate Lives* for Uniform edition, 1927.

CONVERSATIONS IN EBURY STREET (1924, limited edition). *Criticism*
—revised for Uniform edition, 1930.

THE PASTORAL LOVES OF DAPHNIS AND CHLOË. DONE INTO ENGLISH (1924, limited edition). *Translation*
—from Longus. In Uniform edition with *Peronnik the Fool,* 1933.

PERONNIK THE FOOL. New York (1924). *Short Story*
—new limited edition, New York, 1926; revised limited edition, Eure, France, 1928; with engravings by Stephen Gooden, London, 1933; in Uniform edition with *The Pastoral Loves of Daphnis and Chloë,* 1933.

PURE POETRY. AN ANTHOLOGY (1924, limited edition). *Anthology*

ULICK AND SORACHA (1926, limited edition). *Novel*
—included in revised edition of *A Story-Teller's Holiday*, Uniform edition, 1928.

THE MAKING OF AN IMMORTAL. A COMEDY IN ONE ACT. New York (1927).

A FLOOD. New York (1930). *Short Story*

APHRODITE IN AULIS (1930, limited edition). *Novel*
—revised for Uniform edition, 1931.

THE PASSING OF THE ESSENES. A DRAMA IN THREE ACTS (1930)
—limited edition of a further revision of *The Apostle*.

A COMMUNICATION TO MY FRIENDS (1933, limited edition). *Autobiography*
—in Uniform edition with *A Mummer's Wife*, 1933.

DIARMUID AND GRANIA. A PLAY IN THREE ACTS BY GEORGE MOORE AND W. B. YEATS. In the *Dublin Magazine*, xxvi (April-June 1951)
—with an introductory note by William Becker.

Note: Moore also wrote introductions to Zola's *Piping Hot!* (1885), Dostoevsky's *Poor Folk* (1894), and several other books.

Letters:

LETTERS FROM GEORGE MOORE TO EDOUARD DUJARDIN 1886-1922. New York (1929)
—translated by 'John Eglinton' (William Magee).

LETTERS OF GEORGE MOORE. Bournemouth (1942)
—with an introduction by 'John Eglinton'. A frank and convincing picture of Moore as a man.

GEORGE MOORE'S LETTERS TO LADY CUNARD, ed. R. Hart-Davis (1957)
—a record of the great sentimental friendship of Moore's life. Well-edited.

Some Biographical and Critical Studies:

A PORTRAIT OF GEORGE MOORE IN A STUDY OF HIS WORK, by J. Freeman (1922)
—the first full-scale study of Moore's works.

EDWARD MARTYN AND THE IRISH REVIVAL, by D. R. Gwynn (1930)
—appraises Moore's work for the Irish literary revival.

GEORGE MOORE, by H. Wolfe (1931)
—enthusiastic but dated.

EPITAPH ON GEORGE MOORE, by C. Morgan (1935)
—extremely good brief interpretation of Moore as man and writer.

THE LIFE OF GEORGE MOORE, by J. Hone (1936)
—the most important book written on Moore; detached, accurate,
and well written; an admirable biography.

AS I WAS GOING DOWN SACKVILLE STREET, by O. St. John Gogarty (1937)
—a picturesque view of Moore and Yeats.

THE MOORES OF MOORE HALL, by J. Hone (1939)
—describes the life of Moore's brother, Colonel Maurice Moore, as
well as that of the novelist.

'George Moore's Revisions of *The Lake*, *The Wild Goose*, and *Esther
Waters*', by R. A. Gettman, in PMLA, lxix, June 1944
—points out that Moore's habit of revising his work was not confined
to his old age.

GEORGE MOORE: A RECONSIDERATION, by M. Brown. Seattle (1955)
—useful and appreciative.

G. M.: MEMORIES OF GEORGE MOORE, by N. Cunard (1956)
—personal memories, and a friend's appreciation.

THE IRISH WRITERS, 1880-1940, by H. Howarth. New York (1959)
—excellent and informative.

EDWARDIANS AND LATE VICTORIANS, by G. Hough (1960)
—'George Moore and the Nineties', pp. 1-27, is a good survey, setting
Moore in his period.

FROM GAUTIER TO ELIOT, by E. Starkie (1960)
—a good account of French influence on Moore.

'George Moore and literary Wagnerism', by W. F. Blissett, in
Comparative Literature, xiii, Winter 1961
—deals with Moore's use of Wagnerism and his originality.

'A newly discovered drawing by Degas of George Moore', by
R. Pickvance, in the *Burlington Magazine*, June 1963
—useful on Moore's art criticism.

David
Hume

by

MONTGOMERY BELGION

Published for the British Council
and the National Book League
by Longmans, Green & Co.

Three shillings and sixpence net

David Hume has been described as a writer who, 'by incessant labour', made himself 'the one master of philosophic English'. But his English was not exclusively philosophic. His moral, political, and economic essays are outstanding for literary style, and so is his *History of England*, which drew the high praise of a touch of envy from no less a judge than Gibbon. In philosophy Hume's name is coupled with those of his two great predecessors in this country, Locke and Berkeley. He was the greatest of the three in having brought about a turning point in the course of human thought.

Montgomery Belgion is the author of numerous articles and of various books, among the latter being *News of the French*, *Reading for Profit*, and *Victors' Justice*. A work on which he has been engaged for more than ten years, to be called *Megalopolitics*, is now nearing completion. He contributed the essay on H. G. Wells to this series.

Bibliographical Series
of Supplements to 'British Book News'
on Writers and Their Work

★

GENERAL EDITOR
Geoffrey Bullough

DAVID HUME
from a painting by ALLAN RAMSAY *in the*
Scottish National Portrait Gallery

DAVID HUME

by

MONTGOMERY BELGION

PUBLISHED FOR
THE BRITISH COUNCIL
AND THE NATIONAL BOOK LEAGUE
BY LONGMANS, GREEN & CO.

LONGMANS, GREEN & CO. LTD.
48 Grosvenor Street, London, W.1

*Associated companies, branches and
representatives throughout the world*

First Published 1965
© Montgomery Belgion 1965

*Printed in Great Britain
F. Mildner & Sons, London, E.C.1*

CONTENTS

NOTE: For information or references I wish to thank Sir Herbert Read, Mr. Huntington Cairns, and the Rev. Professor Dr. R. Gregor Smith; I also wish to thank Mr. J. S. Burdon and the staff of Kettering public library for obtaining books for me and getting the loan of them extended by the National Central Library.

¶David Hume was born in 1711. He died on 25 August 1776.

DAVID HUME

DAVID HUME—'*le bon David*'—lived from 1711 to 1776, and was the last great British philosopher. He completed the trio which he forms with John Locke (1632-1704), author of *An Essay concerning Human Understanding* (1690), and George Berkeley, Bishop of Cloyne (1684-1753), author of *The Principles of Human Knowledge* (1710 and 1713), and he was greater than they: he went deeper. Sir Leslie Stephen (1832-1904) wrote in 1876:

> Between the years 1739 and 1752 David Hume published philosophical speculations destined, by the admission of friends and foes, to form a turning point in the history of thought.

What Hume did was simply to show that the boundaries between knowledge and belief do not run where it was supposed they did. But for his acumen modern psychology is hardly to be imagined. He is of course the heir of Locke and Berkeley—he too is preoccupied with 'knowledge' and with 'human understanding'—but in addition he has affinities with the leading mediaeval Nominalists, notably William of Ockham (1270-1347). Most of what is negative in his teaching regarding religion and metaphysics has come to be adopted unawares by the masses who have never heard his name. In these islands the literate among us have on the whole preferred Locke. In view of the capital importance of what Hume points out, this may seem curious. He had no disciples, but his legacy did not go unclaimed. It passed to Germany, where it was cultivated and made to fructify as much as the times would allow. There is no doubt regarding the greatness of this last of the great British philosophers, but his philosophical achievement remains subtle and elusive.

Hume added to his complexity in being versatile. He was not only a philosopher. In the catalogue of the British Museum library he is distinguished from another of the same

name by being called 'David Hume the Historian'. Certainly
he achieved greatness and celebrity with his *History of
England*. His essays—moral, economic, and political—are
also remarkable. His chief ambition was indeed to be a good
writer. The *History of England* was the first history in
English to have high literary merit. As late as 1885 the
erudite George Saintsbury (1845-1933) paid tribute to it.
By then there had been other notable histories in English,
Macaulay's, and John Richard Green's *History of the English
People*, and Froude's *History of England from the Fall of
Wolsey;* yet Saintsbury pronounces that Hume's is still the
best written. In the introduction to his *Specimens of English
Prose*, he declares:

> We shall never have a greater historian in style as well as in matter
> than Gibbon; in style at least we have not yet beaten Hume, though
> there has been more than a century to do it in.

The writing may be summed up as lucid, direct, simple, and
elegant. The author felt that the subject was suited to every
capacity, and so 'I composed it', he writes, '*ad populum* as
well as *ad clerum*'. He is content to arouse and sustain the
interest of the reader, and at the same time as he tries to
enter into the individual situation of each of a succession of
selected historical personages he succeeds in being objective
and impartial. It has of course been pointed out more than
once that since his day history has become 'scientific', and is
now based scrupulously on documents (he deliberately uses
no state papers). What is the gain to the general reader? I
was looking at a recently published popular history of
England, and regarding the House of Stuart I found that on
two cardinal matters Hume is more definite than the
twentieth-century historian: to Charles I he is more fair,
and he refuses the benefit of the doubt to Mary Queen of
Scots.

For a writer to expound attractively political and economic theories and principles is even more remarkable than

for him to write good narrative. Hume does both. Unlike philosophy, economics is a progressive science, and the student goes to the latest additions to its literature. Yet so winning is Hume's style that for many years ordinary readers continued to go to his essays for pleasure. He deserves to be called the founder of political economy. Without him his friend and junior, Adam Smith (1723-1790), who is regarded as the first great British economist, could hardly have produced his famous book, *The Wealth of Nations* (1776). As this came in its turn to be superseded, so with its publication Hume's scattered essays on the same subject tended towards eclipse. But they nevertheless continued to be read for their own sake. Here is what J. H. Burton wrote about them in 1846 in his *Life and Correspondence of David Hume* (he refers particularly to the volume entitled *Political Discourses*):

These Discourses are in truth the cradle of political economy; and much as that science has been investigated and expounded in later times, these earliest, shortest, and simplest developments of its principles are still read with delight even by those who are masters of all the literature of this great subject. But they possess a quality which more elaborate economists have striven after in vain, in being a pleasing object of study not only to the initiated, but to the ordinary popular reader.

By now it will be credible that Hume was the first author in England to make writing really pay. A younger son, he did not have to face the world entirely dependent on what he could earn. But his income at the start was only about £40 a year (say, £400 today). He made repeated efforts to eke out this by taking employment, and ultimately retired with a royal pension of £400 a year. In addition, he had some investments. But by 1769 it was what he calls copy-money, and we call royalties, that provided the bulk of his income, so that he then had altogether £1,000 a year. Dr. Samuel Johnson (1709-1784) wrote more for book-sellers, but he did not make as much money. From the

History of England, all rights in which were disposed of, Hume obtained £4,090.

Even to set out philosophical arguments was something that he came to be able to do with felicity, thanks to pertinacity and hard work. In his youth he talked exactly like what he was: a Lowland Scot. He passed through the University of Edinburgh with his speech unpurified, but formed there his lifelong liking for the Latin classics. He graduated, as was then usual, at fifteen. It was by self-tuition that he came to write an English free of dialect. He constantly strove to eliminate Scotticisms, and compiled and published a list of them. The means whereby he was going to change the course of human thought was his first book, *A Treatise of Human Nature*. Upon its publication nobody would have forecast its future celebrity. Confident that he had important things to say, Hume retired to the French provinces from 1734 to 1737 specially in order to write it. Yet, when the first two volumes came out in 1739, they '*fell*', in his own famous phrase, '*dead-born from the press;* without reaching such distinction as even to excite a murmur among the zealots'. The third and last volume which followed in 1740 fared no better. He was not yet thirty. He came to feel that he had begun too young. He decided to recast his ideas in a simpler form. He took great pains to make his philosophy intelligible to the general reader. In 1748 he issued a new version of Book I. It was called *Philosophical Essays concerning Human Understanding*, but in later editions the title was changed and the name *Enquiry* substituted for 'Philosophical Essays'. In 1751 he followed the recast version of Book I of the *Treatise* with one of Book III. He called this, *Enquiry concerning the Principles of Morals*. He regarded it as,'of all my writings, historical, philosophical, or literary, incomparably the best'. Contrasting the distance travelled in point of style between the *Treatise* and this second *Enquiry*, Hume's nineteenth-century editor, T. H. Grose, remarks:

The style of the Treatise is indeed immature, but it reveals the tendencies which were ripened by incessant labour, until Hume was the one master of philosophic English.

Only in F. H. Bradley (1846-1924) has English philosophy had a prose writer worthy of being put by the side of Hume.

To judge by the writings now in print, Hume survives as a sceptic in religion, an economist, and a moral, political, and epistemological philosopher. As philosophy is not a progressive study, some individual contributors to it have a good prospect of speaking to every successive generation, and Plato's *Republic*, Aristotle's *Nicomachean Ethics*, continue available in popular translations. But not every philosopher remains relevant. Father Frederick Copleston, S.J., remarks in Volume IV of his *History of Philosophy:* 'Hume is a living thinker in the sense that Spinoza is not.' Although Hume is so important, he had no direct disciples, but many an English philosopher after him, from John Stuart Mill (1806-1873) to Bertrand Russell (b. 1872), is, in one or more respects, simply a minor Hume. Those philosophers fall into mistakes which Hume is held to have made first. Mill felt too superior to stick his nose inside the *Treatise;* not the author was thereby the loser.

I

If Hume had no direct disciples as a philosopher, he was taken as literary model by a number of later Scottish writers. But his writings have an essence which these literary pupils never distil for themselves. He reflects with his pen his attractive character. He may have been inclined to irascibility in youth, but once adult he became equable, cheerful and sanguine, and such remained his disposition. He says:

I was ever more disposed to see the favourable than the unfavourable side of things, a turn of mind which it is more happy to possess than to be born to an estate of ten thousand a year.

He had a sense of fun, he liked old claret, he was kind-hearted, even generous; he over-estimated the abilities of some of his friends. His living qualities are all in his prose. Of him it is particularly true that *le style, c'est l'homme même.*

We today are in a better position to know about Hume's life than our fathers were, for in recent years there have been new biographies and fresh collections of letters. In 1931 came Mr. J. Y. T. Greig's *David Hume;* in 1932 the same writer's collection in two volumes of the admirably edited *The Letters of David Hume;* in 1954, first, R. Klibansky and E. C. Mossner's *New Letters of David Hume,* and then *The Life of David Hume* by E. C. Mossner. The bare biographical facts were supplied by Hume himself in a short account written six months before his death.

Hume's family was a branch of the Earl of Home's. His father died while he was an infant. He was born in Edinburgh, but grew up in Berwickshire. Life in the Scottish countryside was then primitive and bare. When he found himself with a small income and a strong inclination to study and to write, he was already inured to frugality.

As late as 1748, when he was thirty-seven, he still had to practise economy. In Edinburgh, then, having gone to live in that city, and 'having a fine coat', he was invited out to dinner four or five times a week. It was the custom to tip one's host's servants, and he could not afford to do so. It is reported that his amiability compensated them enough.

How often do English people exclaim 'There we are!' As they quote Shakespeare unawares, few realize that this is a quotation from Hume. The *History of England* came out volume by volume from 1754 to 1761. In 1763, Hume began his second stay in France. He went to Paris as secretary of the British embassy, and by then the book was as well known in France (in translation) as it was at home. In the course of reviewing the French version of Volume I, Voltaire (1694-1778), himself an expert in the writing of history, remarks:

Nothing can be added to the fame of this *History*, perhaps the best ever written in any language. . . . Mr. Hume, in his *History*, is neither parliamentarian, nor royalist, nor Anglican, nor Presbyterian—he is simply judicial.

The moment Hume arrived at Paris he discovered that he was a celebrity. During the twenty-eight months of his stay he was adulated without respite. He was presented to the Dauphin and his three sons—each one to be a king. He became '*le bon David*'. He was a favourite with some of the ladies who ran a *salon*. Even the blind Marquise du Deffand, who was cross with him for visiting her former companion, Julie de Lespinasse (who now had a rival *salon*), had enough affection for him to refer to him by a nickname. For her, he was *le paysan*. Madame Geoffrin, chaffing him about playing the coxcomb, calls him '*mon gros Drôle*'. He was in constant demand for parties and for the opera. One evening he was asked to join in a kind of charade, and was placed on a settee between two dazzling young houris, to whom he was bidden to pay passionate court. He never married, but he was not without experience of laying siege to a woman's heart, and yet now he was tongue-tied. After a long pause, all he managed to stammer was: '*Ah, mes demoiselles, nous voilà!* . . . *Ah, nous voilà ici!*'

This abysmal histrionic failure affected his popularity in Paris not at all. The failure was accepted as he himself had been accepted—with his lumbering frame, his occasional vacuous look which was to frighten Rousseau, and the atrocious Scottish accent with which he spoke French. In the eyes of Paris he continued uninterruptedly to be '*le bon David*'. It should have been as blissful as Bottom wound in Titania's arms.

Earlier in 1763, before Hume went to Paris, the Rev. Thomas Reid (1710-1796), founder of the 'common sense' school of philosophy in these islands, showed him the MS. of a forthcoming book in which he describes Hume's 'principles' as 'the common ones', and declares that in being coherently developed they exhibit 'their futility'. Hume took this with good humour. In returning the MS., he drew attention to a mistake Reid had made in English. He went on:

If you have been able to clear up these abstruse and important subjects, instead of being mortified, I shall be so vain as to pretend to a share of the praise; and shall think that *my errors*, by having at least some coherence, had led you to make a more strict review of my principles, which were the *common ones*, and to perceive *their futility*.

There was but one man whose presence, it is said, he would not tolerate in the same room, a man who had rudely attacked him, without producing evidence, for his not exonerating Mary Queen of Scots in the murder of Darnley. He could be amused by Thomas Reid, but Reid's fellow-critic, James Beattie (1735-1803), and the latter's *Essay on the Nature and Immutability of Truth* (1770), led him to write to his bookseller or publisher in 1775, that he had just drawn up 'a compleat answer to Dr. Reid and to that bigoted silly fellow, Beattie'. It was only a short note or 'advertisement'. If he was normally equable, it was not that he lacked spirit.

He had his share of vicissitudes. In 1745 a young marquis who had read some of his essays wrote inviting him to come and live with him as tutor. In his readiness to take employment so as to improve his finances, he accepted, and then discovered that the marquis was mad and that he was to be less a tutor than a keeper. He had cannily obtained a contract, and under it he was owed, when he left, £75. To recover this sum took him fifteen years. But he persisted till he obtained it.

In 1754 the first volume of the *History* was brought out by a Scottish bookseller who had gone to London. An association or conger of London booksellers put the book under ban, and in a twelvemonth not forty-five copies were sold. Happily, in the end, a London bookseller bought up the unsold copies.

On leaving Paris at the beginning of 1766 he was persuaded to take Jean Jacques Rousseau (1712-1778), then a fugitive from French justice on account of the *Émile* and the *Contrat Social*, to England with him. He set up Rousseau in a country house in Staffordshire with servants and board, for all of which Rousseau was to pay only £30 a year. From George III also he obtained for Rousseau a pension of £100 a year. Rousseau composed the second part of the *Confessions* during this time. Some months later, however, he suddenly wrote to Hume out of the blue accusing him of conspiring to ruin him. Not surprisingly, the sudden attack made Hume rather lose his head. In his letters describing the incident, he calls Rousseau 'a monster' and 'the blackest and most atrocious villain that ever disgraced human nature'; he refers to 'the lying, the ferocity of the rascal'. Both in Paris and London he published 'a succinct account' of the circumstances. It was more than they warranted, and inflicted additional cruelty upon poor Rousseau, who had told him how he was persecuted in Switzerland the year before, but not about what had been attempted against him earlier in France.[1]

In the spring of 1775, Hume was stricken with a disease which had been fatal to his mother. A few months before he died he received from his friend Edward Gibbon (1737-1794) Volume I of the *Decline and Fall of the Roman Empire*, and at about the same time, from Adam Smith, the newly published *Wealth of Nations*. Gibbon was much pleased with Hume's letter of thanks. He notes in *Memoirs of my Life and Writings*: 'A letter from Mr. Hume overpaid the labour of ten years.' And then he prints the letter.

Hume died on 25 August 1776. In the following November Adam Smith wrote to William Strahan, Hume's bookseller, a letter describing his last illness. 'His cheerfulness never abated. . . . He continued to divert himself, as usual, with correcting his own works for a new edition.' Smith recalls further 'the extreme gentleness of his nature', which 'never

---

[1] Cf. F. Macdonald, *La Légende de Jean-Jacques Rousseau rectifiée, d'après une nouvelle critique*, Paris (1909). F. G. Green, *J. J. Rousseau* (1955), has a long account of his relations with Hume, pp. 331-42.

weakened either the firmness of his mind, or the steadiness of his resolutions. His constant pleasantry was the genuine effusion of good nature.'

Such was the man, but not the whole man. He had set himself up in opposition to what in Britain far more than in France was still the current trend. Most of his life he was conscious of being baulked and frustrated. He was confronted with what seemed to be an intangible obstacle. I shall go into this more definitely in Section V below. But the trouble was, for better for worse, in the man himself. As Norman Kemp Smith says in the introduction to *Hume's Dialogues concerning Natural Religion* (1937), allowance has to be made for the defects of Hume's qualities, 'characteristic of his time as well as of himself', and for his limitations of interest and of insight. Not for him, I am sure, to attend, say, a performance of Handel's *Messiah* (composed when he was a boy), to hear the air sung, 'I know that my Redeemer liveth', and then, as the strings take up the air, to burst into tears. No; and not for him either to be affected by the line:

Why, all the souls that were were forfeit once.

It is not that he was cold and insensitive; his emotions had other springs. This needs to be recognized.

In discussing the writings, I shall begin with the *History of England;* then pass to the *Essays Moral and Political* and the *Political Discourses;* next, reach the *Treatise* and the *Enquiries;* and conclude with the *Four Dissertations* and the posthumous *Dialogues concerning Natural Religion.*

II

There is no need to ransack the arcana of Hume's philosophy in order to find a motive for his writing history. He was fascinated by 'human nature'; he was attracted to the past. When he defines the purpose of history in the *Treatise* or in the *Enquiries*, he theorizes; once he settled to being a historian he had to be practical. It was enough that he had an opportunity of writing as well as he was able, for an evident purpose. Narrative can be the easiest kind of reading, especially narrative upon which pains have been lavished. That is all that was required to make him undertake the *History of England*. The work is 'philosophical' only in the sense that Gibbon has in mind when, in his autobiography, he reflects on the merits of Hume's first volume: 'The calm philosophy, the careless, inimitable beauties often forced me to close the volume with a mixed sensation of delight and despair.'

The immediate event that led Hume to set to work was his election in 1752 to be librarian of the Faculty of Advocates in Edinburgh, which gave him the run of 30,000 volumes. The appointment did not long remain agreeable, following in that respect the course of earlier ones, but by the time he wanted to be rid of it he was fully embarked on his task. Later he bought the books he needed.

He began his *History* with the union of the two kingdoms and carried the first volume to the Battle of Newbury. It was, he says, 'an epoch when, I thought, the misrepresentation of faction began chiefly to take place'. (I should mention that, for him, 'faction' is a synonym of 'political party'.) He says:

I thought, that, I was the only historian, that had at once neglected present power, interest, and authority, and the cry of popular prejudices; and as the subject was suited to every capacity, I expected proportional applause.

The first volume appeared in 1754, and even without the London booksellers' boycott to make matters worse, there would have been none of the applause he expected. The volume, on the contrary, was booed. Not surprisingly he was crestfallen:

Miserable was my disappointment: I was assailed by one cry of reproach, disapprobation, and even detestation: English, Scotch, and Irish; Whig and Tory; churchman and sectary, free-thinker and religionist, patriot and courtier, united in their rage against the man who had presumed to shed a generous tear for the fate of Charles I and the Earl of Strafford.

Almost the only praise which he received at the time for the first volume was from the Archbishop of Canterbury, Dr. Herring, and from the Primate of Ireland, Dr. Stone. He was assured that there would always be a bed for him at Lambeth.

In this first volume he can be observed seeking to correct 'the misrepresentation of faction'. He draws his portrait of Charles I. The hour at which to shed a tear over the royal fate has not yet struck, but already the king is being rebuffed by his Commons:

Charles now found himself obliged to depart from that delicacy which he had formerly maintained. By himself or his ministers, he entered into a particular detail both of the alliances which he had formed, and of the military operations which he had projected. He told the parliament, that by a promise of subsidies, he had engaged the king of Denmark to take part in the war; that this monarch intended to enter Germany by the north, and to rouse to arms those princes who impatiently longed for an opportunity of asserting the liberty of the empire; that Mansfeldt had undertaken to penetrate with an English army into the Palatinate, and by that quarter to excite the members of the evangelical union; that the States must be supported in the unequal warfare which they maintained with Spain; that no less a sum than 700,000 pounds a year had been found, by computation, requisite for all these purposes; that the maintenance of the fleet, and the defence of Ireland, demanded an annual expence of 400,000 pounds; that he himself had already exhausted and anticipated in the public service his whole revenue, and had scarcely left sufficient for the daily subsistence of himself and his family; that on his accession to the crown, he found a debt of above 300,000 pounds, contracted by his father in support of the palatine; and that, while prince of Wales, he had himself contracted debts, notwithstanding his great frugality, to the amount of 70,000 pounds, which he had expended entirely on naval and military armaments. After mentioning all these facts, the king even condescended to use entreaties. He said, that his request was the first that he had ever made to them; that he was young and in the commencement of his reign; and if he now met with kind and dutiful usage, it would endear to him the use of parliaments, and would for ever preserve an entire harmony between him and his people.

To these reasons the Commons remained inexorable.

The passage may make the unsophisticated reader more sorry for the king than anxious that the legislature should succeed in asserting that supremacy which it was to be awarded by Locke in his *Second Treatise of Civil Government* half a century later. That will testify to the quality of Hume's narrative, and of course Locke's description of royal absolutism in England is a travesty.

The remaining volumes of the *History* were all published in London. The second came out two years after the first, in 1756. It covered the period from the death of Charles I to the Revolution of 1688. This time Hume, he himself says, gave 'less displeasure to the Whigs', and the instalment was better received. 'It not only rose of itself, but helped to buoy up its unfortunate brother.' Volumes III and IV, dealing with the House of Tudor, were published in 1759, and the last two volumes, which traced the history of Britain from the invasion of Julius Caesar to the Battle of Bosworth in 1485, followed in 1761. A feature of these are the two appendices, one on Anglo-Saxon government and manners, and a second on feudal law and Anglo-Norman government.

In March of that same year, 1761, a letter reached Hume at Edinburgh from the Comtesse de Boufflers (1725-1800) in France. She was a lady of whom he had not previously heard, but he saw at once that her letter was a model of how to address praise to a historian:

The clarity, the majesty, the touching simplicity of your style delight me. Its beauties are so striking that, in spite of my ignorance of the

English language, they cannot escape me. You are, Sir, an admirable
painter. . . . But what expressions shall I employ in order to convey to
you the effect made upon me by your divine impartiality?

In a postscript this new correspondent asked if he might not
be coming over to France.

The Comtesse de Boufflers was famous as a beauty. Hume
was not to pay his respects to her in person till the autumn
of 1763, when he arrived at Paris to be secretary of the
embassy. By then she was thirty-eight, and yet she looked
only thirty, and her complexion was that of a girl ten years
younger still. She was not only ornamental and bewitching.
She was a wit, she was learned, she was a patron of writers,
and she herself composed plays. English, of which she
feigned ignorance in her first letter to Hume, she read, wrote,
and spoke.

She had married in 1746 and borne two sons. But her
husband soon parted from her; in 1751 she was for a short
period principal mistress of the Prince de Conti (1717-1776),
a prince of the blood, the third man in the kingdom. She
was still the hostess at his large dinners and country house
parties. How close was her relationship with Hume does not
have to be pried into. He wrote to her in 1764: 'Among
other obligations, you have saved me from a total indifference to everything in human life.' At one time it was being
said in Paris, and even elsewhere, that he was going to be
her chief friend. He was ready to pass the rest of his days in
France, a country to which he had been ever drawn. Then
in 1765 the countess's absentee husband was unexpectedly
heard of again. He had died. At once her centre of interest
veered, and now her sole ambition was to marry the prince.
Even though she used Hume as a go-between to further her
plans, these did not succeed. Hume remained a faithful and
affectionate correspondent. In spite of her futile moment of
fickleness, she expected apparently that he might soon
return to Paris from having convoyed Rousseau to London
at the beginning of 1766, but it was in vain. Aeneas did not

come back to Carthage. Hume was never to cross the Channel again. Within only a week or so of his own end he heard that the Prince de Conti had died. His last letter to the countess, written a few days before he himself expired, condoles with her over this loss, and salutes her, 'with great affection and regard, for the last time'.

Meanwhile, in London, new editions of the *History of England* had been called for in 1762, 1763 and 1769. It was the most popular of all histories in English before Gibbon. The demand for it was unaffected by a curious rival publication. In 1755—the year after a Scottish bookseller had dared to invade London with Volume 1—the conger of London booksellers commissioned Tobias Smollett (1731-1771), who ran a literary factory at Chelsea, to write a 'complete history of England' in fourteen months. The time limit might have daunted a less well-organized manufacturer. Smollett did not keep strictly to it, but he delivered the MS. of three of the total four volumes during 1757, and that for the fourth in 1758. He carried his narrative down to the peace of Aix-la-Chapelle in 1748, sixty years later than Hume's. The presence in the bookshops of this other *History* did not upset our historian. He saw that, compared with his, it was only journalism, and he did not feel that Smollett was to be reproached with taking part in a scurvy trick. He continued to know him.

Hume's opinion of what happened after he and Smollett were both dead, supposing he had been able to form one, I dare not surmise. In 1793 a bright bookseller thought that the two histories, Hume's and journalist Smollett's, ought to be available together. He had the combined history brought down to the death of George II in 1760. The proceeding was akin to adding two floors of wooden attics to an eighteenth-century Palladian building. As regards the public taste, the bookseller made no mistake. The Hume-cum-Smollett *History* had no fewer than seven editions down to 1877. In 1880 Hume's again appeared by itself. Why does it appear no more?

III

When Hume began writing essays he had in mind a periodical on the lines of the *Spectator* (1711-1712), or of its predecessor, the *Tatler* (1709-1711). The project was dropped, and the essays appeared only in volumes—the first in Edinburgh in 1741, *Essays Moral and Political*—but that accounts for the variety in kind of some of the early ones. The frivolous he did not reprint. From one, 'Love and Marriage', in which, he, a bachelor, boldly speaks for husbands, I rescue the following extract:

> I shall tell the women what it is our sex complains of in the married state; and if they be disposed to satisfy us in this particular, all the other difficulties will easily be accommodated. If I be not mistaken, 'tis their love of dominion.

The contents of the first volume range in subject from 'The Delicacy of Taste and Passion' to the 'Liberty of the Press', from 'Simplicity and Refinement' in writing to 'The Principles of Government'. The essays became mainly moral, political, and economic, and on the whole they are marked by the author's strong sense of balance. Notably in the *Essays Moral and Political* there are pen-portraits of Four Characters—the Epicurean, the Stoic, the Platonist, and the Sceptic. Hume's object in these portraits was, he says, 'to bring out the sentiments of sects that naturally form themselves in the world, and entertain different ideas of human life and happiness'. In the *Critique of Pure Reason* Kant personifies determinism and free will in an Epicurean and a Platonist respectively. Hume is less definite. His Epicurean extols pleasure; his Platonist, contemplation. It is in 'The Sceptic' that he speaks for himself. The following passage reflects the core of his moral philosophy:

> If we can depend upon any principle, which we can learn from philosophy, this, I think, may be considered as certain and undoubted, that there is nothing, in itself, valuable or despicable, desirable or hateful, beautiful or deformed, but that these attitudes arise from the particular

constitution and fabric of human sentiment and affection. What seems the most delicious food to one animal, appears loathsome to another: What affects the feeling of one with delight, produces uneasiness in another. This is confessedly the case in regard to all bodily senses: But if we examine the matter more accurately we shall find, that the same observation holds where the mind concurs with the body. In a word, human life is more governed by fortune than by reason.

In print today are two books, *Hume's Moral and Political Philosophy* (edited by Henry Aiken, 1948) and *Hume's Theory of Politics* (1951). But in fact, as regards politics, Hume formulates no system; he offers no set teaching. His political reflections and recommendations are delivered piecemeal, while he discusses topics of his day. He states his political principles incidentally, enriching his remarks with much illustration drawn from history. For instance, he lays down four principles of government: (1) As force is always on the side of the governed, the governors have nothing to support them but opinion. (If a government can call upon the police or the military, it must still, he holds, have at least persuaded the members of the police and the individual soldiers that it is in the right.) (2) There are opinion of interest and opinion of right. (3) There are two kinds of right, right to power, and right to property. (4) Therefore, upon three opinions—of public interest, of right to power, and of right to property—are all governments founded.

Had Rousseau and he wanted something to quarrel about, their views on the social contract differed completely. They never between them raised the topic. Like Thomas Hobbes (1588-1679) and Locke, Rousseau is positive that there is, and must be, in some form or other, a social contract. Hume is equally downright in proclaiming the contract a phantom. He says:

Would these reasoners look abroad into the world, they would meet with nothing that, in the least, corresponds to their ideas, or can warrant so refined and philosophical a system. On the contrary, we find every where princes who claim their subjects as their property and assert their independent right of sovereignty, from conquest or succession. We find also every where subjects who acknowledge this right in their prince, and suppose themselves born under obligations of obedience to a certain sovereign, as much as under the ties of reverence and duties to certain parents.

It is to be noted that this view of the basis of sovereignty is in harmony with Hume's moral philosophy: what is right is what we approve; wrong, what we condemn. He holds that justice is an artificial conception, since it is adopted, he says, solely in order to make the administration of a commonwealth workable. In the passage which I give above, he speaks of 'subjects who acknowledge' 'in their prince' his 'independent right of sovereignty'; he would no doubt be undisturbed could he see today how citizens of republics acknowledge the same right in an unpersonified state.

I said above that Hume deserves to be called the founder of political economy. I quoted J. H. Burton's tribute to the book, *Political Discourses*, which was first published in 1752, and has had repeated editions right down to the present century. T. H. Huxley (1825-1895), in his short essay on Hume (1878), points out that, on being translated into French immediately on first publication in Britain, it 'conferred a European reputation upon their author; and, what was more to the purpose, influenced the later school of economists of the eighteenth century'. It brought Hume to the attention of Montesquieu (1689-1755), himself the author of original inquiries on the subject. Among the French economists whom Huxley has in mind may be named Quesnay (1694-1774), Mirabeau (1715-1789), Raynal (1713-1796), and Turgot (1747-1781). Mirabeau's *L'Ami des Hommes* disputes Hume's theories of population. I have indicated that the economic essays were the essential stimulus which led Adam Smith to write *The Wealth of Nations*. This had been preceded in 1767 by Sir James Steuart's *Inquiry into the Principles of Political Economy*, but that unfortunately is valueless. How Hume's *Discourses* fathered Smith's treatise is easily seen. Smith sets out from recognition of the fact that wealth is not silver and gold but the goods which men use and consume, and which are produced by their labour. Hume was first in adopting more or less the same starting-point, as he makes clear:

It appears that want of money can never injure any state within itself; for men and commodities are the real strength of any community.

The *Political Discourses* remain pleasant to read, and much of their comment is strikingly up-to-date. At a time when three societies are investigating money and credit in Britain, France, and the United States respectively, and the piling up of national debt gives rise to grave warnings,[1] Hume might be one of ourselves:

In general we may observe that the dearness of everything from plenty of money, is a disadvantage which attends an established commerce, and sets bounds to it in every country by enabling the poorer states to under-sell the richer in all foreign markets.

This has made me entertain a great doubt concerning the benefits of *banks* and *paper-credit*, which are so generally esteemed advantageous to every nation. That provisions and labour should become dear by the increase of trade and money is, in many respects, an inconvenience. . . . There appears no reason for increasing that inconvenience by a *counterfeit money*, which foreigners will not accept in payment, and which any great disorder in the state will reduce to nothing. . . . To endeavour artificially to increase such a credit can never be the interest of any trading nation; but must lay them under disadvantages, by increasing money beyond its natural proportion to labour and commodities, and thereby heighten their price to the merchant and manufacturer.

What national debt really is he sums up in a sentence: 'Our modern expedient is to mortgage the public revenues and to trust that posterity will pay off the incumbrances contracted by their ancestors.' He realizes that 'our national debts furnish merchants with a species of money that is con-

[1] cf., e.g., D. Allhusen and E. Holloway, *Money: The Decisive Factor* (1959).

tinually multiplying in their hands and produces sure gain'. But, counter-balancing the advantages to merchants, 'the taxes which are levied to pay the interest on these debts are apt to be a check upon industry, to heighten the price of labour, and to be an oppression to the poorer sort'. He might be foreseeing the twentieth century where he says: 'The practice of contracting debt will almost infallibly be abused by every government.' And his final conclusion in the matter may yet be verified, for it is: 'Either the nation must destroy public credit or public credit will destroy the nation.'

IV

I come to the philosophy, Hume's chief title to fame. If we want to read him as 'the one master of philosophic English', we have to open the second Enquiry, the *Enquiry concerning the Principles of Morals*, that piece of writing which he himself regarded as 'incomparably' his best. This is from the second Appendix, 'Of Self-Love':

An epicurean or a Hobbist readily allows, that there is such a thing as a friendship in the world, without hypocrisy or disguise; though he may attempt, by a philosophical chymistry, to resolve the elements of this passion, if I may so speak, into those of another, and explain every affection to be self-love, twisted and moulded, by a particular turn of imagination, into a variety of appearances. But as the same turn of imagination prevails not in every man, nor gives the same direction to the original passion; this is sufficient even according to the selfish system to make the widest difference in human characters, and denominate one man virtuous and humane, another vicious and meanly interested. I esteem the man whose self-love, by whatever means, is so directed as to give him a concern for others, and render him serviceable to society: as I hate or despise him, who has no regard to any thing beyond his own gratifications and enjoyments. In vain would you suggest that these characters, though seemingly opposite, are at bottom the same, and that a very inconsiderable turn of thought forms the whole difference between them. Each character, notwithstanding these inconsiderable differences, appears to me, in practice, pretty durable and untransmutable. And I find not in this more than in other subjects, that the natural sentiments arising from the general appearances of things are easily destroyed by subtile reflections concerning the minute origin of these appearances. Does not the lively, cheerful colour of a countenance inspire me with complacency and pleasure; even though I learn from philosophy that all difference of complexion arises from the most minute differences of thickness, in the most minute parts of the skin; by means of which a superficies is qualified to reflect one of the original colours of light, and absorb the others?

But though the question concerning the universal or partial selfishness of man be not so material as is usually imagined to morality and practice, it is certainly of consequence in the speculative science of human nature, and is a proper object of curiosity and enquiry.

That passage seems perfectly straightforward. It is easy to agree with. I need offer no comment. The quality of the writing shows what Hume ultimately achieved. But if we want not simply to admire the style but come to grips with what it is in Hume that formed 'a turning point in the history of thought', we have to go the *Treatise* as well as to *Enquiries;* in fact, to the *Treatise* above all.

In Britain during the author's lifetime the *Treatise* was very generally ignored. No second edition came out till 1817, seventy-eight years after the first appearance of Volumes I and II. The few who tried to understand it failed dismally. Kant, in his *Prolegomena to every Future Metaphysic*, refers to this. He says:

But the perpetual hard fate of metaphysics would not allow Hume to be understood. We cannot without a certain sense of pain consider how utterly his opponents, Reid, Oswald, Beattie, and even Priestley, missed the point of the problem. For while they were ever assuming as conceded what he doubted, and demonstrating with eagerness and often with arrogance what he never thought of disputing, they so overlooked his inclination towards a better state of things, that everything remained undisturbed in its old condition.

I have already mentioned Hume's irritation at the irrelevant attacks of James Beattie. The 'Advertisement' which he drew

up in 1775 out of annoyance at these and other evidences
of complete misunderstanding was for insertion in the next
edition of the *Essays* (with which the *Enquiries* were then
being included), and it actually disowns the *Treatise*!

Today the situation everywhere is different. It may be
that the argument of the *Treatise* continues to be mis-
represented here and there. But, at least since the publication
in 1941 of *The Philosophy of David Hume*, by Norman Kemp
Smith (1872-1958), it is without excuse. Incidentally, Kemp
Smith had already stated the heart of the matter in his
Commentary to Kant's Critique of Pure Reason (1918). In both
places he makes it clear that the *Treatise* cannot be dispensed
with. Happily it is available today in full in two editions,
and a portion of it together with an *Abstract* of the whole
which the author drew up himself, in *Hume's Theory of
Knowledge* (Edinburgh, 1951), and another portion, together
with some of the essays, in *Hume's Theory of Politics* (same
place and date).

Although nobody in Britain during the author's lifetime
could understand what he was driving at in the *Treatise*,
there was one man abroad who did, and that made all the
difference to the turning point in the history of thought. To
quote Kemp Smith's *Commentary*:

> It is a very remarkable historical fact that notwithstanding the clear-
> ness and cogency of Hume's argument, and the appearance of such
> competent thinkers as Thomas Reid in Scotland, and Lambert and
> Crusius in Germany, no less than thirty years should have elapsed before
> Hume found a single reader capable of appreciating the teaching of the
> *Treatise* at its true value.

That single reader was of course Immanuel Kant (1724-
1804). Only the *Enquiries* had been translated into German,
and hence Kant was unacquainted with the *Treatise*. But
presently there came into his hands a translation of Beattie's
Essay, which I referred to above, and in this he found an
essential passage of the *Treatise* quoted, a passage not

repeated in the first *Enquiry* at all. So it was that he made his famous avowal:

> David Hume's teaching . . . first interrupted my dogmatic slumber, and gave my investigations in the field of speculative philosophy a quite new direction.

The passage of the *Treatise* was essential for Kant because it deals with causation fundamentally. In the first *Enquiry* Hume discusses the fact that although whenever anything happens we either assign to it a cause or else expect it to have a particular effect, there is no rational ground for doing so. But it is only in the *Treatise* that he calls in question man's conviction that there always is a relation of cause and effect between things or events. That any two particular events are connected as cause and effect we do not in fact perceive. That is to say, there is nothing in any particular event which implies a cause for it or that it is an effect. Before Hume, the French Oratorian Malebranche (1638-1715) and Locke both insisted on the absence of anything in experience to make us see such a connexion in a particular instance. We simply cannot demonstrate the existence of a thing from the existence of another thing. But Hume goes further, and that is why he is more profound.

Even though we do not perceive the causal bond in particular instances, we could safely assume it in each instance if we had good reason to be sure that all pairs of events, all changes in things, were causally connected. In the *Treatise*, and only in the *Treatise*, Hume points out that we have no such good reason. That is to say, he calls in question the causal axiom: 'Every change must have a cause.' In the categorical character of the 'must' of that axiom there is, he points out, no logic. In fact we do not know that there must always be a cause. Once the impossibility of knowledge in that respect is recognized, a whole set of new epistemological problems comes into view. If causal connexion is not, as had hitherto been taken for granted, within the domain of logic,

then, as Kemp Smith says, 'its true connotation must lie
elsewhere'. We are compelled to believe in necessary connexion, and of course Hume never dreams of disputing the
compulsion. Nobody is more generous with assigning
causes than he in his *History*. Unless we felt sure of causal
connexion, nothing would be intelligible. But to feel sure is
not to be sure. We only believe. That is to say, the boundaries between knowledge and belief are not where it was
thought they were. Furthermore, for Hume, belief differs
radically from knowledge. We acquire knowledge by
reason; belief we attain by feeling. 'Belief', he says, 'is more
properly an act of the sensitive, than of the cogitative part of
our natures.' About causation we only *feel* sure, and this
feeling ensues from custom. As he says again, 'All our
reasonings concerning causes and effects are deriv'd from
nothing else but custom'. And what for individuals is
custom and habit is for society tradition.

The domain of reason, which alone yields knowledge, is
made smaller, but the last thing of which to accuse Hume is
of being irrational. He is no advocate of doing without
reason, like some writers today. He is no fool. He understands that we depend upon reason as far as it will take us.
Only reason can show us the limits of our reason and the
confines of our knowledge. Only thanks to reason do we
discover how much the individual owes to custom and
habit, and society to tradition. Finally we have only our
reason to set bounds to our beliefs.

What are the consequences for ethics and politics? What
for religious faith?

V

Adulation by the wit and beauty of Paris should have been
as blissful as Bottom wound in Titania's arms. But at Paris
from October 1763 to the beginning of January 1766 Hume's
delight was not unalloyed. He contrasted his celebrity in

France with the disappointments and frustrations he had met with at home. To Gilbert Elliot of Minto he wrote from Paris in March 1764: 'I have been accustom'd to meet with nothing but insults and indignities from my native country.' Something which never came fully into view had dogged his career: it was more than the London booksellers' ban on the sale of Volume I of his *History;* more than the refusal of the Edinburgh advocates to let him choose the additions to their library; more than the rancour shown when he refrained from exonerating Mary Queen of Scots and from blackening the memory of Charles I; more than the public's inability to make head or tail of the *Treatise.* Time and again he wanted to speak out, and was prevailed upon to delete or 'to soften' his proposed utterance. But what still went into print under his name sufficed to keep alive and active the hostility which was partly open and avowed, partly busy in the dark behind his back.

Why was he rejected for the chair of pneumatical philosophy at Edinburgh in 1744 and 1745 and for the chair of logic at Glasgow in 1752? He was more than suspected of being religiously unsound. After his funeral two men were put on watch at his tomb for eight nights for fear some enthusiastic churchgoers might, out of their Christian charity, attempt its desecration. The marks of the droppings from the watchmen's candles long commemorated their vigil.

Once there was even talk of taking proceedings against him. In 1755 and again in 1756 it was attempted to have the general assembly of the Church of Scotland pronounce his formal excommunication (and that of his kinsman, Lord Kames, a church elder!), and although the attempts failed they were reinforced by the circulation of grossly written pamphlets against him. In the same year 1755 he proposed to his bookseller, Andrew Millar, a volume to be called *Four Dissertations,* and when, for inclusion in it, he offered one 'Of Suicide'—a justification—and another, 'Of the Immortality of the Soul'—denying any likelihood of it—Millar took advice. There was then talk of a prosecution—by the Lord Chancellor. The two 'dissertations' were withdrawn. They were only published posthumously, and then by pirates. Of the *Four Dissertations* which at last came out in 1757, two were substitutes for those abandoned ones. What remained was still challenging. The first in the volume was entitled 'The Natural History of Religion'. An extract will indicate its tone:

Lucian observes that a young man, who reads the history of the gods in Homer or Hesiod, and finds their factions, wars, injustice, incest, adultery, and other immoralities so highly celebrated, is much surprised afterwards, when he comes into the world, to observe that punishments are by law inflicted on the same actions, which he had been taught to ascribe to superior beings. The contradiction is still perhaps stronger between the representations given us by some later religions and our natural ideas of generosity, lenity, impartiality, and justice; and in proportion to the multiplied terrors of these religions, the barbarous conceptions of the divinity are multiplied upon us.

That 'dissertation' on the history of religion called forth a critical pamphlet, characterized, Hume says, by 'illiberal petulance, arrogance, and scurrility'.

The prime mover in this interference and condemnation was William Warburton, Bishop of Gloucester (1698-1779), who was a man of influence. According to Gibbon, 'the real merit of Warburton was degraded by the pride and presumption with which he pronounced his infallible decrees'. Warburton had praised Alexander Pope's *Essay on Man* (1733), and after Pope's death it fell to him to re-edit Pope's Shakespeare. Of the result there is no improving on George Sampson's description in *The Concise Cambridge History of English Literature* (1941), as follows:

Warburton was one of those bullies of literature whose success is incredible to later ages. His edition (1747) is remarkable alike for its insolence and its ignorance. His conjectures would furnish a curiosity shop of impossible words.

Such was the fellow who, being incapable of suspecting what his actual position was in relation to Hume, adopted towards Hume's writings a tone of ludicrous superiority.

That does not mean that his accusations were baseless. Hume was neither heretic, deist, nor atheist. But he had next to no religion. As a boy in Berwickshire, he had accepted church-going and the corresponding attitude of mind which he was later so vigorously to condemn. He had accepted having Sunday turned into a lugubrious day by the imposition of over-prolonged devotions. Matters are different in Scotland today. Less than a century ago many a Scot was still throwing off all religion on reaching manhood in reaction against the oppression of such Sundays as Hume suffered in boyhood. But Hume's want of religion, once he had grown up, had better grounds. It was by reading and reflecting on what he had read that he lost whatever faith had been his—by reading, for instance, Locke, and also Samuel Clarke (1675-1729), whose *A Demonstration of the Being and Attributes of God* (1704) had on him apparently the opposite of its intended effect.

As with other apostates, however, religion went on pre-occupying him. After he had published Section 10 of the first *Enquiry*, 'Of Miracles', and 'The Natural History of Religion' in *Four Dissertations*, he yet had more to say. Between the years 1749 to 1751 he began writing a set of *Dialogues concerning Natural Religion*. He revised and polished them from time to time, and although he did not attempt to give them to the public himself, he was anxious that after his death they should be duly submitted to the judgement of the world. He entrusted them to his nephew, who brought them out in 1779.

The purpose in them is simple. One of the familiar mediaeval proofs of the existence of God, the argument from design, is subjected to a searching analysis and found worthless. Hume concludes from this in effect to the vanity of all metaphysics.

Kant was not the only citizen of Koenigsberg to come

under Hume's spell. The *Dialogues* were read and translated into German by a friend of his, Johann Georg Hamann (1730-1788). Kant read through the MS. In 'The Transcendental Dialectic' of the *Critique of Pure Reason* all the mediaeval proofs of the existence of God are declared to be entirely unconvincing. Kemp Smith thinks it likely that Kant's reading of Hamann's translation of Hume's *Dialogues* both strengthened him in his rejection of natural theology and enabled him 'to define more clearly than he otherwise would have done, the negative consequences of his own Critical principles'. We know that, unlike Hume, Kant insists on the necessity of metaphysical inquiry for moral reasons. We need to tackle the problems of the existence of God, the freedom of the will, and the immortality of the soul, in our search for a decision regarding what we ought to do. But it seemed to Hamann that in wrestling with these problems Kant surrenders too readily to the rationalism of the Enlightenment. Hamann rose in opposition to the Age of Reason. In 1757, he had come to London from his native Koenigsberg on a business mission, and during his stay he underwent a religious conversion. Thereafter he sets up belief over reason, and finds that constantly the true is the incredible. 'Lies and novels must be plausible', he says, 'also hypotheses and fables; but not the truth.' According to Professor Fritz Blanke, of Zürich, in his *Hamann-Studien*, it was Hamann, more than anybody else, who preserved the evangelical faith in Germany from being corrupted by that rationalism of the Enlightenment, to which Kant, he felt, gives way. What attracted Hamann to Hume was recognition of the limits of the powers of human reason. 'Hume is always my man', he says, 'because he at least honours the principle of belief and has taken it up into his system.' Thus Hume gave rise, chiefly in Germany, to two streams of thought, philosophical and theological, with Kant, on the one hand, leading to G. W. F. Hegel (1770-1831); with Hamann, on the other, as the inspiration of Søren Kierkegaard (1813-1855). If Kant may be reproached with falling in too readily with the current naturalism, Hamann in his writings remains wayward and eccentric.

But neither seems to have carried on, or to have transmitted, Hume's teaching so that it attained to its ultimate conclusion. Hume is under the delusion that the methods of Newtonian physics are appropriate to the study of human nature, and, odder still, that he is applying them. In morality as in physics necessity prevails. We impute responsibility, Hume says, because we are convinced that a man's actions disclose his character and abiding dispositions, and only as they do so can we give them our moral approval or blame. For Hume, the agent simply acts. Only an observer judges what he does. It seems a partial view of what happens. He ignores moral struggle and indecision; he is a stranger to the conquest of temptation:

> 'Tis one thing to be tempted, Escalus,
> Another thing to fall.

But he does hold that feeling, belief, custom are our moral guides. Even so he does not see that this implies admitting moral tradition back into its own, and religion too. For all religion, all propitiation of the Unseen Powers, are what has been transmitted from generation to generation. When he writes of 'our natural ideas of generosity, lenity, impartiality, and justice', his only ground for calling them 'natural' must be Pascal's adage, '*la coutume est une seconde nature*'. Whence do those so-called natural ideas come from to begin with if not from those gods, whose conduct, in the Greek mythology, he declares monstrous?

It is as though he was on the high road to an illumination which lies just round the corner but is brought up short by his rather pedestrian naturalism. That is the significance of his affinities with some of the mediaeval Nominalists, and notably William of Ockham. And he has his affinity also to a sceptical believer nearer his own day, the sceptical but believing Pascal (1623-1662).

Hume is under no illusions about mankind. He does not rise to the tragic view, but he has the needful disposition. In Part XI of the *Dialogues concerning Natural Religion*, Cleanthes speaks of 'the total infirmity of human reason, . . . the great and universal misery and still greater wickedness of men'. Are those words of Cleanthes' so remote from Pascal's *'misère de l'homme sans Dieu'*? We do not interpret the world thanks to our reason, Hume says, but by means of our spontaneous feelings of belief and the inheritance of custom. That is what in effect Pascal says too, but Pascal adds that it is the custom to accept the religion transmitted to us by tradition.

As for the Nominalists, Father Copleston, in Volume III of his *History of Philosophy*, refers to Nicolas of Autrecourt (b. 1300), who, like Hume 450 years later, holds that we have no certainty regarding cause and effect, for from the existence of one thing no other thing can be inferred to exist. Hume successfully disputes the validity of the argument from design. Like Kant, William of Ockham rejects all the so-called metaphysical proofs of the existence of God. But Ockham, suffering too his share of 'insults and indignities', not from his 'native country', but from a succession of Avignon popes—Ockham retains his faith.

VI

David Hume, then, is one of the glories of our prose literature. As historian, essayist, or philosopher, he writes well. He could be proud of being the author of best-sellers, for they were best-sellers of quality. He had sweetness of character, and his character is openly reflected in his writings, particularly in his *History of England*. Through the pages of that sustained work, there flows the milk of human sympathy. Among his numerous essays, a selection are still a pleasure to read. They remain short repositories of wisdom in practical affairs, in politics, economics, and personal relations. His greatest achievement, however, was in philosophy.

He demonstrates that the limits of human knowledge are narrower than had previously been assumed. By 'knowledge' he means not the storehouse of memory but what can be won by means of legitimate inference. He makes us see that we cannot know that either entities or events are bound together in pairs by any system of cause and effect; we must be content to believe it. Likewise, in order to make our way about in daily life as well as in the natural sciences we have to persist in drawing inductive generalizations, although most of them we are unable to justify by evidence. As regards the principles of morality, he makes us see that no valid conclusion can be deduced of what ought to be from apprehension of what is. At first sight those discoveries may seem negative. They are really the opposite, because they have enlarged man's consciousness of what he is and of what he may attempt. They, and they especially, made possible psycho-analysis, and the postulated entities of the subconscious, the unconscious, and the id. Freud, Adler, and Jung may have been largely unaware of his writings; they are nevertheless deep in his debt. He had to open the way in order that they might come after.

Hume had dropped religion for himself, and he tended to scoff at Roman Catholics as superstitious and at Presbyterians as enthusiasts. When his teaching filtered down to the multitude, it encouraged religious indifference. In fact, in those fields where men of learning are in danger of vainglory, his lesson is a reminder to be humble. In the thick of the Age of Reason, in an era of creeping scepticism, he analyzes man's mental capacity so acutely as to restore custom and instinctive belief to the dominant position which they had occupied in the Age of Faith.

DAVID HUME

A Select Bibliography

(Place of publication London unless otherwise stated)

Bibliography:

A BIBLIOGRAPHY OF DAVID HUME AND OF SCOTTISH PHILOSOPHY FROM HUTCHESON TO BALFOUR, by T. E. Jessop (1938)

—writings on Hume from 1938 to 1952 are listed by J. Lameere in *Revue internationale de philosophie*, vi, 1952.

Collected Editions and Selections:

ESSAYS AND TREATISES ON SEVERAL SUBJECTS. 4 vols. (1753-6; 1758; 1760; 1770; 2 vols., with Hume's last corrections, 1764; 1768, and numerous subsequent editions).

THE PHILOSOPHICAL WORKS INCLUDING ALL THE ESSAYS. 4 vols. Edinburgh (1826).

THE PHILOSOPHICAL WORKS, ed. T. H. Green and T. H. Grose. 4 vols. (1874-5)

—these volumes contain the *Treatise* and the *Enquiries*, all the *Essays*, including those withdrawn, *Four Dissertations*, and two long introductions, one by Green, one by Grose.

ESSAYS: MORAL, POLITICAL AND LITERARY (1903, rptd. 1963).

OEUVRES PHILOSOPHIQUES CHOISIES, tr. par M. David. 2 vols. Paris (1912).

HUME'S MORAL AND POLITICAL PHILOSOPHY, ed. H. D. Aiken. New York (1948).

THEORY OF KNOWLEDGE: containing the *Enquiry Concerning Human Understanding;* the *Abstract* and selected passages from Book I of *A Treatise of Human Nature*, ed. D. C. Yalden-Thomson (1951).

THEORY OF POLITICS: containing *A Treatise of Human Nature*, Book 3, parts 1 and 2 and thirteen of the *Essays, Moral, Political and Literary*, ed. F. Watkins (1951).

A TREATISE OF HUMAN NATURE, Book I [abridged]. In *British Empirical Philosophers*, ed. A. J. Ayer and R. Winch (1952)

—containing extracts from *An Enquiry Concerning Human Understanding*.

WRITINGS ON ECONOMICS, ed. E. Rotwein (1955).

HUME ON HUMAN NATURE AND THE UNDERSTANDING: being the complete text of *An Enquiry Concerning Human Understanding*, together with sections of *A Treatise of Human Nature, An Abstract of a Treatise of Human Nature* and two biographical documents, ed. A. Flew. New York (1962).

HUME ON RELIGION, selected and introduced by R. Wollheim (1963).
THE PHILOSOPHY OF DAVID HUME, ed. V. C. Chappell. New York (1963).

Separate Works:

Philosophical:

A TREATISE OF HUMAN NATURE (1739-40)

—Book I, *Of the Understanding;* Book II, *Of the Passions,* 2 vols. (1739); Book III, *Of Morals* (1740; 2nd edn. in 2 vols. 1817); ed. L. A. Selby-Bigge, Oxford (1888; 2nd edn. 1897); ed. A. D. Lindsay, 2 vols. (1911, rptd. 1956); paperback edition, New York (1961), Book I, ed. D. G. C. MacNabb (1962).

AN ABSTRACT OF A TREATISE ON HUMAN NATURE (1740)

—a pamphlet hitherto unknown, rptd. J. M. Keynes and P. Sraffa. Cambridge (1938).

ESSAYS MORAL AND POLITICAL. Edinburgh (1741)

—2nd edn. 2 vols, Edinburgh (1742); rptd. (4th edn.) in *Essays and Treatises,* vol. i, 1753, and in subsequent editions.

PHILOSOPHICAL ESSAYS CONCERNING HUMAN UNDERSTANDING (1748; 2nd edn. 1750)

—rptd. in *Essays and Treatises,* vol. 2, 1756 and in subsequent editions, from 1758 the title being changed to *Enquiry Concerning Human Understanding.* Ed. L. H. Selby-Bigge (1894; 2nd edn. 1902).

AN ENQUIRY CONCERNING THE PRINCIPLES OF MORALS (1751)

—rptd. in *Essays and Treatises,* Vol. 3, 1756 and in subsequent edns. Ed. L. A. Selby-Bigge (1894; 2nd edn. 1902).

POLITICAL DISCOURSES. Edinburgh (1752)

—rptd. (3rd edn.) in *Essays and Treatises,* vol. 4, 1754, and subsequent editions ed. with introduction by W. Bell Robertson (1906).

FOUR DISSERTATIONS (1757), ed. H. E. Root (1956)

—contains: *The Natural History of Religion; Of the Passions; Of Tragedy; Of the Standard of Taste.* Rptd. in *Essays and Treatises,* 3rd edn. (1760) and subsequent edns; *The Natural History of Religion,* ed. H. E. Root (1956).

TWO ESSAYS (1777)

—*Of Suicide* and *Of the Immortality of the Soul,* intended for publication with *Four Dissertations* but withdrawn. Published anonymously.

DIALOGUES CONCERNING NATURAL RELIGION (1779)

—rptd. in *Essays and Treatises,* 1788 edn; ed. N. Kemp Smith (1935;

2nd edn. 1947, rptd. New York, 1963); ed. H. D. Aiken, New York (1948; rptd. 1963).

Historical:

THE HISTORY OF GREAT BRITAIN (UNDER THE HOUSE OF STUART). 2 vols. Edinburgh (1754-7).

THE HISTORY OF ENGLAND UNDER THE HOUSE OF TUDOR. 2 vols. (1759).

THE HISTORY OF ENGLAND FROM THE INVASION OF JULIUS CAESAR TO THE ACCESSION OF HENRY VII. 2 vols. (1762).

THE HISTORY OF ENGLAND FROM THE INVASION OF JULIUS CAESAR TO THE REVOLUTION IN 1688. 8 vols. (1763)

—many further editions and abridgements were issued in the 18th century. The 1778 edn. included the author's last corrections and a short autobiography. In 1793-5 the work was re-issued in 22 volumes with a continuation to 1760 by Tobias Smollett and to 1795 by Joel Barlow. A large number of other expansions and adaptations were published throughout the following century.

Letters:

EXPOSÉ SUCCINCT DE LA CONTESTATION . . ENTRE M. HUME ET M. ROUSSEAU [Paris] (1766)

—correspondence between Hume and Rousseau relating to their famous disputation. Hume wrote the connecting passages.

PRIVATE CORRESPONDENCE . . . BETWEEN THE YEARS 1761 AND 1776 (1820).

LETTERS, ed. T. Murray. Edinburgh (1841).

LETTERS . . . TO WILLIAM STRAHAN, ed. G. Birkbeck Hill. Oxford (1888).

LETTERS, ed. J. Y. T. Greig. 2 vols. Oxford (1932).

NEW LETTERS. ed. R. Klibansky and E. C. Mossner. Oxford (1954).

Some Biographical and Critical Studies:

THE LIFE OF DAVID HUME WRITTEN BY HIMSELF (1777)

—includes Adam Smith's *Letter* to W. Strahan on Hume's last days.

AN ACCOUNT OF THE LIFE AND WRITINGS OF DAVID HUME, by T. E. Ritchie (1807).

LIFE AND CORRESPONDENCE OF DAVID HUME, by J. H. Burton. 2 vols. Edinburgh (1846).

HUME, by T. H. Huxley (1878)

—in the English Men of Letters Series.

HISTORY OF ENGLISH THOUGHT IN THE 18TH CENTURY, by L. Stephen. 3rd edn., 2 vols. (1902).

DAVID HUME, by C. J. W. Francken. Haarlem (1907).

DAVID HUME: SEIN LEBEN UND SEINE PHILOSOPHIE, von A. Thomsen. Berlin (1912).

HUME'S PLACE IN ETHICS, by E. A. Shearer. Bryn Mawr (1915).

'David Hume', by W. R. Sorley. In *A History of English Philosophy*. Cambridge (1920; rptd. 1937).

STUDIES IN THE PHILOSOPHY OF DAVID HUME, by C. W. Hendel. Princeton (1925; rptd. New York 1963).

THE ART OF HISTORY: A STUDY OF FOUR GREAT HISTORIANS OF THE XVIIITH CENTURY, by J. B. Black (1926).

DAVID HUME, LEBEN UND PHILOSOPHIE, von R. Metz. Stuttgart (1929).

'The central problem of David Hume's philosophy: an essay towards a phenomenological interpretation of the first book of the *Treatise of Human Nature*', by C. V. Salmon. In *Jahrbuch für Philosophie und phenomonologische Forschung*, Halle (1929).

FIVE TYPES OF ETHICAL THEORY, by C. D. Broad (1930).

STUDIES IN THE EIGHTEENTH CENTURY BACKGROUND OF HUME'S EMPIRICISM, by M. S. Kuypers. Minneapolis (1930).

LA CRITIQUE ET LA RELIGION CHEZ DAVID HUME, par A. Leroy. Paris (1930).

THE LIFE OF DAVID HUME, by E. G. Braham (1931).

DAVID HUME, by J. Y. T. Greig (1931).

LOCKE, BERKELEY, HUME, by Sir C. R. Morris. Oxford (1931).

DAVID HUME, by B. M. Laing (1932).

HUME'S PHILOSOPHY OF HUMAN NATURE, by J. Laird (1932).

LA FILOSOFIA DELLA ESPERIENZA DI DAVID HUME, di G. della Volpe. 2 vols. Florence (1934-5)

—vol. i, 2nd edn. with title *Hume e il genio dell' empirismo*. Florence (1939).

HUME'S THEORY OF THE UNDERSTANDING, by R. W. Church (1935).

IL PENSIERO FILOSOFICO DI DAVID HUME, di B. Magnino. Naples (1935).

THE CAUSE AND EVIDENCE OF BELIEFS: AN EXAMINATION OF HUME'S PROCEDURE, by F. C. Bayley. Mount Hermon, Mass. (1936).

STUDIES IN HUME'S ETHICS, by P. A. I. Hedenius. Uppsala (1937).

HUME'S THEORY OF KNOWLEDGE, by C. Maund (1937).

HUME AND PRESENT DAY PROBLEMS: PROCEEDINGS OF THE ARISTOTELIAN SOCIETY, Supplementary volume 18 (1939).

HUME'S PHILOSOPHY IN HIS PRINCIPAL WORK, *A Treatise of Human Nature*, AND IN HIS *Essays*, by V. Kruse. Oxford (1939).

DAVID HUME: THE MAN AND HIS SCIENCE OF MAN, by F. H. Heinemann. Paris (1940).

HUME'S THEORY OF THE EXTERNAL WORLD, by H. H. Price. Oxford (1940).

THE PHILOSOPHY OF DAVID HUME: A CRITICAL STUDY OF ITS ORIGINS AND CENTRAL DOCTRINES, by N. K. Smith (1941).

'David Hume: defender of "Nature" against "Reason"', by B. Willey. In *The Eighteenth Century Background* (1941).

'CETTE AFFAIRE INFERNALE': L'AFFAIRE J. J. ROUSSEAU—DAVID HUME, 1766, par H. Guillemin. Paris (1942).

THE FORGOTTEN HUME: LE BON DAVID, by E. C. Mossner. New York (1943).

MAN AND SOCIETY: THE SCOTTISH INQUIRY OF THE EIGHTEENTH CENTURY, by G. Bryson. Princeton (1945).

REASON AND CONDUCT IN HUME'S TREATISE, by R. M. Kydd. Oxford (1946; rptd. New York, 1964).

HUME'S THEORY OF THE PASSIONS AND OF THE MORALS: A STUDY OF BOOKS II AND III OF THE TREATISE, by A. B. Glathe. Berkeley (1950).

DAVID HUME: HIS THEORY OF KNOWLEDGE AND MORALITY, by D. G. C. MacNabb (1951).

DAVID HUME ON CRITICISM, by T. Brunius. Uppsala (1952).

HUME, SA VIE, SON OEUVRE, SA PHILOSOPHIE, par A. Cresson et G. Deleuze. Paris (1952).

HUME'S INTENTIONS, by J. A. Passmore. Cambridge (1952).

EMPIRISME ET SUBJECTIVITÉ: ESSAI SUR LA NATURE HUMAINE SELON HUME, par G. Deleuze. Paris (1953).

DAVID HUME, par A. Leroy. Paris (1953).

'David Hume', by L. Paul. In *The English Philosophers* (1953).

THE LIFE OF DAVID HUME, by E. C. Mossner (1954)
—the standard biography.

DAVID HUME, by A. H. Basson (1958).

'Hume', by F. Copleston. In *Hobbes to Hume*, Vol. V of *A History of Philosophy* (1959).

'David Hume', by F. L. Lucas. In *The Art of Living: Four Eighteenth-century Minds* (1959).

HUME, PRECURSOR OF MODERN EMPIRICISM: ANALYSIS OF HIS OPINIONS ON MEANING, METAPHYSICS, LOGIC AND MATHEMATICS, by F. Zabeeh. The Hague (1960).

HUME'S PHILOSOPHY OF BELIEF: A STUDY OF HIS FIRST INQUIRY, by A. G. N. Flew (1961).

THE MAN OF (ALMOST) INDEPENDENT MIND, by H. MacDiarmid. Edinburgh (1962).

DAVID HUME: A SYMPOSIUM, ed. D. F. Pears (1963).

THE MORAL AND POLITICAL PHILOSOPHY OF DAVID HUME, by J. B. Stewart. New York (1963).

THE MORAL PHILOSOPHY OF HUME, by R. D. Broiles. The Hague (1964).

'David Hume', by B. Willey. In *The English Moralists* (1964).

'David Hume: Reasoning and Experience', by R. Williams. In *The English Mind: Studies in the English Moralists presented to Basil Willey*, ed. H. Sykes Davies and G. Watson (1964).

Elizabeth Barrett Browning

by ALETHEA HAYTER

Published for the British Council
and the National Book League
by Longmans, Green & Co.

Three shillings and sixpence net

The famous love story of the Brownings which continued, rather than ended, with their elopement and uniquely happy marriage, has tended to obscure Elizabeth Barrett Browning's achievement as a poet. When Wordsworth died, her claims to succeed him as Poet Laureate were seriously canvassed; and during her lifetime her work was considered to rank higher than that of her husband. While no one would now claim great genius for her, in Miss Hayter's view 'there are qualities in her poetry which still have power to move and interest us'. Few poets have trained themselves so thoroughly for their chosen profession; fewer have been so widely-read and so versed in scholarship. Mrs Browning's poetry, moreover, reflects her own characteristic freedom from religious, national, class or sex prejudices. Today it is for the 'Sonnets from the Portuguese', those famous love poems to Browning, that Mrs Browning is principally but unjustly known; for she is a far greater poet than these reveal. Many other poems better demonstrate her command of striking and original imagery, her daring—and sometimes outrageous—prosodic experiments, her very excellent mind; while *Aurora Leigh* undoubtedly contains the finest passages she ever wrote. In this illuminating essay Miss Hayter frees Elizabeth Barrett Browning once and for all from 'her legend of invalidism and ringlets'.

Alethea Hayter was awarded the Royal Society of Literature's prize for her *Mrs Browning: a Poet's Work and its Setting* (1962). She is also author of *A Sultry Month: Scenes of London Literary Life in 1846* (1965).

Bibliographical Series
of Supplements to 'British Book News'
on Writers and Their Work

★

GENERAL EDITOR
Geoffrey Bullough

¶ Elizabeth Barrett Browning was born on 6 March 1806, at Coxhoe Hall in Durham. She died in Florence on 29 June 1861.

ELIZABETH BARRETT BROWNING

from a chalk drawing by FIELD TALFOURD *(1859) in the*
National Portrait Gallery

ELIZABETH BARRETT BROWNING

by

ALETHEA HAYTER

PUBLISHED FOR
THE BRITISH COUNCIL
AND THE NATIONAL BOOK LEAGUE
BY LONGMANS, GREEN & CO

LONGMANS, GREEN & CO. LTD.
48 Grosvenor Street, London, W.1

*Associated companies, branches and
respresentatives throughout the world*

First published 1965
© Alethea Hayter 1965

*Printed in Great Britain by
F. Mildner & Sons, London, E.C.1*

ELIZABETH BARRETT BROWNING

I

WHEN Wordsworth died, just half way through the nineteenth century, and a successor for him as Poet Laureate had to be found, the claims of Elizabeth Barrett Browning to succeed him were seriously canvassed. It was suggested that a female Poet Laureate would be particularly suitable when a woman was on the throne of England; but the influential *Athenaeum* flatly stated that in any case no living poet of either sex had a higher claim than Mrs Browning's. This seems to us a startling pronouncement to have been made on the same day—1 June 1850—on which *In Memoriam* was published. Tennyson in fact got the Laureateship, to Mrs Browning's satisfaction though she had thought Leigh Hunt ought to have it; not even she had thought of Browning as a possible candidate.

The suggestion that a female Sovereign should have a female Poet Laureate seemed foolish enough to Mrs Browning. She thought of herself as a poet, not a poetess; she considered that poetry should be judged by its merits, not by the sex of its writers. 'When I talk of women, I do not speak of them . . . according to a separate, peculiar and womanly standard, but according to the common standard of human nature', she said. But it has never been possible for critics to disentangle Mrs Browning from her sex. She was always being classed by her contemporaries as the top woman poet (generally bracketed with Sappho) not simply as a good, or very good, or fairly good, poet. No such woman writer would probably come again for a millennium, wrote Sydney Dobell unprophetically in 1850; but he went on to say that no woman writer, not even Mrs Browning, would ever write a great poem. 'She was a woman of real genius, I know; but what is the upshot of it

5

all? She and her sex had better mind the kitchen and the children', said FitzGerald. Elizabeth Barrett Browning was as much obscured as a poet by her sex and her personal legend as Byron was by his. It is therefore difficult to assess her achievement as objectively as that of other nineteenth-century poets such as Patmore, or Clough, or Meredith, with whom she might reasonably be classed; but she has in fact much more in common with them than with Christina Rossetti or Emily Brontë.

II

Elizabeth Barrett was born on 6 March 1806 at Coxhoe Hall in Durham. She was the eldest of the twelve children of Edward Moulton Barrett and his wife Mary. When she was three years old, the family moved to Hope End in Hereford-shire, and she spent the next twenty-three years of her life in this minaretted country house overlooking a lake and deep in a wooded park. Here she produced her *juvenilia: The Battle of Marathon*, an epic poem written when she was thirteen and privately printed by her father in 1820: *An Essay on Mind, with other Poems*, published in 1826; a number of poems published in magazines; and a good deal of verse, including one long poem 'The Development of Genius', which remained unpublished in her lifetime. Encouraged by two neighbours, the scholars Hugh Stuart Boyd and Uvedale Price, she made a thorough study of Classical and Byzantine Greek literature, and of prosody. Apart from a severe but unidentified illness in 1821, she led a normal social and family life during all these years.

In 1832 financial losses forced her father to sell Hope End and move with his children (his wife had died in 1828) first to Sidmouth, in Devonshire, and then in 1835 to London. In 1833 Elizabeth Barrett published a volume containing a translation of the *Prometheus Bound* of Aeschylus, and some short poems, but neither this nor her earlier volumes (all published anonymously) attracted much notice. Her first real success was achieved with *The Seraphim, and other Poems*, published in 1838 under her own name, which was given long and mainly favourable reviews in the leading journals.

The literary scene on which Elizabeth Barrett entered in the late 1830's was comparatively empty—an undistinguished pause between two great periods of creative writing. Wordsworth, Leigh Hunt and Landor were the patriarchs of the day, but their best work was past; Tennyson, Browning, Dickens, Carlyle, had published their first works, but their great achievement and fame were still to come; Thackeray, Ruskin and the Brontës were still just below the literary horizon. The admired writers of the day were Talfourd, Harriet Martineau, Harrison Ainsworth, Mary Russell Mitford, Thomas Hood, Bulwer Lytton, Barry Cornwall, Mrs Hemans, Letitia Landon, Sheridan Knowles. Among these writers Elizabeth Barrett began to make friends and a place for herself. Her ill-health and her family circumstances prevented her from going out much into the social life of London, but she embarked on exchanges of letters with literary figures which were to influence both her writing and her life. Among her correspondents were Wordsworth, Edgar Allan Poe, Carlyle, Harriet Martineau, Mary Russell Mitford (who gave her Flush, her spaniel), John Kenyon, R. H. Horne and the painter Benjamin Robert Haydon. They exchanged criticisms and appreciations of each other's work, discussed other writers of the day and the ethics and techniques of their profession; Elizabeth Barrett was at last enjoying the stimulus of intellectual equality which had been missing from her secluded childhood and adolescence.

In 1837 her health broke down, her lungs were affected, and she was sent from London to the milder climate of Torquay. Her family took it in turns to stay with her there, and while her eldest brother Edward, nicknamed Bro, was prolonging his stay at Torquay at her entreaty, he went out sailing and was drowned. His sister's lasting grief altered and in some ways strengthened her character.

She came back to London in 1841, still very much of an invalid, and plunged into literary work—book reviews, articles, translations, contributions to symposia. This productive period culminated in the two-volume *Poems* of 1844, the most popular of all her works until *Aurora Leigh* with both the critics and the public. One poem in this collection, 'Lady Geraldine's Courtship', referred favourably to the work of Robert Browning, and he wrote to Elizabeth Barrett to thank her. So began, on 10 January 1845, a correspondence which led to their first meeting four months later. On the day after he had first seen Elizabeth Barrett, Browning sent her a declaration of love, which disturbed her so much that he had to disclaim it before she would consent to receive him again; and it was only gradually, with devoted patience, that he was able to convince her of the reality of his love, to make her avow hers, and to get her consent to an engagement. For a whole year they wrote to each other almost daily, sometimes twice a day, and he called on her every few days. More frequent visits would have aroused suspicion. Mr Barrett's immovable objection to the marriage of any of his children enforced secrecy on Browning and Elizabeth Barrett until they had left for Italy, a week after their marriage on 12 September 1846.

After some months in Pisa, the Brownings moved to Florence, which was to be their base for the rest of Mrs Browning's life; from 1848 they kept a permanent residence there, Casa Guidi, though they were often away from it for many months at a time, on visits to Rome, to Lucca, to Siena. In 1849 the poets' only child, a son christened Wiedeman, but afterwards nicknamed Pennini or Pen, was born. The Brownings visited London four times during the 1850s, and renewed their friendships in the literary world of London. They also spent two winters in Paris, where they got to know many French writers, and were witnesses of some of the most striking events in the rise to power of Napoleon III. Mrs Browning became increasingly absorbed in European politics, particularly the political development of Italy and France, and this preoccupation was reflected in the poetry which she wrote in the last ten years of her life. She also became deeply, almost obsessively, interested in spiritualism, though her credulity was tempered by occasional flashes of common sense.

In the 1840s and 1850s Elizabeth Barrett Browning's poetic reputation was at its height, and made her a serious candidate for the Poet Laureateship. The four books of poetry which she published between 1846 and 1861 were: the first collected edition of her poetry, published in 1850 and including, as well as the best of the 1838 and 1844 poems, some new lyrics and the celebrated 'Sonnets from the Portuguese', addressed to her husband; *Casa Guidi Windows*, a partly political poem about Italy, which appeared in 1851; *Aurora Leigh*, a modern epic or 'novel in verse', as she called it, which was published in 1857 and won immense acclaim; and *Poems before Congress*, 1860, again political in inspiration and deservedly less popular than any other work of her maturity. This was the last book which she published in her life-time. Her health, which had greatly improved with the happiness and the change of climate which her marriage and her move to Italy brought her, weakened again after she had reached the peak of her achievement in *Aurora Leigh*, and she died in Florence on 29 June 1861.

Her *Last Poems*, containing some of her most famous lyrics, were published posthumously in 1862. In the ensuing hundred years, many of her unpublished poems, especially her *juvenilia*, have appeared in small collections, and many volumes of her letters have been published in England and in America, where most of the surviving original letters are now. The most famous of these volumes of correspondence is her exchange of love letters with Robert Browning, a unique interplay of genius and passion. The best of the other collections of Elizabeth Barrett Browning's letters are those to R. H. Horne, Mary Russell Mitford, and Benjamin Robert Haydon, full of comment on contemporary literature, art and social problems; the letters to H. S. Boyd, chiefly concerned with Greek scholarship and metrical experiments; and the letters to her sister Henrietta and her brother George, which give a picture of her family and daily life. The best selection from her general correspondence is still Frederic Kenyon's two-volume one, published in 1898, though it necessarily omits a good deal of interesting biographical material which has appeared since then.

Even the baldest statement of the main events in Elizabeth Barrett Browning's life reveals an exceptional character and destiny. She was a fortunate woman. She had a happy childhood and, even after she grew up, a family life in which she never lacked affection, companionship and admiration for her talents, however much she was deprived of sympathetic understanding and of freedom. She experienced keen pleasure from the study of languages and literature, and had the leisure to indulge the taste fully. In middle life, when she seemed a confirmed invalid, she met and married a great poet who devotedly loved her. She had a charming and intelligent child; she lived in the most beautiful cities of Italy; she never experienced any real want of money; she had many devoted friends, who included most of the great writers of the day. She was convinced that she herself was born to be a poet, she was intensely happy writing poetry, and she had splendid success with her poems when they were published. She died without pain or lingering.

Her good fortune was due to the strength and integrity of her character as much as to her innate talents and her social and economic advantages. She had to overcome crippling ill-health, the loss of a dearly-loved brother, and the unforgiving tyranny and hardness of her father. To achieve this, and to make such a success of her personal and professional life, required a toughness of will, a generosity of heart, a healthiness of mind, which have not always been recognized in Elizabeth Barrett Browning, whose willpower and fierce mental energy have been somewhat obscured by her legend of invalidism and ringlets.

III

'A genuine poetess of no common order' said the *Examiner* of Elizabeth Barrett when reviewing *The Seraphim, and other Poems*, which was published in 1838 and widely praised. The title poem, a lyrical drama on the Crucifixion as seen through the eyes of two mourning archangels, is an ambitious unequal work full of imagination, of mystical visions of the red primaeval heats of creation still forever burning from the heavenly Throne and casting fiery shadows on the crystal sea; of the whole hierarchy of Heaven attendant on the hill of Golgotha:

> Beneath us sinks the pomp angelical,
> Cherub and seraph, powers and virtues, all,
> The roar of whose descent has died
> To a still sound, as thunder into rain.
> Immeasurable space spreads magnified
> With that thick life, along the plane
> The worlds slid out on.

The volume also contained several shorter poems such as 'A Deserted Garden', 'The Sleep', 'Cowper's Grave', which have always been popular with the anthologists. In this volume, too, appeared the first of the ballads which Elizabeth Barrett Browning's contemporaries loved best of all her works. Poems such as 'The Romaunt of Margret', 'Isobel's Child' and 'The Lay of the Brown Rosary' (which was published in 1844), in which the challenge between Love and Death is played out over and over again, with Death always triumphing, have a haunting Gothic strangeness and necromancy which is a persistent mood in nineteenth-century English poetry. From 'Christabel' and 'La Belle Dame Sans Merci' and 'The Lady of Shalott', it runs through Mrs Browning's ballads, and on from them to influence Rossetti's 'Sister Helen' and William Morris's 'The Blue Closet'.

Most of Elizabeth Barrett Browning's religious poetry also dates from the volume of 1838; not only 'The Seraphim', but such lyrics as 'The Soul's Travelling', 'The Virgin Mary to the Child Jesus' and 'Cowper's Grave', in which she meditated on mystical experiences and on the problem of reconciling belief in Divine Love with the suffering and the evils of the world, the problem which tormented so many of her contemporaries, above all Tennyson as he wrote *In Memoriam*. Most of these early religious poems of Mrs Browning's, though intense in feeling, are diffuse and undisciplined in expression, but in a few of the lyrics written at this time she achieved an economy of words which startles the reader by its fineness, as in 'My Doves', her poem about the imprisonment of city streets and the longing for escape. Most of the poem is musically sweet, rather than strong, as when she describes the cooing of the doves who share her imprisonment:

> Of living loves
> Theirs hath the calmest fashion,
> Their living voice the likest moves
> To lifeless intonation,
> The lovely monotone of springs,
> And winds, and such insensate things,

and then she surprises us with the unadorned fitness of her conclusion, in which, renouncing the hope of airy shores and silent dewy fields, she says:

> My spirit and my God shall be
> My seaward hill, my boundless sea.

This concentration is rare in her work; she achieved it in 'A Sabbath Morning at Sea', in 'A Seaside Walk', in snatches of 'The Poet's Vow' and 'Night and the Merry Men', but most completely in 'A Reed':

> I am no trumpet, but a reed,
> Go, tell the fishers, as they spread
> Their nets along the river's edge,

> I will not tear their nets at all,
> Nor pierce their hands, if they should fall;
> Then let them leave me in the sedge.

Elizabeth Barrett's next volumes of poems, published in 1844, showed a development and hardening of her character and style. Illness, bereavement, approaching middle age, had made her less dreamy and more confident, even aggressive in her mannerisms. The 1844 volumes include her most advanced prosodic experiments, some of which seemed barbarous innovations to her contemporaries, but have many parallels in mid-twentieth-century poetry. Her political and social opinions were also growing more definite; two poems in the 1844 volumes, 'The Cry of the Children' and 'The Cry of the Human', were militant attacks on the employment of child labour in factories, and on the Protectionists who kept up the price of bread; the poems were widely commented on, and influenced public opinion in favour of reform. There is more intellect, and a more individual character, in the *1844 Poems* than in Elizabeth Barrett Browning's earlier works, and the volumes had a considerable success with the critics and the public; but in a good many of them there is a note of wildness and exaggeration which has caused subsequent literary historians to class Mrs Browning with the poets who were nicknamed the Spasmodic School, and were attacked for their over-strained hyperbole, subjectivism and lack of discipline. Two of the longer poems in Elizabeth Barrett's 1844 volumes— 'A Drama of Exile', a strange cloudy work on the expulsion of Adam and Eve from Paradise, and 'A Rhapsody of Life's Progress'—do almost justify her classification as a Spasmodic. But these same uneven volumes also contain some of her finest and most disciplined sonnets. Some, like 'Futurity' or the lapidary 'Grief', commemorate her brother's death and her struggle to accept her loss of him; some are analyses of the workings of poetic inspiration, like 'The Soul's Expression' and 'The Prisoner':

> I count the dismal time by months and years,
> Since last I felt the green sward under foot,
> And the great breath of all things summer-mute
> Met mine upon my lips. Now earth appears
> As strange to me as dreams of distant spheres,
> Or thoughts of Heaven we weep at. Nature's lute
> Sounds on behind this door so closely shut,
> A strange, wild music to the prisoner's ears,
> Dilated by the distance, till the brain
> Grows dim with fancies which it feels too fine,
> While ever, with a visionary pain,
> Past the precluded senses, sweep and shine
> Streams, forests, glades,—and many a golden train
> Of sunlit hills, transfigured to Divine.

One poem in the 1844 volumes, 'Catarina to Camoens', was a particular favourite with Robert Browning; he identified Elizabeth Barrett with the Portuguese girl Catarina, the beloved of the poet Camoens, and when his wife's sonnets to him were eventually published, the Brownings chose to call them 'Sonnets from the Portuguese', an ambiguous title which was a disguise from the world but full of secret meaning for the Brownings themselves. These sonnets were published in 1850, four years after the Brownings' marriage, in the first collected edition of Mrs Browning's works. The 'Sonnets from the Portuguese' are her best-known poems, but not her best. The dramatic story of her marriage has given the sonnets something of the fascination of a *roman à clef*, but considered simply as poetry they are unequal and sometimes embarrassing. Individual lines are strong and shapely:

> Beholding, besides love, the end of love,
> Hearing oblivion beyond memory,
> As one who sits and gazes from above
> Over the rivers to the bitter sea

or:

> Yet love, mere love, is beautiful indeed,
> And worthy of acceptation. Fire is bright

> Let temple burn, or flax. An equal light
> Leaps in the flame from cedar-plank or weed.

And there are some whole sonnets, notably XXII and XLIII, which sustain an unforced strength of music. But it is impossible to say of the 'Sonnets from the Portuguese' as a whole, as one can say of the greatest sonnet sequences, that their beauty and interest is self-sufficing, independently of their personal reference. The abiding attraction of these sonnets is the psychological interest of tracing the evolution in love of a thirty-nine-year-old invalid, who at first cannot believe that a brilliant poet, six years younger than herself, can really love her and want to marry her; then, when she begins to believe it, is held back by conscientious scruples at burdening him with her melancholy and ill-health; then is brought to confess her own passion, and to see that he knows what he needs, and loves her for what she really is; then grows happy and luxuriates in the tokens and catchwords and secrets of acknowledged lovers; and at last looks forward to a life-time, an eternity, of enduring love.

Elizabeth Barrett Browning's marked individuality of style and personality makes all her poetry distinctive, but she was at various times much influenced by other poets. Pope was her model in her *juvenilia;* Campbell, Byron, Wordsworth, lent forms and themes to her early lyrics; and after her marriage to Browning, she acquired something of his powers of vivid ironic characterization and comment, an element in her poetry which had been latent since her earliest work but first came to the surface, under Browning's influence, in *Casa Guidi Windows*, published in 1851. This poem, written in a modified *terza rima*, is a reflection on recent political events in Florence and on the character and destiny of the Italians, about whom she is sympathetic but unsentimental:

> We chalked the walls with bloody caveats
> Against all tyrants. If we did not fight
> Exactly, we fired muskets up the air

To show that victory was ours of right.
We met, had free discussions everywhere
(Except perhaps i' the Chambers) day and night.
We proved the poor should be employed . . . that's fair,—
And yet the rich not worked for anywise,—
Pay certified, yet payers abrogated,—
Full work secured, yet liabilities
To over-work excluded.

Six years later, in 1857, she published her masterpiece, *Aurora Leigh*. This immense nine-book poem, longer than *Paradise Lost*, contains the finest passages that Elizabeth Barrett Browning ever wrote, but they are imbedded in an implausible story of a woman poet, a philanthropist who loves her, and a series of misunderstandings and catastrophes which keep them apart till the happy ending. The poem traces the parallel careers of Aurora Leigh, the successful but lonely and dissatisfied poet, convinced that man's salvation must come through the inspired individual, and her cousin Romney Leigh, the social reformer, who believes in progress organized for the people as a whole. He sets up a phalanstery on his ancestral estate, and decides to marry a poor seamstress as a precedent for a classless society. Romney's schemes fail—his bride is tricked away before the wedding, and entrapped into a brothel; the destitute people for whom he set up his phalanstery destroy it, and he loses his sight in the holocaust. When he and Aurora are finally reunited, they conclude that both were partly wrong; he had failed to recognize that to raise men's bodies you must first raise their souls; she had not seen that one must work with, as well as for, humanity.

Mrs Browning took various elements of the story of *Aurora Leigh* from Charlotte Brontë, George Sand and other novelists; but the best way to appreciate the poem is to disregard its story, and to read it—like Wordsworth's *Prelude*, which is perhaps its nearest affinity—not for the narrative, but for the reflections occasioned by the events in the narrative, for the glimpses of distant mountains, for the moments of intense feeling. Elizabeth Barrett Browning said that 'Aurora Leigh' contained her highest convictions on life and art, and in it she was above all concerned with the poet's responsibilities, his call to be a witness to the values of humanity. She was an early propagandist for *la littérature engagée*, maintaining that the sole work of poets is

> to represent the age,
> Their age, not Charlemagne's,—this live throbbing age,
> That brawls, cheats, maddens, calculates, aspires,
> And spends more passion, more heroic heat,
> Betwixt the mirrors of the drawing-rooms,
> Than Roland with the knights at Roncesvalles.
> To flinch from modern varnish, coat or flounce,
> Cry out for togas and the picturesque
> Is fatal,—foolish too. King Arthur's self
> Was commonplace to Lady Guenevere;
> And Camelot to minstrels seemed as flat
> As Fleet Street to our poets.

Aurora Leigh is rich in unusual and glowing imagery, mature and often witty in its comments on contemporary society, compassionate over injustices and the sufferings of the poor, and written in a vigorous and agile blank verse. It had a great and immediate success, though some readers were shocked by its frank sexual references, to prostitution and even to rape. Mrs Browning was not a prude; she thought that social evils were more likely to be abolished by plain speaking about them than by pretending they did not exist.

The last volume of poems which Mrs Browning published in her lifetime, *Poems before Congress*, which appeared in 1860, was a disappointment. It was a small collection of mainly political poems about France and Italy, too much imbued with Mrs Browning's obsessive and often faulty judgements on contemporary political events and person-alities. A year after her death, a further small volume, *Last Poems*, was published. It contained two lyrics, 'A

Musical Instrument' and 'The North and the South', which have found their way into many anthologies, and one remarkable poem, 'Bianca among the Nightingales', which has a story and a refrain like some of the ballads of her youth, but a passion and a sophistication which are quite new.

'*Last Poems* is the last title which anyone could desire to read on a book which bears the name of Elizabeth Barrett Browning', began the *Athenaeum* review of Mrs Browning's posthumous volume, and it went on to call her 'the greatest English poetess that has ever lived' and to say that she had 'the heart of a lion, the soul of a martyr, and the voice of a battle-trumpet. Hers was a great genius, nurtured alike on study of the ancients and instinct for the moderns.' Now, a century later, noone would claim 'great genius' for Elizabeth Barrett Browning, but there are qualities in her poetry which still have power to move and interest us.

IV

Perhaps the best approach to the poetry of Elizabeth Barrett Browning is to note first the thorough training and preparation she underwent in the techniques of her profession. It was a profession to her; she worked full-time, all her adult life, at the business of poetry, and she took seriously the skills and the responsibilities of her trade. In writing of its responsibilities she sometimes lapsed into a shrill didacticism, but at its best her vocation emerges as a genuine poetic impulse to show life, and enable others to see it, as it really is, unobscured by prejudice, self-interest or self-deception. Poets, she said, are 'the only truth-tellers still left to God', and they must speak out against tyranny, against unjust wars, against the exploitation of women and children, against want and slavery, against complacency and ignorance. They must make men think for themselves, must help them to be honest about their emotions, must teach them to outgrow narrow nationalism and sectarianism.

But if poets are to have the power to move men's minds in this way, they must learn the skills which give such power to poetry. She herself gave much time and study to the science of versification; she experimented in many different metres, and was a pioneer in the use of assonantal double rhymes. Her very thorough reading of English poetry, from the earliest to the latest, had convinced her that not enough use was made of the possibilities of rhyme. Double rhymes were almost confined to comic poetry; in any case, regular double rhymes were rare in English. Her innovation was to introduce such assonantal double rhymes as 'trident/silent' and 'benches/influences', or still more extreme ones, matching neither in vowel nor consonant, such as 'angels/candles' or 'burden/disregarding'. These are commonplaces in English poetry of the 1930's and 1940's, but in Mrs Browning's day, and for half a century afterwards, they were considered utterly lawless. Her metrical experiments were less extreme. She used a very wide variety of metres, from the most regular rhymed couplets and Petrarchan sonnets to the loosest accentual verse, approximating to sprung rhythm.

Her prosodic experiments were often more daring than successful, but they were the result of much exploration of Classical and Byzantine Greek literature and of early English poetry. She published a modernized version of a Chaucer poem, and translations of Aeschylus, Theocritus, Apuleius, Nonnus and Anacreon; she also wrote a critical study, illustrated by many translations, of Byzantine poetry from the fourth to the fourteenth century. Greek was the language she loved best, but she also knew Latin, French, Italian, and some German, Spanish and Hebrew, and was so widely read in the literature of these languages that she could trace an image from Lucretius through Saint Basil to Tasso, and draw a parallel between *The Choephoroe* and *Macbeth*, or between an ode of Anacreon and *Romeo and Juliet*. Some of the best known passages in her poetry are her roll-calls of other poets: in *An Essay on Mind*; in 'A Vision of Poets', where she dashes off some notable sketches, such as:

> Bold
> Electric Pindar, quick as fear,
> With race-dust on his cheeks, and clear
> Slant startled eyes that seem to hear
> The chariot rounding the last goal,
> To hurtle past it in his soul

and:

> Lucretius—nobler than his mood;
> Who dropped his plummet down the broad
> Deep universe, and said 'No God',
> Finding no bottom: he denied
> Divinely the divine;

and in *Aurora Leigh*, where she analyses the young poet's reactions to his predecessors, how he loves and imitates them and then finds his own inspiration, and how sometimes there comes a poet like Keats, to whom none of the generalizations about young poets apply; and then she wrote the lines on Keats with which Edmund Blunden has chosen to conclude his study of Keats in this series—

> the life of a long life
> Distilled to a mere drop, falling like a tear
> Upon the world's cold cheek to make it burn
> For ever.

Mrs Browning's knowledge of comparative literature gave her an acute ear for style, and the boldness to refute, on internal stylistic evidence and in an astonishing metaphor, the theory of the multiple authorship of Homer. She possessed a handsome edition of Wolf's *Prolegomena ad Homerum*, on thick white paper with wide margins, and she wrote these memorably indignant lines about 'the kissing Judas, Wolf':

> Who builds us such a royal book as this
> To honour a chief-poet, folio-built,

> And writes above, 'The house of Nobody!',
> Who floats in cream, as rich as any sucked
> From Juno's breasts, the broad Homeric lines,
> And, while with their spondaic prodigious mouths
> They lap the lucent margins as babe-gods,
> Proclaims them bastards. Wolf's an atheist;
> And if the Iliad fell out, as he says,
> By mere fortuitous concourse of old songs,
> Conclude as much too for the universe.

The metaphor of the printed lines sucking the milk of the white page-margins is a good example of another of Elizabeth Barrett Browning's special poetic qualities—her command of striking and original imagery. The richness of her imagination is all the more surprising in view of how few opportunities she had to observe either man or nature. She spent the first twenty-five years of her life in the seclusion of a remote countryside, and most of the next fourteen years shut up in a London house, meeting very few strangers, and ill in bed for whole years. But she made the fullest use of what experience she had—of the conversation and letters of her literary friends, of her long explorations and adventures of the mind between the covers of books, even of her own ill-health and its accompaniments. There is in her work a whole image-cluster derived from her illness—from insomnia, from states of trance, from night silences and transfigurations, from opium visions, from fainting, from the vibrations of a galloping pulse. These made the landscape of her mind; they were to her what external nature was to Wordsworth or Tennyson. She lived in the country as a child, and she travelled widely after her marriage, but it was mostly from one sofa to another. She led an indoor life, and she writes like an indoor poet. Her descriptions of nature often have the freshness of delighted surprise; trees and hills and fresh air were to her not a necessity but a delicious occasional stimulus, like going to the theatre. The spaciousness and dewy greenness of some of her landscape descriptions:

> The mythic oaks and elm-trees standing out
> Self-poised upon their prodigy of shade

remind one of the close dark room in which they were written. What she actually saw from the window of her room was the texture of the London skies—in winter 'wrapped like a mummy in a yellow mist', in summer 'a thick mist lacquered over with light'; the sunsets which 'startle the slant roofs and chimney pots With splashes of fierce colour' and the classic Dickensian spectacle, watching

> the great tawny weltering fog
> Involve the passive city, strangle it
> Alive, and draw it off into the void,
> Spires, bridges, streets, and squares, as if a sponge
> Had wiped out London,

surely a deliberate and ironic echo of Wordsworth's

> Ships, towers, domes, theatres and temples lie
> All bright and glittering in the smokeless air.

Mrs Browning's semantic studies often gave a special turn to her imagery, an interlocking punning ambiguity, as in her description of a man trying to rid himself of the ghost of a dead love:

> He locks thee out at night into the cold
> Away from butting with thy horny eyes
> Against his crystal dreams,

where the adjective 'horny' is used in a double sense: the eyes of the little ghost are horns to butt against a fragile complacency, but also dim horn windows through which an icy memory peers in. Mrs Browning concentrates and interweaves her images so closely that they sometimes defy analysis, and yet have a fierce impact:

> Ten nights and days we voyaged on the deep;
> Ten nights and days without the common face
> Of any day or night; the moon and sun

Cut off from the green reconciling earth,
To starve into a blind ferocity
And glare unnatural; the very sky
(Dropping its bell-net down upon the sea
As if no human heart should 'scape alive)
Bedraggled with the desolating salt.

This passage from *Aurora Leigh* describes how the orphan child, carried away from her home on a miserable voyage to a sad destination, sees all nature turned into the famished wild beasts of some cosmic circus, glaring through the net which has become man's prison, not his protection.

Another of Elizabeth Barrett Browning's special qualities, at once a virtue and a vice, is her great variety. She could plunge from heights of beauty to depths of bathos, sometimes within the same poem. But not all her good work is in one manner, and all her bad in another; even her best work is in several different manners. She could write with classic economy, as in her sonnet on hopeless grief:

Most like a monumental statue set
In everlasting watch and moveless woe,
Till itself crumble to the dust beneath.
Touch it: the marble eyelids are not wet;
If it could weep, it could arise and go

or in her description of Michelangelo's statue of Lorenzo de' Medici:

With everlasting shadow on his face,
While the slow dawns and twilights disapprove
The ashes of his long-established race,
Which never more shall clog the feet of men.

Both these passages are inspired by sculpture, which was always one of Mrs Browning's most potent images; to her, as to Wordsworth, a statue was a 'marble index' of long voyages of the mind. But though she could write marmoreally, much of her most vivid poetry is more like a

modern sculptor's conglomeration of *objets trouvés*—
mechanisms and reptilian forms welded together in flowing
or glutinous structures; as in some passages from *Aurora
Leigh*:

> This social Sphinx
> Who sits between the sepulchre and the stews,
> Makes mock and mow against the crystal heavens,
> And bullies God

or:

> That June-day
> Too deeply sunk in craterous sunsets, now
> For you or me to dig it up alive,—
> To pluck it out all bleeding with spent flame
> At the roots, before those moralizing stars
> We have got instead

a passage which may recall to readers the poetry of
Christopher Fry, rather than of any nineteenth-century
writer.

Mrs Browning's learning and many interests, enriched by
the influence of her husband's still greater erudition, give her
poetry a very wide reference. Religion, philosophy,
politics, social reform, education, classical literature,
scientific discovery, all gave impulse to her poetic inspiration. Indignant at the chicanery of the Great Powers who
concluded the Peace of Villafranca, she dreams of

> the grand solution
> Of earth's municipal, insular schisms,
> Statesmen draping self-love's conclusion
> In cheap, vernacular patriotisms,
> Unable to give up Judaea for Jesus.

She draws a vivid image from the excavations at Pompei,
from Alexander's project to carve Mount Athos into a
colossal statue, from the holy ox of Memphis, from the
mixture of gall and potash on a painter's palette, from the
valves of a dissected hyacinth bulb. She reads Lyell's

Principles of Geology and Chambers's *Vestiges of the Natural History of Creation*, and is prompted to the reflection that

> Good love, howe'er ill-placed,
> Is better for a man's soul in the end,
> Than if he loved ill what deserves love well.
> A pagan, kissing for a step of Pan
> The wild-goat's hoof-print on the loamy down,
> Exceeds our modern thinker who turns back
> The strata . . . granite, limestone, coal and clay,
> Concluding coldly with 'Here's law! where's God?'

Often the imagery in her poetry can be traced back to references in her letters. These are now more read than her poetry, and would be more popular still if they were easily accessible in an up-to-date chronological arrangement. They are a barometer of the intelligent liberal public opinion of her times. Was it true that Newman had gone over to Rome? How long would it be before manhood suffrage was universal? Was Florence Nightingale really making the best use of her powers by being a hospital nurse? Could not prosperous Britain afford schools for all her children? In a letter of April 1846 she argues with Browning over the ethics of duelling. He has agreed with her in condemning capital punishment, and in opposing war, but yet he maintains that 'honourable men are bound to keep their honours clean at the expense of so much gunpowder and so much risk of life—*that* must be, ought to be—let judicial deaths and military glory be abolished never so!'. For her part, setting aside Christian principle, and on merely rational grounds, she 'cannot conceive of any *possible combination of circumstances* which could—I will not say *justify*, but even *excuse*, an honourable man's having recourse to the duellist's pistol, either on his own account or another's . . . His honour! Who believes in such an honour—liable to such amends, and capable of such recovery! *You* cannot, I think—in the secret of your mind. Or if *you can*—*you*, who are a teacher of the world—poor world—it is more desperately wrong than I thought.' When one finds Browning defending the principle of duelling as late as 1846, Pushkin's death in a duel only nine years earlier seems less strange.

Elizabeth Barrett Browning knew, in person or by correspondence, nearly all the eminent writers of her day, and read all the new books of any merit as they came out, and in her letters one can trace the rise and fall of reputations, the literary mysteries and controversies of the day. Could the author of *Adam Bede* really be a woman? How could anyone think Delavigne's poetry superior to Lamartine's, or Monckton Milnes's to Browning's? Could it possibly be true that *Jane Eyre* was by the governess of Thackeray's daughters? New names begin to rise in her literary firmament—Trollope's *Framley Parsonage* is 'really superb'; she is 'thunder-struck' by *Madame Bovary;* she had no idea that Thackeray had such intellectual force as *Vanity Fair* revealed; Matthew Arnold and Clough seem to her full of promise. In her letters one can also chart the rising temperature of her own fame; fan letters addressed to her simply as

Miss Elizabeth Barrett

Poetess

London

find their way to her in Wimpole Street; the terrible arbiters of the *Quarterly* and the *Examiner* begin to treat her with respect; her fellow poets write to congratulate her. But how was she to reply to a letter from Edgar Allan Poe hailing her as 'the noblest of her sex'? Perhaps she might say 'Sir, you are the most discerning of yours'.

This little joke, mocking herself as well as others, is typical of the personal style which makes Mrs Browning's letters, over and above the interest of many of their topics, so delightful. She had trained herself to write letters naturally, as though she were talking; they were indeed her only means of conversation for much of her life, when she was imprisoned by ill-health. And she had a rare ear and memory for the few face-to-face conversations which she did have, such as the misadventure of the Leeds poetess and the dropped H, which she recounted to Browning in a letter of May 1846.

A Miss Heaton had come to call, and had told Miss Barrett that 'the poetess proper of the city of Leeds was 'Mrs A':

'Mrs. A.?' said I with an enquiring innocence.

'Oh' she went on, (divining sarcasm in every breath I drew) 'oh! I dare say, *you* wouldn't admit her to be a real poetess. But as she lives in Leeds, and writes verses, we call her our poetess! and then, really, Mrs. A. is a charming woman. She was a Miss Roberts—and her "Spirit of the Woods", and of the "Flowers" has been admired, I assure you'.

Well, in a moment I seemed to remember something,—because only a few months since, surely I had a letter from somebody who was once a spirit of the Woods or ghost of the Flowers. Still, I could not make out *Mrs A*!

'Certainly' I confessed modestly, 'I never did hear of a Mrs A.—and yet, and yet—' A most glorious confusion I was in, when suddenly my visitor thought of spelling the name. 'H-E-Y' said she. Now conceive that! The Mrs Hey who came by solution, had both written to me and sent me a book on the Lakes quite lately 'by the author of the Spirit of the Woods'. *There* was the explanation! And my Leeds visitor will go back and say that I denied all knowledge of the charming Mrs A. the Leeds poetess, and that it was with the greatest difficulty I could be brought to recognize her existence. Oh, the arrogance and ingratitude of me!'

This anecdote brings out the personality of Elizabeth Barrett—her ability to see herself as others saw her, her compassionate fear to wound competing with her irresistible sense of the absurd; a complex of qualities that made Henry James say 'there is scarce a scrap of a letter of Mrs Browning's in which a nameless intellectual, if it be not rather a moral, grace . . . does not make itself felt'. Elizabeth Barrett Browning's personality, as expressed in her writing, could be maudlin and over-excited; at other times she could be astringent and satirical; but she was not mean or sly. She had that magnanimity which, though it cannot be a substitute for talent, adds a grace to it. She was magnanimous in her freedom from all religious, national, class or sex prejudices, and magnanimous in her personal relationships. The greatest wrong she ever had to suffer was the selfish tyranny of her father, and here is what she said of it:

After all, he is the victim. He isolates himself—and now and then he feels it . . . the cold dead silence all round, which is the effect of an incredible system. If he were not stronger than most men, he could not bear it as he does.

The complement to Elizabeth Barrett Browning's magnanimity, the final quality which distinguishes her poetry—and makes her resemble an Elizabethan poet such as Webster, or a modern one such as Dylan Thomas—is her outrageousness, the fearless unconcern with which she shouts and shocks and exaggerates. In real life she was a quiet-voiced gentle woman, a good listener rather than a good talker, but on paper she would say anything. Christian as she was, she would compare a waltz to the Mass, the unification of Italy to the Resurrection; no squeamishness prevented her from using scalps and tortures and rotting corpses as symbols; no prudery deterred her from talking of the smell of brothels. Like her prosodic experiments, these were deliberate attempts to create a new kind of poetic language, which would startle the reader into full participation. She often overdosed her poetry, and produced a lassitude rather than a stimulus in the reader. Her poems are not tasteful or aristocratic, and will never be appreciated by those who value restraint as a necessary element in good poetry. In thinking of her work, one is reminded of Roy Campbell's memorable lines:

> You praise the firm restraint with which they write—
> I'm with you there, of course;
> They use the snaffle and the curb all right,
> But where's the bloody horse?

Elizabeth Barrett Browning was not very handy with the snaffle or the curb, but the horse was there—a snorting and muscular charger, very liable to do a bolt.

V

In 1856 Ruskin said that Elizabeth Barrett Browning's poetry was 'unsurpassed by anything but Shakespeare'. In 1932 Virginia Woolf said that the only place in literature assigned to Mrs Browning was with Eliza Cook and Alexander Smith and other totally forgotten poets. Today, a century after Elizabeth Barrett Browning's death, her true worth as a poet is still unfixed between these extremes of critical inflation and deflation. Her poetry is very much out of favour with the academic critics and historians of literature. You will not find it among the set books in British university courses in English literature, nor in the latest anthologies. There is not a single poem of hers in John Hayward's *Penguin Book of English Verse* nor in W. H. Auden's *Poets of the English Language*, and a famous Professor is reported to have said that he could not find a poem of hers worth including in his anthology of English poetry. Not every public library in Britain has a copy of her works, and where copies do exist, they are not very often borrowed. No edition of the collected works is in print in Britain, though a new edition of 'Sonnets from the Portuguese' appeared in 1964. Elizabeth Barrett Browning's memory is kept alive at present more by the unending series of plays, films and musical comedies concerned with her private life than by readers of her poetry.

It is still too soon to say whether her fame as a poet will ever return. She may have to wait two hundred years, as Ford and Webster did till Charles Lamb brought them back to life. English literary taste moves in a circle, from extravagance to elegance and round again. It is possible that Elizabeth Barrett Browning's poetry will have a revival of favour at some future time when taste has followed its wonted cycle, and the terms 'gothic' and 'enthusiastic' have once again become terms of praise, not of abuse.

ELIZABETH BARRETT BROWNING

A Select Bibliography

(Place of publication London, unless stated otherwise)

Bibliography:

BIBLIOGRAPHY OF THE WRITINGS IN PROSE AND VERSE OF E. B. BROWNING, by T. J. Wise (1918)
—includes texts of some letters not published elsewhere, but lists as authentic Wise's forged 'Reading, 1847' edition of 'Sonnets [from the Portuguese]'.

A BROWNING LIBRARY. A CATALOGUE OF PRINTED BOOKS, MANUSCRIPTS ETC. OF R. AND E. B. BROWNING, by T. J. Wise (1929)
—the catalogue of Wise's Browning collection, now in the British Museum.

BIBLIOGRAPHIES OF TWELVE VICTORIAN AUTHORS, by T. G. Ehrsam and R. H. Deily. New York (1936)
—Supplement by J. G. Fucilla in *Modern Philology*, *xxxvii*, 1939.

THE LIFE OF ELIZABETH BARRETT BROWNING, by G. B. Taplin (1957)
—contains a List of Principal Manuscripts Sources, and of Contributions to Annuals, Almanacs, Periodicals and Series.

Collected Works:

POEMS. New edition. 2 vols. (1850; 3 vols., 1856; 4 vols., 1864)
—the 1844 *Poems* with many additions, including for the first time 'Sonnets from the Portuguese'.

POEMS, with a prefatory note by R. Browning, 6 vols. (1889)
—first published in 5 vols., 1866.

THE POEMS, with a memoir by Mrs D. Ogilvy (1893).

THE POETICAL WORKS, ed. F. G. Kenyon (1897).

THE POETICAL WORKS. Oxford (1904)
—first edition in the Oxford Standard Authors series.

COMPLETE POETICAL WORKS OF ELIZABETH BARRETT BROWNING, with introduction by L. Whiting. 2 vols. New York (1919).

POETICAL WORKS, WITH TWO PROSE ESSAYS (1920).

Selected Works:

A SELECTION FROM THE POETRY, with a prefatory note by R. Browning.
First Series (1866). Second Series (1880).

POEMS, with an introduction by A. Meynell (1903).

SELECTED POEMS, edited with introduction and notes by E. Lee.
Boston (1904).

POEMS (1912)
—in the World's Classics edition.

POEMS, selected with an introduction by S. J. Looker (1948).

Separate Works:

THE BATTLE OF MARATHON, A POEM (1820)
—published anonymously

AN ESSAY ON MIND, WITH OTHER POEMS (1826)
—published anonymously

PROMETHEUS BOUND, TRANSLATED FROM THE GREEK OF AESCHYLUS, AND
MISCELLANEOUS POEMS (1833)
—with an Introduction by A. Meynell, 1896

THE SERAPHIM, AND OTHER POEMS (1838).

THE POEMS OF GEOFFREY CHAUCER MODERNIZED (1841)
—Elizabeth Barrett contributed a version of 'Queen Annelida and
False Arcite'.

POEMS. 2 vols. (1844)
—by Elizabeth Barrett, Author of *The Seraphim* etc. This edition was
used as the basis for subsequent editions of Elizabeth Barrett
Browning's collected works produced in her lifetime and immediately after her death. The second edition, 1850, included much new
material—a revised version of 'Prometheus Bound', the 'Sonnets
from the Portuguese' (here published for the first time; the so-called
'Reading edition' of 1847 is a forgery), and 35 other sonnets and
lyrics not previously published in book form. There was a third
edition in 1853, a fourth (incorporating 'Casa Guidi Windows') in
1856 (in 3 vols.), a fifth in 1862, a sixth (incorporating 'Aurora
Leigh') in 1864, and a seventh, the final one, in 1866.

A NEW SPIRIT OF THE AGE, ed. R. H. Horne (1844)
—Elizabeth Barrett contributed a number of essays and parts of essays.

CASA GUIDI WINDOWS, A POEM (1851).

AURORA LEIGH (1857)
—with an Introduction by A. C. Swinburne, 1898.

POEMS BEFORE CONGRESS (1860)
—reprinted, New York, 1860, as *Napoleon III in Italy and Other Poems.*

LAST POEMS (1862).

THE GREEK CHRISTIAN POETS AND THE ENGLISH POETS (1863)
—articles reprinted from the *Athenaeum*, 1842; *The English Poets* being a review of an anthology called *The Book of the Poets*.

PSYCHE APOCALYPTÉ, A LYRICAL DRAMA. Projected by E. B. Browning and R. H. Horne (1876)
—an earlier draft of this was printed in *Hitherto Unpublished Poems* (see below).

THE ENCHANTRESS, AND OTHER POEMS (1913).

EPISTLE TO A CANARY, ed. E. Gosse (1913).

LEILA, A TALE (1913).

NEW POEMS BY ROBERT BROWNING AND ELIZABETH BARRETT BROWNING, ed. F. G. Kenyon (1914).

THE POET'S ENCHIRIDION, ed. H. B. Forman. Boston (1914).

HITHERTO UNPUBLISHED POEMS AND STORIES, WITH AN INEDITED AUTO-BIOGRAPHY, ed. H. B. Forman. 2 vols. Boston (1914).

SONNETS FROM THE PORTUGUESE. Centennial Variorum Edition, edited and with an introduction by F. Ratchford and notes by D. Fulton. New York (1950)
—the 1856 text as finally revised by E. B. Browning, but with variant readings from MS texts in the British Museum, Morgan Library and Houghton Library.

Letters:

LETTERS ADDRESSED TO RICHARD HENGIST HORNE, ed. S. R. T. Mayer. 2 vols. (1877).

KIND WORDS FROM A SICKROOM: [FOUR] LETTERS ADDRESSED TO ALLAN PARK PATON. Greenock (privately printed, 1891).

LETTERS OF ELIZABETH BARRETT BROWNING, edited with biographical additions by F. G. Kenyon. 2 vols. (1897).

LETTERS OF ROBERT BROWNING AND ELIZABETH BARRETT, 1845-46. 2 vols. (1899).

ELIZABETH BARRETT BROWNING IN HER LETTERS, by P. Lubbock (1906)
—a selection of the letters with critical commentary.

THE RELIGIOUS OPINIONS OF ELIZABETH BARRETT BROWNING: THREE
    LETTERS ADDRESSED TO WILLIAM MERRY (1906)
—originally printed privately, 1896.

THE ART OF SCANSION: LETTER TO UVEDALE PRICE, with an introduction
    by A. Meynell (1916).

LETTERS REPRINTED BY T. J. WISE (1916 and 1919).

LETTERS TO ROBERT BROWNING AND OTHER CORRESPONDENTS, ed. T. J.
    Wise (privately printed, 1916).

ELIZABETH BARRETT BROWNING: LETTERS TO HER SISTER 1846-1859,
    ed. L. Huxley (1929).

TWENTY-TWO UNPUBLISHED LETTERS OF ELIZABETH BARRETT BROWNING
    AND ROBERT BROWNING, ADDRESSED TO HENRIETTA AND ARABELLA
    MOULTON-BARRETT. New York (1935).

FROM ROBERT AND ELIZABETH BROWNING: A FURTHER SELECTION OF THE
    BARRETT-BROWNING FAMILY CORRESPONDENCE, ed. W. R. Benet
    (1936).

LETTERS TO BENJAMIN ROBERT HAYDON, ed. M. H. Shackford. New
    York (1939).

TWENTY UNPUBLISHED LETTERS TO HUGH STUART BOYD, ed. B. Weaver
    (1950).

ELIZABETH BARRETT TO MISS MITFORD: LETTERS TO MARY RUSSELL
    MITFORD, edited and introduced by B. Miller (1954).

UNPUBLISHED LETTERS OF THOMAS DE QUINCEY AND ELIZABETH BARRETT
    BROWNING, ed. S. Musgrove. Auckland (1954).

ELIZABETH BARRETT TO MR. BOYD: UNPUBLISHED LETTERS TO HUGH
    STUART BOYD, edited and introduced by B. P. McCarthy (1955).

LETTERS OF THE BROWNINGS TO GEORGE BARRETT, ed. P. Landis and
    R. E. Freeman. Urbana (1958).

Some Biographical and Critical Studies:

A NEW SPIRIT OF THE AGE, by R. H. Horne (1844)
—contains a chapter on 'Miss E. B. Barrett and Mrs Norton'.

WORKS OF EDGAR ALLAN POE, ed. E. C. Stedman and G. E. Woodbury.
    Chicago (1895)
—Vol. vi. contains an essay of 1845 on 'Miss Barrett's "A Drama of
    Exile, and other Poems"'.

NOTES SUR L'ANGLETERRE, par H. A. Taine. Paris (1872)
—includes a brief but important study of Mrs Browning's poetry.

TWO GREAT ENGLISHWOMEN: MRS BROWNING AND CHARLOTTE BRONTE,
by P. Bayne (1881)
—critical study with a useful analysis of 'The Seraphim' and 'A
Drama of Exile'.

POÈTES MODERNES DE L'ANGLETERRE, par G. Sarrazin. Paris (1885)
—critical study.

ÉTUDES SUR MISTRESS ELIZABETH BROWNING, par C. des Guerrois.
Paris (1885)
—analysis of Mrs Browning's aesthetic theory, and translations of some
of the poems.

ELIZABETH BARRETT BROWNING, by J. H. Ingram (1888)
—the first biography, inaccurate as to some dates and facts, but sensible
on poetry.

INTRODUCTION, by A. Meynell (1896)
—to edition of *Prometheus Bound and Other Poems*, E. B. Browning's
first translation, originally published 1833.

INTRODUCTION to *Aurora Leigh*, by A. C. Swinburne (1898)

WILLIAM WETMORE STORY AND HIS FRIENDS, by H. James. Edinburgh
(1903)
—includes some short but penetrating references to Mrs Browning.

THE BROWNINGS AND AMERICA, by E. P. Gould. Boston (1904)
—contains a survey of American reviews of E. B. Browning's poetry.

LA VIE ET L'OEUVRE D'E. B. BROWNING, par G. M. Merlette. Paris (1905)
—contains summaries and analyses of all principal poems, and a study
of prosodic experiments.

THE BROWNINGS, THEIR LIFE AND ART, by L. Whiting (1911)
—the first authoritative biography; many of the facts were obtained
from the Brownings' son.

ENGLISH SONGS OF ITALIAN FREEDOM (1911) and ENGLISHMEN AND
ITALIANS: SOME ASPECTS OF THEIR RELATIONS PAST AND PRESENT (1919)
by G. M. Trevelyan
—assesses E. B. Browning's influence on political opinion.

FEMME ET POÈTE: ELISABETH BROWNING, par R. B. Nicati. Paris (1912)
—critical study, includes analysis of E. B. Browning's religion.

ELISABETTA BARRETT BROWNING, di B. Viterbi. Bergamo (1913)
—biography.

THE BROWNINGS, by O. Burdett (1928)
—critical study.

ELIZABETH BARRETT BROWNING, by L. S. Boas (1930)
—biography.

THE COMMON READER, Second Series, by V. Woolf (1932)
—the most important critical study by a 20th-century creative writer.

FLUSH, by V. Woolf (1933)
—ostensibly a biography of E. B. Browning's dog, but contains
  biographical material on her.

AN ENQUIRY INTO THE NATURE OF CERTAIN NINETEENTH CENTURY
  PAMPHLETS, by J. Carter and G. Pollard (1934)
—exposed the 1847 edition of the *Sonnets from the Portuguese* as a
  forgery.

ELIZABETH BARRETT BROWNING: R. H. HORNE: TWO STUDIES, by M. H.
  Shackford. Wellesley, Mass. (1935)
—critical study.

THE FAMILY OF THE BARRETT, by J. Marks. New York (1938)
—history of the Barrett family in Jamaica. Section on E. B. Browning's
  opium addiction.

THE IMMORTAL LOVERS, by F. Winwar (1950)
—biography.

ELIZABETH BARRETT BROWNING, by D. Hewlett (1953)
—biography and critical study.

ROBERT ET ELIZABETH BROWNING, par A. Maurois. Paris (1955)
—the best representative of the disillusioned view of the Browning's
  story.

THE GOLDEN RING: THE ANGLO-FLORENTINES, by G. A. Treves (1956)
—section on the Brownings' lives and friends in Florence.

THE LIFE OF ELIZABETH BARRETT BROWNING, by G. B. Taplin (1957)
—biography, incorporating much new material; valuable bibliography.

AURORA LEIGH, the Fawcett Lecture, by J. M. S. Tompkins (1961)
—analyses E. B. Browning's ideas on women as writers.

MRS BROWNING: A POET'S WORK AND ITS SETTING, by A. Hayter (1963)
—critical study.

Note: Important material on E. B. Browning is contained in Robert Browning's letters and in biographies of him—

RECORDS OF TENNYSON, RUSKIN AND THE BROWNINGS, by Lady Ritchie (Anne Isabella Thackeray) (1892).

ROBERT BROWNING, by G. K. Chesterton (1903).

LIFE AND LETTERS OF ROBERT BROWNING, by Mrs. S. Orr (1908).

LIFE OF ROBERT BROWNING, by W. H. Griffin and H. C. Minchin (1910).

LETTERS OF ROBERT BROWNING, ed. T. L. Hood (1933).

ROBERT BROWNING AND JULIA WEDGWOOD. A BROKEN FRIENDSHIP AS REVEALED IN THEIR LETTERS, ed. R. Curle (1937).

NEW LETTERS OF ROBERT BROWNING, ed. W. C. de Vane and K. L. Knickerbocker (1951).

DEAREST ISA. ROBERT BROWNING'S LETTERS TO ISABELLA BLAGDEN, ed. E. C. McAleer. Austin, Texas. (1951).

ROBERT BROWNING, A PORTRAIT, by B. Miller (1953).

AMPHIBIAN: A RECONSIDERATION OF BROWNING, by H. C. Duffin (1956).

Four Realist Novelists

by VINCENT BROME

Published for the British Council
and the National Book League
by Longmans, Green & Co

Three shillings and sixpence net

English realist novelists in the nineteenth century were interested in character as something essentially idiosyncratic. By the end of the century their work was clearly distinguishable from that of the French naturalist school, headed by Zola, which saw character and event as shaped by environment and other processes which could be scientifically defined. The four representatives of the English realist school treated here, though lesser novelists than their more famous colleagues, deserve reading with attention and interest. While the techniques these men used were not completely successful, Mr. Brome writes, they nevertheless 'showed exceptional skill in evoking the London scene and London characters'. Mr. Brome praises Morrison who, with Gissing, created the first literature of the East End of London as seen from the inside. A craftsman 'who rose occasionally to the heights of original creation', Morrison possessed a sometimes brilliant talent. Mr. Brome also casts sympathetic light on the work of Pugh: complex, often manifesting a clash between his avowed aim to represent average people in average situations, and his liking for melodrama; on that of Whiteing, nearer in spirit to Arthur Morrison in works like *No. 5 John Street*, an 'experimental novel' in organization; and lastly on that of Pett Ridge, a more superficial but genuinely comic writer.

Vincent Brome is author of *H. G. Wells* (1951), *Six Studies in Quarrelling* (1958), and *Frank Harris* (1959). He has written many novels, among them *The Last Surrender* (1954) and *Acquainted With Grief* (1965); and his play, *The Sleepless One*, was produced in the Edinburgh Festival in 1962. Mr. Brome is also a well-known broadcaster.

Bibliographical Series
of Supplements to 'British Book News'
on Writers and Their Work

GENERAL EDITOR
Geoffrey Bullough

¶ Arthur Morrison was born in 1863 and died in 1945; Edwin Pugh was born in 1874 and died in 1930; Richard Whiteing was born in 1840 and died in 1928; and William Pett Ridge was born in 1860 and died in 1930.

ARTHUR MORRISON

FOUR
REALIST
NOVELISTS

ARTHUR MORRISON · EDWIN PUGH
RICHARD WHITEING · WILLIAM PETT RIDGE

by
VINCENT BROME

PUBLISHED FOR
THE BRITISH COUNCIL
AND THE NATIONAL BOOK LEAGUE
BY LONGMANS, GREEN & CO

LONGMANS, GREEN & CO LTD
48 Grosvenor Street, London W.1

*Associated companies, branches and
representatives throughout the world*

First published 1965
© Vincent Brome 1965

*Printed in Great Britain by
F. Mildner & Sons, London, E.C.1*

CONTENTS

Acknowledgments: Our grateful thanks are due to the following for permission to quote from works in copyright: to the owners of the copyright for material from the works of Arthur Morrison, and Messrs Methuen & Co. Ltd. for material from *Tales of Mean Streets;* to Messrs Ward, Lock & Co. Ltd. for material from the works of Edwin Pugh; to the executor of Richard Whiteing for material from *No. 5 John Street;* to Messrs. C. Arthur Pearson Ltd. for material from *Mord Em'ly.*

The frontispiece portrait of Arthur Morrison is reproduced by permission of the Trustees of the British Museum.

FOUR REALIST NOVELISTS

I. ARTHUR MORRISON

A CLOUD OF self-induced obscurity surrounds the life of Arthur Morrison, that small master among the group of English novelists who concentrated their attention on the working classes in their East End *milieu* during the late nineteenth century. The *Times* obituary about him is a bewildered piece of writing. A few lines giving the barest bones of his life are overwhelmed by a laboured examination of his work. According to Morrison himself, he was born in Kent in 1863, but his birth certificate places him immutably in the East End of London. His father he described as an engineer, but he was in fact an engine fitter. Professionally, he identified himself, later in life, as a civil servant and this may be considered a legitimate extension of the fact that he helped to run the People's Palace, a charitable 'mission' founded by Walter Besant in the East End of London in 1887. It was almost as if the man who so vividly evokes the horror, the poverty, the seaminess of late nineteenth century London, wanted to forget or run away from his roots.

His personality is similarly masked. Few interviews or sketches worthy of the name remain, and none reveals what manner of man he was, but there are hints in his contemporaries' comments of a touch of snobbery which might complicate his reasons for concealing his origins. He tired very soon of his life as 'a civil servant' and turned to journalism, becoming a member of the staff of a London daily newspaper. He married in 1892 Elizabeth Adelaide, the daughter of a Dover man. Their one son, Guy, died in 1921 of 'maladies consequent on his war service'. Morrison himself served as an inspector of special Constabulary during World War I, and had the curious distinction of telephoning the warning of the first Zeppelin raid on London. Little else of a personal nature has been recorded.

7

In 1892-3 he drew on his experiences of the East End to
write a number of short stories the first of which, published
in *Macmillan's Magazine*, attracted the attention of W. E.
Henley, who was then steadily building up the reputation of
the famous *National Observer*. Morrison wrote, at Henley's
request, a number of new short stories which were gathered
and published in one volume under the title *Tales of Mean
Streets* in 1894, the year when Henley also discovered H. G.
Wells. Perhaps it is irrelevant to ask for subtlety or depth of
character in stories which set out brutally and bluntly to
depict the darker side of life in the East End of London, but
these early stories are not so effective as Morrison's first
novel, *A Child of the Jago*, which appeared in 1896.

Morrison's intention in writing *A Child of the Jago* can be
given in his own words: 'To tell the story of the horrible
[Jago] . . . and of a boy who, but for his environment would
have become a good citizen.' He sets the scene rapidly in the
opening paragraphs:

> It was past the mid of a summer night in the Old Jago. The narrow
> street was all the blacker for the lurid sky. . . . Below, the hot heavy air
> lay, a rank oppression, on the contorted forms of those who made for
> sleep on the pavement; and in it, and through it all, there rose, from the
> foul earth and grimed walls, a close, mingled stink—the odour of the
> Jago . . . there the Jago, for one hundred years the blackest pit in London,
> lay and festered.

Carefully avoided by most of those who came from the
West End of London, the Jago was an awful Gothic spectacle
of squalor, brutality and crime, which actually existed under
another name in the East End of London, and many of its
inhabitants knew what it meant to be driven by hunger into
extreme behaviour.

A small boy, Dicky Perrott, streaks across this scene with
the hunted vitality of a child whose wits have been sharpened beyond anything childhood should know, and whose
spindly body is alive with the nervous tensions of desperate
need. One day he stealthily insinuates himself into the

ceremony of opening the new wing of the Institute, a procedure which allows Morrison fine scope for satirizing those
West End eminences, including a Bishop, who come to
witness the results of their own charity and congratulate
themselves on the wonderful effects of 'Pansophic Elevation'
among the degraded classes. The canker in their midst, Dicky
Perrot, hides himself behind the curtains of the room
wherein the Bishop and other Eminences will retire to take
tea after the ceremony. Presently the amiable Bishop,
'beaming over the tea-cup . . . at two courtiers of the clergy,
bethought him of a dinner engagement and passed his hand
downward over the rotundity of his waistcoat. "Dear, dear"
said the Bishop glancing down suddenly, "Why—what's
become of my watch".'

When Dicky Perrott bursts in on his family ten minutes
later crying: 'Mother—Father—look! I done a click. I got a
clock—a red un!'—he expects praise, but his father, carefully
pocketing the watch, up-ends and beats him. From now on
the horror of double-dealing, of dirt, crime and brutality
grows as the novel unfolds scene after scene where gang-
warfare outdoes in violence anything known today:

Down the middle of Old Jago Street came Sally Green: red-faced,
stripped to the waist, dancing, hoarse and triumphant. Nail-scores wide
as the finger striped her back, her face, and her throat, and she had a black
eye; but in one great hand she dangled a long bunch of clotted hair, as
she whooped defiance to the Jago. It was a trophy newly rent from the
scalp of Norah Walsh, a champion of the Rann womanhood who had
crawled away to hide her blighted head and be restored with gin.

Against this background, rendered with horrific detail,
Dicky Perrott finds himself torn between Aaron Weech, the
cunning fence who can dispose of anything so long as it is
stolen, and Father Sturt, who gets Dicky a job as a shop-boy
in the Bethnal Green Road and sets him on the path to
respectability. Furious because he has lost a skilful child
operator, Weech engineers the boy's dismissal and Dicky,
once more the bewildered victim of forces he only dimly

comprehends, drifts back to his old haunts and his old ways. Once again the Jago teaches him: 'Spare nobody and stop at nothing, for the Jago's got you, and it's the only way out except the gaol and the gallows.' In due course Josh Perrott, the father, murders Aaron Weech and Dicky is knifed in a street brawl. One solitary principle comes through the murk and the muck. When Dicky is dying Father Sturt asks him—'who did it?'—and he replies, 'Dunno Fa'er'. The lie— the staunch Jago lie. Thou shalt not nark.

Arthur Morrison developed into a distinguished practitioner of a new school of realism in English fiction which derived from Zola, Dickens and Gissing but in his hands became different from any of their work. Descriptions of slums and low life occur in Dickens, Charles Kingsley, Walter Besant and many others but Morrison disdained the quaintness of Dickens's slum characters and recoiled from any attempt to romanticise East End lives. He wanted to record the reality as it was.

Gissing in *The Nether World* gave a description of Pennyloaf Candy's terrible home in the East End of London which leads directly into Morrison's work, but Morrison carefully avoided the self-pity evident in much of Gissing's work:

In my East End stories I determined that they must be written in a different way from the ordinary slum story. They must be done with austerity and frankness, and there must be no sentimentalism, no glossing over. I felt that the writer must never interpose himself between his subject and his reader. I could best bring in real life by keeping myself and my moralizings out of it. For this I have been abused as hard and unsympathetic, but I can assure you it is far more painful for me to write stories than for you to read them.

There was no *explicit* moral anger in Morrison's work as there was with Dickens, and the French naturalism of Zola gave place to the empirical realism of England. The character which dominates *A Child of the Jago* is really the Jago itself. But it is presented without social comment, and for all the

remorseless accuracy with which the author reveals every
corner of this black and hopeless pit, he seldom suggests any
explicit concern for its inhabitants. On the surface, Morrison
seems to shrug his shoulders. Conditions are like this. Slum
life has to be accepted and the destiny of those born within
its precincts is played out under Morrison's direction with a
dreadful inevitability. Take the dialogue in the first chapter
of *A Child of the Jago* between Kiddo Cook and the stranger:

'Ah-h-h-', he said, 'I wish I was dead; and kep a cawfy shop.'
Kiddo Cook felt in his pocket, and produced a pipe and a screw of
paper. 'This is a bleedin unsocial sort o'evenin' party, this is', he said.
'An ere's the on'y real toff in the mob with 'ardly a pipeful left, an' no
lights. D'y'ear me lord',—leaning towards the dozing neighbour—'got
a match?'
'Go t'ell.'
'O wot 'orrid langwidge . . .'
'Go t'ell.'
A lank elderly man who sat with his back to the wall, pushed up a
battered tall hat from his eyes, and producing a box of matches ex-
claimed:
'Hell? And how far's that? You're in it . . .'
'Ah', Kiddo Cook remarked, as he lit his pipe in the hollow of his
hands, 'that's a comfort Mr. Beveridge, anyhow.'

There is another element implicit in the book which tends
to qualify its external realism. A black despair which verges
upon hatred appears in over-emphasized descriptions, and
bursts of emotion are sometimes expressed in acid sarcasm.
For all his protestations, there are times when Morrison
cannot keep his own feelings out of the book. Philanthropy
and its half-sister charity may have brought about changes in
the Jago, but they were full of smugness and humbug which
Morrison exposes. His general method is to describe the
surface reality in detail. He gets his effects by selecting and
reiterating melodramatic episodes, but occasionally he goes
beyond this naturalistic approach and ventures a moral
judgement.

He did not create in Dicky Perrott a child as memorable as George Eliot's Maggie Tulliver because he deliberately foreswore insight into the hidden workings of character. In his view nature reacted on nurture and produced a series of conditioned reflexes in Dicky Perrott. That was sufficient for him. The power of environment was more important than any hidden complex in the psychological makeup of the child.

It is possible to charge the method with superficiality. The wellsprings of human nature are subject to many complicated influences of which topographical environment is only one, if a major one, but it now becomes necessary to explore the theory of English realism in nineteenth-century fiction and its ancestor French naturalism.

One of the most repetitive and confused pieces of writing of which Zola was ever guilty, his prolonged essay, or series of interlocking essays, on 'The Experimental Novel' tries to relate the naturalistic school to the scientific method. It is a pity that no-one at that stage of critical history took the trouble to define clearly the differences between the words naturalistic, realistic and scientific, for the result was that the labels could sometimes be interchanged to the confusion of the whole scene. The main distinguishing feature between French 'naturalism' and English 'realism' was that French writers saw character and event as shaped by environment and other processes which could be scientifically defined. English writers tended to be interested in character as something essentially idiosyncratic, an end in itself, and action as often determined by the operations of chance.

What Zola meant by the *école naturaliste* can be stated fairly simply. Zola saw the late nineteenth century as an age of science, and believed that no subject which was not studied and developed according to the scientific method could claim attention as a serious branch of knowledge. The essence of the scientific method was centred on experiment, and as the scientist had passed from experiment in chemistry and physics to experiment in physiology, so the novelist must pass from the traditional novel to the experimental novel. He saw the novel partly as a means to social reform, and a moral element must therefore prevail in this new approach. The experimental novelist 'must do for man as a whole what the experimenting physiologist does for his body'. He would probe into inherited characteristics, take account of the influence of environment, dissect every action to discover its cause and effect and then, acknowledging the laws of scientific determinism, give an account from beginning to end of the interaction of mind, body and environment.

Strictly speaking, Zola was describing not the application of the scientific method to novel-writing but simply a new departure from an old creative tradition. Granted an overwhelming reverence for the new science, Zola wanted to make it part of literature, but there were only two points where they really met. First the rejection of the romantic tradition and the substitution of a realism which recorded what it saw no matter how nasty or sordid that reality turned out to be, and second, the belief that life and events were mechanistically determined. An experiment carried out under controlled conditions in the laboratory was very different from telling a story in a new way with more realistic observation. Zola wanted novels in future to be closely based on the realities of life and the underlying philosophy of scientific determinism. Henry Norman summed up the desired change in technique in the *Fortnightly Review* for 1 December 1883:

Do not contrive a complicated family or social puzzle of which your novel is to exhibit the process of solution, exhausting your ingenuity in making people misunderstand one another, and in placing obstacles in their way; but take a piece of real life for your basis and let your motives and means be those of our common existence.

The first translations of Zola's novels in England were received with disgust, and a public outcry led to the imprisonment in 1889 of his publisher, Vizetelly. For English readers, with their uneasy Victorian conscience, Zola had overstepped the borderline between the sordid and the pornographic. Always fascinated by the raw material of life, Zola had in fact set out to explore this in a series of novels telling the story of the Rougon-Macquart family and its enormous ramifications during the second Empire. This was intended to be not merely a picture of French life and society but also a study in heredity.

Arthur Morrison read *La Terre*, included in the second half of the series. It is almost certain that he also read Zola's rambling attempt to make a science of literature in *The Experimental Novel*, which was translated into English in 1893, the year before *A Child of the Jago* appeared. Literary periodicals in England also paid attention to the new French school and novels like George Moore's *Esther Waters* were stamped as naturalistic, but the growth of English realism had several distinguishing characteristics. It did not concern itself with science or the scientific method and in the hands of Morrison it had nothing to do with moralizing. Dickens had given it a peculiarly English twist by concentrating on 'characters' but neither Morrison nor Dickens accepted the assumption on which Naturalism as a literary movement was based—that man and his societies can be explained entirely in mechanistic or deterministic terms.

When challenged to explain the precise nature of his brand of realism, Morrison produced a rambling essay in the *New Review* for March 1897 which lost its way in an outburst of pique and failed to answer the question. Stung by an article in the *Fortnightly*, Morrison declared:

I decline the labels of the schoolmen and of the sophisters; being a simple writer of tales who takes whatever means lie to his hand to present life as he sees it; who 'insists' on 'no process' and who refuses to be bound by any formula prescription prepared by the cataloguers and pigeon-holers of literature.

He then gives his definition of realism:

It seems to me that the man who is called a 'realist' is one who, seeing things with his own eyes, discards the conventions of the schools and presents his matter in individual terms of art.

This, of course, will not do. It is not a definition of a realist; it merely describes a particular kind of artist. A man who sees things with his own eyes and presents them in individual terms too often imposes his own vision on the scene observed and loses the documentary quality which is a prime element in realism. Dickens ceases to be a realist when his Cockney characters are converted by his vision into comical caricatures and his slums take on a picturesque or quaint air. Trade unionism in *Hard Times* ceases to be an instrument of working class organization and becomes a form of pointless intimidation, which is very unrealistic.

Not so in the work of Arthur Morrison. If anything he tended to make the Jago more appalling than it was—if that were possible—by over-emphasizing its depravity and squalor. Certainly the London to which he was born provided him with a wealth of realist material. The rabid region east of Aldgate was a catacomb of evil-smelling alleys and tiny shops, of crumbling warehouses and sub-let rooms, of a rancid river slithering furtively to the sea and mud flats which oozed into the city carrying their sour exhalation to the railway arches of Bethnal Green and the grim blackness of the Commerical Road. Thousands of people lived out their pallid lives without leaving the precincts of the slums and many died before they were forty of disease, malnutrition and the hazards of everyday life in places like the Jago. Of course, there were music halls, pubs and gaiety. Of course, on Saturday nights a zest for living burst through all the horrors and insisted on a coarse form of—was it happiness? Arthur Morrison did not deal in the reverse side of the coin. He was concerned with slums, poverty, hardship, to the exclusion of joy, and to that extent could be accused of being an inverted romantic rather than a realist.

He had a second very precise purpose in his writing, which made it necessary to exercise a special technique of selection.

Before Gissing and Arthur Morrison, the literature of the East End of London was a stranger's literature seen from the outside. As V. S. Pritchett has written:

It lies under the melodramatic murk and the smear of sentimental pathos, which in the nineteenth century were generated by the guilty conscience of the middle classes. They were terrified of the poor who seethed in an abyss just beyond their back door. The awful Gothic spectacle of hunger, squalor and crime was tolerable only as nightmare and fantasy—such as Dickens provided—and the visiting foreigner alone could observe the English slums with the curiosity of the traveller or the countenance of the anthropologist.

Gissing and Arthur Morrison broke into this convention to write from *within* the slums, to make internal what had always been external. They looked out through the eyes of men, women and children living in places like the Jago and faithfully recorded what it meant to be involved, day in, day out, in a kind of poverty which was far removed from anything to do with the picturesque. Gissing's novels are full of misery and worthy pathos. Arthur Morrison's dispense with the pathos and convey the impression of a species adapting itself to horrors which should have overwhelmed it. His novels are different from picturesque or nightmare novels and different again from the 'character albums of the writers of low comedy'.

His second novel, *London Town* (1899), another Tale of East End Life 'among the better sort of people in those parts' was not very successful. Dealing with the extremities of East End life Morrison emerged supreme. When he tried to convey a slice of less extravagant life where people were not so hard-pressed and even the beauties of Epping Forest had their place, the note was less urgent, the descriptions less vivid, the narrative rambling.

The powerful colours of squalor and violence inevitably had an impact far greater than the quieter colours of the semi-respectable. It is a severe test of any writer to make the commonplace as interesting as the melodramatic. Morrison did not match up to it. He said, in a note which prefaced this second novel:

I designed this story, and, indeed, began to write it, between the publication of *Tales of Mean Streets* and that of *A Child of the Jago*, to be read together with these books: not that I pretend to figure in all three— much less in any one of them—a complete picture of life in the eastern parts of London, but because they are complementary, each to the two others.

Aware that his first novel had splashed down one kind of East End life in fierce colours, he tried to redress the balance by evoking more neutral scenes which would justify his claim to realism. He did not succeed. As if aware of this his third novel, *Canning Murrell*, was a total departure from what had gone before. It dealt with the activities of a witch doctor in rural Essex in the early 19th century.

Morrison's fourth novel—*The Hole in the Wall*—is his best and stands out among the novels of working class life in the late nineteenth century as a minor masterpiece. It returns once more to the techniques of *A Child of the Jago*. The Hole in the Wall was a public house in the notorious Radcliffe Highway of the East End, and the novel centres upon an orphaned boy, Stephen, brought up by his grandfather in an atmosphere of filth, murder, deception and theft. The viewpoint of the novel shifts from Stephen the boy to the omniscient novelist, one chapter being seen through Stephen's eyes, another taking the wider, third person perspective. It is a clumsy device. It breaks the consistency of the novel and the shifting viewpoint occasionally threatens verisimilitude. It would have been a far more severe test of Morrison as a novelist if he had limited himself to Stephen's viewpoint and seen everything through the boy's eyes. Indeed there are many indications that he intended to do just that, but the intractable material did not easily surrender to the single viewpoint and particularly to the viewpoint of a boy. In an attempt to bring the activities of all the characters into a cohesive whole he was driven to step out of Stephen's shoes.

The central theme of the novel is the effect on Grandfather Nat of the boy's relationship with him. The child is 'sheltered' by Nat, and as he observes the murky life of the pub, he gradually discovers that his grandfather is a receiver of stolen goods. Marr, a defaulting ship owner, disguises himself as a sailor to escape with £800 which eventually comes into the hands of Grandfather Nat. Marr gets drunk and is murdered by Dan Ogle, who at first intended no higher flight of theft than stealing a watch. There is a terrifying scene in which Marr, stunned and tottering between the two men, is dragged towards the river while they sing and bawl at the tops of their voices, pretending they are drunken sailors helping a pal to keep his feet. It is a pity, in one sense, that Morrison introduced that *cliché* character, a blind fiddler, because it modifies the austerity of his realism, but the fiddler finally indulges a form of brutality which lifts him clean away from any romantic tradition. While the wallet with the stolen £800 passes mysteriously to Grandfather Nat, the blind man is double-crossed, assaulted and ridiculed by Dan Ogle. He sets out to track Ogle down across the marshes and when he finds him asleep in a shed concealed by a lime quarry, he attacks him:

Floundering and tumbling against the frail boards of the shed the two men came out at the door in a struggling knot; Ogle wrestling and striking at random, while the other, cunning with a life's blindness, kept his own head safe and hung as a dog hangs to a bull. His hands gripped his victim by ear and hair while the thumbs still drove at the eyes the mess of smoking lime that clung and dripped about Ogle's head. It trickled burning through his hair and it blistered lips and tongue, as he yelled and yelled again in the extremity of his anguish.

The blind man has blinded his enemy. Just one word seems out of place in a description which is much longer and more powerful in the original; the word 'yelled'. It does not adequately convey the reaction of a man whose head is burning from lime and whose eyes are being put out by another man's hands. Such a man undergoing such an experience would have screamed.

The clash between the innocent boy's view of the events he witnesses and the depravity of most of the remaining characters, including Grandfather Nat, gives the novel the tension of moral conflict. As in *A Child of the Jago*, where the clash occurs between the evil of the Jago which itself becomes one of the main characters and the social goodness of Father Sturt, here the child's innocence and unquestioning affection modify Grandfather Nat's degenerate character. The people in *A Child of the Jago* tend to be good or bad, black or white, but in *The Hole in the Wall* they are more complex and the novel, in consequence, more sophisticated.

Once again the River Thames, dragging through its murkiest reaches, the wharves with cranes wheeling a-tiptoe, the marshy flats, sullen skies and the ghastly traffic in human beings trapped in one squalid conspiracy after another, combine to leave a memorable picture of one side of East End life conveyed in the most realistic terms. Only Stephen and Grandfather Nat emerge with any hope for the future:

Dan Ogle, blinded and broken, but silent and saving his revenge; Musky Meg, stricken and pitiable but faithful even if to death; Henry Viney, desperate but fearful and urgently needy; these three skulked at bay in dark holes by Blue Gate.

It remains to guess that Stephen and Dicky Perrot were both embodiments of the shy sensitive boy Arthur Morrison, who had been born into an East End jungle which he wanted to dissociate from his new and cultured life as a writer.

Following *The Hole in the Wall*, Morrison failed to develop as a novelist and produced nothing worthy of comparison. There are obvious reasons for this. In the first place, as a busy journalist his spare time was limited, and another powerful preoccupation had arisen to challenge his interest in creative writing. After the first four novels much of his spare time was spent studying Oriental painting. He left a fine collection of Chinese and Japanese drawings to the British Museum, and wrote a two-volume study of Japanese painting which is still respected by scholars in the field. He also wrote, as early as 1894, a series of detective stories which began with *Martin Hewitt, Investigator*. Within his work itself, however, lay the major reason for his failure to develop. Morrison was a craftsman who rose occasionally to the heights of original creation, but these experiences could not be sustained. Moreover he had stated and re-stated his particular message. He did not have the boundless creative energy of great novelists like Dickens and Zola, and the range of his interests was much more limited. His was a brilliant but minor talent which could not reach beyond the area it had already illumined.

II. EDWIN PUGH

Among the group of writers who followed different creative paths into the lives of the working classes were Edwin Pugh, Pett Ridge, Richard Whiteing and Somerset Maugham. Published in 1897, Maugham's *Liza of Lambeth* was considered very daring, for it dealt with an illicit love affair followed by a miscarriage. Maugham has since become internationally known as a clever story-teller and his novels sell in hundreds of thousands, but Edwin Pugh, Pett Ridge and Richard Whiteing are almost forgotten. Pett Ridge developed the 'mean street' theme with novels which dealt in Cockney comedy as represented by domestic servants, clerks and shop girls, whose lives were very different from the crushed and degraded existence of Morrison's characters.

Edwin Pugh was a much more complicated person and writer. Born to a London where the streets were gas lit, hansom cabs plied for hire, women wore skirts to the ground, men rode penny farthing bicycles and Gladstone dominated the scene, Pugh worked in a city office for eight years and knew at first hand what it meant to be a clerk imprisoned for ten hours a day in return for a pittance. His first book, *A Street in Suburbia* (1895), was a series of sketches of lower

London life which gave little indication of the man who was to attempt an extension of Arthur Morrison's realism.

In an essay 'Real Realism' published in 1916, Pugh criticized those novelists who limited their realism to the sordid, the poverty-stricken and the brutal. Realism, to justify the term must include the lovely as well as the unlovely, he said, the idealistic as well as the corrupt. He soared away into rhetorical flights proclaiming:

Our hearts do realize that there is, all said and done, more idealism than materialism upon earth and more nobleness than depravity in man. In short—*real realism* consists in giving a picture of life in which the light and shade are in their due proportions.

Throughout the essay there are bursts of highly emotional overstatement: 'Real art seizes life at its richest moments and presents it, preserved forever by its immaterial essence, from inconstancy and degradation.' Pugh's general theories, however, are much more sharply defined and formalized than those of Arthur Morrison, even if, in the end, he contradicts himself. In the essay 'Real Realism', he emphasizes that the novelist must observe life as a highly sensitized photographic plate and receive and record impressions without bias. Any alteration or faking of the picture is equivalent to treason, and even the inevitable process of selection must not be guided by personal prejudice. Pugh does not define at what point choice, or personal taste become personal prejudice. He simply states: 'A specific purpose . . . should have no place in any work of art that aspires to any kind of impersonal treatment.'

When he wrote this essay (1916) he must have completely forgotten an earlier one on 'The Charles Dickens Originals' (1912), where he speaks of Dickens as an idealist as well as a realist with obvious approval. In the collection of essays which include 'Real Realism' he remarks in another essay on Dickens: 'It was Dickens who invented that fine and wholly admirable thing: the Novel with a Purpose.'

His essay entitled 'The Novelist as Expert' states ambitiously that there is 'no phase of modern life upon which some novelist or other is not a supreme authority', and he recommends all those solemn investigators of social conditions who operate under the guise of commissions or charitable bodies to summon as witnesses the novelists. He then defines the qualities required in a realistic novelist. He must not merely be capable of understanding in the highest degree the experiences of his fellows, but able to share their feelings imaginatively, in any given situation. He should be charitable, sympathetic, large-minded, tolerant and capable of making impartial judgements. There follow even more exacting requirements which, when brought together, create an Olympian figure with such multiple talents as rarely find embodiment in any but the greatest novelists; and Pugh was not a great novelist.

Does his work measure up to any of his own requirements? Certainly in *A Street in Suburbia* the fundamental requirement of photographic accuracy is overlaid by sentimentality. *Tony Drum* is another matter. On the surface the novel remains a somewhat sentimental account of a crippled boy, Tony Drum, born to lowly circumstances, who undergoes one tragic deprivation after another. It is worth noticing how many of these novelists set innocence against evil by choosing a child as one of the main protagonists. Dicky Perrot and Stephen in Morrison's novels are here replaced by Tony Drum, a boy of sickly health, with a hump-back, who is quickly subjected to the horrors of a butcher's boy's life. Unlike the emotional climate of Morrison's work, there is a spontaneous affection in the family relationship between Tony, his sister Honor and his father Michael, which permeates the whole novel. The picture of the boy in the butcher's shop vividly evokes its horror:

'None o' that lolling about Boy, I won't have it', cried the butcher.
'I'm so tired sir', pleaded Tony.

'*Tired*, are you. Well, its healthy to be tired. An' you'll be worse 'fore you've done. Ther's another three hours yet.'

Tony had been hoping that the shop closed at eleven. He felt he should never be able to stand upright for three more hours. He could have whimpered in his despair but he was too much a man. The meat stank in his nostrils. The buzzing of the gas deafened him. Every passerby who jostled him, he hated from his heart. To see the misery of some filled him with vindictive glee; the gaiety of others stirred his bile. How his head throbbed and swam! . . . He felt he must go mad of his weariness. . . .

'Buy, buy! buy!' shouted the butcher. 'Ere's a nobby bit of pork for you, ladies!'

Tony turned and looked at the clock. It was six minutes past nine! He looked again and rubbed his eyes. Six minutes past! He was furious at Time's tardiness and sick to his very heart.

Within the sentimental approach, one disaster after another overtakes Tony, each new tragic impact being ghoulishly reinforced by the note of loving kindness in the narrator's voice.

Tony survives the butcher's shop only to become involved in an accident with a gig on a rare day's outing in the country, which kills his mother and mangles his father. He is used by his father to make a childish appeal for money to the grandfather, only to find that his grandfather is more interested in his sister. He discovers the word 'love', but when he goes in search of its meaning his sister, on the verge of womanhood, blushes and simpers—'You're too young to worry about such things'—and no one else seems to know the answer. In the end he is driven back on the simple-minded girl known as Silly-H, and when she discloses that she is a love-child, Tony asks her to become his 'fyanky'—or sweetheart—but this, too, goes wrong. Once they have formalized their relationship the old intimacy weakens, they are shy and silent together, and at last Tony is forced to write her a note which says: 'I release you from our engagement.'

Nothing could possibly go right for the pale little hunchback who would, in any other novelist's hands, have found some compensations. Still surrounded by an atmosphere of sweetness and light, he is taken away from school because of ill health, loses his new girl friend to a rival, humiliates himself in a fight to win her back, and returns home one night to find his sister gone away. The grandfather has taken Honor off to 'make a lady of her'. The one human being with whom Tony really communicates in depth has been smuggled away in his absence. 'He bowed his head in the darkness and wept.'

Still, life has not finished with him. After one brief, inarticulate letter, his sister ceases to write to him and day after day he looks for her scrawled handwriting, in vain. The one gleam of hope in the black night of existence is a chance to see the sea, for the first time in his life. The ending comes sharply and suddenly: 'In life Tony Drum was very intimate with Death, and when his time came Death called to him with the voice of a friend. He never saw the sea. Saturday was the day fixed for his departure from London; on Friday he died.'

If the Jago becomes a black monster forcing the lives of its inhabitants into a debased mould, Pugh contrives to show the effect of poverty on human relationships in a different way. There are no gang fights, no brutality, but people who love one another are torn apart because they are poor, and aspiring neighbours develop a sad sense of snobbery.

It can easily be held against Pugh that he does not practise what he preaches. He suggested that representative average types involved in average situations should be the stuff of which realistic novels are made, but the hunch-back son of an impoverished flute player does not fit these requirements. Similarly, the average evangelical lay preacher does not kill the man who has seduced and deserted the woman he loved as Peter Cowcross does in *The Spoiler*. As for Harry Weaver who breaks away from poverty, escapes vulgarity and becomes an M.P., he would be more believable if he did not acquire a sensitivity for which we are not prepared and were satisfied with the letters M.P. after his name without coveting and adding the distinction K. C. as well.

However, in contradiction to his theories about the realistic novel, Pugh's philosophy of life easily embraces every quirk and oddity within his novels. In *The Enchantress* he found the world very much like a theatre,

in which most of the exciting incidents take place behind the scenes; in which the cues are often missed or taken up so tardily that the whole interest of the piece flags and wilts away to nothing whilst the call-boy wanders around in the outer darkness summoning the appointed player to appear before the footlights. The scenery is often hopelessly inappropriate too; the properties are so ill made that they break off short in the hand. . . . And the prompter has generally lost his script; the curtain never falls at the opportune moment: and when the author is called for he has invariably left the house.

In everyday life Pugh found that people were hopelessly inconsistent, and time and again some unexpected action from a person one had known for years, forced a reassessment of his character. Zola's attempt to introduce science into fiction was doomed to failure because nothing could be predicted about people with any certainty. Life was illogical, improbable, full of the unexpected. In the final analysis the biologists came closest to the truth when they traced the confusing surface patterns of human behaviour down to the primitive self-preservative and herd instincts, one directing human behaviour in totally unexpected areas and the other demanding a stereotyped uniformity which some individuals found crippling.

Pugh has two types of hero in his works—the aspiring Cockney who emerges successfully from his environment, and the debased hero who does not. Pallister, in *The Shuttlecock*, is an example of the former, and the novel has a universal theme which would delight the heart of modern psychiatrists. Here is David Pallister, the plaything of a restless search for love, constantly driven to achieve fresh conquests. When he has reached the point of making love to his latest paramour, he never says—'I love you', but asks instead 'Do you love me?' Yearning to be mothered by a woman who can devote her whole attention to him, once she has satisfied his vanity with her self-sacrifice and brought his confidence to the highest possible point, he desires nothing better than to set forth again in search of fresh conquests. If women respond to his advances he is delighted, but when the game comes dangerously close to marriage he desires one thing only; to be released from the possibility of any ties. Romance, love, passion, these are the life blood of existence but the need to remain free is no less a necessity and the essence of living is to remain a shuttlecock in the 'game of love'.

David Pallister is a novelist, and it is possible that many parts of *The Shuttlecock* are autobiographical, but we know too little of Pugh's life to judge with any certainty. Whatever autobiographical strains break through the novels there is no mistaking the uncompromising presence of topographical realism, like those scenes at the beginning of *The Man of Straw*, where a description of a Saturday night street market is followed by another of a music hall where the bar bursts with blousy women and dubious puffy-faced men. The orchestra cannot keep time and every other instrument is out of tune; a singer said to be young, but prematurely wizened, howls 'The Gorgonzola Cheese' only to have an echoing howl thrown back by men in greasy evening dress and women in a state of obvious debauchery, while drunken youth, foul age and anaemic manhood pour a flood of ribald song and comment from the gallery. Pugh makes it clear that to him everything about the London music hall is not merely vulgar but false. The audience can be moved to easy tears by pathos and sentimentality, but they rarely carry this over into their everyday lives. About the life of English pubs he is divided, but most of them appear in his novels as unsympathetic dens.

Once more he calls in question his own concept of realism. This is no sensitive photographic plate recording without comment what it finds. It is the clash of middle-class values on working class values. He does not record the genuine enjoyment which these people drew from the rough, ribald life of music hall and public house, but recoils in middle class distaste from *what* they enjoyed. There are exceptions. The Cockney landlord, Jim Scratch of *The Purple Head* is drawn sympathetically. The Prince of Denmark in *Empty Vessels*, also receives warm treatment:

There the clerk or respectable artisan takes his sweetheart for a stirrup cup of port, there married couples whose social status may range from that of a meek roundsman to that of a chartered accountant, are in the habit of resorting regularly as other married couples resort to one another's front parlours, for recreation and refreshment. There is seldom any least disturbance of the almost cloistral air of calm repose which pervades those gilded haunts of vice as they have been called; there is always a plenitude of good fellowship and innocent laughter.

For the rest pubs and music halls are anathema.

III. RICHARD WHITEING

Of the remaining novelists of the working classes Richard Whiteing is nearest in spirit to Arthur Morrison and the English realist school in novels like *No. 5 John Street*. He was born in 1840 and his father 'held a modest place in the Inland Revenue Office at Somerset House'. He lived in Norfolk Street, Strand, when it consisted of a 'double line of Georgian houses and was the classic land of the London lodging house'. Once again, Richard Whiteing first worked as a journalist, but there is no indication that he gave any special attention to the East End of London in his search for copy. His autobiography carefully avoids giving any dates which could be of the slightest help to the literary historian, but he seems to have come to literature fairly late in life after a long and successful journalistic career. His output was not nearly so prolific as that of Pett Ridge and his reputation stands or falls by two novels, *The Island* and *No. 5 John Street*.

His most successful novel was *No. 5 John Street* and it is not difficult to understand why it was so widely read. It would appeal to all literate people, but most of all to those among two of the three classes which were represented in the book —the middle and upper classes—who disliked the poverty and hardship on which their comfortable lives were built, and salved guilty consciences by vicariously sharing the way of life of London's East End.

The narrator in the novel is a well-to-do gentleman with a manservant who decides to abandon his West End life to work and live like a working class person. He goes to live in a tenement house and quickly discovers a totally different scale of values about violence:

> A sudden tumult in the back yard. A shriek of 'Murder' and evidently a shriek in good faith. . . .
>
> I knock at my friend Low Covey's door and rush in without waiting for an answer. . . .
>
> 'What's up now!' he asks with something of the impatience of a prima donna disturbed in her scales.
>
> 'Did you hear that fearful cry?'
>
> 'Ah! I 'eerd somethink.'
>
> 'There's murder going on—a woman, I think.'
>
> 'Dessay. It's Sat'dy night.'

His ability to stay in a factory job for £1. 2s. od. a week is the envy of his new friend Covey, who does not like regular employment, but he cannot quite discard his gentlemanly habits and asks for a washerwoman to wash his clothes. Covey immediately suspects him of being a toff, which should have been self-evident long before from his accent.

Throughout the whole novel, the scenes are seen through the 'gentleman's' eyes, and this gives the stimulus of contrast but robs the narrative of the realism which distinguished Morrison's work. The novel comes perilously close to deserving the charge of slumming, of representing a gentleman who indulges a charitable expedition into the Abyss. Certainly it would have displeased Morrison because it represented the external approach.

Many episodes in *No. 5 John Street* stop short of the logically conclusive, final horror. Murder is not committed, Covey does not starve, the narrator is sacked but promptly goes back to his luxury life, and the flower girl Tilda at first escapes the disasters which her altruism invites. In the end she dies from an anarchist's bomb. Nance too, a pale thin girl working in a factory where the atmosphere slowly poisons her, also dies:

'The vitality has gone [the doctor says]; gone through persistent slow poisoning. She has been as surely poisoned as if she had taken a dose. I know the place where she worked. We had hundreds of cases from it at Gray's in my student days. It's a murder trap. . . . It's pneumonia now, if I had to give it a name for a certificate. But it would be sheer poisoning in small doses if I had to lecture on it as a hospital case.'

The narrator asks—why not tell the truth for once and record the exact nature of her death? The doctor answers: 'The law won't stand any nonsense about first causes. Half the certificates we write are mere anodynes for the public conscience.' Scenes of this kind achieve a realism like Arthur Morrison's. Similarly, there are passages which effectively satirize those charitable figures who never come into real contact with the lives they hope to change:

The brain reels with it still. The message which bears the news of progress to three hundred and fifty millions with one touch of an electric button makes no mention of Sir Marmaduke. But his dominant personality is still implicit in that Royal and Imperial salutation to a fifth of the population of the globe. The native runners who are even now tearing along with it from Tropical and Antipodean receiving offices, to every hole and corner of the wondrous system, really carry the glad tidings that Sir Marmaduke kisses his hand to the human race.

No. 5 John Street is more like an 'experimental novel' in its organization than any other novel considered here. It juxtaposes long descriptions of slum life with a return to luxury living and interlards these again with 'reports to the Governor' of what the narrator has found in that black hell beyond Shoreditch. Irony underlines many passages:

This however only brings out the wonders of our mechanism of social administration into greater relief. The Law, the Churches, the more fortunate classes, are all busy in their several ways; and when by chance they miss a case of absolute starvation, the Press invariably makes it the subject of a paragraph exhorting them to greater vigilance. And in all such cases there is reason to believe the unhappy sufferers are only those who have steadily refused to work. . . . We cannot give better than we have, and we must search our hearts deeply to feel sure that we are equal to the high mission of putting others to death for their own good. . . .

The reply of the Governor to the final report is a fine piece of ironic amazement at the way in which the London economic system works.

IV. WILLIAM PETT RIDGE

There remains, among the four novelists I have chosen, Pett Ridge. He is commonly assumed to translate the Cockney scene more into comedy than tragedy, but the opening of one of his most successful books, *Mord Em'ly*, gives a description of a fight between two rival gangs of girls which borders on the brutal. Mord Em'ly is one of those feminine products of the East End with toughened bodies, sharpened wits, and a flow of racy Cockney slang which baffles even the local police. The shock of growing up first presents itself in the need to find a job and she goes 'after a place as a servant', only to astound the genteel household with her bold Cockney speech.

Within a short time domestic service bores her to distraction and one night when she is supposed to be on duty she suddenly recalls the joys of The Mont, a music hall where Flo Macgomery, known as Britain's Brilliant and Beautiful

Brunette, and Mr. Pat Foley, Ireland's Brightest Gem, sing and dance in unmusical unison:

Mord Em'ly started up from her chair. Her breath came erratically, her hand trembled as she unpinned her cap. . . . 'I'll be back in arf-an hour', she whispered to the loud-ticking little American clock 'if anybody asks for me'.

She closed the front door gently. . . . About five minutes took her to Queen's Road; and, as she stood there breathless, in the lighted thoroughfare, a tram went by . . . a tram from New Cross to Waterloo. She felt hastily in her pocket and found some coppers.

'*Now* then Kinductor!' said Mord Em'ly, as she swung herself on the platform of the tram. 'Why don't you pull up when you see a lady like me asking of you?'

Arrested for stealing a handful of cakes, Mord Em'ly is taken off to a home of correction, as defiantly witty as ever. Unfortunately, throughout the whole novel she is so deliberately 'written up' as a character that she becomes a caricature of what the real Mord Em'ly should have been, and sentimentality lies close to the surface in the worst moments of tragedy. The Cockney slang proves to be not slang as modern students know it, but the romanticized imposition of what the middle classes take to be a cockney idiom.

Such was the social guilt of many well-to-do readers of the middle classes that they read with avidity any novel whose heroine cunningly and with considerable humour outwitted the worst the fates could bring against her, and Mord Em'ly was no exception. Unconsciously, in his fiction, Pett Ridge provided an opium for the middle classes somewhat as Marx declared religion to be the opium of the people.

Mord Em'ly has many skirmishes with jobs, authority, the Salvation Army and men until that last moment when the stoutest reaches of her Cockney spirit are strained as she emigrates to Australia and faces the loss of her oldest and closest friend Miss Gilliken.

Behind the simple parting is a tragedy of deeper proportions. Too many people from the worst parts of the East End finally fled in despair from their homeland and emigrated to new countries like Australia and New Zealand. Pett Ridge was content to treat the parting as one minute segment of sentimentality and never implied the whole. He was a writer unaware of the wider implications of what he wrote. This lack of depth of awareness marks the limitations of his work. In some of his novels he was the expositor of one popular Victorian myth. Born to the worst kind of street life Mord Em'ly triumphs over everything and represents the truism that aspiring Cockneys can transcend their environment. In other words, given enough character, circumstances do not matter. It was one of the precepts by which many Victorians lived.

V. CONCLUSION

None of the techniques used by the lesser novelists of the English realist school was completely successful. Inevitably a photographic representation of events lacked depth. The isolation of the murderous side of slum life overlooked its better aspects. Most working class people in the East End lived dull rather unoriginal lives within a framework of hard work and respectability far removed from the purple melodrama of murder, starvation and gang warfare. No single novelist in this group achieved a completely representative picture of East End life, but all vividly evoked different aspects. If one took the Gothic horror of Arthur Morrison's novels, added a dash of Edwin Pugh's complexity, and impregnated the scene with something of Pett Ridge's sentimentality and Cockney humour, the picture still would not be complete. This is not to put a sad limitation on literature. It is simply to recognize that these were lesser novelists, who nevertheless showed exceptional skill in evoking the London scene and London characters. With the work of Arthur Morrison, the *genre* achieved its most significant expression.

FOUR REALIST NOVELISTS

A Select Bibliography

(Place of publication London, unless stated otherwise)

ARTHUR MORRISON

TALES OF MEAN STREETS (1894). *Short Stories*

MARTIN HEWITT INVESTIGATOR, etc. (1894). *Short Stories*

CHRONICLES OF MARTIN HEWITT (1895). *Novel*

A CHILD OF THE JAGO (1896). *Novel*

ADVENTURES OF MARTIN HEWITT (1896). *Novel*

THE DORRINGTON DEED BOX (1897). *Short Stories*

TO LONDON TOWN (1899). *Novel*

THE HOLE IN THE WALL (1902). *Novel*

RED TRIANGLE (1903). *Novel*

THAT BRUTE SIMMONS. A Play in One Act
—adapted with Herbert Sargent from a story in *Tales of Mean Streets*
(1904).

THE GREEN EYE OF GOONA (1904). *Novel*

DIVERS VANITIES (1905). *Short Stories*

THE DUMB-CAKE: a play in one act
—adapted with Richard Pryce from a story in *Tales of Mean Streets*
(1907).

GREEN GINGER (1909). *Short Stories*

THE PAINTERS OF JAPAN, 2 vols. (1911). *Criticism*

SELECTED TALES (1929). *Short Stories*

FIDDLE O'DREAMS (1933). *Short Stories*

EDWIN PUGH

A STREET IN SUBURBIA (1895). *Short Stories*

THE MAN OF STRAW (1896). *Novel*

TONY DRUM, A COCKNEY BOY (1898). *Novel*

KING CIRCUMSTANCE (1898). *Short Stories*

MOTHER-SISTER (1900). *Novel*

THE STUMBLING BLOCK (1903). *Novel*

THE FRUIT OF THE VINE (1904). *Novel*

THE PURPLE HEAD (1905). *Short Stories*

THE SPOILERS (1906). *Novel*

THE SHUTTLECOCK (1907). *Novel*

THE ENCHANTRESS (1908). *Novel*

THE BROKEN HONEYMOON (1908). *Novel*

PETER VANDY (1909). *Novel*

THE CHARLES DICKENS ORIGINALS (1912). *Essays*

PUNCH AND JUDY (1913). *Novel*

THE PROOF OF THE PUDDING (1913). *Short Stories*

THE COCKNEY AT HOME (1914). *Short Stories*

THE QUICK AND THE DEAD (1914). *Novel*

THE PHANTOM PEER (1914). *Short Stories*

SLINGS AND ARROWS (1916)

THE EYES OF A CHILD (1917). *Novel*

THE WAY OF THE WICKED (1921). *Short Stories*

THE SECRET YEARS (1923). *Novel*

THE WORLD IS MY OYSTER (1924). *Short Stories*

EMPTY VESSELS (1926). *Novel*

RICHARD WHITEING

THE ISLAND; OR, AN ADVENTURE OF A PERSON OF QUALITY (1888). *Novel*

NO. 5 JOHN STREET (1899). *Novel*

THE YELLOW VAN (1903). *Novel*

RING IN THE NEW (1906). *Novel*

ALL MOONSHINE (1907). *Novel*

LITTLE PEOPLE (1908). *Novel*

A LITTLE BOOK ABOUT LONDON (1911). *Essays*

MY HARVEST (1915). *Autobiography*

WILLIAM PETT RIDGE

A CLEVER WIFE (1895). *Novel*

MINOR DIALOGUES, etc. (1895). *Short Stories*

THE SECOND OPPORTUNITY OF MR. STAPLEHURST (1896). *Novel*

AN IMPORTANT MAN AND OTHERS (1896). *Short Stories*

SECRETARY TO BAYNE M.P. (1897). *Novel*

MORD EM'LY (1898). *Novel*

A SON OF THE STATE (1899). *Novel*

OUTSIDE THE RADIUS (1899). *Short Stories*

A BREAKER OF LAWS (1900). *Novel*

LONDON ONLY (1901). *Short Stories*

THE STORY OF MAGGIE CANNON (1902). *Novel*

LOST PROPERTY (1902). *Novel*

ERB (1903). *Novel*

GEORGE AND THE GENERAL (1904). *Novel*

MY NEXT DOOR NEIGHBOURS (1904). *Short Stories*

MRS. GALEN'S BUSINESS (1905). *Novel*

ON COMPANY'S SERVICE (1905). *Short Stories*

NEARLY FIVE MILLION (1907). *Novel*

SPEAKING RATHER SERIOUSLY (1908). *Short Stories*

NAME OF GARLAND (1908). *Novel*

LIGHT REFRESHMENT (1910). *Short Stories*

LOVE AT PADDINGTON (1912). *Novel*

DEVOTED SPARKES (1912). *Novel*

THE REMINGTON SENTENCE (1913). *Novel*

THE HAPPY RECRUIT (1914). *Novel*

THE KENNEDY PEOPLE (1915). *Novel*

BOOK HERE (1915). *Short Stories*

MADAME PRINCE (1916). *Novel*

THE AMAZING YEARS (1917). *Novel*

TOP SPEECH (1918). *Novel*

THE BUSTLING HOURS (1919). *Novel*

JUST OPEN (1920). *Short Stories*

RICHARD TRIUMPHANT (1922). *Novel*

MISS MANNERING (1923). *Novel*

A STORY TELLER: FORTY YEARS IN LONDON (1923). *Autobiography*

LEAPS AND BOUNDS (1924). *Novel*

RARE LUCK (1924). *Novel*

JUST LIKE AUNT BERTHA (1925). *Novel*

I LIKE TO REMEMBER (1925). *Autobiography*

AFFECTIONATE REGARDS (1929). *Novel*

Some Biographical and Critical Studies:

'Theories and Practice of Modern Fiction', by H. Norman, in the *Fortnightly Review*, vol. 34, 1883.

THE EXPERIMENTAL NOVEL, by E. Zola. New York (1893)
—contains an essay which is a useful introduction to the Naturalist School in France.

THE NEW FICTION AND OTHER ESSAYS, by D. H. Traill (1897)
—useful introduction to the English Realist School.

'What is a Realist?' by A. Morrison, in *New Review*, xvi, March 1897.

THE QUARTERLY REVIEW, vol. 196. 1902.

NATURALISM IN FRENCH FICTION, by W. C. Frierson. Columbus (1930).

THE WORKS OF EDWIN PUGH, 1874-1930, by T. E. M. Boll. Philadelphia (1934).

THE LIVING NOVEL, by V. S. Pritchett (1946)
—contains a chapter on Arthur Morrison.

WHAT IS LITERATURE? by J. P. Sartre (1950)
—deals interestingly with the French Naturalist School.

'A Study of Arthur Morrison', by J. Bell, in *Essays and Studies*, 1952

Edward Lear

by JOANNA RICHARDSON

Published for the British Council
and the National Book League
by Longmans, Green & Co

Three shillings and sixpence net

Edward Lear is famous for his nonsense verses, and has often been compared with that other Victorian master of nonsense, Lewis Carroll. Yet, as Miss Richardson puts it, 'Carroll approached his nonsense by way of logic and mathematics, Lear approached it through his paintings and through poetry, and . . . through life itself'.

He first became prominent as a draughtsman and topographer; indeed, throughout his life, he was a prolific landscape painter, and the author of delightful travel-books illustrated by himself. These books record the wanderings of a lonely, restless man, afflicted with epilepsy, asthma, bronchitis and weak sight. In the gayest of his letters, as in the most fantastic of his nonsense verses, there runs a streak of melancholy, the reflection of his unhappiness and insecurity. The self-contained world which he invented was a recompense for his failure to find stability and emotional fulfilment in life. Miss Richardson's essay on the man, the topographer, the painter and the poet elucidates the complexity of his life and work.

Joanna Richardson has already published a number of books on nineteenth-century figures. Among them are *Fanny Brawne: a Biography* (1952); *Théophile Gautier: his Life and Times* (1958); *The Pre-Eminent Victorian: a Study of Tennyson* (1962); and *The Everlasting Spell: a Study of Keats and his Friends* (1963). She has also edited a selection from the works and letters of Edward FitzGerald (1962), and is the author of *Edward FitzGerald* in the *Writers and Their Work* series.

Bibliographical Series
of Supplements to 'British Book News'
on Writers and Their Work

GENERAL EDITOR
Geoffrey Bullough

EDWARD LEAR
the last photograph of the author, 1887

EDWARD LEAR

by

JOANNA RICHARDSON

PUBLISHED FOR
THE BRITISH COUNCIL
AND THE NATIONAL BOOK LEAGUE
BY LONGMANS, GREEN & CO

LONGMANS, GREEN & CO LTD
48 Grosvenor Street, London, W.1

*Associated companies, branches and
representatives throughout the world*

First Published 1965
© Joanna Richardson 1965

*Printed in Great Britain
F. Mildner & Sons, London, E.C.1*

CONTENTS

Acknowledgement: The frontispiece portrait of Edward Lear is reproduced by permission of the Trustees of the British Museum.

¶ EDWARD LEAR was born at Highgate on 12 may 1812 and died at San Remo on 29 January 1888.

'How pleasant to know Mr. Lear!'
    Who has written such volumes of stuff!
Some think him ill-tempered and queer,
    But a few think him pleasant enough.

His mind is concrete and fastidious,
    His nose is remarkably big;
His visage is more or less hideous,
    His beard it resembles a wig.

He has ears, and two eyes, and ten fingers,
    Leastways if you reckon two thumbs;
Long ago he was one of the singers,
    But now he is one of the dumbs.

He sits in a beautiful parlour,
    With hundreds of books on the wall,
He drinks a great deal of Marsala,
    But never gets tipsy at all.

He has many friends, laymen and clerical,
    Old Foss is the name of his cat;
His body is perfectly spherical,
    He weareth a runcible hat.

When he walks in a waterproof white,
    The children run after him so!
Calling out, 'He's come out in his night-
    gown, that crazy old Englishman, oh!'

He weeps by the side of the ocean,
    He weeps on the top of the hill;
He purchases pancakes and lotion,
    And chocolate shrimps from the mill.

He reads but he cannot speak Spanish,
    He cannot abide ginger-beer:
Ere the days of his pilgrimage vanish,
    How pleasant to know Mr. Lear!

EDWARD LEAR

EDWARD LEAR

I. THE LIFE

Edward Lear was born in Highgate, a picturesque village north of London, on 12 May 1812. He was one of the youngest of the twenty-one children of Ann (*née* Skerrit) and Jeremiah Lear. Mr. Lear was of Danish origin. 'My own name', Edward would explain, 'is really LØR, but my Danish Grandfather picked off the two dots and pulled out the diagonal line, and made the word Lear.' The Danish grandfather had become a naturalized Englishman; Lear's father, Jeremiah, was conventional enough to be a stockbroker in the City of London. And nothing could have been more English than Edward's own first memory: it was the summer of 1815, he was just three years old, and he was wrapped in a blanket and taken out of bed to see the illuminations celebrating Waterloo.

He once declared that he could remember '*every particle*' of his life from the time he was four years old; and his earliest recollections were probably quite happy. The house was large and comfortable, the family well-to-do, there were pleasant drives through the Highgate lanes, and walks on Hampstead Heath. In the big painting-room at Bowman's Lodge (the house has long since been destroyed), Edward pored over illustrated books of natural history, and learnt how to draw and paint from his sister Sarah.

Soon after his seventh birthday, he began to suffer from what he was to call the 'Terrible Demon': the epilepsy which pursued him for the rest of his life. Its attacks were frequent (sometimes as many as eighteen in a month); and it had a deep effect on his character. 'It is', he wrote, 'a most merciful blessing that I have kept up as I have, and have not gone utterly to the bad mad sad.' His infirmity made him embarrassed in the presence of strangers, reticent, and often deeply depressed. It also made him gentle and considerate; and it was to help him, as a man, to understand the problems

9

and needs of childhood, and to be perfectly at ease with
children. 'He knew a great deal about children', wrote one
who remembered him, J. St. Loe Strachey,

... and they knew that he knew it, and he knew that they knew that he
knew it, and so a complete and (as he might have said) abject harmony
was established. The sympathy of which I speak is written large in all
Mr. Lear's books; in every word of the letterpress and in every line, deep
or narrow, straight or wavy, of his drawings. It was also shown in his
personality. . . . I have a peculiarly vivid recollection of seeing Lear
when he was stopping at my father's house, when I was about 8 or 9
years old. . . . I remember perfectly the towering, bearded, spectacled
man, standing in the drawing-room at Sutton Court, and talking in a
way which made one feel at once that he was 'all right'. . . .

Lear was not only beset in childhood by the Terrible
Demon, epilepsy; he was already liable to attacks of asthma
and bronchitis. His sight was poor; and he was very conscious that his nose was large, and that he was plain. These
were personal causes for sadness; but, when he was thirteen,
disaster struck the whole Lear family. Mr. Lear went
bankrupt, the house at Highgate had to be sold, the servants
and the carriages dispersed. Mr. Lear was imprisoned, and
his wife moved the family into London, within reach of the
jail. The two eldest sons emigrated to America, the third
son went as a medical missionary to West Africa, and some
of the daughters were sent out to earn their living as gover-
nesses and companions. Several of them died, unable to bear
the hardships of their new life. Four years later, having paid
off Jeremiah's debts, Mrs. Lear retired with him to Graves-
end. She seems to have been more devoted to her husband
than to her children; from the moment of the tragedy, she
had entrusted Edward to his eldest sister, Ann. His education
and upbringing lay entirely in her hands.

Ann was fortunate in having a small private income (her
grandmother had left her £300 a year); she was high-
principled, gentle, and extremely understanding. As Lear
would write, later, 'she has always been as near to Heaven as

it is possible to be'. But he was too frail to go to school, and Ann's teaching could only be a poor substitute for education. 'Please believe', Lear once explained, 'that the irritation of an artist's life produces much which works its possessor bitterness, when that individual's brain has been so little guided in youth as mine was.'

He spent much time writing verse, and studying books of natural history; he worked hard at drawing and painting. At the age of fifteen he began to earn his living as a draughts-man. He made morbid disease drawings for doctors and hospitals, and he coloured prints, screens and fans. By the time he was eighteen, he was taking pupils. Soon afterwards, through a friend, he was asked by the Zoological Society to draw the parrots in the London Zoo. The result was *Illustrations of the Family of Psittacidae, or Parrots*: a magnificent folio with 42 coloured lithographs of birds. It appeared in 1832; and the delicacy and beauty of the drawings led Dr. J. E. Gray, of the British Museum, to ask Lear to illustrate his volume *Tortoises, Terrapins and Turtles* (which eventually appeared in 1872). The parrot book was to have a result of far more importance. The Earl of Derby, an eager naturalist, had assembled a private menagerie at his country house, Knowsley Hall, near Liverpool. He wanted to publish a book about his collection, and needed a suitable artist to illustrate it. Lear was recommended. Lord Derby watched him at work in the Parrot House in the Zoological Gardens, and commissioned him at once to come to Knowsley. Lear spent most of the next four years in the enormous stately house in Lancashire, drawing the menagerie and finding friends and patrons he could hardly otherwise have met. The product of his four years' work appeared in 1846: a handsome volume called *Gleanings from the Menagerie and Aviary at Knowsley Hall*.

During those four years Lear had also stumbled on his immortality. A 'valued friend' had shown him a children's book called *Anecdotes and Adventures of Fifteen Gentlemen*, and they had pointed out a limerick:

There was an Old Man of Tobago,
Lived long on rice gruel and sago;
   But at last, to his bliss,
   The physician said this—
To a roast leg of mutton you may go.

The limerick caught Lear's imagination; and, urged on by the grandchildren of Lord Derby, who showed their quite 'uproarious delight', he struck off one limerick after another. The nonsense poet had found himself. The first *Book of Nonsense* appeared in 1846, the same year as the book on the Knowsley menagerie.

During his years at Knowsley, Lear had travelled to the Lakes and to Ireland. His growing interest in landscape, and his indifferent eyesight, led him to make an important decision. He would do no more exacting drawings of parrots and turtles. He would earn his living by landscape painting; he would improve his health by living in a southern climate. His decision to go abroad for an indefinite period must have hurt his sister Ann; and Lear felt a certain guilt at leaving her to an empty life. But in 1837 he set out for Italy, and there he stayed for the next three years. The first result, *Views in Rome and Its Environs*, a fine collection of lithographs, was published in 1841.

It was in Rome, in 1845, that he met a handsome, ebullient, gifted Irishman, Chichester Fortescue, who was just down from Oxford and making the Grand Tour before he entered Parliament. 'Lear a delightful companion', wrote Fortescue, 'full of *nonsense*, puns, riddles, everything in the shape of fun. . . . I don't know where I have met anyone to whom I have taken so great a liking.' The liking was mutual. Lear and Fortescue were drawn to each other at once, and their friendship continued until Lear's death.

Circumstances had made it hard for Lear to lead a normal life. As a friend observed, he needed marriage, 'especially if it should give him children of his own instead of all the world's'. Lear probably knew that he needed marriage; but his epilepsy and plainness seemed to him to put it out of the question. When Fortescue once complained of loneliness, Lear answered: '*You*, it appears to me, might put an end to all chance of such blacknesses, by asking any young Lady to marry you, which if *you* asked her she instantly *would*, whereas if *I* asked her she instantly *wouldn't*.' For most of his life, Lear refused to think of marriage; but he was affectionate by nature, and he longed for close relationships. Chichester Fortescue and, later, Franklin Lushington, the judge, were the two dearest friends in his life; and in these friendships he found considerable happiness. But his happiness could not be complete. He could not be everything to Fortescue, who enjoyed a late but perfect marriage to Countess Waldegrave. 'Every marriage of people I care about', wrote Lear, in dejection, 'rather seems to leave one on the bleak shore alone.' As for Lushington, for whom he conceived an even deeper love, he did not merely get married: he was incapable of showing Lear affection. 'I am older than Babylon in many ways', wrote Lear, in misery. 'I wish sometimes I grew hard and old at heart, it would I fancy save a deal of bother.'

But if his closest friendships gave him only partial pleasure, Lear did enjoy professional success. When his *Illustrated Excursions in Italy* appeared in 1846, he himself was in London; and Queen Victoria summoned him to Osborne, in the Isle of Wight, to give her a course of twelve drawing-lessons. Prince Albert showed him the model of Osborne House, part of which was still under construction; and the Queen herself made a deep impression on him. Nearly forty years later, he wrote warmly:

To my mind, [she] is one of the most remarkable women of this century or perhaps any other. . . . She is a true and fine woman in every respect. . . . I don't know if it is proper to call a sovereign a duck, but I cannot help thinking H. M. a dear and absolute duck, and I hope she may live yet thirty or forty more years, for every year she lives will be a blessing to her country. . . .

Queen Victoria's drawing master returned to Rome late

in 1846; the following spring he toured Sicily (his drawings of it were to be published fifty years after his death). That summer, with the same companion, Lord John Proby, he toured Calabria and Naples, and his accounts of these tours appeared, with many lithographs, in 1852, as *Journals of a Landscape Painter in Southern Calabria*.

For the last ten years Lear had made Rome his head-quarters; in 1848 the political situation grew disturbing, and he decided it was time to move. 'I strongly long to go to Egypt for the next winter as ever is', he told Fortescue. 'I am crazy about Memphis & On & Isis and crocodiles and opthalmia & nubians, and simooms & sorcerers, & sphingidoe. Seriously the contemplation of Egypt must fill the mind, the artistic mind I mean, with great food for the rumination of long years. . . .' He stayed briefly in Corfu, and then, on the invitation of Sir Stratford Canning, the British Ambassador in Turkey, he went to Athens and to Constantinople; he travelled on to Albania, Malta and Egypt. During 1848 and 1849 he covered the whole Greek peninsula from Salonika in the north-east to Suniu in Attica. For the next two years hem made lithographs from his sketches, and wrote up his diaries. The result was *Journals of a Landscape Painter in Albania etc.*, which appeared in 1851. It was well received, and rightly, for it was illustrated with style, and written with infectious, original gusto; and those who knew Lear's infirmities must have respected him for his willingness to live rough, his constant eagerness for adventure.

From 1849 to 1853 Lear was living in England. During the winters he worked in London, and held exhibitions (his painting *Claude Lorrain's House on the Tiber* was hung at the Royal Academy in 1850); and in the summer he visited friends in the country. Among these friends were the Tennysons, in the Isle of Wight. But, left to himself, in an English winter, Lear was sometimes unable to work, and weighed down by his inescapable melancholy. Fortescue suggested marriage. 'No, my dear Fortescue', answered Lear,

I don't mean to marry—never. In my case I should paint less and less well, and the thought of annual infants would drive me wild. . . . I only wish I could dub and scrub myself into what I wish to be, and what I might be I fear if I took proper pains. But chi sa? How much will be allowed for *nature*, and early impressions, and iron early tuition? Looking back, I sometimes wonder I am even what I am. I often wonder how I have made so many certainly real friends as I have. . . .

One of his real friends had recently come into his life: Holman Hunt, the Pre-Raphaelite painter. Hunt was fifteen years younger than Lear, but Lear looked up to him with the admiration of a pupil, and came to believe himself, as a landscape-painter, to be a child of the Pre-Raphaelite School. It was during a stay with Holman Hunt that he conceived the idea of illustrating Tennyson's poems; the project was to occupy him, intermittently, for the rest of his life. 'I don't want to be a sort of pictorial Boswell', Lear explained, 'but to be able to reproduce certain lines of poetry in form and colour.' None of Tennyson's contemporaries more nearly reproduced his verbal pictures than Lear did, in the book that has come down to us.

In 1855, at last, Lear settled in Corfu; and though he made numerous journeys, Corfu remained his headquarters for the next three years. But his unequal friendship with Lushington (who was preoccupied with his work as a judge) was a constant source of anxiety; and, in his noisy lodgings, feeling little but dislike for the limited society of the island, he was more frustrated and miserable than ever:

Just figure to yourself [he told Fortescue] the condition of a place where you never have any breath or extent of intellectual society, & yet cannot have any peace or quiet. . . .
The constant walking and noise overhead prevents any application to any sort of work, & it is only from 6 to 8 in the morning that I can attend really to anything. . . . And then, if I can't sleep, my whole system seems to turn into pins, cayenne-pepper, & vinegar & I suffer hideously. You see I have no means of carrying off my irritation: others have horses, or boats, in short:—I have only walking, and that is beginning to be impossible alone. . . .

From 1858–60, Lear was living in Rome; from 1861–4 he was back in Corfu. In 1867 he settled for three years in Cannes. The long list of his wanderings emphasizes his persistent loneliness. But at last, in the winter of 1870, at the age of fifty-eight, when he had saved some £3,000, he began to look for a permanent home. He chose San Remo, bought some land, and arranged for a house to be built. He spent the summer of 1870 at an hotel in the mountains near Turin, writing up his Egyptian journals and preparing *Nonsense Songs, Stories, Botany and Alphabets* (which appeared in 1871). When he returned to San Remo that autumn, he found his house, the Villa Emily, rapidly nearing completion. Two 'damsels' were soon making curtains, the carpets were laid, and Lear moved in with his servant Giorgio, and the bandy-legged gardener Giuseppe; before long the household received the distinguished addition of Foss, the cat. A new nonsense book, *More Nonsense*, was published just before Christmas 1871. It belied the feelings of its author. 'I am very glad you all like the "More Nonsense" ', Lear wrote to Fortescue. 'It is queer (and you would say so if you saw me) that I am the man as is making some three or four thousand people laugh in England all at one time,—to say the least, for I hear 2,000 of the new Nonsense are sold.'

Early in 1872 Lear's relative domestic peace was broken. His friend Lord Northbrook, who had just been appointed Viceroy of India, offered to take him to India, with him, give him a year's sightseeing, and pay for his journey back to San Remo. To an elderly man who had recently settled in a house of his own, the prospect must have seemed a little daunting; but in 1873 Lear embarked on his two-year tour of India and Ceylon (his viceregal travels were described in his *Indian Journal*, published as recently as 1953). In 1877 appeared *Laughable Lyrics*, the last book of nonsense to be published in his lifetime. In 1881, when a new 'diametrical damnable blazing 5 Story Hotel' was built at the end of his garden, and his peace and privacy were gone, he moved from the Villa Emily to the Villa Tennyson, San Remo. He continued his landscape painting, for, as he observed, 'a man can but "try", and the mere act of "trying" goes, I take it, a long way to stave off mental and fizzicle maladies'. But his melancholy would not leave him. He failed to take his chance of happiness, when at last it came: he failed to ask Augusta Bethell in marriage; and in his nonsense, as will be seen, lies the record of his love and of his failure.

He waited for death with equanimity:

> I cannot say I find any terror in the contemplation of death [he told Fortescue in 1882]; I have lived to ascertain positively that much of the evil of my life has arisen from congenital circumstances over which I—as a child—could have had no control; a good deal too has been the result of various ins and outs of life vagaries, and what is called chance—which chance I don't believe in, for if I did I must give up all idea of a God at all. I know also that I owe an immensity to the assistance of friends; and neither do I put that down to chance. So, on the whole, I am tolerably placid....

Two years later he wrote sadly, to the same correspondent: 'The grasshopper has become a burden, and the quick-pace downhill transit to indifference and final apathy is more and more discernible as month follows month.'

Edward Lear died on 29 January 1888. He was buried at San Remo.

II. THE ARTIST, TOPOGRAPHER AND LETTER-WRITER

Such is the outline of Lear's life. 'And thinking over all', he wrote, 'I have long since come to the conclusion that we are *not wholly* responsible for our lives, *i.e.*, our acts, *in so far as* congenital circumstances, physical or psychical, over which we have no absolute control, prevent our being so.' Lear's destiny had virtually been decided for him. He was convinced he could not marry; he had to live abroad, he was compelled to travel constantly, not only in search of subjects for his brush, but in search of temporary forgetfulness. 'I

am convinced of this more and more', he told Fortescue in
1859, 'If you have a wife, or are in love with a woman, . . .
then you may stay in any place and in any circumstances. . . .
But if you are absolutely alone in the world, and likely to be
so, then move about continually and never stand still.'

Lear himself very rarely stood still. He travelled with
astonishing energy, considering his ill-health, to produce his
pictures and travel books. And here, perhaps, it is time to
consider the artist and the 'Globular foolish Topographer'.

Lear's immortality as a writer of nonsense has obscured his
very real gifts as a serious draughtsman and an artist. His
Illustrations of the Family of Psittacidae, or Parrots, published in
1832, had been of more than ornithological interest. Lear's
delicate likeness of the salmon-crested cockatoo had been a
picture in its own right; his red and yellow macaw, with the
vain and stupid look in its little eye, had shone quite un-
forgettably from the page; and it had been hard to choose
between the pair of glowing crimson-winged parakeets and
the New Holland parakeets, subtle and almost Chinese in
effect. Lear's watercolours of foreign lands were less intense
in hue; but they showed a delicate colour sense, a sophisticated simplicity. His painting of the Eubœan landscape near
Castella (reproduced in *Later Letters of Edward Lear*) suggest
how exquisitely dreamy, how subtly Romantic he could be.
The illustrations in his *Indian Journal* show that he used the
medium with decision and fluency, and his meticulous
notes: 'Temples. Brown oker', or 'River more intricate, and
brighter', reveal how he insisted on accuracy.

But it is not true that, in his landscapes, the pupil of
Holman Hunt paid Pre-Raphaelite attention to minutiae.
His details may be scrupulously accurate, but he limits them
to essentials, and some of his impressionistic lithographs
suggest the rich, strange world that we sometimes see in the
paintings of Samuel Palmer. Lear is especially sensitive to the
forms of trees: to 'the endlessly varying groups of olive
trees', the 'wildly twisted olive-trunks' in the Ionian Islands.
He loves the contrast between the cumulus olive and the

spiral cypress. He is haunted, too, by the barren, jagged rocks, by cliffs and caves reflected in the sea, by the grim heights of Sappho's Leap, the majestic, ruined walls of ancient Samos. The lithographs in his *Journals . . . of Southern Calabria* catch the fairytale romance of the square, towering rock of Palizzi, and the double fortress rock of Rocella. The lithographs in the *Illustrated Excursions in Italy* show no Victorian insistence on trivia : they are drawn freely, in the grand manner, and it is clear that the hillside town of Città di Penna, the clouded silhouette of Civita d'Antino, struck deep at Lear's imagination :

> Illyrian woodlands, echoing falls
> Of water, sheets of summer glass,
> The long divine Peneïan pass,
> The vast Akrokeraunian walls,
>
> Tomohrit, Athos, all things fair,
> With such a pencil, such a pen,
> You shadow forth to distant men,
> I read and felt that I was there.

As Tennyson emphasized, in his poem 'To E. L., on his Travels in Greece', Lear did more than record the facts: he recalled an atmosphere. In his lithograph of Tempe, in his painting of the pale blue and violet mountains of Thermopylae, in his impressions of the crags of Suli, the huddled mountain buildings of Pentèdátilo, we feel a haunting, melancholy, deeply Romantic poetry. It is, at times, akin to that of 'The Princess' and 'Œnone'; and it confirms how perfectly Lear was suited to his task of illustrating Tennyson. But the poetry that Lear expressed in painting was not merely Tennysonian. It was poetry which was natural to himself.

If Lear deserves far more acclaim for his natural history illustrations, for his accomplishments as a landscape artist, he also deserves more recognition as a writer of travel books. He himself dismissed the Albanian *Journal* as 'memoranda of an artist's mere tour of search among the riches of far-away Landscape'; and the remark contains a certain truth. Lear's travel books are, first and foremost, the works of a draughtsman and painter. 'You have majestic cliff-girt shores', he writes of Albania; 'castle-crowned heights, and gloomy fortresses; palaces glittering with gilding and paint; mountain-passes such as you encounter in the snowy regions of Switzerland; deep bays, and blue seas with bright, calm isles resting on the horizon.' The Tennysonian vision was, none the less, the vision of Lear, the artist. Lear's visual sense is always evident: he has an eye for colour, form and composition. In Corsica he finds it good 'to sit below huge brown-armed trees, full-foliaged, shading a green slope of freshest turf and fern'. In India he revels in 'the rich colour of woods, ilex and pine, and the vast blue space of hollow mountain'.

Lear's books of travel are certainly searches for the riches of landscape; but they are not merely that. They are amused, appreciative, gay. Lear revels in the 'torrents of pigs' rushing down from the hills for their supper in Arezzano; he is amused by his primitive lodgings: 'a large raftered room, of a bewildering aspect, . . . strewed with articles of female dress, intermixed rather oddly with fowls of all sizes, fluttering about in every direction, over and under two very misshapen beds.' At Trasacco, he records, 'we stood at the end of a fearfully hot slip of white pebbles, bordered by a fringe of meditative green frogs'. At Città di Penna he was woken at daybreak 'when a sound of Choc! choc! choc! pervaded the room, and forthwith numbers of little chanticleers rushed from all corners'. And, touring the Ionian Islands, describing the Plain of Currant-Vines near Galáro, the familiar Lear breaks through at last: the Plain, he decides, 'may be, in truth, called one unbroken continuance of future currant-dumplings and plum-puddings'. Lear's nonsense is never very far away.

It is certainly never far from his letters; and his correspondence was massive. 'Every human being', he wrote, 'capable of writing ever since the invention of letters must have written to me, with a few exceptions perhaps, such as the prophet Ezekiel, Mary Queen of Scots, and the Venerable Bede.' The number of his correspondents puzzled him. 'Either all my friends must be fools or mad; or . . . there must be more good qualities about this child than he ever gives or has given himself credit for possessing.' The fact was that he was immensely endearing. It *was* pleasant to know Mr. Lear, and receive a letter in his 'meandering mash-potato manner'; and so the volume of correspondence was such that in 1864 Lear declared: 'I abhor the sight of a pen, and if I were an angel I would immediately moult all my quills for fear of their being used in calligraphy.'

Lear's letters are inimitable, and he was an industrious writer. It is strange that there are only two published volumes of his correspondence. But since they cover forty years of his life (1847–87), and since the letters are nearly all addressed to Chichester Fortescue, one of the few, wrote Lear, 'who understand this queer child', they bring us very close to the writer.

They reveal, more than anything else, Lear's constant loneliness. 'I think', he wrote to Lady Waldegrave in 1870, 'as I can't help being alone it is perhaps best to be altogether, jellyfish-fashion caring for nobody.' The remark, made in desperation, did not ring true. For the letters, which show us Lear's loneliness, also make it plain that he was intensely affectionate. He had no time for a vapid, superficial social life; but he loved his family, he was devoted to children, and he was very fond of his friends. 'I am coming to England fast as I can', he wrote to Fortescue, when Lushington proved an unresponsive companion. 'Why are you coming say you? because I can't stay here any longer—without seeing friends & having some communion of heart & spirit— with one who should have been this to me, I have none. . . . And I can't bear it. And I want to see my sister. . . . And *you*. And my dear Daddy Holman Hunt, & other people. So I'm off.' Lear was a deeply serious man; and the letters he wrote to Fortescue (then Lord Carlingford) on the death of his wife show the gentle understanding, the complete, affectionate sympathy he was capable of feeling.

However, he did not enjoy any one complete relationship; he was never supremely important to another human being. And this ultimate lack of love was the bane of Lear's life. Time and again, in his correspondence, he bursts out in depression. 'I must leave off, I feel like 5 nutmeg-graters full of baked eggshells—so dry & cold & miserable.' 'For all I write cheerfully I am as savage and black as 90,000 bears.' Sometimes he seeks refuge from his loneliness in his books and correspondence: 'I am writing this from Certosa del Pesio, a Mountain Pension twenty-four hours above S. Remo, to which . . . I have come for a week or two to be out of the great heat by the sea-shore, to complete my child's nonsense-book for Xmas, and to write letters, and a fair copy of two Egyptian journals, 1854 and 1867, for future publication.' Sometimes he attempts to forget his loneliness in his painting, working long hours in his studio, or tramping miles to record a landscape. 'Did I tell you of my visit to Oudesh, vulgarly called Gozo?' he asks Lady Waldegrave in 1866. 'I drew every bit of it, walking fifteen or twenty miles a day.' And then, again, Lear attempts to be philosophic about his solitude. 'As I grow older', he writes, 'I as it were prohibit regrets of all sorts, for they only do harm to the present and thereby to the future. By degrees one is coming to look on the whole of life past as a dream, and one of no very great importance either if one is not in a position to affect the lives of others particularly.' It was a brave but futile attempt to pretend indifference.

But though Lear's gayest letters are still permeated with sadness, though they leave a haunting sense of melancholy, they are far from being a mere record of natural grievances. They have an unmistakable style; only Lear could have written them. They are intimate, fluent, vivid, discursive, and, as he would say, spongetanious.

And here and there in his correspondence, when he is

particularly moved, Lear finds himself, suddenly, writing poetry. Like many sensitive people, he tries to hide his feelings under a cloak of flippancy, but the feelings carry him away. In Damascus, on 27 May 1858, he sits down to write to Lady Waldegrave, and to tell her about his visit to Jerusalem. He is moved to write one of the finest of his letters:

There is enough in Jerusalem to set a man thinking for life, & I am deeply glad I have been there. O my nose! O my eyes! O my feet! How you all suffered in that vile place! for let me tell you, physically Jerusalem is the foulest and odiousest place on earth. A bitter doleful soul-ague comes over you in its streets. And your memories of its interior are but horrid dreams of squalor & filth, clamour & uneasiness, hatred & malice & all uncharitableness. But the outside is full of melancholy glory, exquisite beauty & a world of past history of all ages:—every point forcing you to think on a vastly dim receding past, or a time of Roman war & splendour, (for Ælia Capitolium was a fine city) or a smash of Moslem & Crusader years, with long long dull winter of deep decay through centuries of misrule. The Arab & his sheep are alone the wanderers on the pleasant vallies & breezy hills round Zion: the file of slow camels all that brings to mind the commerce of Tyre and other bygone merchandize. . . .

Poetry lay deep in Lear: a sense of significance, of the natural music of writing. He had a strong sense of colour, too; and the landscape-painter's letters are punctuated with bright little pictures: like the verbal watercolour of the way to Ramleh, 'through one almighty green lovely cornfield', with 'the long unbroken line of blue-lilac hills'. 'Nubia delighted me', he writes from Cairo. 'Sad, stern, uncompromising landscape, dark ashy purple lines of hills, piles of granite rocks, fringes of palm and ever and anon astonishing ruins of oldest temples: above all wonderful Abou Simbel, which took my breath away.' 'Imagine 16 worlds of gardens rolled out flat', he writes to Lady Waldegrave, 'with a river and a glittering city in the middle, & you have a sort of idea of what the Damascus pianura is like'. And then, sitting in Trieste in November 1861, he tells Fortescue:

I shall employ my last hours on earth,—*i.e.* before I embark on the oshun, in writing to you. . . .

All the traffic of Trieste is like gold & silver set in lapis lazuli & emerald, & the air is as lovely as the wision & spectacles . . . .

For with this sense of poetry, this sense of form and colour, went a sense of humour: sometimes gentle, sometimes wild, and at times disguising some profound affection or depression. After a visit to Farringford in 1859, when he had enjoyed the comfort of a normal domestic life, the motherly care of Mrs. Tennyson, Lear wrote to Fortescue:

I should think, computing moderately, that 15 angels, several hundreds of ordinary women, many philosophers, a heap of truly wise and kind mothers, 3 or 4 minor prophets, and a lot of doctors and school-mistresses, might all be boiled down, and yet their combined essence fall short of what Emily Tennyson really is. . . .

'A twitching regret' bothered him on leaving Farringford. 'At present', he added, sadly, 'I am doing little, but dimly walking on along the dusty twilight lanes of incomprehensible life. I wish you were married. I wish I were an egg and was going to be hatched.' And then, years later, when Fortescue was married to Lady Waldegrave, Lear found himself reflecting on their after-life:

Perhaps in the next eggzi stens you and I and My Lady may be able to sit for placid hours under a lotus tree a eating of ice creams and pelican pie, with our feet in a hazure coloured stream and with the birds and beasts of Paradise a sporting around us.

It would be a mistake to look, all the time, for a deeper meaning in Lear's humour. Much of it is straightforward enough. One need only recall his account of his hunger after an illness: 'Hunger! did you ever have a fever? No consideration of morality or sentiment or fear of punishment would prevent my devouring any small child who entered this room now. I have eaten everything in it but a wax-candle and a bad lemon.' Then there is the wild account of Nice, with its play on words:

I never was in so dry a place in all my life. When the little children cry, they cry dust and not tears. There is some water in the sea, but not much: —all the wetnurses cease to be so immediately on arriving:—Dryden is the only book read:—the neighbourhood abounds with Dryads and Hammerdryads: and weterinary surgeons are quite unknown. . . .

At the caves of Ipeica, on his Italian travels, Lear becomes 'acquaint with a family of original Froglodytes: they are', he wrote, 'very good creatures, mostly sitting on their hams, & feeding on lettuces & honey.' When he has visited the monasteries of Athos, he decides:

More pleasing in the sight of the Almighty I really believe, & more like what Jesus Christ intended man to become, is an honest Turk with 6 wives, or a Jew working hard to feed his little old clo' babbies, than these muttering, miserable, mutton-hating, man-avoiding, misogynic, morose, & merriment-marring, monotoning, many-mule-making, mocking, mournful, minced-fish & marmalade masticating Monx.

Yet this play on words is not the kind of humour we really expect of Lear. What we expect is his familiar non-sense. Sometimes we find it in a phrase, as when he de-scribes the scenery of Gozo as 'pomskizillious and grom-phibberous'; but sometimes, to our delight, we recognize Lear's nonsense *in extenso*. Here and there in the letters, we come across one of those 'spongetanious' passages which only the inventor of the Jumblies could have written:

When the 300 [Tennyson] drawings are done, I shall sell them for £18,000: with which I shall buy a chocolate coloured carriage speckled with gold, and driven by a coachman in green vestments and silver spectacles,—wherein, sitting on a lofty cushion composed of muffins and volumes of the Apocrypha, I shall disport myself all about the London parks, to the general satisfaction of all pious people. . . .

And then, on 6 September 1863, Lear makes a heartfelt request to Chichester Fortescue:

I want you to write to Lord Palmerston to ask him to ask the Queen to ask the King of Greece to give me a 'place'. As I never asked anything of you before, I think I may rely on your doing this for me. I wish the place to be created a-purpos for me, and the title to be Lord High Bosh and Nonsense Producer, with permission to wear a fool's cap (or mitre)— 3 pounds of butter yearly and a little pig,—and a small donkey to ride on. Please don't forget all this, as I have set my heart on it.

And this remark is not so flippant as one might suppose. Lear wanted credit for his nonsense. 'I wish', he wrote, 'I could have all the credit due to me, small as that may be.' And again: 'If you are asked ever about that Book of Nonsense, remember I made *all* the verses.' Lear took his nonsense in all seriousness. And, beneath his nonsense verse, as beneath the nonsense in his letters, there is sometimes unexpected gravity and truth.

III.   THE NONSENSE POET

As we have seen, it was during the 1830s, at Knowsley Hall, that someone had shown Lear the lines beginning: 'There was an Old Man of Tobago . . .' The greater part of the first *Book of Nonsense* was then, as he tells us, 'struck off with a pen'. It was in this verse-form and the delight of Lord Derby's grandchildren that the nonsense poet discovered himself:

> There was an old Derry down Derry,
> Who loved to see little folks merry;
>   So he made them a Book,
>   Till with laughter they shook,
> At the fun of that Derry down Derry.

That verse introduced the first *Book of Nonsense* in 1846. But the Derby children were not the only ones that Lear loved to amuse. In his *Mid-Victorian Memories*, R. E. Francillon, the son of a judge at Cheltenham, remembered: 'We children were delighted eye-witnesses of some of the earliest poems of the first *Book of Nonsense*. We possessed a good share of the original drawings, made while we stood by the artist's knee, and their attendant limericks were household words, long before there was any thought of their publication.'

But, whoever he wrote for, it is plain that Lear was doing more than amusing a young audience. He was escaping from reality, ridding himself of his worries and haunting in-hibitions. Lear, understandably, found life hard, and society in general unsympathetic. 'They' did not understand the sensitive, 'they' did not appreciate the original and enter-prising; and again and again in his limericks he lamented and ridiculed the philistine cruelty of the world:

> There was an Old Man of Whitehaven,
> Who danced a quadrille with a Raven;
> But they said—'It's absurd, to encourage this bird!'
> So they smashed that Old Man of Whitehaven.

> There was an Old Person of Chester,
> Whom several small children did pester;
> They threw some large stones, which broke most of his bones,
> And displeased that Old Person of Chester.

But Lear did more than ridicule the harshness of society. In his letters he writes about his uncertainty, his restlessness, his financial insecurity, and, above all, about his ugliness. Again and again, in his limericks, as a kind of release, he jokes about the same things. He laughs at enormous beards, poor eyesight, excessively long legs, fatness, thinness. And, above all, because it is his own most obvious shortcoming, he makes fun of enormous noses:

> There was an Old Man in a Barge,
> Whose nose was exceedingly large;
> But in fishing by night, it supported a light,
> Which helped that Old Man in a Barge.

Holman Hunt tells us that Lear was terrified of dogs. And that, I think, is why the characters in Lear's limericks own dogs far larger than themselves; they are chased by horrible cows, virulent bulls, or—like the Young Lady of Clare—by a ferocious bear. Lear's laughter is a kind of nervous defiance.

Lear earned his hard living by landscape painting; but it is doubtful whether he cared more about his paintings than his nonsense. From the first moment he was delighted by the popularity of his nonsense verse. When the revised edition of his book appeared in 1861, he reminded Chichester Fortescue: 'Tell me when you have seen the new *Book of Nonsense*. Please recommend it all you can. . . . Over five hundred copies have already been sold. Please do what you can to increase the sale by axing and talking about it. . . .' He was proud of the £125 he earned from the *Book of Nonsense*—it was almost all he earned from a book which went into nearly 30 editions even in his lifetime; and he was gratified by the eccentric in Corfu 'who has taken a kind of monomaniac fancy to my Nonsense Book, and declares that he knew *personally* the Aunt of the Girl of Majorca!! I hear it is more than humanity can bear to hear him point out how exactly like she is—and how she used to jump the walls in Majorca with flying leaps.'

So far, Lear had only published limericks. He had not invented the form, but he had introduced it to general notice; henceforward it was to be associated, *par excellence*, with his name. Now his nonsense was to take other forms. At Cannes, in the winter of 1868, he met a little girl who inspired him with a masterpiece. Janet Symonds was three years old, the daughter of John Addington Symonds, the author of the *History of the Italian Renaissance*. 'Did I tell you how much we see of Mr. Lear?' Symonds asked a friend. 'He comes here nearly every day, and nearly every day he brings Janet a fresh picture or poem—a portrait of the *Blue Bird* or the *Red Bird*. . . .' In these birds we can see distinct reminiscences of the salmon-crested cockatoo, the red and yellow macaws, wistfully distorted into nonsense birds with runcible names. It was for Janet Symonds that Lear invented the most famous bird in his aviary; for Symonds recorded that 'one original illustrated song about the Owl and the Pussy-cat who went to sea and got married, she is very fond of and has by heart':

The Owl and the Pussy-Cat went to sea
In a beautiful pea-green boat,
They took some honey, and plenty of money,
Wrapped up in a five-pound note.
The Owl looked up to the stars above,
And sang to a small guitar,
'O lovely Pussy! O Pussy, my love,
What a beautiful Pussy you are,
You are,
You are!
What a beautiful Pussy you are!'

We owe much of Lear's nonsense to the children he knew; and the next child to inspire him was Hubert Congreve, the son of a former Rugby master living at San Remo. Congreve recalled his first meeting, in the early autumn of 1869, with this tall, bearded, bespectacled gentleman, who asked at once 'if I knew who he was, and without waiting for a reply proceeded to tell me a long, nonsense name, compounded of all the languages he knew'. From that day to his death, wrote Congreve, 'Lear was my dearest and best friend of the older generation. . . . He was always full of interest in our doings, and a week seldom passed without his bringing us a drawing of some event in our lives or of some plant which had flowered in our gardens.' And this, perhaps, was the origin of Lear's nonsense botany: of Manypeeplia Upsidownia, of Jinglia Tinkettlia and Nasticreechia Krorluppia. Occasionally the Congreves were invited to dine with him, and he always sent a nonsense menu. It was only natural that nonsense cooking should fascinate him, too:

To make Gosky Patties. Take a Pig, 3 or 4 years of age, and tie him by the hind leg to a post. Place 5 pounds of currants, 3 of sugar, 2 pecks of peas, 18 roast chestnuts, a candle, and 6 bushels of turnips, within his reach; if he eats these, continually provide him with more. Then procure some cream, some slices of Cheshire cheese, four quires of foolscap paper, and a packet of black pins. Work the whole into a paste. . . . Visit the paste and beat the Pig alternately for some days, and ascertain if at the end of that period the whole is about to turn into Gosky Patties. If it does not then, it never will.

In the summer of 1870, Lear went to stay at a hotel in the mountains near Turin, to complete his *Nonsense Songs, Stories, Botany and Alphabets*. There he met Margaret Terry, the little daughter of an American artist. The child whispered to her mother that she would like to have Lear for an uncle. Lear, delighted, 'glowed, bubbled and twinkled more than ever'. He became the child's devoted friend and 'adopty duncle'; they went for walks in the chestnut forests, where they kicked the chestnut burrs before them, the 'yonghy-bonghy-bòs', as they called them, and Lear sang 'The Owl and the Pussycat' 'to a funny little crooning tune of his own compostition'. He drew a complete nonsense alphabet for Margaret Terry, and every day she found a letter of it on her plate at luncheon. Lear's nonsense alphabets must be a quite unforgettable way of learning reading: we should remember the letter D for ever once we had seen 'The Dolomphious Duck, who caught Spotted Frogs for her dinner with a Runcible Spoon'; we should know the letter F for all time, once we had met the Fizzgigious Fish.

It is strange that Lear should have chosen to call the chestnuts the 'yonghy-bonghy-bòs'. A year and more later, on Christmas Day, 1871, when his third book, *More Nonsense*, had just appeared, he told Chichester Fortescue that he had just written a poem on the Yongy-Bonghy-Bò. It was the most significant poem he had put on paper. There had been glimpses of Lear himself in his limericks; but 'The Courtship of the Yonghy-Bonghy-Bò' takes us much deeper into his private life. It was autobiography that he dared not express in serious writing. He had written the tale of the four little children who went round the world, with a cat and a Quangle-Wangle, for the four children of Lord Westbury, the Lord Chancellor; and Lord Westbury's unmarried daughter, Augusta Bethell, had inspired him with such affection that, for the only time in his life, he had seriously thought of marriage.

Augusta Bethell was, appropriately, a writer of children's books. She was extremely fond of Lear, and would almost certainly have accepted him. But the need for decision made Lear all the more aware of his infirmities. He could not bring himself to propose to her. By some irony of fate, she married a Mr. Parker, who was completely paralysed—a much more hopeless invalid than Lear himself. When she was widowed, a few years later, she and Lear met often, and with the greatest pleasure on both sides. In 1883 she came to San Remo, and when she had gone, he wrote: 'I miss her horridly. So ends the very last possible chance of changing this life.' Within a year of his death, he asked her to come again; she came, and he very nearly proposed. 'But nothing occurred beyond her very decidedly showing me how much she cared for me. . . . This, I think, was the death of all hope':

'Lady Jingly! Lady Jingly!
Sitting where the pumpkins grow,
Will you come and be my wife?'
Said the Yonghy-Bonghy-Bò.
'I am tired of living singly,—
On this coast so wild and shingly,—
I'm a-weary of my life;
If you'll come and be my wife,
Quite serene would be my life!'—
Said the Yonghy-Bonghy-Bò,
Said the Yonghy-Bonghy-Bò . . .

Lady Jingly answered sadly,
And her tears began to flow,—
'Your proposal comes too late,
Mr. Yonghy-Bonghy-Bò!
I would be your wife most gladly!'
(Here she twirled her fingers madly)
'But in England I've a mate!
Yes! you've asked me far too late,
For in England I've a mate,
Mr. Yonghy-Bonghy-Bò!
Mr. Yonghy-Bonghy-Bò!' . . .

From the Coast of Coromandel
Did that Lady never go;
On that heap of stones she mourns

For the Yonghy-Bonghy-Bò.
On that Coast of Coromandel,
In his jug without a handle,
Still she weeps and daily moans;
On that little heap of stones
To her Dorking Hens she moans
For the Yonghy-Bonghy-Bò,
For the Yonghy-Bonghy-Bò.

The poem appeared in 1877 in *Laughable Lyrics*. This was the fourth and last nonsense book to be published in Lear's lifetime, and it is not only an epitome of his art, it is also a pathetic commentary on a life of unhappiness and escape. The old man with his 'purely original dress', set upon by children and animals, makes Lear's final comment on the cruelty of society. Mr. and Mrs. Discobbolos seek asylum on the top of a wall, for that is the only place where they are safe from trouble and sorrow. But, above all, it is clear from this book that Lear has now created a complete and self-contained nonsense world. The Quangle-Wangle who had once sailed round the world with the four little children now had a permanent home on the top of the Crumpetty Tree; and the hills of the Chankly Bore, that the Jumblies had once visited, the Great Gromboolian Plain, where the pelicans' daughter was living, were now inhabited by one of Lear's saddest creations. The Dong with a Luminous Nose is Lear himself, still aware of his ugliness; the Dong, in his vain and constant search for his Jumbly girl, is Lear still dreaming of Augusta. This may be nonsense, but, once again, it is poetic nonsense. It is nonsense with a flavour of Tennyson, the friend whom Lear had consistently admired:

When awful darkness and silence reign
  Over the great Gromboolian plain,
    Through the long, long wintry nights:—
When the angry breakers roar,
As they beat on the rocky shore:—
    When Storm-clouds brood on the towering heights
Of the Hills on the Chankly Bore:—

Then, through the vast and gloomy dark,
There moves what seems a fiery spark,
    A lonely spark with silvery rays
    Piercing the coal-black night,—
    A meteor strange and bright:—
Hither and thither the vision strays,
    A single lurid light.

Slowly it wanders,—pauses,—creeps,—
Anon it sparkles,—flashes and leaps;
And ever as onward it gleaming goes
A light on the Bong-tree stems it throws.
And those who watch at that midnight hour
From Hall or Terrace, or lofty Tower,
Cry, as the wild light passes along,—
    'The Dong!—the Dong!
  'The wandering Dong through the forest goes!
    'The Dong!—the Dong!
  'The Dong with a luminous Nose!'

In March 1884 Lear fell very ill with pleurisy and in flammation of the lungs; it was May before he could leave San Remo, and even then his manservant had to lift him in and out of railway carriages, because his feet were too swollen for him to walk. Early in June, he sent Chichester Fortescue, now Lord Carlingford, 'a few lines just to tell you how your aged friend goes on':

    O my aged Uncle Arley!
    Sitting on a heap of Barley
Through the silent hours of night!
    On his nose there sate a cricket,—
    In his hat a railway ticket—
    But his shoes were far too tight—
    Too! Too!
        far too tight!

'My Aged Uncle Arley', Lear told John Ruskin, was 'the last Nonsense poem I shall write.'

A manuscript copy of 'My Aged Uncle Arley' had been

sent to Ruskin in gratitude for his letter to the *Pall Mall Magazine*. Asked to choose his favourite books, Ruskin had decided: 'Surely the most beneficent and innocent of all books yet produced is the *Book of Nonsense*, with its corollary carols—inimitable and refreshing, and perfect in rhythm. I really don't know any author to whom I am half so grateful, for my idle self, as Edward Lear. I shall put him first of my hundred authors.' Lear was enchanted by Ruskin's praise; he was delighted when the *Spectator* called his verse 'meloobious', and set examination questions on his work:

1. Comment, with illustrations, upon Mr. Lear's use of the following words: Runcible, dolomphious, borascible. . . .
2. Enumerate accurately all the animals who lived on the Quangle-Wangle's hat. . . .

In a life that was often unhappy, Lear did at least enjoy the beginnings of his immortality.

What is the secret of this immortality? Where is the charm of Lear? It lies (as it always does with poets) in his love of words: their cadences, their very look on the page, their mystery, their endless, exciting power of evocation. Lear played delightedly with language; and if, at times, he deliberately misused it (where else have we heard 'a promiscuous oration'?), even his misuse seems to have a meaning. When the Queen's English proved to be restricting, or inadequate, he simply invented a word for his purpose:

> There was an old person of Grange,
> Whose manners were scroobious and strange. . . .

Far be it from us to observe that Lear applies the identical epithet to a snake. Runcible is an adjective which is cheerfully accorded to a spoon, a raven and a hat. But what does that matter? It is a word, like many others in Lear, which gives us unique, indescribable delight.

Lear coined a vocabulary, and he did so with gusto. I think it is in his gusto that he differs most from Carroll. One never feels with Lear that his nonsense is an intellectual recreation; one never has the sense of contrivance. We can almost hear him pottering round his garden at San Remo, spontaneously christening his plants Sophtsluggia Glutinosa, or Minspysia Deliciosa. We can hear the limericks tossed off the moment the first line is given. And yet what art, deliberate or natural, lies behind those apparently casual verses! Lear is the master of the incompatible, the wildly impossible:

> There was an Old Man of Blackheath,
> Whose head was adorned with a wreath,
> Of lobsters and spice, pickled onions and mice,
> That uncommon Old Man of Blackheath.

He is master, too, of the totally unexpected: of the line which catches the reader unawares:

> There was an Old Man of Three Bridges,
> Whose mind was distracted by midges,
> He sate on a wheel, eating underdone veal,
> Which relieved that Old Man of Three Bridges.

Lear understands every kind of humour: the humour of words and the humour of situation; he can be dry, rumbustious, zany, slapstick, and, sometimes, macabre. Occasionally he anticipates—and parodies in advance—the 'automatic writing', the irrational inspiration of the Surrealists:

> Mrs. Jaypher found a wafer
> Which she stuck upon a note;
> This she took and gave the cook.
> Then she went and bought a boat
> Which she paddled down the stream
> Shouting: 'Ice produces cream,
> Beer when churned produces butter!
> Henceforth all the words I utter
> Distant ages thus shall note—
> From the Jaypher Wisdom-Boat.'

But the magic of Lear cannot really be analysed. The

wisest comment on it was made by a critic who, in his nursery days, had come face to face with Edward Lear himself. 'As far as I can understand', wrote St. Loe Strachey, talking of *The Lear Coloured Bird Book for Children*,

... the charm is due to the fact that in some incomprehensible way Lear has managed to get his personal feeling for childhood to run along the lines of his brush and into the hearts of children. ...

The fact that remains is that children love Lear's pictures and that Lear meant them to love them, and that is enough.

Perhaps these remarks should also apply to Lear's written nonsense. But if, as adults, we seek further, we may learn more of Lear by a comparison. Lear is often compared with his contemporary in nonsense, Lewis Carroll; but a world divides them. Carroll approached his nonsense by way of logic and mathematics, Lear approached it through his paintings and through poetry, and—which is most important—through life itself. Lear was intensely human—and his humanity, warm and honest and spongetanious, cannot ever fail to be endearing.

EDWARD LEAR

A Select Bibliography

(Place of publication London, unless stated otherwise)

Bibliography:

EDWARD LEAR ON MY SHELVES, by W. B. O. Field. New York (privately printed, 1933)
—a biography of Lear, a bibliography, and lists of original drawings, watercolours, lithographs, engravings and woodcuts. Many quotations from reviews, and from Lear's diaries, which cover a period of 30 years. Limited to 155 numbered and signed copies.

Collected Works

EDWARD LEAR'S NONSENSE OMNIBUS. With all the Original Pictures, Verses, and Stories of his *Book of Nonsense*, *More Nonsense*, *Nonsense Songs*, *Nonsense Stories* and *Alphabets*. With an Introduction by Sir E. Strachey, Bart. (1943).

THE LEAR OMNIBUS, ed. R. L. Mégroz (1945).

THE COMPLETE NONSENSE OF EDWARD LEAR. Edited and introduced by H. Jackson (1947).

Selected Works:

EDWARD LEAR'S NONSENSE SONGS (1938)
—with the author's own illustrations.

A BOOK OF LEAR, ed. R. L. Mégroz (1939).

EDWARD LEAR'S PARROTS, by B. Reade. With twelve reproductions of coloured lithographs from Lear's *Psittacidae*. Foreword by E. L. Warre (1949)
—a scholarly account of Lear's interest in natural history; but the lithographs lose immeasurably by poor reproduction.

EDWARD LEAR'S JOURNALS: A SELECTION, ed. H. Van Thal (1952).

Separate Works:

ILLUSTRATIONS OF THE FAMILY OF PSITTACIDAE, OR PARROTS: the greater part of them hitherto unfigured, containing forty-two lithographic plates, drawn from life, and on stone (1832).

37

VIEWS IN ROME AND ITS ENVIRONS. Drawn from Nature and on Stone (1841).

GLEANINGS FROM THE MENAGERIE AND AVIARY AT KNOWSLEY HALL. Knowsley (printed for private distribution, 1846).

ILLUSTRATED EXCURSTIONS IN ITALY. 2 vols. (1846).

A BOOK OF NONSENSE, by Derry Down Derry [Edward Lear] (1846).

JOURNALS OF A LANDSCAPE PAINTER IN ALBANIA, etc. (1851).

JOURNALS OF A LANDSCAPE PAINTER IN SOUTHERN CALABRIA, &c. (1852)
—reprinted as *Edw ard Lear in Southern Italy*, with an introduction by Peter Quennell, 1964.

VIEWS IN THE SEVEN IONIAN ISLANDS (1863).

JOURNAL OF A LANDSCAPE PAINTER IN CORSICA (1870).

NONSENSE SONGS, STORIES, BOTANY, AND ALPHABETS (1871).

MORE NONSENSE PICTURES, RHYMES, BOTANY, &c. (1872)
—this book appeared just before Christmas, 1871, but was dated 1872.

TORTOISES, TERRAPINS, AND TURTLES. Drawn from Life by James de Carle Sowerby, F.L.S., and Edward Lear (1872).

LAUGHABLE LYRICS. A Fourth Book of Nonsense Poems, Songs, Botany, Music, &c. (1877).

POEMS BY ALFRED, LORD TENNYSON. Illustrated by Edward Lear (1889).

QUEERY LEARY NONSENSE. A Lear Nonsense Book. Edited by Lady Strachey of Sutton Court. With an Introduction by the Earl of Cromer (1911)
—certain unpublished pieces, including three additional illustrations for 'The Owl and the Pussycat', appear here for the first time. The bird plates are reproduced from the drawings made by Lear for the eldest son of Lord Cromer.

THE LEAR COLOURED BIRD BOOK FOR CHILDREN. With a Foreword by J. St. Loe Strachey (1912)
—this book was originally contained in *Queery Leary Nonsense*, and is now published separately.

LEAR IN SICILY. Twenty line drawings by Edward Lear, illustrating a tour made in May-July 1847 in the company of John Joshua Proby, with a coloured frontispiece signed by both the travellers and a full introduction by Granville Proby (1938)
—unpublished drawings of Sicily, with a commentary taken from Lear's letters, &c.

TEAPOTS AND QUAILS. And Other New Nonsenses. By Edward Lear, edited and introduced by A. Davidson and P. Hofer (1953)
—all the material in this book had hitherto been unpublished, except for a few of the limericks which were published in 1933 by Wm. B. Osgood Field in *Edward Lear on my Shelves*.

EDWARD LEAR'S INDIAN JOURNAL. Watercolours and extracts from the diary of Edward Lear, 1873–1875, ed. R. Murphy (1953).

Letters:

LETTERS OF EDWARD LEAR, Author of 'The Book of Nonsense', to Chichester Fortescue (Lord Carlingford) and Frances Countess Waldegrave, ed. Lady Strachey (1907).

LATER LETTERS OF EDWARD LEAR, Author of 'The Book of Nonsense', to Chichester Fortescue (Lord Carlingford), Frances Countess Waldegrave and Others, ed. Lady Strachey (1911).

Some Biographical and Critical Studies:

EDWARD LEAR. LANDSCAPE PAINTER AND NONSENSE POET (1812–1888), by A. Davidson (1938)
—this is the only full-scale biography of Lear; it contains a great deal of material not available elsewhere. It was reprinted as a Penguin Book in 1950.

THE FIELD OF NONSENSE, by E. Sewell (1952)
—a general study of nonsense writing, which draws comparisons and contrasts between Lear, Lewis Carroll, etc.

WRITERS AND THEIR WORK: NO. 185

Susan Ferrier

and

John Galt

by W. M. PARKER

Published for the British Council
and the National Book League
by Longmans, Green & Co

Three shillings and sixpence net

Susan Ferrier and John Galt, who were contemporaries of Sir Walter Scott, invented a literary genre—the Scottish novel of manners and of parochial life. Susan Ferrier, by birth, environment and temperament, was well fitted to observe and to delineate the habits and the foibles of upper middle class society in Edinburgh. John Galt was at his best when portraying the political and commercial life of the countryside and small towns of Western Scotland.

Although she lived to be over seventy, Susan Ferrier published only three novels, *Marriage*, *The Inheritance* and *Destiny*. Despite the paucity of her writings she was much esteemed by her contemporaries, including Scott, and was even considered by the *Edinburgh Review* to be the equal of Jane Austen. She prided herself on her ability to detect faults in other people, and was particularly averse to vulgarity, which was, in her view, a marked characteristic of John Galt's novels.

Galt was a prolific writer who, in his own words, 'put together many books'. His varied experience of life in the Mediterranean and in Canada gave him an understanding of the motives and ambitions which animate men of affairs. He drew on this experience in a series of novels about his native Scotland, the most accomplished of which are *Annals of the Parish*, *The Provost* and *The Entail*. His two most successful political novels are *The Radical* and *The Member*, satirical descriptions of the manoeuvres and the jobbery which accompanied the passing of the Reform Bill of 1832.

W. M. Parker was co-editor of *Letters of Sir Walter Scott* (12 vols. 1932-7) and of *The Journal of Sir Walter Scott* (1950). He is also the author of numerous articles on Scott and Thomas Hardy, of *Modern Scottish Writers*, and of *On the Track of the Wessex Novels*, as well as editor of Waverley Novels in Everyman's Library. He has been a literary research reader in the National Library of Scotland for over 35 years.

Bibliographical Series
of Supplements to 'British Book News'
on Writers and Their Work

★

GENERAL EDITOR
Geoffrey Bullough

¶ Susan Ferrier was born in Edinburgh on 17 September 1782 and died there on 5 November 1854.

¶ John Galt was born at Irvine, Ayrshire on 2 May 1779 and died at Greenock on 11 April 1839.

SUSAN FERRIER

SUSAN FERRIER

and

JOHN GALT

by

W. M. PARKER

PUBLISHED FOR
THE BRITISH COUNCIL
AND THE NATIONAL BOOK LEAGUE
BY LONGMANS, GREEN & CO

LONGMANS, GREEN & CO LTD
48 Grosvenor Street, London W.1

*Associated companies, branches and
representatives throughout the world*

First published 1965
© W. M. Parker 1965

Printed in Great Britain by
F. Mildner & Sons, London, E.C.1

CONTENTS

Frontispiece: The portrait of Susan Ferrier is after a miniature by Robert Thorburn; the portrait of John Galt is from the painting by Charles Gray in the Scottish National Portrait Gallery.

For

ELIZABETH MARY

SUSAN FERRIER and JOHN GALT

INTRODUCTORY

Among the Scottish novelists who were contemporaries of Sir Walter Scott two especially made a considerable impact on fiction; indeed, they diverted the trend of the Scottish Novel into new channels. Hitherto there had been Smollett's picaresque vagaries and Henry Mackenzie's tales that wallowed in sentimentality. Scott had not as yet established the historical romance. Susan Ferrier and John Galt appeared on the literary horizon and became preoccupied with entirely different genres.

The Scottish Novel of manners and of ordinary parochial life thus came into being with those two authors. Later, the contrasts between their outlook as well as the literary treatment in their works will be considered. But what immediately strikes us on approaching them is difference of personality and temperament, conditioned, to some extent, by environment, upbringing, and social status. We can sense a certain detachment in Susan Ferrier's observation of sections from the human scene. She is the Edinburgh female 'chield takin' notes'. And we are just as aware of a sympathetic absorption in John Galt's interpretation of parochial and commercial life. He has the warm characteristics of his native Ayrshire.

I. SUSAN FERRIER

SUSAN Edmonstone Ferrier was born in Edinburgh on 17 September 1782. Her birthplace was a flat in Lady Stair's Close which had been recently inhabited by Sir James Pulteney and his wife Lady Bath. Susan was the youngest of the ten children of James Ferrier, who, through the influence of John, fifth Duke of Argyll, was appointed a Principal Clerk of Session and had Sir Walter Scott as a colleague and friend. Her mother was Helen Coutts, a famous beauty who, before her marriage, had lived at Holyrood Palace. There is little record of Susan's education, but we know that at an early age she attended Mr. Stalker's Academy in George Street, an infant school for boys and girls.

James Ferrier, a man of indomitable perseverance, which urged him on to the top of his profession, became manager of Argyll's estates. His duties entailed frequent visits to Inveraray Castle on Loch Fyne whither, in her girlhood, Susan accompanied him. These visits had significance, for they opened up to the young girl vistas upon which she was to draw when she came to engage in authorship. She saw county fashion and high life at close quarters. Moreover, she formed friendships which were to help in shaping her literary career.

The Duke's younger daughter, Lady Charlotte Campbell (later Lady Charlotte Bury) was accustomed to do the honours of Scotland to contemporary literary notabilities. She made a deep impression on Susan Ferrier's imagination, and they remained on intimate terms for the rest of Susan's life.

But the most important friendship at this stage was with Charlotte Clavering, the Duke's niece. She and Susan Ferrier found continuous amusement in observing the frequenters of the Castle. There were, for instance, red-haired Highland

8

chiefs, snuffing, sneezing, and condemning everything that was not Scottish. There were London ladies who brought their parrots, lap-dogs, macaws, and doctors. Surely such human oddities would provide rich material for a novel. Indeed, they so impressed the young ladies that Charlotte suggested Susan ought to make a book about them. Accordingly, it was planned that they would collaborate in writing a story based on their observations. This was the genesis of Susan Ferrier's first novel, *Marriage*.

When her mother died Susan Ferrier looked after the household and her father, after whose death in 1829 she lived a retired existence between the semi-rural Morningside House and Edinburgh, where she mixed in social circles. During her later years her eyesight failed and she had to spend her days in a darkened room. One who knew Susan Ferrier in her youth described her as 'dark, tall, and handsome, a most attractive personality, and a brilliant conversationalist'. But with age her expressive face showed irregular features. She died at 38 Albany Street, Edinburgh, on 5 November 1854, and was buried in St. Cuthbert's Churchyard. Allan Cunningham, the Scots poet and man of letters, paid tribute to her warm heart, her lively fancy, and her great powers of discrimination.

During the composition of *Marriage* in 1810 an exciting correspondence passed between the prospective collaborators. The moral message of the book would be, as Susan confided, 'to warn all young ladies against runaway matches . . . I expect it will be the first book every wise matron will put into the hand of her daughter . . . I hear the enchanting sound of some sentimental miss, the shrill pipe of some antiquated spinster, or the hoarse grumbling of some incensed dowager as they severally inquire for me at the circulating library, and are assured by the master that 'tis in such demand that though he has thirteen copies, they are insufficient to answer the calls upon it, but that each of them may depend upon having the very first that comes in ! ! !' Then she added in great trepidation: 'One thing let me entreat of you: if we engage in this undertaking let it be kept a profound secret from every human being. If I was suspected of being accessory to such foul deeds my brothers and sisters would murder me, and my father bury me alive.' Charlotte Clavering gave her every encouragement and wrote enthusiastically regarding one of the characters. 'I must tell you that I approve in the most signal manner of "Lady McLaughlan". The sort of character was totally unexpected by me, and I was really quite transported with her . . . Let me have the continuation of Lady McLaughlan directly.'[1]

Susan Ferrier, still apprehensive, again wrote: 'I've taken a remorse of conscience about Lady MacLaughlan and her friends: if I was ever detected, or even suspected, I would have nothing for it but to drown myself. I mean, therefore, to let her alone . . . as I think we might compound some other kind of character for her that might do as well and not be so dangerous.' But the Lady was retained.

Soon, however, Charlotte withdrew from the collaboration, her one contribution being the rather uninteresting portion called 'the History of Mrs. Douglas'. Meanwhile she had read some of Susan's MS. to Lady Charlotte Campbell who declared that it was 'without the least exception the cleverest thing of the kind that ever was written, far surpassing Fielding'. Reporting this to Susan, Charlotte Clavering added: 'I am sure you will be the first author of the age.'[2]

Provisionally entitled *The Chiefs of Glenfern*, the work was submitted to William Blackwood who accepted it for publication. On 6 May 1817, he wrote to Susan Ferrier: 'The whole construction and execution appear so admirable that it would almost be presumption in any one to offer corrections to such a writer.'

The book, retitled *Marriage*, appeared anonymously in

---

[1] *Memoir and Correspondence*, pp. 76, 77, 103, 105.

[2] Ibid, p. 106.

1818.[1] It achieved a popularity far beyond Edinburgh. In London it was attributed to Scott, who later praised the novel in a valedictory postscript to *A Legend of Montrose* in these words: 'I retire from the field, conscious that there remains behind not only a large harvest, but labourers capable of gathering it in ... If the present author, himself a phantom, may be permitted to distinguish a brother, or perhaps a sister, shadow, he would mention, in particular, the author of the very lively work entitled *Marriage*.'

What was the nature of this 'very lively work'? Unequal in execution, with a weak plot, the narrative concerns the silly, selfish Lady Juliana who elopes with the penniless but handsome Scots captain, Henry Douglas. He takes her to Glenfern, his dreary Highland castle, where there is not even loaf bread, where she is nearly poisoned with a Scotch broth, where she is deafened by bagpipes and bewildered by aunts and sisters-in-law.

After she has given birth to twin daughters, she and Henry move to London and get into debt. Henry is imprisoned, and on his release he joins a regiment in India, permanently separated from his wife. The interest is then concentrated on the daughters: Mary, who eventually marries a Scotsman, and Adelaide, who captivates an unattractive English duke. The underlying theme dwells on their respective happy and unhappy marriages.

It happened that before the book appeared Susan Ferrier's father, who had no use for female authors, was ill in bed. He asked her to read something to him. As she wanted his opinion of her maiden effort she read her MS. behind curtains so that he could not see the script. He was so delighted with the tale that he told Susan to get another by the same author. Susan informed him there was no other. 'I am sorry to hear that,' he said, 'for it is the best book you have ever brought me.' 'Then what will you say when I tell you it was written by a woman?' 'Nonsense', he replied, 'no

[1] On 2 March 1818, Blackwood paid Susan Ferrier £150 for the copyright. The MS. agreement is in the National Library of Scotland.

woman could ever write a book like that.' Susan then confessed to its authorship.

The novel suffers from an excess of characters. Susan Ferrier deals with human absurdities. She attacks the tiresome, the vulgar, the selfish. Her barbs are often inflicted unsparingly. Although she possesses masculine sagacity and shrewd observation, her real distinction is in comic exaggeration. Saintsbury considered her studies of the ridiculous were 'a collection of exceedingly clever caricatures, some of which deserve a higher title and the best of which will rank with the best originals in English fiction'.[1]

If the sketches of fashionable life in *Marriage* have a superficial air about them nevertheless they ring truer than those which Scott attempted in *St. Ronan's Well*. His Lady Penelope Penfeather is unconvincing when she is compared with Susan Ferrier's Lady MacLaughlan although Susan, it cannot be denied, was unable to create a Meg Dods. Indeed, Scott himself realised he had failed in the genre. On 28 July 1826, he entered in his *Journal* after rereading his novel: 'I must allow the fashionable portraits are not the true thing. I am too much out of the way to see and remark the ridiculous in society.'[2]

It is the redoubtable Lady MacLaughlan who is the dominant personality in the tale. Blunt but good-hearted, she does not refrain from making rude speeches to her husband, Sir Sampson, and to her friend Miss Grizzy. She is involved in two especially humorous scenes: one in which she shortens her visit to Glenfern Castle in high dudgeon and the other in which the unfortunate spinsters, the laird's

[1] *The Collected Essays and Papers of George Saintsbury*, vol. I (1923) p. 314.

[2] *The Journal of Sir Walter Scott*, edited by J. G. Tait and W. M. Parker (1950), p. 207. Discussing *St. Ronan's Well*, W. P. Ker remarked that 'Scott makes the same mistake as (now and then) his contemporaries Galt and Miss Ferrier—whom we naturally think of when we find Scott approaching the world of *The Entail* and *Marriage*. All three novelists have fits of melodrama, which does not agree well with their humorous comedy of Scottish life and manners.'—*Scott Centenary Articles* (1932), p. 135.

three elderly sisters, Grizzy, Nicky, and Jacky, mistaking the day, arrive to visit her when they are not expected. Indeed, Lady MacLaughlan is a memorable figure in fiction.

Hardly less successful is the epicurean physician, Dr. Redgill, quietly and steadfastly selfish. His contempt for Scottish scenery is balanced by his admiration of Scottish breakfasts and his aversion to churches, which he thinks are 'highly prejudicial to health'. Blackwood assured Susan Ferrier that 'anyone who has ever associated with the English of a certain class will at once recognise in Dr. Redgill the living portrait of hundreds, though never before hit off so well'. In addition, Jacky, the most sensible woman and the best orator in the parish, Grizzy the platitudinous, and Nicky almost as sensible as Jacky, provide much entertainment. The trio represent a bygone social order. Not the least effective of Susan Ferrier's parodies is that of a blue-stocking conversation at Mrs. Bluemit's in Bath.[1]

When we come to consider her second novel, *The Inheritance*, we recall the claim made that Susan Ferrier was doing for Scotland what Jane Austen and Maria Edgeworth had done respectively for England and Ireland, namely, producing characters that live in the hearts and minds of readers. A further claim, that she is the Scottish Jane Austen, cannot be readily accepted. If she never indulged in Maria's extreme didacticism she was equally incapable of Jane's delicate irony. Susan Ferrier's satire is robust and hard-hitting in comparison.

She knew *Emma* and had heard of *Pride and Prejudice*. In 1816 she wrote to Charlotte Clavering: 'I have been reading *Emma*, which is excellent; there is no story whatever, and the heroine is no better than other people; but the characters are all so true to life, and the style so piquant.'[2] And in

---

[1] 'As for *Marriage*, that is indeed a much superior book to any that Hogg or Cunningham, or any of that sort will ever write.' *John Bull's Letter to Lord Byron*, attributed to J. G. Lockhart, edited by Alan Lang Strout (Norman, University of Oklahoma Press (1947), p. 95.

[2] *Memoir and Correspondence*, p. 128.

1813 she had written: 'I should like amazingly to see that same *Pride and Prejudice* which everybody dins my ears with.'

When, therefore, Susan Ferrier began *The Inheritance* we may guess that Jane Austen was at the back of her mind. Moreover, emulation of Miss Austen's expression seems to occur in one instance at least. We find this in the first sentence of the novel which corresponds, almost word for word, with the opening sentence of *Pride and Prejudice*. Susan Ferrier begins: 'It is a truth universally acknowledged that there is no passion so deeply rooted in human nature as that of pride.' Jane Austen opens with 'It is a truth universally acknowledged that a single man in possession of a good fortune must be in want of a wife.' These two sentences with the same initial six words appear to be a remarkable coincidence.

Again, it might be argued that Susan Ferrier was indebted to Jane Austen for the comic Miss Pratt whose endless stream of gossip bears a marked resemblance to that of the garrulous Miss Bates in *Emma*. The very ribbons of Miss Pratt's bonnet 'seemed to vibrate with impatience'; she forced her way in everywhere, invited or not; and made herself at home wherever she went.

Whereas *Marriage* was a rich promise of what Susan could do, *The Inheritance*, published anonymously in 1824, was a successful fulfilment of that promise. Here there are a central unity, a well-knit plot, and a better style.

Gertrude St. Clair, the supposed heiress of her uncle, Lord Rossville, is brought by her mother to live at the Earl's castle. The Earl is a petty, benevolent tyrant, composed of little thoughts, little plans, little ideas, little prejudices, little whims. He sits 'behind the teapot like a cackling hen', observes Miss Pratt. He is determined that Gertrude shall marry Mr. Delmour, the next heir-male to the Rossville estates. But Gertrude falls in love with the wrong man, Delmour's brother the colonel.

The climax is reached when the Earl dies and Gertrude finds herself a countess. Meanwhile, a mysterious, vulgar person called Lewiston hovers about demanding money. In the end he forces himself into the castle and announces that he is really Gertrude's father. It is revealed that the ambitious Mrs. St. Clair, despairing of issue, had adopted the daughter of a servant and passed her off as her own child. Colonel Delmour immediately decamps on hearing the news. Gertrude loses her inheritance only to find another, for she is taken up by testy Uncle Adam Ramsay with his £70,000, and eventually marries Edward Lyndsay, an excellent if rather colourless young man.

Undoubtedly, *The Inheritance* shows greater skill and dexterity than were exhibited in *Marriage*. The characters are drawn with slightly less exaggerated humour, the descriptions are true to nature, and there are several unique situations such as Miss Pratt's arrival at the castle in a hearse drawn by eight horses in which she sought shelter from a snowstorm.

In Susan Ferrier's gallery of originals, or, as Saintsbury characterises them, 'her museum of abnormalities', Uncle Adam Ramsay is prominent. The portrait was based on Susan's father, at whose death Scott wrote: 'Honest old Mr. Ferrier is dead at extreme old age . . . We used to call him Uncle Adam after that character in his gifted daughter's novel.' Perhaps Susan meant to express a kind of retaliation for her father's dislike of women novelists in creating this irritable old man, who plays a considerable part in the tale.

There is the scene depicting Adam in his turret room at Rossville so absorbed in *Guy Mannering* that he delays, and at last postpones, his departure indefinitely so that he may see poetic justice done on Glossin:

In a paroxysm of *ennui* one bad day he had taken up the first volume of Guy Mannering with little expectation of deriving either amusement or instruction from it; but, once fairly entered upon it, he found himself compelled, *nolens volens*, to proceed, which he did, however, in the most secret and stealthy manner. Uncle Adam had been no novel-reader even in his younger days, and with him, as with many other excellent, but we must suppose mistaken people, novels and mental imbecility were ideas inseparably united in his brain. Novel-writers he had always conceived to be born idiots, and novel-readers he considered as something lower in the scale of intellect. It was, therefore, with feelings of the deepest humiliation he found himself thus irresistibly carried along on a sort of *King's-cushion*, as it were, by Meg Merrilies and Dominie Sampson. Not that he traversed the pages with the swiftness of a modern reader—or that he read them probably with half the rapidity with which they were written—for he was one of those solid, substantial readers who make what they read their own—he read and re-read, and paused and pondered—and often turned back, but never looked forward, even while experiencing the most intense anxiety as to the result—in short, Uncle Adam's whole being was completely absorbed in this (to him) new creation, while, at the same time, he blushed even in private at his own weakness in filling his head with such idle havers, and, indeed, never could have held it up again if he had been detected with a volume in his hand.

Uncle Adam meditated his leavetaking on the following day but as

the thoughts of Guy Mannering came over him, he staggered in his resolution: leave it he could not—to borrow it he would have been ashamed—to abstract it never entered his primitive imagination; for, in his day, it had not been the fashion for ladies and gentlemen to take other people's books, or to lose other people's books, or, in short, to do any of the free and easy things that are the privilege of the present age. True, there were libraries in Barnford; but to have recourse to a circulating library!—to have it through the town that he was a *novelle* reader! there was distraction in the thought! Perish Dumple and Dandie Dinmont, Dominie Sampson, and the whole host of them, before he would stoop to such a measure! But then, not to see the end of that scoundrel Glossin, whom he could have hanged with his own hands, only that hanging was too good for him—ay, there's the rub! . . . Before he could make up his mind, therefore, the time came for adjourning to the drawing-room; but, instead of repairing there, Uncle Adam stole away to his own apartment, to try whether another chapter would not set the matter at rest.

Later Lady Rossville finds him in his turret room. She has come to announce the arrival of Major and Mrs. Waddell

(Adam's niece) with whom she knows the old man will not want to be under the same roof:

> She looked in, and there sat Uncle Adam, with spectacles on nose, so intent upon a book, that all his senses seemed to be completely lapt in its pages . . . She ventured to lay her hand on his shoulder, and—Guy Mannering dropt upon the floor.
>
> 'You seem to be much interested in your studies', said Lady Rossville . . .' 'It's just a wheen idle havers', Mr. Ramsay replied, 'They maun hae little to do that tak up their heids writing sic nonsense.'
>
> 'I never heard the author accused of idleness before', said Lady Rossville, with a smile; 'and no one need be ashamed to own the interest excited by these wonderful works of genius.' 'Interest—hugh!—Folk may hae other things to interest them, I think, in this world. I wonder if there's ony o't true? I canna think how ae man could sit down to contrive a' that. I dinna misdoot that scoondrel Glossin at a'. I would gie a thoosand pound out o' my pocket to see that rascal hanged, if hanging wasna owre gude for him!' 'Well, you may be at ease on that head, as even worse befalls him', said Lady Rossville. 'Weel, I rejoice at that! for if that scoondrel had gotten leave to keep that property, by my troth, I believe, I would have burnt the book . . . But it's a' nonsense thegither, and I'm no gaun to fash my head ony mair about it.'

Lady Rossville tries to prevail on him to meet his relatives, but in vain. 'No sooner had she left the room, than Mr. Ramsay locked and bolted the door, to prevent any further intrusion, and after a few glances at Lizzie [a picture of his long-loved Lizzie Lundie], his ruffled pinions were smoothed, and he returned with unabated ardour to his studies.'

This episode is unique among the incidents in Susan Ferrier's novels by reason of the acute analysis of Uncle Adam's personality and also because of the restrained manipulation of dialect.

Commenting on *The Inheritance* in January, 1842, the *Edinburgh Review* noted that Susan Ferrier 'had learned . . . to feel her own strength, and to confide in her command over the higher passions and more tender emotions as well as over the ludicrous and the grotesque'. But she had not

sufficient control over her exaggerations. Even in this more
moderate novel they thrust themselves in, permeate here
and there.

Destiny, which was dedicated to Scott, came out in 1831.
Susan's third and last novel, it shows a marked decline in
her powers, and the construction is loose.

The scene of the action is the Scottish Highlands into
which some members of fashionable London society in the
early nineteenth century are introduced. The tone is mainly
serious but the atmosphere is enlivened by the ludicrous
humour of a narrow-minded and conventional society. The
reader laughs at the proud, arrogant chief, Glenroy, growing
more childishly obstinate and bigoted; at his echo and
retainer Benbowie; at the uncouth, self-sufficient pastor,
McDow; and at the supercilious Lady Elizabeth who thinks
herself always *recherchée*. The moral of this too diffuse novel
is, that no man can escape his destiny.

Exaggeration is still almost an obsession. Glenroy, for
instance, is described as having 'a vague, confused apprehension that an evangelical pastor was a sort of compound
of a Popish priest, a stiff-necked Presbyterian, a sour-faced
Covenanter, a lank-haired Seceder, a meddling Jesuit, a
foul-tongued John Knox, a what not that had evil in its
composition'.

The clergyman, the Rev. Duncan McDow, is the one
really impressive character. He delights in stale jokes, bad
puns, and horse laughter, and is so thick-skinned as to be
impervious to snubs. At the end of the memorable lunch
which he gives to Captain and Miss Malcolm, he presses
Malcolm to have a dram:

'I never drink spirits', the Captain replied. 'Hoot, toot', said McDow,
'that's a very bad rule and the sooner it's broken the better. Come, let
me persuade you.' 'Pray keep your powers of persuasion for a better
cause . . . I have seen too much of the evils of such socialism.'

This passage and especially this early use of the word
'socialism' occur in the one-volume edition (1841) of

Destiny, which was revised by the author, who appears to be one of the first writers to employ the word. The sense in which the Captain uses it is 'sociality'.

Much of *Destiny* was written at Stirling Castle while Susan Ferrier was on a visit to the Governor's wife. It was her one pecuniary success. As a result of Scott's financial negotiations on her behalf, she received £1,700 for it. The book was widely read, Sir James Mackintosh being so absorbed in it during the dissolution of Parliament that he had no thought for King or Parliament. Mrs. Eliza Fletcher, the wife of Archibald Fletcher, the reformer, urged Susan to continue her fiction-writing. 'Go on, dear Miss Ferrier . . . go on to detect selfishness in all its various forms and foldings, to put pride and vanity to shame, to prove that vulgarity belongs more to character than condition, and that all who make this world their standard are essentially vulgar and low minded, however polished their exterior or refined their manners may be.'[1] But *Destiny* was an artistic disappointment, and Susan wisely decided that she would write no more fiction.

In this her swan song a lively sense of the ridiculous is still maintained and the satire continues to be hard. It might have been well had Susan Ferrier taken to heart her own warning in chapter vii: 'Many a pure and generous feeling is stifled in the young heart by the withering breath of ridicule.' Yet *Destiny* is not without attraction. Again we meet the usual quaint characters, hit off in customary style, and we come upon almost Trollopian descriptions of everyday occurrences. The caustic presentation of Mrs. Malcolm, one of the redeeming passages in the book, anticipates descriptive touches in Dickens:

In a few minutes the door opened, and the lady entered. She was arrayed in a bright amber-silk gown, a full dress cap, decorated with scarlet ribbons, and even more than the usual number of bows that tied nothing, and ends that evidently had no ends to answer, save that of

1 *Memoir and Correspondence*, p. 222.

swelling the milliner's bill. She had a mean, vacant countenance, and a pair of most unhappy-looking hands, crossed before her, clothed in bright purple gloves, with long empty finger-ends, dangling in all directions . . . Mrs. Malcom's hands were perfectly characteristic; they proclaimed at once that they could do nothing; that they were utterly helpless, and morally, not physically, imbecile.

Occasionally Susan Ferrier gives way to affected diction. Such an artificial expression as 'when the overflowings of a generous heart are confined within the narrow limits of its own bosom, and the offerings of love are rudely rejected by the hand most dear to us' is scarcely forgivable.

The portrait of McDow is worthy of a place in the gallery of clerics in English fiction. His ministry resulted in an empty kirk, a much-frequented ale house, a neglected school, a careless, uncared-for people. When he officiated at the burial of Glenroy, the ceremony resembled more 'a clumsy heathen apotheosis than a Christian rite'. We feel that had Susan Ferrier written a Disruption novel she would have found ample material in the social problems of ministers and their wives who quitted the manse and a secure social position for uncertain prospects in the wilderness of 'vulgar, unendowed dissent'.

The *Edinburgh Review* of January 1842 rated *Destiny* too highly when the critic declared that the presentations of the establishments at Glenroy and Loch Dhu 'are conceived and executed with a skill which no female writer of the present day has surpassed', and, reviewing Susan Ferrier's three novels in the same article, the writer placed them 'on a level with those of Miss Austen', and, indeed, 'considerably above those of Miss Burney'. Such praise was surpassed some thirty years later by William Forsyth, Q.C. and man of letters, who considered that Susan's three novels, '*Marriage, Inheritance, and Destiny*, especially the two former, are among the best in the English language'.[1] While we may not agree with

1 In Forsyth's *The Novels and Novelists of the Eighteenth Century* (1871), and quoted in *Thomas Hardy's Notebooks*, edited by Evelyn Hardy (1955).

these extravagant eulogies nevertheless the novelist who could create Lady MacLaughlan, Uncle Adam, Miss Pratt, and the Rev. McDow was certainly not devoid of the gift of successful characterisation.

Scott recorded his impression of Susan Ferrier's personality. 'This gifted personage, besides having great talents, has conversation the least *exigeant* of any author, female at least, whom I have ever seen among the long list I have encountered with, simple, full of humour, and exceedingly ready at repartee, and all this without the least affectation of the blue stocking.'[1]

A late nineteenth-century writer observed that though Susan Ferrier has not flattered the Scots 'she has put them down as she found them to be, with their faults and their virtues, their crotchets and their prejudices; and yet with that strong, sturdy independence and true-heartedness, which, in spite of individual exceptions, make the Scotch nation what it has proved itself to be'.[2] She herself thought that 'perhaps, after all, the only uncloying pleasure in life is that of fault-finding'. That declaration should not be taken too literally, but it seems to hint at the source of her satire. She did not spare acid comments on the pretentious and eccentric society of Edinburgh. Of her kind of satire we find an analogy in art. Hogarth, who could exaggerate with ludicrous intent, commented on the absurdities of fashion and polite gesture in society in his picture, *Taste in High Life*.

Susan Ferrier's moral attitude requires some consideration. On examination it is seen to be an extraneous feature although she firmly believed that 'the only good purpose of a book is to inculcate morality, and convey some lesson of instruction as well as delight. I do not see that what is called a *good moral* can be dispensed with in a work of fiction.' Unfortunately, when she did moralise she was apt to become sententious. In furthering a moral sentiment she can make a

[1] *Scott's Journal* (1950), pp. 739–40.
[2] *Women Writers, etc.*, by C. J. Hamilton (1892), p. 242.

character use the most stilted language of the period, such as that spoken by poor Mary, admiring the view from Edinburgh's Calton Hill: 'The ideas which are inspired by the contemplation of such a spectacle as this are far—oh, how far!—superior to those excited by the mere works of art. There, I can, at best, think but of the inferior agents of Providence: here, the soul rises from nature to nature's God.' How different that is from the usual lively, pointed speech which suffuses most of *Marriage*.

If we compare the knowledge of Scottish Presbyterianism exemplified in, say, Lockhart's *Adam Blair*, with anything of the kind in Susan Ferrier's novels we realise the paucity of religious atmosphere in them. Only in her later years did she acquire a marked religious outlook.

Like that of Galt, Susan Ferrier's reputation suffered somewhat from being overshadowed by the fame and popularity of Scott. Nevertheless, in 1842 the *Edinburgh Review* could inform its readers that though her novels appeared while the public mind was attracted by Scott's romances 'yet her fictions were at once felt to possess peculiar and sterling merits of their own . . . the rare gift of genuine humour as opposed to mere wit and smartness . . . These qualities secured to the writings of Miss Ferrier, even during the ascendency of Scott, not indeed a noisy popularity, but yet an enviable place in the opinion of those whose opinion in such a question was most valuable.' Not only did Edinburgh enjoy *Marriage*, for instance, as something new in contemporary fiction, but it discussed the book with animation at interminable bluestocking tea-parties, trying to identify the characters. Lady MacLaughlan must be Mrs. Damer, the sculptor, or Aunts Grizzy, Jacky, and Nicky were recognizable as the Misses Edmonstone of George Street, distantly related to the Duke of Argyll, and so on.

Despite Susan Ferrier's satirical criticism of Scottish deficiencies she did not conceal her deep attachment to her native land and to its folk. For her no country could surpass

Scotland, which, she remarked, 'with all its faults, will ever
be to its own children the land of our love, our fathers'
home'.

This essay on Susan Ferrier would be incomplete if it
omitted to cite one or two of her uninhibited opinions of
other novelists' works. Her attitude to Scott's romances
vacillated. In 1816 she wrote: 'I've read *My Landlord's Tales*,
and can't abide them; but that's my shame, not their fault.'
But by 1823 she began to relent, to fall into line with
contemporary Scott enthusiasts. She then wrote: 'I am
reading *Peveril*, and like it, as I do all that author's works
for the imagination, wit, and humour that pervade them.'[1]
On Lockhart's *Adam Blair* she commented: 'It is powerfully
written, but painful and disagreeable to the greatest degree
and in other respects not fit to be mentioned.' As we have
seen, vulgarity had always been one of her pet aversions,
and so when she came upon the 'vulgar' elements in Galt's
work she was naturally shocked and expressed her dislike
in no uncertain terms. 'I have not read *Sir Andrew Wylie*,
as I can't endure that man's writings, and I'm told the
vulgarity of this beats print.'[2] We shall attempt an estimate
of the object of her censure in the essay that follows.

[1] *Memoir and Correspondence*, pp. 132, 165.
[2] A. Grant, *Susan Ferrier of Edinburgh*, (1957) p. 114.

II. JOHN GALT

On turning to John Galt we are confronted with several easily perceived contrasts between him and Susan Ferrier. Whereas she belonged to the professional class, Galt's social background was commercial. Her existence was comparatively serene; Galt's life was restless. His kindly humour differs from her rather merciless satire. He never set out to denigrate his fellowcountrymen; she, as we have seen, was not averse to passing severe strictures on Scottish vulgarity and uncouthness. There are few Scotticisms in her narratives; Galt indulged in a too free use of Scots dialect, on which something will be said later. Finally, Susan Ferrier wrote but three novels; John Galt expended his gifts in a too prolific output of miscellaneous writings.

The son of a shipmaster, he was born at Irvine, Ayrshire, on 2 May 1779. His family removing to Greenock, he there completed his education and became engaged as an office clerk in the Customs House, at the same time contributing mediocre verse and prose to local periodicals.

Becoming dissatisfied with his business connection at Greenock, he migrated to London, studied law and entered at Lincoln's Inn, although he was never called to the bar. He then obtained employment on the Continent in order to ascertain how far British goods could be exported in defiance of the Berlin and Milan Decrees. During his travels in the Mediterranean he met Byron in 1809. His commercial schemes did not prosper. Later (c. 1819) he was instrumental in getting passed through Parliament a bill promoted by the Union Canal Company of Scotland.

It was in Canada, however, that he expended most energy in practical affairs, but to little purpose as transpired. There he acted as agent for the claims of Canadians for losses incurred during the war of 1814 and as Secretary of the Canada Company for the purchase of crown land in the

24

colony. He was one of a commission to investigate the matter in Upper Canada. He was then appointed the Company's Canadian superintendent and founded the town of Guelph. But there was no immediate profit, stock fell, and Galt was superseded.[1] Returning to England, he had to meet heavy claims. In 1832 he was Secretary of the British American Land Company. His last years were spent at Greenock where he died on 11 April 1839.

Of a naturally unsettled temperament, Galt made an unpromising start in literature. He began by writing worthless poetry and plays that have gone to deserved oblivion. It was after the publication of *The Majolo*, an amateurish production of 1816, that Galt realised he would have to write for money. In *The Literary Life* (Vol. I, p. 185), he wrote: 'Hitherto I had written only to please myself, and had published more to acquire the reputation of a clever fellow than with the hope of making money; but . . . I saw that hereafter I was destined to eke out my income with my pen.' Eventually he produced about sixty books, several of a mixed miscellaneous nature (mostly hackwork) as well as some novels of inferior merit. Consequently, the corpus demands a winnowing of the grain from the chaff.

Before we comment on his major works, however, three books merit notice. In *Voyages and Travels* (1812) he gave his reactions to places of classical antiquity during his Mediterranean tour. An example is his comment on Syracuse, 'one of the very strongest fortresses in the kingdom [of Sicily]. The garrison was a British regiment, consisting of about six hundred men. In the town, there were upwards of twelve hundred ecclesiastics; therefore, it was necessary to have a garrison of foreigners.' As for the Temple of Concord and the Temple of Juno in Agrigentum, they seemed to Galt 'hardly worth a sabbath day's journey'. The church of St. Martin's in the Fields, London, was 'larger than both

---

[1] Galt is one of those to whom the authorship of 'The Canadian Boat Song' has been dubiously attributed. See E. MacCurdy's *A Literary Enigma* (1935), pp. 58–61.

of them put together, and infinitely more magnificent'.

The Member (1832) and *The Radical* (1832) are brief satirical novels with political themes which appeared during the controversy over the famous Reform Bill. The first concerns Archibald Jobbry, a canny, good-humoured Scot, who buys a seat in the House of Commons as member for Frailtown. In Parliament he maintains an independent position and manages to bestow high-salaried positions and annuities upon many of his relatives and friends. Latterly, he becomes a liberal Tory with moderate views. The concluding pages contain his opinions on taxation, rents, banking, the coming of the machine age, farm problems, and other economic subjects. Eventually he retires from the political arena and views the political scene as a spectator.

In *The Radical*, which Thackeray thought very clever but dull, Galt presents a broad satirical portrait of Nathan Butts, whose early business and domestic duties prevent his advancing the Radical cause. But when his mother dies he is free to promulgate Radical principles. By bribing the right people, he is sent to Parliament to represent the village of Mothy. Gradually he comes to view the Reform Bill as a 'mile-stone in the highway of perfectibility, and . . . worthy of all acceptation'. Although he is suddenly disqualified from voting because he has been elected by 'flagitious perjury', he is nevertheless sure of being 'returned with triumph and glory' at the first election under the Reform Bill. An interesting comparison could be made out between Nathan Butts and Harold Transome, the conventional Radical politician in George Eliot's *Felix Holt*. When Transome stands for Parliament his political convictions are not incompatible with 'treating' and other demoralising practices. Galt is competent enough, but he lacked the moral intensity that inspired George Eliot's vision of life.

Let us now consider those novels which have placed Galt in a peculiar and honourable niche in Scottish fiction. It has been asked if he was a major or a minor writer, and if he was overshadowed by Scott. Concerning the first query, we have no hesitation in concluding that the author of *The Ayrshire Legatees*, *Annals of the Parish*, *The Provost*, and *The Entail* cannot be regarded as a second-rate writer. At the same time, he has not that irresistible creative urge, those soaring flights of imagination, of the master novelist. As regards the second query, while Scott has definitely over-shadowed him in width or range and in that wizardry to which he alone had an indefinable access, the fact must be borne in mind that Galt's idiom was of a completely different complexion from that of Scott. Moreover, he was incapable of Scott's inexhaustible imagination, his wide appeal, his powers of characterisation. The 'Big Bow-Wow strain', as Scott characterised his own *métier*, was beyond Galt.

Nevertheless, within his circumscribed orbit, Galt did a distinct service to Scottish fiction by his absorption in his own age and by giving expression to the parochial outlook of the humbler Scottish middle-class. He was one of the first novelists to create and to popularise Scottish merchants, ministers, lairds and their ladies—all of them douce, pawky, and fond of clishmaclavers (i.e. gossiping). That in itself was no mean achievement, but it did not justify Galt's temerity in declaring that 'his literary resources were far greater in extent than those of Sir Walter Scott'.[1] By the later nineteenth century the merits of his fiction were recognised in some unlikely quarters. The intellectual George Meredith, for example, a novelist far removed from Galt's qualities, remarked in his *Essay on Comedy* that 'in our prose literature we have had delightful Comic writers . . . Galt's neglected novels have some characters and strokes of shrewd comedy.'

When Galt first addressed himself to what we now regard as his best fiction his aim was to represent realities faithfully, insisting on a close relationship to real life in style, character-ization, and incident. In 1820 he submitted *The Ayrshire Legatees* to William Blackwood, who, perceiving the

---

[1] As reported by R. P. Gillies in his *Memoirs of a Literary Veteran* (1851), Vol. III, p. 59.

originality of the work, accepted the MS. for publication in *Maga* from October 1820 to March 1821.

It is possible to discern a model for the book in Lockhart's *Peter's Letters to His Kinsfolk*. The epistolary forms of both have certain similarities. But an even more obvious prototype is Smollett's *Humphry Clinker*. Mrs. Pringle in the *Legatees*, for instance, makes the same vulgar misspellings as do Tabitha and Winifred Jenkins in *Humphry Clinker*. Winifred is capable of speaking about 'the holy bands of mattermoney' and Mrs. Pringle intimates that she is deeply involved in her daughter's 'matteromoneal affair'.

The tenuous plot of the *Legatees* concerns the Pringle family. Having received a letter from India informing him that his cousin, Colonel Armour, has died at Hyderabad and named him residuary legatee, Dr. Pringle goes with his family to London to settle the transference of the inheritance with Colonel Armour's agents. Finding himself heir to more than a hundred thousand pounds, the patriarch settles temporarily in London. Andrew Pringle, his son, having been called to the Scottish bar, obtains an intimate view of official and Parliamentary functions. Rachel, his romantically inclined daughter, marries the dashing young Captain Sabre, whom she had first met aboard the Leith smack on the way to London. In the end Dr. and Mrs. Pringle return home, Andrew goes to Paris, and Rachel departs on her honeymoon.

Though the *Legatees* is not a *great* work, nevertheless it reveals Galt's ability to delineate vividly Scottish men and manners in a true domestic environment. Dr. Pringle the clergyman, Galt's earliest lifelike character, has affinities with Fielding's Parson Adams. Both of them are gentle and naïve. Already, too, Galt uses satire in a kindly manner.

The *Legatees* was such an immediate success that Galt desired to follow it up with a tale as good. His initial idea for this was to write a village schoolmaster's register of local events. But, after a few years' interval, he altered his conception to a village minister's record of his parish. The book was to be a kind of Scottish *Vicar of Wakefield*, to which, however, the work in its final shape bore no resemblance. Had Crabbe turned to prose narrative he might have produced something akin to Galt's realistic treatment of the rural theme.

During its composition Galt informed Archibald Constable, the publisher, of his project; but the reply came that Scottish novels would never do. *Waverley*, be it remembered, had not yet appeared. The unfinished MS. was put aside. Later, Galt rediscovered it, read it over, thought well of it, and sent it to Blackwood. At first it was designated *The Pastor of His Parish*, but was eventually issued by Blackwood in 1821 under the title, *Annals of the Parish: or the Chronicle of Dalmailing, during the Ministry of the Rev. Micah Balwhidder*.[1]

This is the most balanced of Galt's Scottish stories. Strictly speaking, it is not a novel with a unified plot but rather a series of fictional sketches, or episodes, adroitly strung together. There is almost a complete absence of conspicuous intrusions by the author; the whole is moulded with an art that appears to be spontaneous. The fact should not be overlooked, of course, that a certain quota of the literary construction that shaped the *Annals* was as much due to Blackwood's careful revisions and alterations as to Galt's own invention. These changes were implemented with the author's permission although he did not always take kindly to Blackwood's supervision.

The parson's little troubles and triumphs are revealed in frank reflections in his journal. 'When we enjoy most, we have least to tell. I look back on this year [1784] as on a sunny spot in the valley, amidst the shadows of the clouds of time.' Again: 'I could mark a visible darkness of infidelity spreading in the corner of the vineyard committed to my keeping . . . But I said nothing. I knew that the faith could not be lost, and that it would be found purer and purer the more it was tried.' Or again: 'I am apt to confound the

---

1 The work is frequently misnamed *The Annals of the Parish*.

things of one occasion with those of another, which Mrs. Balwhidder says is an admonishment to me to leave off writing. But, please God, I will endeavour to fulfil this as I have through life tried, to the best of my capacity, to do every other duty . . . I have seen, in my time, many mutations and turnings, and ups and downs . . . But, in my own estate, I have had a large and liberal experience of goodness.'

The *Annals* reflects the social transformations—the influx of wealth, and the growth of commerce, farming, industry, the educational system, local government, administration— which invaded Scotland in the eighteenth century. The aim was appreciated by Mrs. Christian Isobel Johnstone, the novelist, who, in the year of its publication, noted that the design of the book 'is to present a lively record of that change in manners and national character which has within the last sixty years wrought such miracles around us', adding that 'the Statistical Account of Scotland will never be complete till the faithful annals of this homely and veracious chronicler are added to the appendix'.

The account of far-reaching events alternates, or becomes interwoven, with local gossip. What may be called the boom period in industry, 1785–95, saw large-scale establish- ments at New Lanark (famous as the scene of Robert Owen's socialistic experiments) and Blantyre in Lanarkshire. 'The factory system had arrived with its attendant problems in health, morals, and education.' Galt's fictitious 'Cayenne- ville' is typical of the growing transformation. The new town was built for the workers of the cotton-mill on the land of Mr. Cayenne, an American loyalist.

The Rev. Micah Balwhidder discovers that 'with wealth come wants, like a troop of clamorous beggars at the heels of a generous man, and it's hard to tell wherein the benefit of improvement in a country parish consists, especially to those who live by the sweat of their brow . . . In the midst of all this commercing and manufacturing, I began to discover signs of decay in the wonted simplicity of our country ways. Among the cotton-spinners and muslin-weavers of Cayenneville were several unsatisfied and ambitious spirits.'

Nevertheless, the effects of improved conditions in Dalmailing parish are summed up in the pastor's eloquent words: 'The minds of men were excited to new enterprises; a new genius, as it were, had descended upon the earth, and there was an erect and outlooking spirit abroad that was not to be satisfied with the taciturn regularity of ancient affairs.' We find a similar pronouncement at the close of *The Provost* where the narrator declares that he has endeavoured 'to show and to acknowledge, that there is a reforming spirit abroad among men, and that really the world is gradually growing better . . . and the main profit of the improvement will be reaped by those who are ordained to come after us.'

As in Galt's other major novels, the accretions of idio-syncratic character contribute piquancy to the variety of interest, which includes great events like the American Rebellion and the French Revolution as they affect the Dalmailing community, also the spread of tea-drinking and the prevalent smuggling trade.

Balwhidder and Cayenne are the most effective characters. The pastor's egocentricity and loneliness are stressed in bold relief. Moreover, his parochialism finds outlet, as in his comment on Charlie Malcolm's friend: 'How, indeed, could Mr. Howard know anything of sound doctrine, being educated, as he told me, at Eton school, a prelatic establish-ment.'

The pastor is of course the presiding genius of the book. The peaceable minister has his troubles with the hot-tempered, heretical Cayenne, whose redemption he tries to effect after many struggles. Cayenne's blasphemous reply, as Justice of the Peace, to two young democratic weavers is said to be based on a celebrated real event in which the judge was the brutal Lord Braxfield, who figures in R. L. Stevenson's *Weir of Hermiston*.

The episode is related by the parson in these words:

Mr. Cayenne, who had been some time before appointed a justice of
the peace, came over from Wheatrig-house to the Cross Keys, where he
sent for me and divers other respectable inhabitants of the clachan, and
told us that he was to have a sad business, for a warrant was out to bring
before him two democratic weaver lads, on a suspicion of high treason.
Scarcely were the words uttered, when they were brought in, and he
began to ask them how they dared to think of dividing, with their
liberality and equality principles, his and every other man's property in
the country. The men answered him in a calm manner, and told him
they sought no man's property, but only their own natural rights; upon
which he called them traitors and reformers. They denied they were
traitors, but confessed they were reformers, and said they knew not how
that should be imputed to them as a fault, for that the greatest men of all
times had been reformers. 'Was not', they said, 'our Lord Jesus Christ a
reformer?' 'And what the devil did he make of it?', cried Mr. Cayenne,
bursting with passion. 'Was he not crucified? . . .'[1] Nothing, however
was found against the weaver lads; but I never, from that day, could
look on Mr. Cayenne as a Christian, though surely he was a true
Government-man.'

Perhaps the most impressive, powerful, and daring scene
is that in which Cayenne exhibits peculiar behaviour when
Balwhidder visits him on his deathbed. The pastor, antici-
pating that he might turn him from his unregenerate state,
said that he hoped 'he would soon be more at ease, and he
should bear in mind that the Lord chasteneth whom he
loveth'.

'The devil take such love,' was his awful answer . . . However, I was
resolved to do my duty to the miserable sinner, let him say what he
would. Accordingly, I stooped towards him with my hands on my
knees, and said in a compassionate voice, 'It's very true, sir, that you are
in great agony, but the goodness of God is without bound.'

[1] At the trial of Joseph Gerrald, the political reformer, in 1794, he said
to Lord Braxfield, the presiding judge: 'All great men have been reformers
—even our Saviour himself!' To which Braxfield added 'Muckle he made
of that; he was hanged!'—*The Real Weir of Hermiston* by W. D. Lyell
(1903), pp. 19–20.

'Curse me if I think so, doctor', replied the dying uncircumcised Philistine. 'I am, however, no saint, as you know, doctor, so I wish you to put in a word for me, doctor; for you know that in these times, doctor, it is the duty of every good subject to die a Christian.'

'I knelt down and prayed for him with great sincerity, imploring the Lord . . . that it would please him to lift up . . . the chastening hand which was laid so heavily upon his aged servant . . . at which Mr. Cayenne cried out, 'None of that stuff, doctor; you know that I cannot call myself his servant.'

'I made no reply, but continued, 'Thou hearest, O Lord! how he confesses his unworthiness. Let not thy compassion, therefore, be with-held, but verify to him the words that I have spoken in faith, of the boundlessness of thy goodness, and the infinite multitude of thy tender mercies.' . . . Mr. Cayenne raised his head, and giving me a queer look, said, 'That last clause of your petition, doctor, was well put, and I think, too, it has been granted, for I am easier . . . I have, no doubt, doctor, given much offence in the world, and oftenest when I meant to do good; but I have wilfully injured no man, and as God is my judge, and his goodness, you say, is so great, he may perhaps take my soul into his holy keeping.' In saying which words, Mr. Cayenne dropped his head upon his breast, his breathing ceased, and he was wafted away out of this world with as little trouble as a blameless child.'

At the close of the chronicle an arresting passage might be construed as prophetic of present-day aims at Church unity. Balwhidder perceives that there 'has come a spirit of greater liberality than the world knew before, bringing men of adverse principles and doctrines into a more humane communion with each other, showing that it's by the mollifying influence of knowledge the time will come to pass when the tiger of papistry shall lie down with the lamb of reformation, and the vultures of prelacy be as harmless as the Presbyterian doves.' The rounding-off is more satisfactory than that of the companion novel, *The Provost*. The pastor wishes that he may soon be gathered to his fathers where he expects to meet 'all the old and long-departed sheep of my flock'. It sounds a 'dying fall'. Galt was never to recapture the natural spontaneity with which he invested the *Annals*.

Although *Sir Andrew Wylie* (1822) was Galt's first full-length Scottish novel, it does not call for an extensive survey. Only the early chapters are in Galt's best vein; the rest is more or less *pastiche*. The contemporary political background is etched in deftly. Evidence of Galt's indebtedness to the novel of sensibility is apparent. As for the gipsy scenes, they remind us of those in *Guy Mannering*.

Turning now to *The Provost* (1822), which Galt misjudged a better work than the *Annals*, we may perhaps conjecture that the author relied, to some extent, upon documentary records for his supposedly authentic material. His insight into country-town life provides a sociological theme.

The *Annals* had shown the progress of improvement in a rural district of the West of Scotland; *The Provost* describes a similar process in a township of the same region. It is the autobiographical success-story of Provost Pawkie who, having 'thrice reached the highest station of life in his line', outlines the main events of his career from the time of his apprenticeship to Mr. Remnant, a tailor, until his retirement after representing for many years 'the supreme power and authority of Majesty in the royal borough of Gudetown'.

As bailie, Pawkie had succeeded in subduing the rivalry between two factions of the Town Council, and with pride he points to the improvements he has supervised after having become Provost of the burgh: corruption in business and politics decreased, new roads were made, sanitary measures were enacted, etc. The accounts of these developments form the major part of the book, and the total impression they convey lends vividness to the narrative. *The Provost* is as intimate a revelation of Scottish municipal life as the *Annals* is that of a Scottish rural community.

Provost Pawkie aims at reform even if he has an eye to the main chance in the process. We obtain glimpses of old burgh customs which, however, will soon dwindle to decay. Relations between countryside and town are changing. Wealth (economics has become one of Galt's preoccupations) is passing from lairds and land-owners to the merchant burgesses so that, to quote the author, 'the bit prideful lairdies were just looked down upon by our gawsie [jolly] big-bellied burgesses, not a few of whom had heritable bonds on their estates'. In this book the entanglements of eighteenth-century phraseology with which the narrative is embellished, although they are attractive in themselves, impede the flow and sequence of the prose.

Galt's next considerable performance, *The Entail* (1823), is the study of a dominant character, Claud Walkinshaw, whose vaulting ambition to regain the land lost by his grandfather, his inflexible self-assertion, pangs of conscience, and attacks of remorse are traits not unlike some of those in Hardy's Michael Henchard, the Mayor of Casterbridge. The grim subject and the improbability of certain incidents, too, presage Hardy's fiction. Despite obvious limitations in creative invention, the novel's merits entitle it to rank as superior to any of Galt's work with the exception of the *Annals*.

The story turns upon the disinheriting, for estate reasons, by Claud Walkinshaw, Laird of Grippy, of his eldest son Charles, and on the events which result therefrom. Walkinshaw, the representative of an old but ruined family, has suffered from penury, but at an early age he aims at the reconquest of the family estates. To achieve this he sacrifices every secondary consideration.

His youth was spent as a pedlar, and when, having established himself in trade, he decides to marry he goes 'where money is'. Charles is his favourite son, but paternal affection gives way before the ruling passion. Watty, the second son, a half-wit from birth, is heir to the estate of his maternal grandfather. It is only through a transaction depending on the possession of this property that a Walkinshaw can be reinstated in possession of the undiminished Walkinshaw estates.

To these circumstances Charles is sacrificed, and his father's dream seems at last to be realized. But, though he has gained his point, the old man finds he is further than ever from contentment. In the midst of his woes Claud is carried off by a paralytic shock. The evil he has done, however, lives after him. The calculating business man, the youngest of the sons, succeeds to the role of principal character.

Galt's naturalistic treatment in this book has been compared with Zola's, Balzac's, and Galsworthy's in *The Forsyte Saga*, but Galt's kind of humour is foreign to these other writers.

A particularly dramatic episode is that in Chapter lxviii where James Walkinshaw, Charles's son, who wishes to give up the proposed match with his cousin Robina as he has bestowed his affections on one Ellen Frazer, gives way to an outburst about 'interest':

'Do think, James, how prejudicial it must be to your interests to quarrel with my father?,' said Robina.

'Curse that eternal word "interests"!' was the unceremonious answer. 'Your father seems to think that human beings have nothing but interests; that the heart keeps a ledger, and values everything in pounds sterling. Our best affections, our dearest feelings, are with him only as tare, that should pass for nothing in the weight of moral obligations.'

'But stop', said Robina . . . 'tell me what all this means—what has affections and dear feelings to do with your counting-house affairs?—I thought you and he never spoke of anything but rum puncheons and sugar cargoes.'

'He is incapable of knowing the value of anything less tangible and vendible!' exclaimed her cousin—'but I have done with both him and you . . . Interest seems the everlasting consideration of our family—interest disinherited my father—interest made my uncle Walter consign my mother to poverty—interest proved the poor repentant wretch insane—interest claims the extinction of all I hold most precious in life—and interest would make me baser than the most sordid of all our sordid race.'

Apart from Claud, all the portraits of the Walkinshaw family are admirable, especially the remarkable delineation of Watty, the half-wit. Even the minor character of Betty

Bodle is distinguished for her boldness, frankness, and freedom of conduct.

The general outlook is tinged with an almost Hardyan sense of disillusionment, and Galt's recourse to sensational incident was to be a characteristic of Hardy's plot contrivances. The development of a dramatic situation, however, is not really helped by Galt's excessive use of dialect. Objections had already been raised concerning the Scots idiomatic style in *The Provost*, but Galt defended his own use of the Scots vernacular in these words: 'What has thus been regarded as a fault by some, others acquainted with the peculiarities of the language may be led to consider as a beauty.' There can be no bad taste in using Scots to express 'sentiments and feelings entirely Scottish'.[1]

Here, for instance, is Watty's comment on his wife's (Betty Bodle's) funeral which he refuses to attend: 'I canna understand what for a' this fykerie's about a lump o' yird? Sho'elt intil a hole, and no fash me.'[2] It is hardly surprising that Henry Mackenzie (author of *The Man of Feeling*) confessed his inability to understand the language of Galt's characters or that Scott declared: 'Mr. Galt, though a man of very considerable powers, sometimes out-Scottifies the Scotch dialect.' Scott himself never abused his superb command of the vernacular by distortion or exaggeration.

The elucidation of Claud's complex personality is a *tour de force*. Having become isolated from society, he grows introspective, and feels unable to cope with the trend of events:

He began to think there was something in the current of human affairs over which he could acquire no control, and that, although, in pursuing so steadily the single purpose of recovering his family inheritance, his endeavours had, till this period, proved eminently successful, he yet saw, with dismay, that, from the moment other interests came to be blended with those which he considered so peculiarly his own, other causes also

---

[1] *Ringan Gilhaize* (1823), pp. 311, 312.

[2] 'I cannot understand what for all this petty trouble about a lump of earth. Shove it into a hole and don't trouble me.'

came into operation, and turned, in spite of all his hedging and prudence, the whole issue of his labours awry. He perceived that human power was set at nought by the natural course of things.

Galt's first historical novel, *Ringan Gilhaize* (1823), was in the nature of a challenge. He intended to counteract, in some measure, what he considered was Scott's levity and ridicule in his treatment of the Covenanters in *Old Mortality*. The book is a family chronicle ranging through three generations, covering part of the Reformation period and the Covenanting days from the Restoration to Claverhouse's death at Killiecrankie. The conflict between Presbyterians and Royalists is presented with consistency. We are not spared, of course, the revelation of hardship and misery which were caused by heartless oppression.

Galt himself was no religious fanatic, but he despised hypocrisy. The Covenanters are depicted in a favourable light. To strengthen his understanding of the Presbyterian norm Galt relied largely on Knox's *History of the Reformation in Scotland*. Where he differed most from Scott was in interpreting Claverhouse. 'The implacable rage with which Claverhouse persecuted the Covenanters', Ringan observes, 'has been extenuated by some discreet historians, on the plea of his being an honourable officer deduced from his soldierly worth elsewhere; whereas the truth is, that his cruelties in the shire of Ayr, and other of our western parts, were less the fruit of his instructions, wide and severe as they were, than of his own mortified vanity and malignant revenge.'[1]

While we may agree with Sir George Douglas's summary of the work, viz. that 'few incidents are omitted and the skill shown by the Author in stringing the pearls of history upon the thread of his narrative is not the least of the merits he displays', we must also concede that Galt had not Scott's learning, he could not cast Scott's peculiar romantic aura over the scenes he describes, and he did not command Scott's living characterisations—there are no figures in

[1] *Ringan Gilhaize*, III. pp. 88 f.

Ringan Gilhaize equal to Scott's Poundtext, Mucklewrath, Macbriar, Bessie McLure, Guse Gibbie, and, above all, Mause Headrigg.

In *The Last of the Lairds* (1826) Galt reverted to auto-biographical narrative and to further exploration of the Scottish scene but he did not seem to have his former confidence in tackling his subject. Indeed, the execution of the tale resulted in a prolonged quarrel between him and Blackwood. While Galt was grateful for suggested altera-tions regarding scenes and incidents, he would not brook interference with plot and characters. Blackwood wanted the novel to contain more grace in form and matter. D. M. Moir, another Blackwood author, altered the MS. of the *Lairds* and expressed his prudish objections to Galt's alleged vulgarity in the novel. 'The only set out against all these excellencies', he commented, 'is the leaven of vulgarity and uncleanness but too frequently to be met with in these pages; and indeed the only objection I ever hear advanced against the writings of Galt, which from the nature and true tone of feeling can never cease to interest. I humbly opine that for readers of delicate nerves we have still too much in the Laird of tramping claes with kilted petticoats, bare ancles, and cutty stools.'[1]

It is a pity that Galt repeated, with less success, the social theme he had already portrayed with his anti-romantic vision. Throughout the unsatisfactory plot, with not a few cynical touches, Galt pictures the waning of the wealth and influence of landed families and the rise of a class which came to be designated the *nouveau riche*. The laird himself is not as attractive as Sir Andrew Wylie. Notwithstanding, the *Lairds* is valuable as further evidence of Galt's steadily maintained middle-class attitude.

For much of his literary career Galt found it necessary to continue pot-boiling. Such works as *Southennan*, depicting Scottish manners and customs in Queen Mary's reign, or

---

[1] Short three-legged stools; 'stools of repentance'.

the much-abused *Life of Lord Byron*, are quite inferior manifestations of his capabilities. As will have been gathered from this survey, *The Ayrshire Legatees*, *Annals of the Parish*, *The Provost*, and *The Entail* constitute the best of his literary achievement.

To a certain extent Galt was the founder of a school of Scottish literature in which he still maintains eminence. D.M. Moir's *Mansie Wauch* (1828) is akin to Galt's work in manner, though its humour tends more to caricature and its sentimentality is more extreme than anything in Galt. But there is really little justification for the assumption that Galt was a forerunner of the Kailyard story-tellers. His vigorous feeling is in direct contrast to the Kailyarders' saccharine, lachrymose sentiment.

Galt's moral purpose is always implied; there is never pure didacticism; rigid, orthodox, even conventional, morality is inconspicuous. Exaggeration and caricature were eschewed by him as much as they were courted by Susan Ferrier, and in contradistinction to her repeated attacks on vulgarity, we find unmistakable distillations of *petit-bourgeois* vulgarity in many of Galt's works. Jeffrey, that exacting critic of *The Edinburgh Review*, considered there was too much vulgarity, as in *The Last of the Lairds*. But we must remember that as Galt set out to present character realistically in the surroundings of the time, he could not well dispense with the coarse vulgarisms which were natural accompaniments to the way of life he was depicting.

Though Galt's inventive powers are limited, though he rarely touches on the love theme, though he is addicted to diffuseness and writes in an uneven, sometimes inelegant, style which has no poetic vein running through it, despite these defects he comes out triumphant in his keen observation of parochialism. That is perhaps his main feature. His comic relief occasionally savours of knock-about humour reminiscent of Smollett's; his sprinklings of tragedy have little in common with, say, Hardy's challenge to the injustice of the human lot.

For most of his life, Galt linked literary pursuits with practical ones. He was no dedicated author. His attitude to the literary vocation, which he considered an occupation secondary to that of practical affairs, was self-confessed in his *Autobiography* with all the emphasis of Trollope. He states his view when referring to his friend James Park, who

seemed to consider excellence in literature as of a more sacred nature than ever I did, who looked upon it as a means of influence; indeed it is but few authors who are very enviable; it is a poor trade.

Notwithstanding I have put together many books, and become so various an author, it has been rather in consequence of the want of active engagements than from a predominant predilection for the art. I would, no doubt, unless my time had been fully occupied with business, have still been an author, but would have followed the promptings and impulses of my own taste instead of thinking of what might be profitable.[1]

It was for his ill-arranged *Autobiography* that Galt reserved what views he entertained concerning art. In general, he was singularly deficient in aesthetic feeling. In his fiction we never come upon allusions to famous artists as we do when perusing the Waverley and the Wessex Novels wherein Scott and Hardy advert to the other arts for apt similes.

His view of Nature was more Wordsworthian than the neo-classical ideal of general, universal Nature as opposed to what is local and particularised. In his *Literary Life* he remarks specifically: 'I can see nothing in Nature that is not systematic—a continual preordination of causes and effects demonstrating that some incomprehensible intelligence must have been exercised from the beginning.'[2]

Galt had independence, self-confidence, self-assertiveness. There are more substance, inquiry, and speculation in his mental make-up than in that of Susan Ferrier. He penetrated to the heart of sociological thought. True, Elizabeth Hamil-

[1] In *The Literary Life* he asserts definitely: 'I have ever held literature to be a secondary pursuit'—Vol. I, p. 351.

[2] Vol. I, p. 60.

ton's *The Cottagers of Glenburnie* (1808) had attempted to
expose the dirt and squalor that were typical of many a
Scottish village in those days in order to voice her views on
a practical branch of reform, but she had little penetration
or foresight. It remained for Galt to consider thoroughly
the implications of social trends.

He was no believer in systems of a theoretical nature.
When, in the *Annals*, Balwhidder says he has often thought
'that love and charity, far more than reason or justice,
formed the tie that holds the world, with all its jarring
wants and woes, in social dependence and obligation
together', he is probably expressing one of the author's
ideals. Galt seemed to maintain that self-interest should be
linked with a disposition favourable to social welfare. He
had implicit faith in social progress. Taking stock of
contemporary problems, at the same time he recognised
the value of the past. Like Provost Pawkie he thought 'that
if we judge of past events by present motives, and do not
try to enter into the spirit of the age when they took place,
and to see them with the eyes with which they were really
seen, we shall conceit[1] many things to be of a bad and
wicked character, that were not thought so harshly of by
those who witnessed them, nor even by those who, perhaps,
suffered from them ... The spirit of their own age was
upon them, as that of ours is upon us.' Galt's eminent
service to Scottish fiction was in seeing the spirit of his own
age and giving it permanent memorial.

He disliked the current 'marvellous' novels; he wished
his own stories of contemporary, or near-contemporary,
Scottish life to be considered as 'theoretical histories' rather
than 'novels or romances', and he rightly claimed to have
been one of the first practitioners of the genre. 'Many,
I am very free to allow', he wrote in his *Autobiography*,
'have vastly surpassed my endeavours in the historical
novel, but I do not think that I have had numerous pre-

[1] Imagine, think.

cursors, in what I would call my theoretical histories of society, limited, though they were required by the subject, necessarily to the events of a circumscribed locality.'

Conflicting personal impressions of Galt the man are on record. In 1813 Byron entered in his *Journal*: 'Galt called ... We are old fellow-travellers, and, with all his eccentricities, he has much strong sense, experience of the world, and is, as far as I have seen, a good-natured philosophical fellow.' But J. G. Lockhart and John Wilson ('Christopher North') 'found the author of the *Legatees* prosy and pompous, and put no faith in his knowledge of the world'. Much later, in 1832, after he had met Galt, Carlyle wrote in his note-book: 'Galt looks old, is deafish; has the air of a sedate Greenock Burgher; mouth indicating sly humour, and self-satisfaction; the eyes old and without lashes gave me a sort of wae [sorrowful] interest for him. He wears spectacles, and is hard of hearing: a very large man; and eats and drinks with a certain west-country gusto and research. Said little; but that little peaceable, clear, and gutmüthig [good-natured].' An even more favourable impression was set down by William Jerdan, the Scots journalist, who, praising Galt's sense of humour, his shrewdness, and credulity, pronounced him 'entirely modest, unaffected, and not in the least opinionated'.

In conclusion, it would be a mistake to dismiss Susan Ferrier and John Galt as spent forces. They survive as pioneers in the establishment of a new type of Scottish fiction which they enriched with their own examples in the kind.

SUSAN FERRIER and JOHN GALT

A Select Bibliography

(Books published in London, unless stated otherwise)

SUSAN FERRIER

Collected Works:

MISS FERRIER'S NOVELS. 6 vols. (1882).

THE NOVELS OF SUSAN FERRIER, ed. R. B. Johnson. 6 vols. (1894).

THE WORKS OF SUSAN FERRIER, with an Introduction by Lady M. Sackville. 4 vols. (1928).

Separate Works:

MARRIAGE, a Novel. 3 Vols. Edinburgh (1818)
—published anonymously. New edition, with biographical preface by A. Goodrich-Freer and critical notices by Walter, Earl of Iddesleigh. 2 vols. 1902. In Everyman's Library with an Introduction by H. L. Morrow, 1928, reprinted, 1953; and in Nelson's Classics, 1953.

THE INHERITANCE. 3 vols. Edinburgh (1824)
—published anonymously. New edition, with biographical preface by A. Goodrich-Freer and critical notices by Walter, Earl of Iddesleigh, 2 vols. 1903.

DESTINY: OR, THE CHIEF'S DAUGHTER, 3 vols. Edinburgh (1831)
—a new one-volume edition, revised and corrected by Susan Ferrier, 1841.

Some Biographical and Critical Studies:

WOMEN WRITERS, THEIR WORKS AND WAYS, by C. J. Hamilton, First Series (1892).

THE BLACKWOOD GROUP, by Sir G. Douglas. Edinburgh (1897).

MEMOIR AND CORRESPONDENCE OF SUSAN FERRIER 1782–1854 (1898)
—based on her Private Correspondence, collected by her grand-nephew, John Ferrier, edited bv J. A. Doyle; reissued, 1929.

THE WOMEN NOVELISTS, by R. B. Johnson (1918).

'Miss Ferrier', by G. Saintsbury. *Collected Essays and Papers*, vol. 1, 1923.

SUSAN FERRIER OF EDINBURGH, A BIOGRAPHY, by A. Grant, Denver, Colorado (1957).

JOHN GALT

Bibliography:

'The Bibliography of John Galt', by H. Lumsden. *Records of Glasgow Bibliographical Society*, vol. ix, 1931
—obviously incomplete, it includes contributions to periodicals, miscellanies, etc.

Collected Works:

WORKS OF JOHN GALT, edited by D. S. Meldrum, with an Introduction by S. R. Crockett, 8 vols. Edinburgh (1895, 1896).

THE WORKS OF JOHN GALT, ed. D. S. Meldrum and W. Roughead. 10 vols. Edinburgh (1936).

Separate Works:

VOYAGES AND TRAVELS IN THE YEARS 1809, 1810, AND 1811; CONTAINING STATISTICAL, COMMERCIAL, AND MISCELLANEOUS OBSERVATIONS ON GIBRALTAR, SARDINIA, SICILY, MALTA, SERIGO, AND TURKEY. (1812).

THE MAJOLO: A TALE. 2 vols. (1816)
—published anonymously.

THE EARTHQUAKE: A TALE. 3 vols. Edinburgh (1820)
—published anonymously.

THE AYRSHIRE LEGATEES: OR THE PRINGLE FAMILY. Edinburgh (1821)
—published anonymously. Frequently reprinted with *Annals of the Parish*.

ANNALS OF THE PARISH: OR THE CHRONICLE OF DALMAILING, DURING THE MINISTRY OF THE REV. MICAH BALWHIDDER. Edinburgh (1821)
—published anonymously. Edited by G. S. Gordon, 1908; with an Introduction by G. Baillie MacDonald in Everyman's Library, 1910, reprinted 1920, 1926; with a Preface by W. M. Parker in Nelson's Classics, Edinburgh, 1952. There have been several other reprints.

SIR ANDREW WYLIE, OF THAT ILK. 3 vols. Edinburgh (1822)
—published anonymously. Reprinted 1841, 1850, 1854, 1868, etc.

THE PROVOST. Edinburgh (1822)
—published anonymously. Reprinted with *The Steamboat* and *The Omen*, Edinburgh, 1842, 1850, 1869.

THE ENTAIL: OR THE LAIRDS OF GRIPPY. 3 vols. Edinburgh (1823)
—in The World's Classics, edited by J. Ayscough, 1913.

RINGAN GILHAIZE: OR THE COVENANTERS. 3 vols. Edinburgh (1823)
—published anonymously. New edition, edited by Sir George Douglas, 1899.

THE LAST OF THE LAIRDS: OR THE LIFE AND OPINIONS OF MALACHI MAILINGS, ESQ. OF AULDBIGGINGS. Edinburgh (1826)
—reprinted, 1926.

THE RADICAL: AN AUTOBIOGRAPHY (1832).

THE MEMBER: AN AUTOBIOGRAPHY, by Archibald Jobbry (pseud.) (1832).

THE AUTOBIOGRAPHY OF JOHN GALT. 2 vols. (1833).

THE LITERARY LIFE AND MISCELLANIES. 3 vols. Edinburgh (1834)
—contains essays, poems, tales, etc.

Some Biographical and Critical Studies:

'Biographical Memoir of John Galt', by D. M. Moir
—prefixed to *Annals of the Parish* and *The Ayrshire Legatees* in Blackwood's Standard Novels, Vol. 1, Edinburgh (1841).

THE BLACKWOOD GROUP, by Sir G. Douglas. Edinburgh (1897).

JOHN GALT, by R. K. Gordon, with bibliography. Toronto (1920).

JOHN GALT, by J. W. Aberdein (1936).

'John Galt, Social Historian', by W. M. Brownlie. *Papers of the Greenock Philosophical Society*, 1952
—the John Galt Lecture for 1951. This is a detailed survey of social change and industrial development within the period of *Annals of the Parish*.

JOHN GALT'S SCOTTISH STORIES 1820–1823, by E. Frykman. Uppsala (1959)
—the most comprehensive analysis not only of the stories under discussion but of Galt's literary merits and demerits in general.

WRITERS AND THEIR WORK: NO. 186

The
Restoration
Court Poets

by VIVIAN de SOLA PINTO

Published for the British Council
and the National Book League
by Longmans, Green & Co

Three shillings and sixpence net

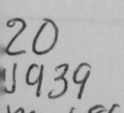

The court wits and poets of the Restoration have usually been regarded as talented debauchees. Macaulay's reference to their 'outrageous profaneness and licentiousness' is typical of the moralistic condemnation to which they have been subjected. Professor Pinto argues that 'the merry gang', as Marvell called them, were no mere idle profligates, but intellectuals reacting against the formality of the elder Cavaliers and the narrowness of the Puritans.

He examines the writings of four Court poets, all of whom practised two chief kinds of poetry: the love lyric, and the satire. Although they were amateurs they were not *dilettanti*, and they rendered certain valuable services to English poetry. In particular, they preserved the lyrical spirit in an age dominated by the new scientific movement; and they ensured the continuance in English poetry of a tradition of vernacular and colloquial verse which might otherwise have vanished.

V. de S. Pinto is Emeritus Professor of English at the University of Nottingham. His *Restoration Carnival* (1954) is a detailed study of the poets of the period, and he has edited the poems and written the life of Rochester. His most recent publications in other fields include *Crisis in English Poetry 1880-1940* (1951), *The Common Muse* (1957), which he edited with A. E. Rodway, and an edition, with Warren Roberts, of *The Complete Poems of D. H. Lawrence* (1964).

Bibliographical Series
of Supplements to 'British Book News'
on Writers and Their Work

GENERAL EDITOR
Geoffrey Bullough

JOHN WILMOT 2nd EARL OF ROCHESTER
from the painting attributed to J. HUYSMANS in the National Portrait Gallery

THE
RESTORATION
COURT POETS

JOHN WILMOT, EARL OF ROCHESTER
CHARLES SACKVILLE, EARL OF DORSET
SIR CHARLES SEDLEY · SIR GEORGE ETHEREGE

by
VIVIAN de SOLA PINTO

PUBLISHED FOR
THE BRITISH COUNCIL
AND THE NATIONAL BOOK LEAGUE
BY LONGMANS, GREEN & CO

LONGMANS, GREEN & CO LTD
48 Grosvenor Street, London W.1

*Associated companies, branches and
representatives throughout the world*

First published 1965
© Vivian de Sola Pinto 1965

*Printed in Great Britain by
F. Mildner & Sons, London, E.C.1*

CONTENTS

¶ JOHN WILMOT, 2nd EARL OF ROCHESTER was the son of a Cavalier general. Born in 1647, he was educated at Wadham College, Oxford, where he took his M.A. in 1660. He then travelled in France and Italy, returning to England in 1664, when he appeared at court and earned a reputation for wit and dissipation. He served at sea in the Dutch war in 1665-6. Charles II enjoyed his company but he was banished from court more than once for his outspoken satires on the king. His health declined in the late sixteen-seventies and in 1679 he made the acquaintance of Gilbert Burnet, afterwards Bishop of Salisbury, with whom he had a series of conversations on religion in the winter of 1679-80. After a dramatic conversion to Christianity, he died on 26 July 1680.

¶ CHARLES SACKVILLE, 6th EARL OF DORSET, born in 1643, became Lord Buckhurst in 1652 when his father inherited the title of Earl of Dorset. After spending a year at Westminster School, he travelled on the Continent, returning to England soon after the Restoration. He collaborated with Sedley and others in a translation of a tragedy of Corneille, which was produced in 1663, and in June of that year took part with Sedley in a wild frolic at the Cock Tavern in Covent Garden. He served at sea against the Dutch in 1665, and in 1677 inherited the earldom of Dorset. In the House of Lords in 1689 he voted in favour of offering the throne to William and Mary and he became Lord Chamberlain to the new monarchs. He was a generous patron to many men of letters. He died in January 1705/6.

¶ SIR CHARLES SEDLEY (or SIDLEY), born in 1639, was the son of a Kentish baronet. He was educated at Wadham College, Oxford and inherited the baronetcy on the death of his brother in 1656. After the Restoration he became a lively member of the 'merry gang' at court. His comedy The Mulberry Garden was staged in 1668, his tragedy Antony and Cleopatra in 1677 and a second comedy Bellamira in 1687. He was M.P. for New Romney and was a frequent and vigorous speaker in the Commons after the Revolution. He died in August 1701.

¶ SIR GEORGE ETHEREGE, born in 1635, probably spent part of his early life in France, where his father died in 1649. He was apprenticed to a London attorney in 1653 and made the acquaintance of Buckhurst (Dorset) through the success of his play The Comical Revenge in March 1664. His second comedy She Wou'd If She Cou'd was staged in February 1667-8 and in August 1668 he went to Constantinople as secretary to the British ambassador. He was in London in 1671 and his best comedy The Man of Mode was produced with great success in 1676. In 1679 he was knighted, and in 1685 he went to Ratisbon (Regensburg) as British envoy to the Diet of the Empire. At the Revolution he relinquished his post at Ratisbon and went to Paris, where he died in May 1692.

THE
RESTORATION COURT POETS

I

INTRODUCTION

THE last group of English courtier poets belonged to a set of lively young people in whose company Charles II spent much of his time after the Restoration. In 1661 the Duke of Ormonde described them to the Chancellor Clarendon as 'confident young men who abhorred all discourse that was serious, and, in the liberty they assumed in drollery and raillery, preserved no reverence towards God or man, but laughed at all sober men, and even at religion itself'. The historian Burnet gives us the names of some of these 'confident young men': 'the three most eminent wits of that time . . . the earls of Dorset and Rochester and Sir Charles Sidley'. A brilliant addition to the group was George Etherege, who became acquainted with Lord Buckhurst (afterwards Earl of Dorset) as a result of the success of his first play, *The Comical Revenge*, in March 1664. These young men together with the slightly older and immensely rich Duke of Buckingham and a number of less distinguished figures formed the circle known as the Court Wits, described by Andrew Marvell as 'the merry gang', who led a gay, dissipated life in the sixteen-sixties and -seventies, the period called by Dryden 'A very Merry Dancing, Drinking, Laughing, Quaffing, and unthinking Time'. Legends clustered round the personalities of the Wits, and they were built up into figures of diabolical wickedness in the age of the new puritanism which followed the Revolution. Macaulay in the second chapter of his *History of England* speaks in horrified tones of 'the open profligacy of the court and Cavaliers' after the Restoration and 'the outrageous profaneness and licentiousness of the Buckinghams and the Sedleys'. Unfortunately criticism of their writings was for long coloured by this moralistic condemnation of their lives. Now that the great flood of

7

English puritanism has subsided it is possible to see the Wits
and their writings in a truer perspective.

They were certainly no mere idle profligates. Their
diversions included music, the theatre, reading and translating the classics, and literary discussion as well as women and
drinking. Both Rochester and Buckhurst fought as volun-
teers at sea in the Dutch war. Rochester, surprisingly,
seems to have been an affectionate, if not a faithful, husband
and a good landlord. Dorset (Buckhurst) was a generous and
discerning patron of poets and dramatists. Sedley, after a
riotous youth, became a useful member of the House of
Commons, and Etherege was a successful dramatist and later,
by seventeenth-century standards, an efficient diplomat.
They were men living between two worlds, on the one hand
the old hierarchical universe mirrored in the traditional life
of the Court, on the other the new materialistic philosophy
and science and the atomized society of free individuals.
They can be seen now not, as they have been traditionally
pictured, a set of young royalists indulging in wild orgies
as a reaction from the austerity of the Rule of the Saints, but
as a post-war generation reacting as much against the stiff
formality of the old cavaliers as against the narrow religiosity
of the puritans. They were intellectuals as well as gay young
men about town. Both Rochester and Sedley received part
of their education at Wadham College, Oxford, one of the
cradles of the new experimental science, and they all read
and admired the works of Thomas Hobbes, the first English
philosopher to propound a purely materialistic and utili-
tarian system. Hobbes was to them something very much
like what Marx was to the young English poets of the
nineteen-thirties, a symbol of liberation from antique inhibi-
tions and out-worn ideas. Sedley, addressing a typical Court
Wit, wrote:

> Thou art an Atheist, Quintus, and a Wit,
> Thinkst all was of self-moving Attoms made.

If Hobbes was right and the universe consisted merely of

atoms governed by mathematical laws, it was surely only
sensible to enjoy the good things of this world and ignore
the croakings of killjoys, whether they were anglican parsons,
puritan preachers or old fashioned cavaliers. The age was
one of experiment, and the Wits tried the experiment of
living in a little pagan paradise of sensual, aesthetic and
intellectual pleasure. Behind the experiment there was a
vision and a theory. The vision was well described by
Charles Lamb as 'the Utopia of gallantry, where pleasure is
duty and the manners perfect freedom'. The theory was
that which was known in seventeenth-century Europe as
'libertinism',[1] a term which implied a revolt against traditional morality and institutions and a way of life based on the
satisfaction of natural passions and appetites. Rochester,
who had the most philosophical mind of the group summed
up the libertine theory in the following lines:

> Thus, whilst 'gainst false reas'ning I inveigh,
> I own right Reason, which I wou'd obey;
> That Reason, which distinguishes by sense,
> And gives us rules of good and ill from thence:
>
> * * *
>
> Your Reason hinders, mine helps t' enjoy,
> Renewing Appetites, yours wou'd destroy.

The attempt to live in accordance with these principles was
bound to fail in the face of the realities of the human
condition, but the vision which lay behind it, as well as the
contradictions which it involved, provided material for the
best comedies of the period as well as for the poetry of the
courtiers.

The Wits must not be judged as professional poets. Like
their predecessors, the Cavalier poets of the Court of Charles
I, they were gentlemen amateurs and their verses, which
were mostly 'occasional', were written not for publication

[1] It is well described by Dale Underwood in *Sir George Etherege and the
Seventeenth Century Comedy of Manners* (1957), pp. 10-36.

in the modern sense of the word but for circulation in manuscript among their friends. This does not mean that they were mere *dilettanti*, for whom the writing of verse was simply an elegant game. This was, doubtless, true of the minor figures in the Court circle, but, for the leading Wits, poetry was an art and a vital expression of a truly creative culture founded on a knowledge of books and experience of life. They aimed at what they called 'ease' or colloquial naturalness in poetry and were well aware that this could only be achieved by craftsmanship, even though their practice was sometimes marred by gentlemanly carelessness. Their poetry belongs to the courtly-classical or polite tradition, which descends from Ben Jonson through the Cavalier poets of the reign of Charles I. This tradition underwent a change somewhere about the middle of the century, when it began to acquire the character which we call Augustan. The change is apparent in the poetry of Waller and Cowley, two poets of the mid-century whose work was greatly admired by the Wits. Hobbes, who was influential both as a literary critic and a philosopher, had close connections with both these poets, and in their best work they are trying to carry into effect his demand for a new 'perspicuity', worldliness and realism in poetry.[1] They saw themselves as new Augustans renovating English poetry after the English Civil War as Virgil and Horace renovated Latin poetry after the Civil Wars of Rome. This new 'Augustan' movement could tend either towards a greater actuality and realism in accordance with the spirit of the new science and the new philosophy, or towards an elegant rococo neo-classicism not without charm but always in danger of becoming pompous and insipid. Both tendencies are apparent in the poetry of the Wits. At its worst it is not very far removed from Etherege's parody of the fashionable love lyric in *The Man of Mode* (1676):

[1] See his 'Answer to Davenant' (1650) in *Critical Essays of the Seventeenth Century*, ed. J. E. Spingarn, II, 63.

How Charming Phillis is, how fair!
Ah that she were as willing,
To ease my wounded heart of Care
And make her Eyes less killing.

But in their best poetry they were saved from this kind of thing by their good sense, their wit and their irony. They were helped, too, by their contact with a tradition which is commonly ignored by the literary historians. This was the tradition of the street ballad and popular song, that lusty growth of English vernacular poetry found in innumerable broadsides sold in the streets and taverns and in the popular verse miscellanies such as the *Drolleries* and *Academies of Compliments*, which were best-sellers in the Restoration bookshops.

The two chief kinds of poetry which they practised were the love lyric and the satire or 'libel'. The two kinds often tend to shade into each other in their work and one of its distinguishing marks is the combination of the singing voice of the lyric with the critical and ironic spirit of satire. They were the last English poets to use successfully the pastoral convention as part of the courtly love-game. This convention had lost the imaginative grandeur with which it was invested in the High Renaissance, but it remained a symbol for a non-moral dream-world of delicate charm and grace. At the end of the century it had become absurd when Lady Wishfort in Congreve's *The Way of the World* (1700) proposed to 'retire to deserts and solitudes, and feed harmless sheep by groves and purling streams'. The Wits in their best lyrics avoid this sort of silly escapism by disinfecting the pastoral with what Ezra Pound called 'a dash of bitters'. With them reality, like cheerfulness in the philosophy of Dr. Johnson's friend, kept breaking in. At times, too, their realistic temper enables them to use the convention to express a human situation when it becomes clear that Thirsis or Strephon is a real man feeling a genuine affection for his Celia and Phillis. The 'libel', lampoon or satire was a feature of Restoration court life as common as the love-song.

It could be simply a string of witty and usually bawdy insults in verse, but, in the hands of its ablest practitioners, notably Rochester, it became a vehicle for genuine social criticism based on a perception of the glaring contradictions between the smooth exterior of court life and the sordid actualities which lay behind it.

The Wits were a small, fairly closely knit community. Professor J. H. Wilson has estimated that about fourteen persons can be reckoned as belonging to the inner circle. As far as we know, they never authorized the printing of any of their works and a large quantity of their songs, 'libels' and other verses have survived in manuscript miscellanies, printed broadsides, contemporary anthologies, and editions, often of doubtful authenticity, published after their deaths. The result has been that it is extremely difficult for modern editors to establish either a reliable text or an authentic canon of the writings even of the leading figures.

As with the circle of Wyatt and Surrey in the early sixteenth century and that of the 'Sons of Ben Jonson' in the early seventeenth, there is a kind of basic poetic voice common to all the Restoration Wits who wrote verse. We can hear it in the following opening lines of a poem ascribed rather doubtfully to Dorset:

> Though, Phillis, your prevailing charms
> Have forc'd me from my Celia's arms,
> That kind defence against all powers,
> But those resistless eyes of yours:
> Think not your conquest to maintain
> By rigour and unjust disdain;
> In vain, fair Nymph, in vain you strive,
> For love does seldom hope survive . . .

This sort of rather thin, graceful poetry of conventional gallantry, strongly influenced by Waller and the slightly earlier French poetry of writers like Voiture and Sarrazin, could be written by almost any member of the circle including such minor poetasters as Lords Mulgrave and

Roscommon, Sir Car Scroop or Sir Fleetwood Shepherd. The 'most eminent wits', to use Burnet's expression, all sometimes make use of this 'basic' poetic voice but they are distinguished from their fellow courtiers by their power of speaking (or singing) in other voices covering wider and more interesting areas of experience.

II

JOHN WILMOT, EARL OF ROCHESTER

Rochester had by far the most powerful and original mind of all the Wits. His distinguishing characteristics are an unusual capacity for intellectual and sensual experience, a profound scepticism and a share in that quality of 'terrifying honesty' which T. S. Eliot ascribed to Blake. He began his career as a wholehearted disciple of Hobbes, but this was only the starting point for an intellectual voyage which ended with his conversion on his death bed to Christianity and his total rejection of what he then described as 'the absurd and foolish philosophy that the world so much admired, propagated by Mr. Hobbes and others'. In a letter to his wife he writes of 'so great a disproportion 'twixt our desires and what it has ordained to content them' and of those who are 'soe intirely satisfyed with theire shares in this world, that theire wishes nor their thoughts have not a farther prospect of felicity & glory'. One of his admirers called him an 'Enthusiast in Wit', and, if we interpret this as meaning that he combined intellectual toughness with a passionate aspiration to 'felicity and glory', the description is apt.

In the lyric he can play the game of the courtly pastoral and can also enjoy the fun of deflating its sentiment by substituting for the languishing swain and the chaste nymph a pair of cynical sensualists:

How perfect, Cloris, and how free
    Would these enjoyments prove,
But you with formal jealousy
Are still tormenting Love.

Let us (since Wit instructs us how)
    Raise pleasure to the top,
If Rival bottle you'll allow,
I'll suffer rival fop.

There's not a brisk insipid spark
    That flutters in the Town
But with your wanton eyes you mark
Him out to be your own . . .

Such a poem as this is obviously a deliberate 'shocker'. We can hear in it the voice of the hard-boiled 'confident young men' who made people like the Duke of Ormonde shudder. J. M. Synge wrote in 1908 that 'before verse can become human again it must learn to be brutal'. These words can be applied to the age when seventeenth-century romanticism was dying as well as to that which saw the collapse of Victorian romanticism.

Rochester is writing from a far deeper level of experience in the following poem, where he gives a philosophic dimension to a favourite theme of the Wits, inconstancy:

LOVE AND LIFE
All my past Life is mine no more,
    The flying hours are gone:
Like transitory Dreams giv'n o're,
Whose Images are kept in store,
    By Memory alone.

The Time that is to come is not,
    How can it then be mine?
The present Moment's all my Lot,
And that, as fast as it is got,
    Phillis, is only thine.

Then talk not of Inconstancy,
    False Hearts, and broken Vows;

> If I, by Miracle, can be
> This live-long Minute true to thee,
>   'Tis all that Heav'n allows.

This attitude is very different from that of the thoughtless pleasure-seeker. The plangent cadences of the opening lines convey a sense of the mystery of the time-process and the whole poem is suffused with melancholy for the precariousness of the artificial paradise which the lover finds in the arms of his Phillis.

Rochester's break-through to reality in the lyric can take the form of passionate tenderness as well as brutality. This is found in a handful of lyrics which F. R. Leavis has well described as 'peculiarly individual utterances' and which were aptly compared by Sir Herbert Grierson to the songs of Burns:

> My dear Mistress has a Heart
>   Soft as those kind looks she gave me;
> When with Love's resistless Art,
>   And her Eyes she did enslave me,
> But her Constancy's so weak,
>   She's so wild, and apt to wander;
> That my jealous Heart wou'd break,
>   Should we live one day asunder.
>
> Melting Joys about her move,
>   Killing Pleasures, wounding Blisses;
> She can dress her Eyes in Love,
>   And her Lips can arm with Kisses.
> Angels listen when she speaks,
>   She's my delight, all Mankind's wonder:
> But my jealous Heart would break,
>   Should we live one day asunder.

Here the 'ease' and unaffected naturalness which the Wits prized are combined with a note of rapture and a crystalline perfection of phrase and form of which Rochester alone among them knew the secret.

His satiric poems are of two kinds. Some, like his attacks on Lord Mulgrave and Sir Car Scroop, are simply 'libels' in the fashion of the day and only distinguished from the numerous other contemporary squibs by their greater pungency and literary force. His lampoons on the king deserve special mention. The character of Charles II seems to have fascinated him, perhaps, because, like his own, it was full of paradoxes. The contrast between the traditional view of the monarch hedged by divinity and the actual person of the 'sauntering', informal Charles Stuart was a never-failing source of ironic amusement to the poet. It is neatly embodied in his celebrated extempore epigram:

> We have a pritty witty king
> And whose word no man relys on:
> He never said a foolish thing,
> And never did a wise one.

Charles's good-humoured reply is said to have been that what Rochester observed was easily explained. He was responsible for his words but his ministers for his actions. This epigram, however, is mild compared with some of the longer lampoons on the King ascribed to Rochester. What seemed to him especially despicable in the King was not that he took his pleasure with his mistresses but that he allowed himself to be governed by them:

> Restless he rolls about from Whore to Whore,
> A merry Monarch, scandalous and poor.

Rochester's more serious work in satire, however, deserves to be called philosophic; it can be seen as reflecting the dialectical process which transformed the gay young spark of the sixties into the dying penitent of 1680. One characteristic of these poems is his intense and vivid perception of the 'waste land' of the world revealed by the new materialistic philosophy together with the sordidness of a society vulgarized by the growth of the money power. The other is the creative use of his reading. He was the first poet to use the Augustan method of 'imitation', afterwards brilliantly exploited by Oldham, Pope and Johnson. Not only his fine

'Allusion to the Tenth Satire of the Second Book of Horace' but each of his major satiric works is at once a criticism of contemporary life and in some measure an 'imitation' or re-creation of a work of ancient or contemporary poetry often with a touch of parody. His famous lines 'Upon Nothing' are a kind of inversion of Cowley's 'Hymn to Light' and at the same time he makes use of the conception of Nothing as an active force found in the Renaissance Latin poems quoted by Johnson in his account of Rochester in *The Lives of the Poets;* behind the poem, too, lie still more august antecedents: the Book of Genesis, the first verses of the Fourth Gospel and the Aristotelian doctrine of form and matter:

> Nothing! thou Elder Brother ev'n to Shade,
> That hadst a Being e're the World was made,
> And (well fixt) art alone, of ending not afraid.

In the last stanzas the irony is transferred from metaphysics to contemporary society:

> Nothing who dwell'st with Fools in grave Disguise,
> For whom they rev'rend Shapes, and Forms devise,
> Lawn Sleeves and Furs and Gowns, when they like thee
> look wise.
>
> *   *   *   *
>
> The great Man's Gratitude to his best Friend,
> King's Promises, Whore's Vows, tow'rds thee they bend,
> Flow swiftly into thee, and in thee ever end.

The emptiness that lies behind the façade of human institutions and social life is visualized here as a kind of evil abstract deity (Blake's 'Nobodaddy'), and Swift's doctrine of man as a 'micro-coat' (see *A Tale of a Tub*) is clearly foreshadowed. Pope must have studied this poem carefully, for he wrote a clever imitation of it in his youth and the Triumph of Dullness at the end of *The Dunciad* probably owes much to Rochester's Triumph of Nothing.

'The Maim'd Debauchee', described by Charles Whibley as a 'masterpiece of heroic irony', recalls Davenant's epic

Gondibert as 'Upon Nothing' recalls Cowley's 'Hymn to Light'. The stately metre and diction of Davenant's 'heroic' poem are used to exhibit the old age of a gentlemanly rake, who is ironically equated to a superannuated admiral watching a naval battle from a safe position on shore. Like all Rochester's best satiric work this poem is not a statement but a vision. We are made to see the absurdly ferocious old sailor:

> From his fierce Eyes flashes of Rage he throws
> > As from black Clouds when Lightning breaks away,
> Transported thinks himself amidst his Foes,
> > And absent, yet enjoys the bloody Day.

This image is, as it were, superimposed upon that of the old *roué* inciting his young friends to the life of pleasure:

> My pains at last some respite shall afford,
> > While I behold the Battels you maintain:
> When Fleets of Glasses sail around the Board,
> > From whose Broad-Sides Volleys of Wit shall rain.

Are we looking at a riotous banquet or a naval battle? It is impossible to say; the two images are fused into a simple whole.

In his most powerful social satire 'A Letter from Artemisa in the Town to Cloe in the Country', Rochester shows us the obverse of the Utopia of Gallantry in which the Wits and ladies of Whitehall spent their time. In this poem the horror of the life of a prostitute in Restoration London is etched with the mordant realism of a Hogarth or a Goya:

> That wretched thing Corinna, who has run
> Through all the sev'ral ways of being undone:
> Cozen'd at first by Love, and living then
> By turning the too-dear-bought-cheat on Men:
> Gay were the hours, and wing'd with joy they flew,
> When first the Town her early Beauties knew:
> Courted, admir'd, and lov'd, with Presents fed;
> Youth in her Looks, and Pleasure in her bed.

★ ★ ★

Now scorn'd of all forsaken and opprest,
She's a *Memento Mori* to the rest:
Diseas'd, decay'd, to take up half a Crown
Must Mortage her Long Scarf, and Manto Gown;
Poor Creature, who unheard of, as a Flie,
In some dark hole must all the Winter lye:
And want, and dirt, endure a whole half year,
That, for one month, she Tawdry may appear.

This is a glimpse of the hell over which the heaven of the Strephons and Cloes of Whitehall was precariously constructed.

The culmination of contemporary society is seen in his 'Satyr against Mankind', where the revolt is extended to an attack on the human condition itself. The poem was suggested by the eighth satire of Boileau, reinforced by hints from Montaigne and La Rochefoucauld. Nevertheless, it is a profoundly original work, for Rochester, like Pope, is never so original as when he is making full use of his reading. The poem is stamped with the peculiar strength of his personality in every line and expresses with an almost frightening intensity his mood of indignation and disillusionment. He never created a more striking image than that of mankind at the opening of the poem as the Lost Traveller, who, deceived by Reason, 'an *Ignis fatuus* in the Mind',

Stumbling from thought to thought, falls head-long down
Into doubts boundless Sea, where like to drown,
Books bear him up awhile, and make him try,
To swim with Bladders of Philosophy;

* * *

Then Old Age, and experience, hand in hand,
Lead him to death, and make him understand,
After a search so painful, and so long,
That all his Life he has been in the wrong;
Hudled in dirt, the reas'ning Engine lyes,
Who was so proud, so witty, and so wise.

Nowhere in the English poetry of the seventeenth century is the moral crisis of the age expressed with such force and precision; in the new mechanico-materialist universe of Descartes, Hobbes and the scientists, man is only a 'reas'ning Engine' (the phrase is probably suggested by an expression of Robert Boyle, the great contemporary chemist), yet the pitiful creature has the presumption to call himself witty and wise and seek an explanation of a universe in which he seems to be little better than an irrelevant accident. The central passage of the poem containing a comparison between man and the beasts is one of the most searching pieces of moral realism in English poetry:

> Be Judge your self, I'le bring it to the test,
> Which is the basest Creature Man or Beast?
> Birds feed on Birds, Beasts on each other prey,
> But Savage Man alone does Man betray:
> Prest by necessity, they Kill for Food,
> Man undoes Man to do himself no good.
> With Teeth and Claws by Nature arm'd they hunt,
> Nature's allowances, to supply their want;
> But Man with smiles, embraces, Friendships, praise,
> Unhumanely his Fellows life betrays;
> With voluntary pains works his distress,
> Not through necessity, but wantonness.
> For hunger, or for Love, they fight or tear,
> Whilst wretched Man is still in Arms for fear;
> For fear he arms, and is of Arms afraid,
> By fear, to fear, successively betray'd,
> Base fear, the source when his best passions came,
> His boasted Honor, and his dear bought Fame.
> That lust of Pow'r, to which he's such a Slave,
> And for the which alone he dares be brave . . .

Rochester is here piercing the defences of his aristocratic readers and showing the real passions that lay behind their highflown talk of 'Honor' and 'Fame'. It is a passage that communicates forward to the Swift of *Gulliver's Travels*: the King of Brobdingnag's denunciation of the Europeans and the superiority of those wise and humane quadrupeds, the Houyhnhnms to the filthy, cowardly Yahoos.

Rochester's reputation, like Byron's, has suffered from the blaze of notoriety which surrounded his life and personality. Andrew Marvell, no mean judge, declared that he was 'the best English satyrist and had the right veine', and Voltaire went further and called him 'a man of genius and a great poet'. As a craftsman in verse, compared with his contemporary John Dryden, he is a brilliant amateur. His place is among the daring thought-adventurers of English poetry, whose work lives by the intensity of their passion, the forthrightness of their speech and the searching clarity of their vision.

III

CHARLES SACKVILLE, EARL OF DORSET

Dorset (known throughout the early part of his career as Lord Buckhurst) was the least productive, though by no means the least gifted, of the Restoration Wits. The works which can be certainly attributed to him are a translation of one act of a tragedy of Corneille, a few lampoons, prologues and epilogues, a ribald parody, the well known ballad 'Song Written at Sea, in the first Dutch War' and a small sheaf of lyrics. He was rich and indolent and delighted in the company of men of letters, to whom he was a munificent host and patron. The condition of such a wealthy and universally flattered nobleman, 'fed', like Pope's Bufo, 'with soft dedication all day long', was perhaps even worse for a creative artist than the poverty and obscurity of an Oldham or an Otway. When Dryden couples his name with those of Virgil, Shakespeare and Donne, and Prior tells us that 'There is a Lustre in his Verses, like that of a Sun in Claude Loraine's Landskips' we are listening to the courtly hyperboles of the grateful recipients of his bounty. Pope, however, who was under no obligation to him, rated his poetry very highly, and if we can trust Spence's *Anecdotes*, surprisingly preferred it even to Rochester's. His own work shows that he studied it carefully.

Dorset's celebrated ballad deserves its reputation. An excellent example of the benefit which the Wits derived from their contact with the vernacular tradition, it is a true street-ballad written to be sung to the traditional tune of Shackerley Hay, and we know from the Stationer's Register and Pepys's Diary (2 Jan. 1664/5) that it was actually published under the title of 'The Noble Seaman's Complaint' as a broadside and was a popular hit. In this poem, as can be judged from the following quotation of the three opening stanzas, the rhythmic vitality of vernacular poetry is happily combined with the sophisticated wit and irony of the courtier, producing an effect that remains fresh and sparkling after three centuries:

> To all you Ladies now at Land,
>   We Men at Sea indite;
> But first wou'd have you understand
>   How hard it is to write;
> The Muses now, and Neptune too,
> We must implore to write to you.
>
> For tho' the Muses should prove kind,
>   And fill our empty Brain;
> Yet if rough Neptune rouze the Wind,
>   To wave the azure Main,
> Our Paper, Pen and Ink, and we,
> Roll up and down our Ships at Sea.
>
> Then if we write not by each Post,
>   Think not we are unkind;
> Nor yet conclude our Ships are lost
>   By Dutchmen, or by Wind:
> Our Tears we'll send a speedier way,
> The Tide shall bring 'em twice a day.

Another lyric in the ballad style and metre has a touch of the sturdy vulgarity and sensuality of popular art:

Methinks the poor Town has been troubled too long,
With Phillis and Chloris in every Song;
By Fools, who at once can both love and despair,
And will never leave calling 'em cruel and fair;
Which justly provokes me in Rhime to express
The Truth that I know of bonny black Bess.

This Bess of my Heart, this Bess of my Soul,
Has a Skin white as Milk and Hair black as Coal,
She's plump, yet with ease you may span her round Waste,
But her round swelling Thighs can scarce be embrac'd:
Her Belly is soft, not a word of the rest;
But I know what I think when I drink to the best.

The Plowman and 'Squire, the arranter Clown,
At home she subdu'd in her Paragon Gown;
But now she adorns the Boxes and Pit,
And the proudest Town-gallants are forc'd to submit;
All hearts fall a-leaping wherever she comes,
And beat Day and Night, like my Lord Craven's Drums.

Perhaps Dorset's most original and distinctive work is seen in the sequence of his four little poems on Katherine Sedley, the daughter of his friend Sir Charles. The character of this bold, witty young woman, who became the mistress of the Duke of York, afterwards James II, seems to have fascinated him. In these verses Dorset is creating a new kind of poem in which lyrical movement is combined with satiric force. It was, doubtless, of them that Rochester was thinking when he called him 'the best good Man, with the worst natur'd Muse'. The following poem has an economy of language and a classic perfection of form unrivalled in English poetry outside the works of Landor:

Dorinda's sparkling Wit and Eyes,
United, cast too fierce a Light,
Which blazes high, but quickly dies,
Pains not the Heart, but hurts the Sight.

Love is a calmer, gentler Joy.
Smooth are his Looks, and soft his Pace;

> Her Cupid is a black-guard Boy,
> That runs his Link full in your Face.

The metaphor of a painfully dazzling fire links the two
stanzas together with admirable art and the sudden transition
in the last two lines from the rococo cupid to the 'black-
guard Boy' with his flaming 'Link' (i.e. torch) takes us with
a pleasurable shock from the dreamworld of the pastoral
convention to the actuality of night in the murky streets of
Restoration London, where there were no street lamps and
the only illumination was provided by the torches of link-
boys. In another poem on Katherine Sedley the same verbal
economy and felicity of imagery gives force to a penetrating
piece of social satire:

> Tell me, Dorinda, why so gay,
>   Why such embroid'ry, fringe and lace?
> Can any Dresses find a way,
> To stop th' approaches of decay,
>   And mend a ruin'd Face.
>
> Wilt thou still sparkle in the Box,
>   Still ogle in the Ring?
> Canst thou forget thy Age and Pox?
> Can all that shines on Shells and Rocks
>   Make thee a fine young Thing?
>
> So have I seen in Larder dark
>   Of Veal a lucid Loin
> Replete with many a brilliant Spark,
> As wise Philosophers remark,
>   At once both stink and shine.

This is not merely an attack on Katherine Sedley. It is a
dramatization of a true social criticism which sees all the
glittering apparatus of court life ('embroid'ry, fringe and
lace' and 'all that shines on Shells and Rocks') as a mockery
masking the hideous realities of venereal disease and decaying
flesh. There is a sharp visualization of ugly and sordid
images in this poem revealing a new kind of poetic sensibility
which was to be exploited with remarkable results by Pope

and Swift. A similar quality is found in one of Dorset's lampoons on the Hon. Edward Howard, a contemporary dramatist who was one of the favourite butts of the Wits:

> Thou damn'd Antipodes to Common sense,
> Thou Foil to Flecknoe, pry'thee tell from whence
> Does all this mighty Stock of Dullness spring?
> Is it thy own, or hast it from Snow-Hill,
> Assisted by some Ballad-making Quill?
> No, they fly higher yet, thy Plays are such
> I'd swear they were translated out of Dutch,
> Fain wou'd I know what Diet thou dost keep,
> If thou dost always, or dost never sleep?
> Sure hasty-pudding is thy chiefest Dish,
> With Bullock's Liver, or some stinking Fish;
> Garbage, Ox-cheeks, and Tripes, do feast thy Brain
> Which nobly pays this tribute back again,
> With Daisy roots thy dwarfish Muse is fed,
> A Giant's body with a Pygmy's head.

* * *

> Think on't a while, and thou wilt quickly find
> Thy Body made for Labour, not thy Mind.
> No other use of Paper thou should'st make,
> Than carrying Loads and Reams upon thy Back.
> Carry vast Burdens till thy Shoulders shrink,
> But curst be he that gives thee Pen and Ink:
> Such dang'rous Weapons shou'd be kept from Fools,
> As Nurses from their children keep Edg'd-Tools:
> For thy dull Fancy a Muckinder[1] is fit
> To wipe the slabberings of thy snotty Wit.

Dr. Johnson rightly saw in these lines evidence of 'great fertility of mind'. They show a strength and a freedom of imagination which make us think of *The Dunciad* and regret that Dorset's birth and fortune prevented him from developing his considerable literary potentiality.

---

1 Muckinder=a handkerchief.

IV

SIR CHARLES SEDLEY

Pope described Sedley as 'a very insipid writer; except in some few of his little love-verses'. This is not quite fair to Sedley, who wrote some good poetry besides his 'little love verses', but it is possible to understand what Pope meant. Sedley's poetry has neither Rochester's passionate intensity and intellectual energy nor the satiric bite and sensuality of Dorset's best work. He uses the old stereotypes of the courtly pastoral convention with grace and wit, sometimes with tenderness, but rarely with passion. His attitude to the sex-relationship is rational and humorous:

> Phillis, let's shun the common Fate
> And let our Love ne'r turn to Hate.
> I'll dote no longer than I can
> Without being call'd a faithless Man.
> When we begin to want Discourse
> And Kindness seems to taste of Force,
> As freely as we met we'll part
> Each one possest of his own Heart.

In two poems he uses the theme of the address to a very young girl, treated already with imaginative richness by Marvell and courtly grace by Waller. The following are the opening stanzas of the song to Cloris in Sedley's comedy, *The Mulberry Garden*:

> Ah Cloris! that I now could sit
>   As unconcern'd as when
> Your Infant Beauty cou'd beget
>   No pleasure, nor no pain.
>
> When I the Dawn us'd to admire,
>   And prais'd the coming Day;
> I little thought the growing fire
>   Must take my Rest away.

Your Charms in harmless Childhood lay,
   Like metals in the mine,
Age from no face took more away,
   Than Youth conceal'd in thine.

But as your Charms insensibly
   To their perfection prest,
Fond Love as unperceiv'd did flye
   And in my Bosom rest.

My passion with your Beauty grew,
   And Cupid at my heart,
Still as his mother favour'd you,
   Threw a new flaming Dart.

This is, perhaps, a little too pretty. It might be described a boudoir poetry, recalling some erotic French eighteenth-century painting of the school of Boucher. More astringent and satisfying to a modern taste in its delicate, playful humour is the poem addressed 'To a Devout Young Gentlewoman':

Phillis, this early Zeal asswage,
   You over-act your part;
The Martyrs, at your tender Age,
   Gave Heaven but half their Heart.

Old Men (till past the Pleasure) ne're
   Declaim against the Sin;
'Tis early to begin to fear
   The Devil at Fifteen.

The World to Youth is too severe,
   And, like a treacherous Light,
Beauty, the Actions of the Fair,
   Exposes to their sight.

And yet the World, as old as 'tis,
   Is oft deceiv'd by't too;
Kind Combinations seldom miss,
   Let's try what we can do.

The first two stanzas of this poem are nearly flawless but the last two are marred both by banality of thought and verbal clumsiness, seen in the awkward inversions and the slipshod grammar of the penultimate stanza. A similar failure of inspiration mars the lyric beginning with the following often-praised and beautiful lines:

> Love still has something of the Sea,
> From whence his Mother rose;

The expectation aroused by this rich opening is immediately damped by the next two lines with their hackneyed imagery and inversion for the sake of the rhyme:

> No time his Slaves from Doubt can free,
> Nor give their Thoughts repose

After a series of stanzas filled with frigid allegory the poems ends with lines almost worthy of its superb opening:

> And if I gaz'd a thousand Years
> I could no deeper love.

None of the weaknesses noted in these poems is found in two of Sedley's songs which for long retained their popularity through the contemporary musical settings. In the following poem the courtly convention is most happily wedded to the appreciation of an exquisite moment of actual experience:

> Hears not my Phillis, how the Birds
> Their feather'd Mates salute?
> They tell their Passion in their Words;
> Must I alone be mute?
> Phillis, without Frown or Smile,
> Sat and knotted all the while.
>
> The God of Love in thy bright Eyes
> Does like a Tyrant reign;
> But in thy Heart a Child he lyes,
> Without his Dart or Flame.
> Phillis, without Frown or Smile,
> Sat and knotted all the while.

So many Months in Silence past,
And yet in raging Love,
Might well deserve one Word at last
My Passion shou'd approve.
Phillis, without Frown or Smile,
Sat and knotted all the while.

Must then your faithful Swain expire,
And not one look obtain,
Which he to sooth his fond Desire
Might pleasingly explain?
Phillis, without Frown or Smile,
Sat and knotted all the while.

This lyric must be heard sung to Purcell's exquisite setting if its full effect is to be realized, but even on the printed page it succeeds in conveying the poet's delight in the ballet-like situation, in the movement of the verse and the conventional images, which his emotion endows with a surprising freshness and vitality. Equally successful is an even more famous song which shows an originality of metrical invention unusual in Sedley's work and due, doubtless, in some measure to the music:

Phillis is my only Joy,
Faithless as the Winds or Seas;
Sometimes coming, sometimes coy,
Yet she never fails to please;
If with a Frown
I am cast down,
Phillis smiling,
And beguiling,
Makes me happier than before.

Tho', alas, too late I find,
Nothing can her Fancy fix;
Yet the Moment she is kind,
I forgive her all her Tricks;
Which tho' I see,
I can't get free;

She deceiving,
I believing;
What need Lovers wish for more?

In one lyric Sedley achieves the expression of tender feeling
in language of diaphanous simplicity that almost equals that
of Rochester's best songs, though, as so often in his poetry,
the magnificent promise of the opening lines is hardly
sustained:

Not, Celia, that I juster am
    Or better than the rest,
For I would change each Hour like them,
    Were not my heart at rest.

But I am ty'd to very thee
    By every Thought I have,
Thy Face I only crave to see,
    Thy Heart I only crave.

All that in Woman is ador'd
    In thy dear self I find,
For the whole Sex can but afford
    The Handsome and the kind.

Why then should I seek farther Store,
    And still make Love anew?
When Change itself can give no more,
    'Tis easie to be true.

Sedley is not, however, exclusively what Ben Jonson calls
'a woman's poet'. There is a more masculine quality in some
of the poems probably written in the later part of his life.
This quality is found especially in his translations and imitations of Latin poetry. Prior with true critical insight described
him as 'Sir Charles that can write and better Translate'. His
version of the eighth Ode of the Second Book of Horace is
one of the finest verse translations of the seventeenth century.
It is one of those rare translations that reads like an original
poem. Horace's dangerous old harlot is transmuted into one
of the glittering, rapacious courtesans of the Court of

Charles II and the poem is as vivid, incisive and carefully controlled as the Latin original:

Did any Punishment attend
   Thy former Perjuries
I should believe a second time
   Thy charming Flatteries:
Did but one Wrinkle mark this Face,
Or hadst thou lost one single Grace.

No sooner hast thou, with false Vows,
   Provok'd the Powers above;
But thou art fairer than before
   And we are more in love.
Thus Heaven and Earth seem to declare,
They pardon Falshood in the Fair.

Sure 'tis no Crime vainly to swear,
   By ev'ry Power on high,
And call our bury'd Mother's Ghost
   A witness to the Lye:
Heaven at such Perjuries connives,
And Venus with a Smile forgives.

The Nymphs and cruel Cupid too,
   Sharp'ning his pointed Dart
On an old hone besmear'd with Blood,
   Forbear thy perjur'd Heart.
Fresh Youth grows up, to wear thy Chains,
And the Old Slave no Freedom gains.

Thee, Mothers for their eldest Sons,
   Thee, wretched Misers fear,
Lest thy prevailing Beauty should
   Seduce the hopeful Heir.
New-marry'd Virgins fear thy Charms
Should keep their Bridegroom from their Arms.

A similar strength is found in a series of adaptations of epigrams of Martial, one of the best of which is cast in the form of a Shakespearian sonnet and must be one of the very few poems in this form written between the early seventeenth and early nineteenth centuries:

> Thou art an Atheist, Quintus, and a Wit,
>   Thinkst all was of self-moving Attoms made,
> Religion only for the Vulgar fit,
>   Priests Rogues, and Preaching their deceitful Trade;
> Wilt drink, whore, fight, blaspheme, damn, curse and swear:
>   Why wilt thou swear by God, if there be none?
> And if there be, thou shouldst his Vengeance fear:
>   Methinks this Huffing might be let alone;
> 'Tis thou art free, Mankind besides a Slave,
>   And yet a Whore can lead thee by the Nose,
> A drunken Bottle, and a flatt'ring Knave,
>   A mighty Prince, Slave to thy dear Soul's Foes,
> Thy Lust, thy Rage, Ambition and thy Pride;
> He that serves God, need nothing serve beside.

This poem shows that Sedley was capable not only of living in the libertine 'Utopia of Gallantry' but of outgrowing it and criticizing it, though his criticism lacks the philosophic depth and fierce irony of Rochester's.

At the end of his life he wrote a long poem on marriage called 'The Happy Pair'. In spite of some rather banal theorizing, the passages denouncing mercenary and loveless marriages have a note of actuality due, no doubt, to the poet's own bitter experience; he was married at the age of seventeen to a woman who became a paranoiac. The conclusion of the poem with its praise of quiet domesticity shows that the wild gallant of the sixteen-sixties had by the end of the century developed into an Augustan 'man of feeling'. In the following lines there is a sensuous perception of 'images of external nature' which foreshadows the rural-sentimental poetry of the eighteenth century:

> Love, like a cautious fearful Bird, ne'er builds,
> But where the Place Silence and Calmness yields:
> He slily flies to Copses, where he finds
> The snugging Woods secure from Blasts and Winds,
> Shuns the huge Boughs of a more Stately Form,
> And Laughs at Trees tore up with ev'ry Storm.

V

SIR GEORGE ETHEREGE

Unlike the other members of the Court circle Etherege did
not come from a wealthy, aristocratic background. His
grandfather was a 'vintner', or publican, at Maidenhead and
his father, after spending some time in the Bermudas, held a
small appointment at the Court of Charles I and died in
exile in France after the royalist defeat. The only fact that we
know about the young George Etherege is that he was
apprenticed by his grandfather to a London attorney in 1653
at the age of eighteen. Eleven years later his first play was
produced with great success at the Duke's Theatre; he
dedicated it to Lord Buckhurst (Dorset) and there is no
doubt that it was through his friendship with that nobleman
that he was accepted as a member of the 'merry gang'. This
experience was the central fact of his life. Like Oscar Wilde
two centuries later, he was a wit and an artist in comedy,
who was admitted into aristocratic circles, and was enchanted
by the ideal of the man of fashion and leisure who was
master of the art of living. In each of his three comedies we
find this figure, beginning with the sketch of the gay and
charming Sir Frederick Frollick in *The Comical Revenge*,
proceeding to the two attractive young sparks, Courtall and
Freeman, in *She Wou'd If She Cou'd* and culminating in the
finished portrait of Dorimant in *The Man of Mode*, said to be
based on the character of Rochester. Contrasted with
Dorimant in this play is Sir Fopling Flutter, that 'eminent
Coxcomb', who embodies all that is absurd in the fashionable
ideal. Etherege himself was probably something halfway
between Dorimant and Sir Fopling. Just as Wilde called
himself a *poseur*, so Etherege called himself a fop. In one of
his letters he writes: 'I confess I am a fop in my heart; ill
customs influence my senses, and I have been so used to
affection [affectation] that without the air of the Court
nothing can touch me'. Unlike the other members of the

merry gang he never outgrew the courtly-libertine ideal of
the sixteen-sixties. Like Wilde he was never so much himself
as when he was acting a part and the part of the 'fop' or perfect aesthetic hero became second nature to him. It might be
imagined that such a man, when he wrote verse, would speak
only in the 'basic voice' of the court poet. Actually, however,
in Etherege's poetry, slight as it is in quantity, we can hear
other and more individual voices. John Palmer acutely
ascribed to him 'a worldly simplicity captivating from its
entire lack of self-consciousness' and this describes very well
the quality of his best lyrics. His poem addressed 'To a very
Young Lady' has none of the playfulness and boudoir
eroticism of Sedley's 'Song to Cloris' but a kind of innocent
freshness which brings him nearer to Marvell or even
Vaughan than to Waller or Sedley:

> Sweetest bud of beauty, may
> No untimely frost decay
> The early glories that we trace,
> Blooming in thy matchless face;
> But kindly opening, like the rose,
> Fresh beauties every day disclose,
> Such as by nature are not shown
> In all the blossoms she has blown—
> And then what conquest shall you make
> Who hearts already daily take?
> Scorched in the morning with thy beams,
> How shall we bear those sad extremes
> Which must attend thy threatening eyes
> When thou shalt to thy noon arise.

The following lyric is more characteristic. Here the voice is
that of a *persona*, the 'shepherd' or ideal poet of the court
pastoral, a fairy tale or tapestry world. The attitude of the
'shepherd', we may notice, is highly ambiguous. Ostensibly
he is issuing a warning against the love of women, but we
are told that love's 'chain' is 'imperial' and its 'pain'
'enchanting', and it seems obvious that the loss of 'quiet' by

those who gaze on 'beauteous Eyes' is a not unenviable condition:

> Ye happy youths, whose hearts are free
>   From Love's imperial chain,
> Henceforth be warned and taught by me
>   T'avoid the enchanting pain.
> Fatal the wolves to trembling flocks,
>   Sharp winds to blossoms prove,
> To careless seamen hidden rocks,
>   To human quiet Love.
>
> Fly the fair sex if bliss you prize,
>   The snake's beneath the flower;
> Whoever gazed on beauteous eyes
>   That tasted quiet more?
> How faithless is the lover's joy!
>   How constant is his care!
> The kind with falsehood do destroy,
>   The cruel with despair.

The craftsmanship of this poem is remarkable. The common ballad quatrain is enlivened by a subtle pattern of alliteration and assonance and the cadences ('human quiet Love', 'gazed on beauteous eyes', 'tasted quiet more') are the work of a fine artist in verbal music. He is equally successful with flowing anapaests in the song called 'Silvia'. Here the feeling is genuine but it is of the kind that can be called operatic like that of Tom Moore's best songs, the manner of which is remarkably foreshadowed in this poem. It is interesting to find that it was immensely popular as 'words for music' and was set by no fewer than four different contemporary composers:

> The nymph that undoes me is fair and unkind,
> No less than a wonder by Nature designed;
> She's the grief of my heart, the joy of my eye,
> And the cause of a flame that never can die.
>
> Her mouth, from whence wit still obligingly flows
> Has the beautiful blush and the smell of the rose;

Love and destiny both attend on her well,
She wounds with a look, with a frown she can kill.

The desperate lover can hope no redress
Where beauty and rigor are both in excess:
In Silvia they meet, so unhappy am I,
Who sees her must love and who loves her must die.

Etherege can speak in other voices in his poetry besides that
of the courtly gallant. In some of the lyrics in his plays we
can hear the voice of the man of the street, the tavern and
the coffee-house, using the idiom of the popular song, catch
and street-ballad. The following lines, trolled by the sharper
Palmer in the tavern scene in *The Comical Revenge* (II. 2),
have the salty tang of vernacular speech and the hearty
sensuality of popular poetry:

If she be not fair as kind
    But peevish and unhandy,
Leave her—she's only worth the care
    Of some spruce Jack-a-dandy.

I would not have thee such an ass,
    Hadst thou ne'er so much leisure
To sigh and whine for such a lass
    Whose pride's above her pleasure.

Make much of every buxom girl
    Which needs but little courting;
Her value is above the pearl,
    That takes delight in sporting.

The song sung by the 'wanton' Gatty in the first scene of the
fifth act of *She Wou'd If She Cou'd* is a genuine street-ballad
which was reprinted in two broadsides. It is poetry that
springs as directly from the life of Restoration London as an
entry in Pepys's Diary:

To little or no purpose I spent many days,
In ranging the Park, the Exchange, and the Plays;
For ne'er in my rambles till now did I prove
So lucky to meet with the man I could love.

Oh! how I am pleased when I think on this man,
That I find I must love, let me do what I can!

How long I shall love him, I can no more tell
Than had I a fever when I should be well.
My passion shall kill me before I will show it,
And yet I would give all the world he did know it;
But oh how I sigh when I think he would woo me,
I cannot deny what I know would undo me.

As a poet Etherege is seen at his best in his lyrics; his few complimentary and erotic poems in the heroic couplet are polished but undistinguished. His lines to the Marchioness of Newcastle 'after the Reading of Her Incomparable Poems' might have been written by any competent imitator of Waller:

Those graces nature did till now divide
(Your sex's glory and our sex's pride)
Are joined in you, and all to you submit,
The brightest beauty and the sharpest wit.
No faction here or fiercer envy sways,
They give you myrtle, while we offer bays.
What mortal dares dispute this wreath with you,
Armed thus with lightning and with thunder too.

He is said to have written lampoons railing at women, but no 'libel' can be certainly ascribed with him. If he is the author of 'Mrs Nelly's Complaint', a satire on Nell Gwynn attributed to him in *The Miscellaneous Works of the Duke of Buckingham*, he cannot be credited with a satiric talent beyond that of those whom Dryden calls 'our common libellers'. The best passage in the poem gives an amusing glimpse of the strangely variegated company that was to be found in the royal presence at Whitehall in the reign of Charles II:

Let mountebanks make market houses ring
Of what great feats they've done before the King,
Let learned Sir Sam his Windsor Engine try,
Before great Charles let quacks and seamen lie.

He ne'er heard swearers till Mall Knight and I,
Never heard oaths less valued, or less true
(And yet 'tis said, he has paid for swearing too)
Loudlier we swore than plundering dragoons,
'Sblood followed 'Sblood, and Zoons succeeded Zoons.

A more individual note is heard in a series of verse epistles written by Etherege to his friends in the tumbling four accent 'Hudibrastic' metre popularized by Butler's famous poem. In this metre he conducted a witty but obscene correspondence with Buckhurst and, later, when he was British Envoy at Ratisbon, wrote verse epistles to his friend and official superior Lord Middleton. One of these epistles contains a description of one of 'rough Danube's beauties' which combines the picturesque with the comic in a manner that Byron would not have despised:

How would the ogling sparks despise
The darling damsel of my eyes,
Did they behold her at a play,
As she's tricked up on holiday,
When the whole family combine
For public pride to make her shine.
Her hair which long before lay matted
Are on this day combed out and platted
A diamond bodkin in each tress
The badges of her nobleness;
For every stone as well as she
Can boast an ancient pedigree.
* * * *
No serpent breaking in the air
Can with her starry head compare.
Such ropes of pearls her hands encumber
She scarce can deal the cards at ombre;
So many rings each finger freight,
They tremble with the mighty weight:
The like in England ne'er was seen
Since Holbein drew Hal and his Queen.
But after these fantastic sights
The luster's meaner than the lights

> She that bears this glittering pomp
> Is but a tawdry ill-bred ramp
> Whose brawny limbs and martial face
> Proclaim her of the Gothic race,
> More than the painted pageantry
> Of all her father's heraldry . . .

Unlike the other 'eminent wits' Etherege never goes beneath the surface in his poetry. It is all 'light verse' but, at the same time, it is the work of a true artist and it succeeds in transmitting across three centuries his gaiety, insouciance and attractive mixture of innocence and sophistication.

VI

CONCLUSION

The pattern of life and writing of the 'merry gang' arose from a particular phase of society and culture and could not be repeated. Men like George Granville, Lord Lansdowne and William Walsh, who tried to reproduce it after the Revolution, appear now as Young Pretenders, mere pale and colourless imitations. By the end of the century the character of the libertine Court Wit had become the absurd anachronism which Swift caricatures in *A Tale of A Tub* when he describes the activities of the three brothers in high society: 'they writ and rallied, and rhymed and sung and said, and said nothing: they drank and fought, and slept, and swore, and took snuff: they went to new plays on the first night, haunted the chocolate houses, beat the watch, lay on bulks, and got claps: they bilked hackney-coachmen, ran in debt with shopkeepers, and lay with their wives: they killed bailiffs, kicked fidlers downstairs, eat at Will's, loitered at Locket's . . .'. The men who did these things in Swift's time were, to use his own expression, mere microcoats, imitators of the externals of what had once been a life of gaiety, poetry and adventure. Alone among men of the post-Revolution generation William Congreve caught the authentic note of the Restoration Wits in a few poems such as the following lyric, the first stanza of which, at least, Rochester would not have disowned:

> False though she be to me and love,
>   I'll ne'er pursue revenge;
> For still the charmer I approve
>   Though I deplore her change.
>
> In hours of bliss we oft have met,
>   They could not always last;
> For though the present I regret,
>   I'm grateful for the past.

The best of the poetry of the Wits lives to-day by virtue of its youthfulness, insouciance, direct and unaffected speech, irreverence and sensuality. These qualities are, perhaps, more acceptable now than at any time since the latter part of the seventeenth century. For long the aura of scandal surrounding the personalities of the Wits obscured the historical significance of their writings. They rendered two great services to English poetry. One was to keep the singing voice of the lyric alive in an age of mathematics and scientific positivism. Boileau said that Descartes had cut the throat of poetry. It was to a large extent due to the 'merry gang' that the positive spirit of Descartes, Hobbes and the scientists failed to cut the throat of the English lyric. Their other memorable achievement was to diversify and invigorate the Augustan tradition by preserving the happy freedom of colloquial, informal English poetry, a heritage which they handed on to the Queen Anne Wits, Swift, Pope, Prior and Gay, and through them to the Byron of 'Beppo', 'The Vision of Judgment' and 'Don Juan'.

THE RESTORATION COURT POETS

A Select Bibliography

(Books published in London, unless otherwise stated)

Abbreviations

CHEL   *Cambridge History of English Literature*
ESMEA   *Essays and Studies by Members of the English Association*
MLN   *Modern Language Notes*
NQ   *Notes and Queries*
PQ   *Philological Quarterly*
RES   *Review of English Studies*
RMS   *Renaissance and Modern Studies*

JOHN WILMOT, EARL OF ROCHESTER

Bibliography:
   JOHN WILMOT, EARL OF ROCHESTER, HIS LIFE AND WRITINGS, by J. Prinz.
      Leipzig (1927)
   —contains a full descriptive bibliography of Rochester's writings.
   ROCHESTER'S POEMS ON SEVERAL OCCASIONS, ed. J. Thorpe. Princeton
      (1950)
   —deals with the complex status and order of the so-called 'Antwerp'
      editions (see below). This and the following work contain valuable
      bibliographical information not in Prinz.
   ATTRIBUTION IN RESTORATION POETRY, by D. Vieth (1963).

Collected Works:
   POEMS ON SEVERAL OCCASIONS. 'Antwerp' (1680)
   —the 'Antwerp' imprint is almost certainly spurious. At least ten
      editions (fewer than twenty copies of which have survived) were
      surreptitiously printed from 1680 onwards, either dated or ante-
      dated 1680, or without date. It includes a number of poems which
      are not by Rochester. A facsimile of the Huntington Library copy,
      ed. J. Thorpe, Princeton, 1950, contains a valuable introduction and
      notes.

POEMS ON SEVERAL OCCASIONS (1685)

—omits nine poems which appeared in the preceding collection but adds five others. Reprinted, 1701, 1712.

POEMS &C. ON SEVERAL OCCASIONS, WITH VALENTINIAN, A TRAGEDY (1691)

—an expurgated text but contains additional authentic poems. Published by Jacob Tonson with Preface by Thomas Rymer. Reprinted, 1696, 1705.

THE MISCELLANEOUS WORKS (1707)

—printed and sold by B. Bragge. Pirated by E. Curll, 1707, 1709. Contains poems by other authors besides Rochester. The 'Life of Rochester' is not (as stated in the title) by Saint Evremond.

THE WORKS (1714)

—a reprint of Tonson's edition of 1705 including a number of Rochester's letters. For later editions, notably of the 2-vol. collection of poems by Rochester, Roscommon, Dorset, &c., 1714 (many times reprinted with or without 'The Cabinet of Love' appendix during the 18th century), see Prinz's bibliography.

THE COLLECTED WORKS, ed. J. Hayward (1926)

—contains almost everything that has been attributed to Rochester, including a number of spurious poems. A Nonesuch limited edition.

POEMS, ed. V. de S. Pinto (1953)

—in the Muses' Library. The first attempt to establish a reliable canon, though not a definitive text, of the poems. Includes an appendix of poems attributed to Rochester on doubtful authority. Revised edition, 1964.

Separate Works:

A SATYR AGAINST MANKIND WRITTEN BY A PERSON OF HONOUR [c.1679]
—a folio poem published according to Anthony à Wood in June 1679. Several of Rochester's poems were published separately in folio towards the end of his life (v., as examples, the two following entries).

UPON NOTHING BY A PERSON OF HONOUR [c.1679]
—two undated folios published about 1679. Reprinted by E. Curll, 1711, and by R. H. Griffiths, Texas, 1946.

A LETTER FROM ARTEMISA IN THE TOWN TO CHLOE IN THE COUNTRY (1670, also undated)
—two editions in folio exist.

VALENTINIAN A TRAGEDY AS 'TIS ALTER'D BY THE LATE EARL OF ROCHESTER (1685—two issues)
—contains an important preface by Robert Wolseley, reprinted in *Critical Essays of the Seventeenth Century*, edited by J. E. Spingarn, vol. iii, 1909.

FAMILIAR LETTERS. 2 vols. (1697 *bis*)
—reprinted 1699, 1705.

THE ROCHESTER-SAVILE LETTERS 1671-1680, ed. J. H. Wilson. Columbus, Ohio (1941)
—a modern edition of the letters to Henry Savile in *Familiar Letters* together with Savile's extant letters to Rochester.

THE FAMOUS PATHOLOGIST OR THE NOBLE MOUNTEBANK, by Thomas Alcock and John Wilmot Earl of Rochester, ed. V. de S. Pinto. Nottingham (1961)
—Rochester's 'Mountebank Bill' printed from the MS of his servant T. Alcock with Alcock's preface telling how he masqueraded as the Italian quack doctor 'Bendo'. A contemporary, possibly the original, printed edition of Alexander Bendo's Advertisement (no place, printer, or date) has survived in an apparently unique copy.

Some Biographical and Critical Studies:

A SERMON PREACHED AT THE FUNERAL OF THE RT. HONORABLE JOHN EARL OF ROCHESTER, by R. Parsons. Oxford (1680)

SOME PASSAGES OF THE LIFE AND DEATH OF THE RIGHT HONOURABLE JOHN EARL OF ROCHESTER, by G. Burnet (1680)
—reprinted in numerous 18th-century editions (and in *English Biography of the Seventeenth Century*, edited by V. de S. Pinto, 1951), and the basis of many hortatory tracts and pious pamphlets issued as religious propaganda up to the end of the 19th century.

THE LIVES OF THE MOST EMINENT ENGLISH POETS, by S. Johnson (1781)
—includes Johnson's Life of Rochester.

'John Wilmot Comte de Rochester', par E. D. Forgues. In *La Revue de Deux Mondes*, Aug.-Sept. 1857.

ROCHESTERIANA, collected and edited by J. Prinz. Leipzig (1926).

JOHN WILMOT, EARL OF ROCHESTER, HIS LIFE AND WRITINGS, by J. Prinz. Leipzig (1927).

ROCHESTER, by C. Williams (1935).

BEAST IN VIEW, by F. Whitfield. Cambridge, Mass. (1939).

'Rochester and the Right Veine of Satire', by V. de S. Pinto. In *ESMEA*, N.S. v, 1953.

'Rochester's "Scepter Lampoon" on Charles II', by D. Vieth. In *PQ*, 37, 1958.

'Rochester and Dryden', by V. de S. Pinto. In *RMS*, v, 1961.

ENTHUSIAST IN WIT: A PORTRAIT OF JOHN WILMOT EARL OF ROCHESTER, by V. de S. Pinto (1962)

—revised and enlarged edition of *Rochester: Portrait of a Restoration Poet*, by the same author, 1935.

CHARLES SACKVILLE, EARL OF DORSET

Bibliography:

'A Check-List of Dorset's Poems', by H. A. Bagley. In *MLN*, xlvii, November 1932, pp. 454-61.

'Some Additions to the Poems of Lord Dorset', by R. G. Howarth. In *MLN*, l, November 1935, p. 457.

Collected Works:

THE WORKS OF THE EARLS OF ROCHESTER, ROSCOMMON, DORSET &C. 2 vols. (1714)

—vol. ii contains the earliest known collection of 'Poems by the Earl of Dorset'.

THE WORKS OF THE MOST CELEBRATED MINOR POETS. 2 vols. (1749)

—vol. i contains 'Poems by the Earl of Dorset'. Reprinted Dublin, 1751.

A SUPPLEMENT TO THE WORKS OF THE MINOR POETS PART I (n.d.)

—contains additional poems by Dorset.

Separate Works:

POMPEY THE GREAT (1664)

—translation of *La Mort de Pompée* of P. Corneille. See below under 'Sir Charles Sedley'.

THE NOBLE SEAMANS COMPLAINT TO THE LADIES AT LAND TO YE TUNE OF SHACKERLEY HAY

—broadside ballad entered in the Stationers' Register, 30 December 1664. No copy is known to survive. This is Dorset's famous ballad usually known as 'Song Written at Sea in the First Dutch War'. The earliest extant printed version is that which appears in *Wit and Mirth or Pills to Purge Melancholy*, Vol. V, 1714, pp. 168-70 under the title 'A Ballad by the Late Lord Dorset when at Sea'. There is an early manuscript version of this poem in Br. Mus. Harl. MS 3991, printed by N. Ault in his *Seventeenth Century Lyrics*, 1928, p. 333.

A COLLECTION OF POEMS WRITTEN UPON SEVERAL OCCASIONS BY SEVERAL PERSONS (1672)

—printed for Hobart Kemp. Contains three poems probably by Buckhurst (Dorset). This important collection was the predecessor or a number of other Restoration miscellanies containing a few poems by Dorset.

POEMS ON AFFAIRS OF STATE (1697)

—contains Dorset's 'The Duel of the Crabs', a parody of Sir Robert Howard's 'The Duel of the Stags'.

Some Biographical and Critical Studies:

THE LIVES OF THE MOST EMINENT ENGLISH POETS, by S. Johnson (1781)

—includes Johnson's Life of Dorset.

CHARLES SACKVILLE, SIXTH EARL OF DORSET PATRON AND POET OF THE RESTORATION, by B. Harris. Urbana, Illinois (1940).

SIR CHARLES SEDLEY

Bibliography:

THE POETICAL AND DRAMATIC WORKS, ed. V. de S. Pinto. 2 vols. (1928)

—contains a bibliography of Sedley's writings.

Collected Works:

THE MISCELLANEOUS WORKS, ed. Capt. Ayloffe (1702)

—reprinted with additional material, not all of which is by Sedley, 1707 and 1710.

THE WORKS, 2 vols. (1722)

—contains an account of the Life of Sedley, possibly by Defoe. Reprinted, 1776 and 1778.

THE POETICAL AND DRAMATIC WORKS, ed. V. de S. Pinto. 2 vols. (1928).

Separate Works:

POMPEY THE GREAT (1664)

—translation of *La Mort de Pompée* of P. Corneille by Waller, Buckhurst, Sedley, Godolphin and Filmer. Act III possibly by Sedley.

THE MULBERRY GARDEN (1668)

—reprinted, 1675 and 1688.

A COLLECTION OF POEMS WRITTEN UPON SEVERAL OCCASIONS BY SEVERAL PERSONS (1672)

—printed for Hobart Kemp. Contains about thirty poems by Sedley, including some of his best lyrics. Reprinted for T. Collins and

J. Ford, 1673. Contains some additional matter. Reprinted with
further additional matter and some alterations for F. Saunders, 1693.
ANTONY AND CLEOPATRA (1677)
—reprinted, 1696.
BELLAMIRA OR THE MISTRESS (1687).
THE HAPPY PAIR (1702)

Biographical and Critical Study:
SIR CHARLES SEDLEY, by V. de S. Pinto (1927).

SIR GEORGE ETHEREGE
Bibliography:
THE DRAMATIC WORKS, ed. H. F. B. Brett Smith. 2 vols. Oxford (1927)
—contains a bibliography of the plays.
THE POEMS, ed. J. Thorpe. Princeton (1963)
—contains valuable bibliographical information about the poems.

Collected Works:
THE WORKS (1704).
THE WORKS, ed. A. W. Verity (1888).
THE DRAMATIC WORKS, ed. H. F. B. Brett Smith. 2 vols. Oxford (1927).
THE POEMS, ed. J. Thorpe. Princeton (1963).

Separate Works:
THE COMICAL REVENGE OR LOVE IN A TUB (1664)
—reprinted 1667, 1669, 1689, 1697.
SHE WOU'D IF SHE COU'D (1668)
—reprinted 1671, 1693, 1710.
THE MAN OF MODE OR SIR FOPLING FLUTTER (1676)
—reprinted 1684, 1693, 1711.
THE LETTERBOOK OF SIR GEORGE ETHEREGE, ed. S. Rosenfeld. Oxford
(1928).

Some Biographical and Critical Studies:
SEVENTEENTH CENTURY STUDIES, by E. Gosse (1883).
THE COMEDY OF MANNERS, by J. Palmer (1913).
ESSAYS IN BIOGRAPHY, by B. Dobrée (1925).
Contributions by Dorothy Foster to *NQ*, vols. cliii, 1927 and cliv,
1928, and *RES*, vol. viii, 1932.
ETHEREGE AND THE SEVENTEENTH CENTURY COMEDY OF MANNERS, by
D. Underwood. Oxford (1957).

GENERAL WORKS

Bibliography:

A BIBLIOGRAPHY OF ENGLISH POETICAL MISCELLANIES 1521-1750, by A.
E. Case (1935).

ENGLISH SONG BOOKS 1651-1702, A BIBLIOGRAPHY, by C. L. Day and
E. Boswell. (1940).

Some Biographical and Critical Studies:

ATHENAE OXONIENSES, by Anthony à Wood. 2 vols. (1691-2)

—edited by P. Bliss, 4 vols. 1813-20.

THE LIVES OF THE MOST EMINENT ENGLISH POETS, by S. Johnson. 4 vols.
(1781)

—revised edition of 1783 edited by G. B. Hill, 3 vols. Oxford, 1905.

ANECDOTES, OBSERVATIONS AND CHARACTERS OF BOOKS AND MEN
COLLECTED FROM THE CONVERSATION OF MR. POPE AND OTHER
EMINENT PERSONS OF HIS TIME, by Joseph Spence, ed. S. W. Singer
(1820)

—a definitive edition of *Spence's Anecdotes*, edited by J. M. Osborn,
will shortly be published by the Oxford University Press.

BRIEF LIVES, by John Aubrey, ed. A. Clark, 2 vols. Oxford (1898)

—edited by A. Powell, 1949.

CRITICAL ESSAYS OF THE SEVENTEENTH CENTURY, ed. J. E. Spingarn.
3 vols. Oxford (1908).

'The Court Poets', by C. Whibley. In *CHEL*, viii (1912).

REVALUATION, by F. R. Leavis (1936).

THE COURT WITS OF THE RESTORATION, by J. H. Wilson. Princeton
(1948).

RESTORATION CARNIVAL, by V. de S. Pinto (1954)

—a Folio Society limited edition.

Historical and Social Background:

MÉMOIRES DU CHEVALIER DE GRAMONT, par A. Hamilton. Cologne
(1713)

—translated by Peter Quennell, 1930. Edited by C. Engel, Monaco
1958.

THE HISTORY OF MY OWN TIME, by Gilbert Burnet, 2 vols. (1724-34)

—edited by O. Airy, 2 vols. Oxford, 1897-1900.

THE LIFE OF EDWARD EARL OF CLARENDON WRITTEN BY HIMSELF. Oxford
(1759)

—2nd edition, 2 vols. Oxford, 1857.

THE DIARY OF JOHN EVELYN, ed. E. S. de Beer, 6 vols. Oxford (1955).

THE DIARY OF SAMUEL PEPYS, ed. H. B. Wheatley. 10 vols. (1893-9).

KING CHARLES II, by A. Bryant (1931).

ENGLAND IN THE REIGN OF CHARLES II, by D. Ogg. 2 vols. Oxford (1956).

POETRY AND POLITICS UNDER THE STUARTS, by C. V. Wedgwood (1960).

POEMS ON AFFAIRS OF STATE vol. I 1660-1678, ed. G. de F. Lord (1963).

WRITERS AND THEIR WORK: NO. 187

Louis MacNeice

by JOHN PRESS

Published for the British Council
and the National Book League
by Longmans, Green & Co

This is the first considerable study of Louis MacNeice to be published since his death in 1963. John Press, who knew MacNeice and is himself a poet, skilfully draws attention to the complex and contradictory elements in MacNeice's character and life which influenced his poetry. A prolific and versatile writer in many fields, including radio drama, he first became known, with Spender, Auden and Day Lewis, as one of the leading 'Poets of the Thirties'. Though his attitude towards the world did not change fundamentally as he grew older, the poetry of his final years displayed a new gravity and astringency. In the last few years of his life he was again beginning to win widespread esteem after a period of comparative neglect.

In this interpretation of a contemporary 'poet of genius', as T. S. Eliot called him, John Press surveys every aspect of his work. His essay and his bibliography will prove invaluable to all students of MacNeice.

John Press has published two books of poems and three works of criticism, the most recent of which is *Rule and Energy* (1963). He is the author of *Andrew Marvell* and *Herrick* in the *Writers and Their Work* series.

Acknowledgments: Our thanks are due to the following for permission to quote from works in copyright: to the executors of Louis MacNeice and to Messrs. Faber & Faber for material from *Collected Poems 1925-1948*, *Visitations*, *Solstices* and *The Burning Perch*; to Mr. Geoffrey Grigson and to Phoenix House for material from *Poetry of the Present*.

Bibliographical Series
of Supplements to 'British Book News'
on Writers and Their Work

GENERAL EDITOR
Geoffrey Bullough

¶ LOUIS MACNEICE was born in Belfast on 12 September 1907, and died in London on 3 September 1963.

LOUIS MACNEICE

LOUIS MACNEICE

LOUIS MACNEICE

by

JOHN PRESS

PUBLISHED FOR
THE BRITISH COUNCIL
AND THE NATIONAL BOOK LEAGUE
BY LONGMANS, GREEN & CO

LONGMANS, GREEN & CO LTD
48 Grosvenor Street, London, W.1

*Associated companies, branches and
representatives throughout the world*

First Published 1965
© John Press 1965

*Printed in Great Britain
F. Mildner & Sons, London, E.C.1*

LOUIS MACNEICE

I. LIFE

LOUIS MACNEICE was born in Belfast on 12 September 1907, and when he was still almost an infant his father, John Federick MacNeice (who later became a Bishop), was appointed rector of Carrickfergus. The family, being unable to take immediate possession of the rectory because the retiring incumbent was on his death-bed, moved for a while into a house overlooking the harbour, where the child used to sit watching the sailing-boats as they moved westward. MacNeice once remarked that most poets have access to a poetic landscape which is the constant background of all their work, and certainly he was haunted throughout his life by memories of childhood scenes. He serves indeed as a perfect illustration of Cyril Connolly's dictum that 'the one golden recipe for Art is the ferment of an unhappy childhood working through a noble imagination'.

His mother died when he was young and, despite his father's remarriage, he was often left in the charge of domestic servants, who were unsympathetic to a lonely, sensitive child. Some of his early memories were awesome, but not horrifying. He never forgot the sight of the *Titanic* as she passed down Belfast Lough on her maiden voyage: the image of the doomed ship's drifting towards the iceberg is prominent in a late poem, 'Death of an Old Lady', and recurs in *The Administrator*, one of his last plays for radio. Other memories were more disturbing, and some of the mythologies which he wove round the red-brick rectory influenced his dreams until his death. We know from his own account that he was afraid of blindness, of long corridors, of light glancing off a mirror; his loneliness, the old wives' tales recounted by the servants, his familiarity with the terrifying imagery of the Bible and his frequent nightmares must have accentuated his predisposition to fear:

5

> When I was five the black dreams came;
> Nothing after was quite the same.
>
> *Come back early or never come.*
>
> The dark was talking to the dead;
> The lamp was dark beside my bed.

Moreover, as he tells us,

> I also had certain early contacts with both mental illness and mental deficiency (these latter may explain the *petrification* images which appear pretty often in my poems, e.g. in *Perseus*). I should add that our house was lit by oil lamps (not enough of them) and so was full of shadows .... These circumstances between them must have supplied me with many images of fear, anxiety, loneliness or monotony (to be used very often quite out of a personal context). They may also explain—by reaction— what I now think an excessive preoccupation in my earlier work with things dazzling, high-coloured, quick-moving, hedonistic or up-to-date.

MacNeice recognized the fact that his childhood experiences had left an ineffaceable mark upon him:

> I was the rector's son, born to the anglican order,
>   Banned for ever from the candles of the Irish poor;
> The Chichesters knelt in marble at the ends of a transept
>   With ruffs about their necks, their portion sure.

Even in the Chichester transept there was a source of fear: above the huge monument there hung a coat-of-arms which took on the shape of an evil man looking down at the rector's son. And long before Jimmy Porter delivered his tirade against church bells in *Look Back in Anger*, Louis MacNeice saw them as skulls' mouths.

Yet it would be wrong to suppose that MacNeice gained nothing of positive value from his upbringing. His father was a man of some distinction, who played a prominent part in settling a local dock-strike, and who in the years before 1914 showed his independence of mind by being a home-ruler and a pacifist. He later scandalized Belfast by refusing to allow the Union Jack to be hung in perpetuity over Carson's tomb in St. Patrick's Cathedral. Louis MacNeice also remembered with gratitude that he had grown up in a household where commercial values were not supreme, where he had a good deal of time to himself, and where books were plentiful.

He was educated at Marlborough and then went up to Oxford, where he dressed foppishly, grew long side-whiskers and cultivated an admiration for Nietzsche. His tutor, deceived by MacNeice's apparent neglect of his work, prophesied that he would get a Third, and was confounded when he obtained a First in Mods and in Greats. Over thirty years afterwards MacNeice explained that two undergraduates (Quintin Hogg and R. S. Crossman) were pointed out to him as men certain to get Firsts. He thereupon decided that if such dull-looking people could do so he would emulate them, but 'I will lounge my way in like Petronius Arbiter'.

Even as an undergraduate he had begun to prefer Aristotle to Plato. Looking back on this youthful preference, he quoted Shelley's lines from 'Adonais':

> Life, like a dome of many-coloured glass,
> Stains the white radiance of eternity

and commented: 'Aristotle, being among other things a zoologist, never let a transcendental radiance destroy the shapes of the creatures or impose a white-out on everything.' His undergraduate days were perhaps, as he put it, 'a limbo period spent in slouching', but his abilities and opinions had already started to ripen.

After leaving Oxford he became a lecturer in Classics, first at Birmingham, where he was a prominent member of a remarkably talented circle, and then at Bedford College, London. His youthful marriage did not last long, and the outbreak of war found him lecturing at Cornell. Characteristically, for he was a man of vivacious, stubborn pugnacity, he chose to come back to England in 1940. Equally characteristically, he wrote a cool, unsentimental article, printed in *Horizon*, February 1941, about those British writers who had sailed for the United States in the late 1930s and had decided to stay there. A writer, he argued, can best serve his country by writing, and only he can judge where his imagination enjoys its fullest play. MacNeice admitted that although he never felt at home in England he found it more stimulating to live there than in Ireland or elsewhere. He had therefore returned to England but, as an ex-expatriate, he defended those writers who had remained in America: 'They have consciences of their own, and the last word must be said by their own instinct as artists.'

Soon after his return to England he married Hedli Anderson, for whom W. H. Auden had written some of his early cabaret songs. He began to work for the B.B.C., and remained in its employ until his death over twenty years later. He gave devoted service, and the Corporation proved in its turn a generous employer, granting him leave of absence so that he could take temporary posts in South Africa, India and Greece, where he spent a year as Director of the British Institute in Athens.

MacNeice wrote and produced a large number of feature programmes for the B.B.C. When recording one of these in the summer of 1963, he insisted on accompanying the engineers down a pot-hole, got soaked, and sat about in wet clothes. He contracted a chill, but on 26 August wrote a cheerful letter, enclosed with a note about his forthcoming volume, *The Burning Perch*, which was to be the Poetry Book Society's Autumn Choice. His chill took a turn for the worse, and he died in hospital on 3 September.

II. PROSE, DRAMA AND TRANSLATIONS

MacNeice was a prolific, versatile, highly professional writer, and it is worth examining his work in other branches of literature before we consider his original poetry. He was the author of two works of criticism, a number of lively

critical essays, numerous reviews, a score of radio scripts
(mostly unpublished), several plays (also mostly unpublished), translations of Aeschylus and of Goethe, a pseudony-
mous novel, a children's story, a book on astrology, a
booklet on the American army, and two or three volumes
which can best be described as gallimaufries. One of these,
Letters from Iceland, published in 1937 and written in
collaboration with W. H. Auden, still repays study as a
document of the times. It contains some of the silliest bits
of facetious writing ever committed by either author, some
admirable descriptive prose, a few good poems, Auden's
coruscating 'Letter to Lord Byron', which unfortunately
he has never reprinted, and a joint 'testament', crammed
with personal allusions, cultural chit-chat and bawdy jokes.

Zoo and *I Crossed the Minch* were two pot-boilers, both
of which appeared in 1938. Their ostensible themes are,
respectively, the London Zoo and the islands of the Outer
Hebrides, but both contain many digressions and autobiographical reminiscences, which are, indeed, the most
valuable portions of the books. Two passages from *Zoo*
are interesting for the light they throw upon MacNeice's
response to the visible world and upon his philosophical
outlook:

The pleasure of dappled things, the beauty of adaptation to purpose,
the glory of extravagance, classic elegance or romantic nonsense and
grotesquerie—all of these we get from the Zoo. We react to these with
the same delight as to new potatoes in April speckled with chopped
parsley or the lights at night on the Thames of Battersea Power House,
or to cars sweeping their shadows from lamp-post to lamp-post down
Haverstock Hill or to brewer's drays or to lighthouses and searchlights
or to a newly cut lawn or to a hot towel or a friction at the barber's or
to Moran's two classic tries at Twickenham in 1937 or to the smell of
dusting-powder in a warm bathroom or to the fun of shelling peas into
a china bowl or of shuffling one's feet through dead leaves when they
are crisp or to the noise of rain or the crackling of a newly lit fire or the
jokes of a street-hawker or the silence of snow in moonlight or the
purring of a powerful car.

Original Sin won for us a life of progress, pattern of dark and light, the necessity of winning our bread which builds our wits, the tension without which there is no music and the conflict without which there is no harmony.

MacNeice's other miscellaneous writings need not detain us. His booklet on the American servicemen is sensible, the children's story is unremarkable, and the novel is dull, although it has a promising theme—the attempt of a young intellectual to escape from the futility of life at Oxford, his elopement and marriage with the daughter of the nerve specialist who has certified him as unbalanced, and his return to Oxford as a don, partially reconciled with himself and his environment. *Astrology*, published posthumously in 1964, testifies to its author's life-long interest in chance, superstition and the irrational aspects of human nature. When he was a young man MacNeice was adept at telling fortunes by cards, and he never lost his fondness for blarney or his delight in man's credulity.

His critical work, on the other hand, deserves to be studied with some attention. He did not make inflated claims about the value of criticism, as the following passage may suggest:

The best criticism, like the best philosophy, tends to be negative. It is inferior philosophy, like pragmatism, that influences action, and it is a narrow and limited criticism that encourages the production of art. What the artist and the reader need is an Aristotle or a Dr. Johnson.

His own criticism is, within the limits which he set himself, acute and illuminating. He believed that a reviewer should not pontificate about poetry in the abstract, but concentrate on singling out specific faults and merits in the individual poems. Even in his full-scale critical works the most valuable portions are those in which MacNeice is speaking as a craftsman, and drawing on his knowledge of technique.

Thus in *Modern Poetry: a Personal Essay*, he continually tests abstruse theories of rhythm by reference to specific lines of verse, and suggests that even Gerard Manley Hopkins sometimes allows his passion for elaborate speculation about metrics to distort the movement of his verse. He agrees with G. M. Young that a whole poem written to the pattern of 'Put your knife and your fork across your plate' would be intolerable, but argues that in a melodramatic passage about an impending murder the heavy, irregular stresses would produce an admirably sinister effect, if cunningly employed:

> The dark is falling and the hour is late:
> *Put your knife and your fork across your plate.*

It is context and normal speech that determine whether or not a particular metre is appropriate. Thus he observes that

'Pussy-cat, Pussy-cat, where have you been?' is a good line rhythmically, but I should not like to write, 'Polar Bear, Polar Bear, where have you been?' For (a) in ordinary speech we say 'Pólar Béar' and (b) 'bear' is here a more important syllable than '-cat' both for sound-value and meaning.

Again, MacNeice remarks that 'The Polar Bear prowled on the ice' is a more satisfactory line than 'The Polar Bear was prowling on the ice', since the former throws the proper stress on the important words and gives the right effect of weight.

MacNeice always emphasizes the supreme value of rhythmical vitality in poetry. After quoting Nijinsky's cryptic utterance, 'I am going to dance the war', he comments: 'In the same way the poet dances his experiences in words.' He never abandoned his belief that rhyme, strongly-marked rhythmical patterns, artifice and technical inventiveness were desirable elements of poetry. In a review of Reuben Brower's critical study, *The Poetry of Robert Frost*, printed in the *New Statesman*, 12 July 1963, a few weeks before his death, MacNeice displays an astringent contempt for some fashionable theorizing on these matters:

Thus several reviewers of Thom Gunn's last book seemed to assume that his abandonment of recognisable rhythmical patterns for unrecognisable syllabic ones *automatically* marked an advance and betokened an increase in profundity. Similarly some idiot recently stated that rhyme in English poetry was now a thing of the past.

He quotes with approval Frost's dictum: 'I had as soon write free verse as play tennis with the net down', and adds a rider of his own:

A sentence in prose is struck forward like a golf ball; a sentence in verse can be treated like a ball in a squash court. Frost is a master of angles.

This recalls his comparison, made in *Modern Poetry*, between poetry and one of his favourite games:

The mere arranging of verse in lines serves the same purpose as the offside rule in rugger and the rule against forward passes; instead of the meaning being passed vertically down the field as it is in prose, each line in verse when it comes to an end passes back to the beginning of the next (and I am not only thinking of typography). This method, as in rugger, gives a sweeping movement, an impression of controlled speed and power—an impression which is enhanced when the verse is on a recognisable rhythmical pattern.

MacNeice's critical wit, though seldom unkind, is occasionally devastating. After quoting Eliot's remark about the ordinary man who 'falls in love, or reads Spinoza', MacNeice drily observes: 'It is typical of Eliot that his ordinary man should read Spinoza.' And one of his aphorisms makes abundantly clear the distinction between poetry and propaganda which MacNeice maintained throughout his life: 'Others can tell lies more efficiently; no one except the poet can give us poetic truth.'

MacNeice's book, *The Poetry of W. B. Yeats* (1941), was the first full-length study of the poet to be published after Yeats's death. It was written before any collection of Yeats's letters had appeared, and before the industrious Yeatsian research-workers had begun to burrow in the archives preserved by the poet's widow. In a sense, therefore, it is an unscholarly work based on insufficient evidence. Yet it exhibits certain qualities unequalled by later tomes on Yeats: it is by a man who was both a poet and an Irishman and who could look at the published verse and prose of Yeats undistracted by the mass of secondary and often irrelevant documents which all subsequent commentators have felt bound to digest. MacNeice's chapter on the Irish background remains an admirable introduction to the subject; his discussion of Yeats's political beliefs avoids the uneasy special pleading to which some apologists have been driven. MacNeice acknowledges the distasteful truth that Yeats came to adopt 'his own elegant brand of fascism', however tempting it may be to pretend that all he really wanted was a revival of eighteenth-century aristocratic values. Nor does MacNeice burke the fact that Yeats was in some ways a *poseur*. Yet he has no doubt that, despite his flaws, he was a great poet. It is easy to dismiss MacNeice's view of Yeats as the shallow judgement of a young Left-wing poet writing soon after the outbreak of war; but his summing-up is likely to commend itself to all those who, while accepting Yeats as a major poet, are not disposed to revere him as a political guide or as an expounder of esoteric wisdom.

MacNeice occasionally anticipates in a couple of sentences the elaborate disquisitions of more ponderous Yeatsian scholars. Thus he remarks of Yeats's early verse dramas: 'Aristotle would not have considered them plays at all. They are pieces of tapestry.' Now that Yeats is sometimes spoken of in the same breath as Shakespeare it is refreshing to read the comments of a man who loved the poetry of Yeats this side idolatry:

When Yeats was an old man he was not, according to his friends, in the least tortured by fear of death and even welcomed jokes about his own. Being a vain man he was well pleased with himself and with his latter-day fame and even with the publicity of the Senate House. He also drew strength from two new kinds of adventuring—into the world of sense and sensuality on the one hand, and into the magical philosophical world of *A Vision* on the other. His poetry kept pace with these adventures and his poetic energy accumulated.

Yeats's later poetry contains an element that is very like humour. When he attempted humour in his plays he usually failed, but in private life he had not only wit and an Irish joy in hyperbole, but a fine supply of animal spirits which made him relish blasphemy, indecency, and malicious personal gossip . . . .
The humour in his later poems seems to be a blend of whimsicality, bravado, canniness and sadism.

Whatever the Yeatsian experts may say, MacNeice's book is a stimulating account of a great poet, and a salutary corrective to the adulation which has been lavished upon him for the past twenty-five years.

Although most of MacNeice's dramatic works were in the form of radio scripts, he wrote a number of plays for the stage. *Eureka* and *One for the Dead: a Modern Morality Play* remain unpublished and unperformed; *Station Bell*, of which all traces seem to have vanished, was given one performance in the 1930s by the University English Club at Birmingham; *Traitors in Our Way*, an unpublished drama about treason in a society threatened by Communism, was staged by the Group Theatre, Belfast in 1957. *Out of the Picture* was written for the Group Theatre, London, and performed there in 1937, with production by Rupert Doone, music by Benjamin Britten, sets and costumes by Robert Medley. It was, in short, a highly characteristic period piece.

The protagonist is a neurotic painter, whose picture of Venus is bought by a film star, Clara de Groot. In a confusing sequence of episodes, performed while the radio announces the coming of war, the painter falls in love with Clara, shoots a Cabinet Minister and goes to bed with a model called Moll O'Hara, who first gives him a drug that will kill him after two hours, as an act of mercy.

It cannot be described as a successful play. Some of the

favourite tricks of the Thirties' repertoire are trotted out:
surrealist humour, Freudian clichés, a fantastic plot, card-
board characters indulging in buffoonery, satirical attacks
on society, and long monologues which mingle farcical
parody and hysterical rhetoric. And all these are packed into
a ramshackle vehicle, whose dramatic machinery makes
loud, creaking noises and moves jerkily. MacNeice takes
over the Radio Announcer, beloved of Auden and Isherwood, and invents one or two symbolic figures, such as a
sinister Auctioneer, who turns up again in one of his last
radio-plays, *The Mad Islands.*

MacNeice salvaged a few lyrics from this play and reprinted them in his *Collected Poems.* There are also some
passages which are typical of his youthful preoccupations,
notably Venus's speech about those who have gone into the
land of death:

> Their heads and their eyes are of stone,
> Being no longer organisms of nature
> But final versions of an artist's vision.

We get also some characteristic passages about the sheer
pleasure of being alive:

> The dog stares into the fire, beatitude of platitude,
> God be praised that things are as they are,
> That grass is green, that water is wet, that trees are tall,

and an expression of MacNeice's reverence for courage,
uncomplaining endurance and energy:

> Blessed are the reckless spendthrifts of vitality
> But blessed also are all who last the course,
> Blessed are those who endure as a point of etiquette
> And blessed are the cynics who carry their cross as a gesture.

Another passage seems to anticipate the fire-raids on London
which were soon to become a potent image in MacNeice's
verse:

There is nothing to stem the mechanical march of fire.
Nothing to assuage the malice of the drunken fire.
FIRE FIRE FIRE FIRE.

Most of MacNeice's dramatic writing took the shape of radio scripts, a medium in which he laboured for over twenty years. Charles Lamb said that his true *Works* lay in the ledgers of the East India Company, and much of MacNeice's literary output is yellowing in the files of the B.B.C. It is difficult to judge the merits of his work in this field, since most of it is unpublished, including *Prisoner's Progress*, which won the *Premio Italiano* in 1954; but those scripts which have been printed are, for all their ingenuity and skill, unsatisfying and strangely insubstantial.

MacNeice devoted considerable thought to drama in general and to radio drama in particular. In an unpublished lecture delivered at Cambridge in 1959, entitled 'Lyric into Drama', he discussed the reasons for the decay of verse in the theatre, and suggested that the finest 'poetic' effects in the drama of our time had been created by dramatists using the medium of prose. In his introduction to the 1963 edition of his radio play, *Christopher Columbus*, which had been first published in 1944, he reverts to this theme, explaining his development as a writer for radio:

> In most of my later radio plays (for the same reason I suppose as the more *poetic* of contemporary writers for the theatre) I avoided verse and preferred a kind of sleight-of-hand colloquial dialogue.

Although he continued to write radio scripts, MacNeice admitted that the medium was transitory and limited. The introduction already quoted reads like a valediction to the form on which he had lavished his talents:

> Many years later, re-reading both the play itself and my own introduction to it, I feel I am returning to an innocent but quaint and archaic period. The nickname 'steam radio' is properly nostalgic: rarely has an up-to-date medium matured, and indeed aged, so rapidly.

But there are more fundamental reasons for the disappointing quality of MacNeice's radio scripts. His introduction to the 1944 edition makes a damaging avowal:

With a literature as old as ours and a contemporary diction so vulgarised, precise and emotive writing comes to depend more and more upon twists—twists of the obvious statement or the hackneyed image. To do this on the printed page requires constant ingenuity and often leads to an appearance of being too clever by half.

The temptation to rely on twists and sleight-of-hand was dangerous to a writer of MacNeice's facility and quickness of wit. The use of radiophonic devices concealed the structural weakness of the writing, while the music composed for *Christopher Columbus* by William Walton, and for *The Dark Tower* by Benjamin Britten carried the reader over the thinner patches of the drama. As MacNeice acknowledged, the music of these composers supplied a dimension which the scripts otherwise lacked.

In *Christopher Columbus* there is no attempt to survey the life of Columbus, or even to portray accurately the complicated dispute between him and the Commissioners who opposed his voyage of exploration. MacNeice concentrates on Columbus's fanatical resolve to find the Western route to Asia, and on the triumphant conclusion of his Quest—the discovery of a New World. This is, in many ways, MacNeice's most successful radio script, because he has eschewed all trickiness, and allowed his theme to unfold itself in its simplicity and grandeur.

Unfortunately, the medium of the radio script encouraged MacNeice's predilection for the slightly portentous symbol and for the resonant trumpet-call urging us to go onwards and upwards. *The Dark Tower* resembles *Christopher Columbus* in being a play about a Quest. Its hero, Roland, like the hero of Browning's poem, 'Childe Roland', sets out to challenge a Dragon, who is reputed to live in a Dark Tower. Before the play opens, Roland's brothers have, one by one, undertaken a similar Quest and have never returned from their mission.

The Dark Tower is a repository of well-worn symbols from the common stock of the Thirties and from MacNeice's private treasury. There is the Mother who, like the formidable matriarch in Auden and Isherwood's *The Ascent of F6*, drives on her son to achievement or to vengeance (she appears again in another Quest play, *The Mad Islands*, published in 1964 and broadcast two years before). Then we have a Parrot, the voice of negation and defeat, who pops up again in *Autumn Sequel*, and once more we encounter MacNeice's obsession with stone. He feels obliged to write a Note about this image, which had baffled his radio audience:

> The Child of Stone puzzled many listeners. The Mother in bearing so many children only to send them to their death, can be thought of as thereby bearing a series of deaths. So her logical last child is stone—her own death. This motif has an echo in the stone in the ring.

This stone in the ring plays a crucial part in the unfolding of the action. For when it ceases to burn, thereby signifying that the Mother no longer wants her son Roland to pursue the Quest, he throws away the ring, which strikes a stone bearing an inscription:

> To Those Who Did Not Go Back—
> Whose Bones being Nowhere, their signature is for All Men—
> Who went to their Death of their Own Free Will
> Bequeathing Free Will to Others.

Inspired by this message, he goes on, summons the Dragon to come out of the Dark Tower, which has mysteriously arisen from the ground, and blows the Challenge Call. The voice of the Sergeant Trumpeter, a cross between a family retainer and a Regular Non-Commissioned Officer, repeats the instruction which he gave at the opening of the play: 'Hold that note at the end.' The text then continues:

> The trumpet holds it, enriched and endorsed by the orchestra. They come to a full close and that is THE END.

MacNeice took his radio scripts seriously and, in his Introductory Note to *The Dark Tower*, defends his use of symbols and his attempt to revivify the legend of the Quest:

Man does after all live by symbols . . . I have my beliefs and they permeate *The Dark Tower*. But do not ask me what Ism it illustrates or what Solution it offers.

The trouble is that the symbols lack the power to arouse much interest or to command imaginative assent. One can only agree with W. H. Auden's observation that a good libretto is likely to survive even the best radio script, and regret that MacNeice never collaborated with Britten, Walton or some other gifted composer in the writing of an opera. His radio scripts may be revived from time to time, but their probable fate is to lie neglected in the B.B.C. archives or, at best, to achieve the status of cultural exhibits, like the Masques of the early seventeenth century.

MacNeice produced various programmes of translations from both Classical and modern European poets, and was himself the author of two large-scale translations, *The Agamemnon of Aeschylus* and Goethe's *Faust*. It is a commonplace that all translations date, so it is not astonishing that certain features of MacNeice's version of Aeschylus are stamped with the hall-marks of the 1930's—the anti-militarism, the determination to make the speeches sound colloquial, the deliberate avoidance of the loftily heroic. But MacNeice has very largely succeeded in his difficult task. The characters are both credible human beings and also ritualistic figures of Greek mythology; they remain men and women who are remote from us in speech and thought, but who are no mere resurrected mummies intoning platitudes in wooden verse; the drama is at once a representation of human passions and the working out of a preordained divine pattern. MacNeice unites a contemporary sharpness and directness with a formal dignity that suggests the mode of life in the Ancient World. Although the version must be judged as a whole, two brief passages may serve as an index of his skill, the first being part of a Chorus, the second an extract from a speech by Clytemnestra:

> But the money-changer War, changer of bodies,
> Holding his balance in the battle
> Home from Troy refined by fire
> Sends back to friends the dust
> That is heavy with tears, stowing
> A man's worth of ashes
> In an easily handled jar.
>
> The man who outraged me lies here,
> The darling of each courtesan of Troy,
> And here with him is the prisoner clairvoyante,
> The fortune-teller that he took to bed,
> Who shares his bed as once his bench on shipboard,
> A loyal mistress. Both have their deserts.
> *He* lies so; and she who like a swan
> Sang her last dying lament
> Lies like her lover, and the sight contributes
> An appetizer to my own bed's pleasure.

Aeschylus is notoriously difficult to translate. Walter Headlam's literal prose version of the second passage quoted suggests how hard it is to produce a rendering that shall be faithful to the original and yet sound tolerable in English:

Low lies the injurer of me, his wife, the comfort of Chryseus' daughters before Troy, and with him she, the bond-servant and auguress, the divining—concubine, the trusty—bed-fellow, practised—equally in the matter of ship's benches. But the pair have fared after their deserts: this is *his* condition; while *she*, after carolling swan-like her last dying lamentation, she, the lover of him, lies there; she, the trivial by-morsel to my lawful bed, hath only afforded me the luxury of triumph.

Headlam's version merely helps the reader to construe the Greek original: MacNeice, without departing far from the text of Aeschylus, has given us a passage of acceptable English verse.

In MacNeice's version of Goethe's *Faust* the 12,000 lines of the original are cut to 8,000, yet even so this shortened text is longer than *Paradise Lost*. The sheer size of the undertaking would have daunted most writers, and probably the most praiseworthy aspect of the venture was the dogged persistence which MacNeice brought to his task. He seems not to have regretted the labours it involved: 'It gave me a long and strenuous exercise in the craft of writing and also revealed to me a master who, for all his glaring faults, is a great one.'

He made things even more difficult than they might have been by his decision on a technical matter:

I aimed at a line-for-line translation and also (which was made easier by the kinship of German and English) at a prosody equivalent to or, if possible, identical with Goethe's. Some of my friends regretted that I did not turn the whole thing into blank verse or 'free verse' but in my opinion that would have ruined the sense of it. For the rhymes in Goethe are part of the sense and he uses them again and again to clinch his point.

This recalls the self-imposed penances of another Irish poet, Austin Clarke, who, when asked by Robert Frost what kind of verse he wrote, replied, 'I load myself with chains and try to get out of them.'

MacNeice's fidelity to the original German leads at times to a grotesque deformation of the English language. At its clumsiest the verse is little better than doggerel, as in this dialogue between Nereus and Thales while they watch spirits fly past in the form of doves:

> *Nereus* Already over, they pass over
> In oscillation and gyration;
> What reck they of my consternation?
> Ah could they take me with them yonder!
> And yet one single glimpse can cheer
> And last me for another year.
>   *Thales* Hail! Once more hail!
> How I bloom and regale
> On beauties' and truths' penetration!

Everything live is water's creation!
Water keeps all things young and vernal!
Ocean grant us thy rule eternal.
Clouds—were it not for thee sending them,
Nor fertile brooks—expending them,
Rivers—hither and thither bending them,
And streams—not fully tending them,
Then what would be mountains, what plains and earth?
'Tis thou giv'st livingest life its birth.

This is, admittedly, one of the feeblest passages in the translation, but only on rare occasions does it rise above a pedestrian dullness. One successful portion is Gretchen's song at the spinning wheel:

> My peace is gone,
> My heart is sore,
> I shall find it never
> And never more.
>
> He has left my room
> An empty tomb,
> He has gone and all
> My world is gall.
>
> My poor head
> Is all astray,
> My poor mind
> Fallen away.

This reads like an original lyric, not like the rendering of a foreign text into operatic English. The bulk of MacNeice's version resembles an ambitious but cumbersome libretto which might be tolerable were it set to music by a composer of genius.

It may be that Goethe is untranslateable into English and that MacNeice's venture was foredoomed to fail. One regrets that he did not devote his energies to the translation of Horace, Catullus, Tibullus, Propertius and Petronius Arbiter: the version of Horace, *Odes*, I, 4 which he wrote in the mid-1930's demonstrates his brilliance and sureness of touch when translating a congenial poet. He evokes with the utmost delicacy the coming of spring sketched so vividly and economically by Horace:

> Winter to Spring: the west wind melts the frozen rancour,
>   The windlass drags to sea the thirsty hull;
> Byre is no longer welcome to beast or fire to ploughman,
>   The field removes the frost-cap from his skull.

And he manages to endow the weighty Horatian common-places about the coming of death and the transitoriness of worldly pleasure with a resonance and an evocative melancholy that somehow combine the plangency of modern Romantic verse with the clarity and grave precision of classical antiquity:

> Equally heavy is the heel of white-faced Death on the pauper's
>   Shack and the towers of kings, and O my dear
> The little sum of life forbids the revelling of lengthy
>   Hopes. Night and the fabled dead are near

> And the narrow house of nothing past whose lintel
>   You will meet no wine like this, no boy to admire
> Like Lycidas who today makes all young men a furnace
>   And whom tomorrow girls will find a fire.

III. THE EARLY POETRY

There are some poets whose work seems to alter radically at various times throughout their careers, and others whose development, though steady, is so gradual that the superficial reader is scarcely aware of it. MacNeice belongs to this second class; he is, moreover, a poet whose temperament and attitude towards the world do not fundamentally change as he grows older. He constantly recurs to scenes, images and fears remembered from his childhood; at different stages of his life he writes poems that are variations on one or two basic themes; he persistently celebrates the same human virtues and qualities. Even his characteristic modes of expression do not undergo a dramatic transformation. His technique in many ways becomes more assured, his experiments grow bolder, his range widens, but the curve of his achievement is gradual, nor does he re-make himself in the manner of W. B. Yeats. It is, therefore, advisable to consider the forces which, in his youth, formed his poetic nature, and to examine the background of poetry in the 1930's, the decade in which he began to gain a reputation.

We have seen that his childhood was in some respects unhappy, and that it was of the kind to stimulate his imagination, but it would be a mistake to overemphasize these early experiences. MacNeice himself, in *Modern Poetry*, gives due weight to other causes when drawing up a list of factors that influenced his poetry:

... having been brought up in the north of Ireland, having a father who was a clergyman; the fact that my mother died when I was little; repression from the age of six to nine; inferiority complex on grounds of physique and class-consciousness; lack of a social life until I was grown up; late puberty; ignorance of music (which could have been a substitute for poetry); inability to ride horses or practise successfully most of the sports which satisfy a sense of rhythm; an adolescent liking for the role of 'enfant terrible'; shyness in the company of young women until I was twenty; a liking (now dead) for metaphysics; marriage and divorce; Birmingham; an indolent pleasure in gardens and wild landscapes ... a liking for animals, an interest in dress.

MacNeice became well known as one of the leading 'Poets of the Thirties', a term often applied to certain poets of the time who were popularly supposed to form a movement, the most prominent figures reputedly being Auden, Day Lewis, Spender and MacNeice. It is not easy to disentangle the truth from the legend, but certain facts are well established. There was no school or group, in the continental sense, no working-out of a coherent aesthetic doctrine, no manifesto, no organized campaign. Indeed there is no record of all four poets' meeting together in the same room during the entire decade. Undoubtedly the members of this alleged cabal were not averse to the publicity which they received, and they did what they could to boost one another's reputation. But MacSpaunday, the name bestowed by Roy Campbell on his archetypal Left-wing poet, was a misnomer.

It is true that MacNeice was a friend and collaborator of W. H. Auden, that he regarded the ruling classes in Britain as ineffectual and contemptible, that he viewed the rise of Nazism with horror and disgust. Yet he was far from being an orthodox Left-wing poet, or even a writer whose poetry had an overt social purpose. It is significant that Michael Roberts omitted him from his two influential anthologies, *New Signatures* (1932) and *New Country* (1933), both of which were designed to hasten the birth of a new social order and the advent of a new Lenin (ambitions later disavowed by Roberts).

MacNeice, by temperament and by conviction, was always hostile to Communism. He was, in politics as in religion, a sceptic who mistrusted lofty idealism and self-righteousness, in no matter what disguise they draped themselves. Nor did he trust any creed which exalted a bureaucratic hierarchy, whether of priests or of politicians, at the expense of the individual. In such poems as 'Turf Stacks', 'To a Communist' and 'The Individualist Speaks', MacNeice explicity dissociates himself from those who proclaim the millennium:

—But I will escape, with my dog, on the far side of the Fair.

Moreover, although he remained all his life a radical, a satirical observer of the established order, and a mocker of shams and pomposities, he was too honest to deny that he enjoyed the pleasures and shared many of the values of upper-middle-class life:

My sympathies are Left. On paper and in the soul. But not in my heart or my guts . . . . With my heart and my guts I lament the passing of class. Of class, property and snobbery. A man for me is still largely characterised by what he buys—by his suits, his books, the meals he gives you, his chair-covers.

Finally, even in the mid-1930s', when it was fashionable
for public-school boys to proclaim their adherence to
Communism, MacNeice recognised the equivocal nature
of many such conversions:

> So many left-wing comrades, at least in England, suffer from the
> masochism of the puritan . . . . A future of Esperanto, Sunday School
> treats and homage to the Highest Common Factor. Not that this was
> Lenin's ideal.

> Comradeship is the communist substitute for bourgeois romance; in
> its extreme form (cp. also fascism and youth-cults in general) it leads
> to an idealisation of homosexuality.

Writing in 1957, MacNeice remarked that even in the
early work of Auden, Day Lewis and Spender, a large
proportion of the poems cannot be properly described as
'social' or 'political'. This is still more true of his own early
verse. He called his youthful volume, published in 1929,
Blind Fireworks, because the poems in it 'are artificial and
yet random; because they go quickly through their antics
against an important background'. MacNeice came to
judge his own *juvenilia* pretty harshly; the best description
of his verse in the late 1920's and early 1930's is to be found
in Geoffrey Grigson's *Poetry of the Present* (1949):

> Compared with Auden . . . all of MacNeice's fireworks and icicles
> were alien. Ixion, Pythagoras, Persephone, Orestes, de Sade, Origen—
> were mixed up in poems of a blatant cleverness. Still, cleverness it was,
> words were courted; and there in these juvenilia were stretched to
> tautness criss-crossing wires of form with this spangled acrobat perform-
> ing on them; and the cleverness . . . grew and strengthened itself into
> a capable and convincing rhetoric, beholden to much, yet chiefly to
> MacNeice himself. The wires were still silvery and still glittered. The
> icicles, the ice-cream, the pink and white, the lace and the froth and the
> fireworks were still there, but underneath the game was the drop, the
> space, and the knowledge.

What one notices above all in these poems is MacNeice's
responsiveness to the brilliance, the glitter, of the visible
world:

In that Poussin the clouds are like golden tea,
And underneath the limbs flow rhythmically,
The cupids' blue feathers beat musically.

('Poussin')

The yokels tilt their pewters and the foam
Flowers in the sun beside the jewelled water.
Daughter of the South, call the sunbeams home
To nest between your breasts.

('Mayfly')

And the street fountain blown across the square
Rainbow-trellises the air and sunlight blazons
The red butcher's and scrolls of fish on marble slabs.

('Morning Sun')

'Leaving Barra' is both a philosophical poem and a declaration of love, yet when one has forgotten the argument, and the avowal has faded from one's mind, a single image, characteristic of MacNeice, lingers in the memory—'the dazzle on the sea, my darling'.

Nevertheless, MacNeice was unable to enjoy unquestioningly the sensuous world, or to believe that the mere recording of phenomena was adequate. He had, as we have seen, rejected while still at Oxford the metaphysical assumptions of Plato, and he continued to assert the irreducible diversity of things:

World is crazier and more of it than we think,
Incorrigibly plural. I peel and portion
A tangerine and spit the pips and feel
The drunkenness of things being various.

('Snow')

He distrusted all neat philosophical systems, all 'the nostrums Of science art and religion'; he had abandoned his father's Christian beliefs; he regarded the world of scholarship and of museums as an attractive but slightly disreputable escape from reality:

Museums offer us, running from among the buses,
A centrally heated refuge, parquet floors and sarcophaguses.

Yet, despite his frequently expressed desire to live in the present, his resolve to cease constructing moral or philosophical codes, his longing to throw off the burden of introspection—'I do not want to be reflective any more'—he was never able to abdicate from the responsibility of being a rational, moral creature. He remained all his life his father's son, often indeed weakening the impact of his poems by his tendency to preach a lay sermon, to expound the necessity of decency, courage, endurance.

Thus in a series of long poems, written between 1933 and 1937, MacNeice wrestles, like a stern Victorian agnostic, with a host of moral and political problems. 'The Hebrides' is less an impressionistic picture of a beauty-spot than a celebration of human dignity; and his four Eclogues are also musings on the condition of man. The closing lines of 'An Eclogue for Christmas' sum up what was to be a life-long preoccupation with the relationship between flux and permanence, the allure of transient phenomena, the possibility of a permanent, divine order:

A. Let the saxophones and the xylophones
And the cult of every technical excellence, the miles of canvas in the
        galleries
And the canvas of the rich man's yacht snapping and tacking on the seas
And the perfection of a grilled steak—
B. Let all these so ephemeral things
Be somehow permanent like the swallow's tangent wings:
Goodbye to you, this day remember is Christmas, this morn
They say, interpret it your own way, Christ is born.

Twenty years later, in *Autumn Sequel*, he was to make the same half-questioning affirmation.

The tension in these early poems springs from MacNeice's intuitive response to physical stimuli, and his simultaneous awareness of the need for reflection and moral judgement. He was also profoundly moved by the political events of the time, and watched with a sickening helplessness the senile inability of the Western democracies to preserve the

liberties of Europe, or even to understand the nature of the
threat to themselves. His 'Postcript to Iceland: For W. H.
Auden' expresses his personal loneliness and his sense that
human liberty and decency are imperilled throughout the
world:

> For the litany of doubt
> From these walls comes breathing out
> Till the room becomes a pit
> Humming with the fear of it
>
> With the fear of loneliness
> And uncommunicableness;
> All the wires are cut, my friends
> Live beyond the severed ends.
>
> So I write these lines for you
> Who have felt the death-wish too,
> But your lust for life prevails—
> Drinking coffee, telling tales.
>
> Our prerogatives as men
> Will be cancelled who knows when;
> Still I drink your health before
> The gun-butt raps upon the door.

All the themes which run through these early poems
recur in *Autumn Journal*, published in the spring of 1939.
Written in irregular metre, and in a flexible rhyme-scheme,
the poem is capacious enough to accommodate a mixed
assortment of descriptive passages, autobiographical reflections, political rhetoric, memories of a broken marriage,
social satire, potted history, philosophical argument and
random jottings about a variety of topics. It still remains a
delightfully readable, though uneven poem, and the most
intelligent record of what it was like to be young, sceptical,
radical and pleasure-loving in England just before the
Second World War. It contains one or two passages of
memorable virtuosity, notably Section IX, an evocation
of Ancient Greece and an ironical commentary on the way

in which pedants distort the truth about that savage, vital
civilization:

> So the humanist in his room with Jacobean panels
>   Chewing his pipe and looking on a lazy quad
> Chops the Ancient World to turn a sermon
>   To the greater glory of God.
> But I can do nothing so useful or so simple;
>   These dead are dead
> And when I should remember the paragons of Hellas
>   I think instead
> Of the crooks, the adventurers, the opportunists,
>   The careless athletes and the fancy boys,
> The hair-splitters, the pedants, the hard-boiled sceptics
>   And the Agora and the noise
> Of the demagogues and the quacks; and the women pouring
>   Libations over graves
> And the trimmers at Delphi and the dummies at Sparta and lastly
>   I think of the slaves.
> And how one can imagine oneself among them
>   I do not know;
> It was all so unimaginably different
>   And all so long ago.

Two of MacNeice's poems written in the 1930's have
become popular anthology pieces. Surrealism had little
influence on English poetry, and the only good English
poet to take seriously this fashionable Continental theory was
David Gascoyne. But just as the Marx Brothers employed
modified surrealistic devices in their films, so MacNeice,
contemplating the crazy fabric of capitalist Britain, gave
vent to his despair and disgust in the high-spirited fantasy
of 'Bagpipe Music':

> It's no go the Yogi-Man, it's no go Blavatsky,
> All we want is a bank balance and a bit of skirt in a taxi . . .
>
> Willie Murray cut his thumb, couldn't count the damage,
> Took the hide of an Ayrshire cow and used it for a bandage.
> His brother caught three hundred cran when the seas were lavish,
> Threw the bleeders back in the sea and went upon the parish . . .

It's no go the picture palace, it's no go the stadium,
It's no go the country cot with a pot of pink geraniums,
It's no go the Government grants, it's no go the elections,
Sit on your arse for fifty years and hang your hat on a pension.

In 'The Sunlight on the Garden', MacNeice shapes his
private fears, his sense of coming doom, his delight in the
pleasures of the moment into a lyric which, beneath the
surface elegance, has a disturbing power:

> The sunlight on the garden
> Hardens and grows cold,
> We cannot cage the minute
> Within its nets of gold,
> When all is told
> We cannot beg for pardon.
>
> Our freedom as free lances
> Advances towards its end;
> The earth compels, upon it
> Sonnets and birds descend;
> And soon, my friend,
> We shall have no time for dances.
>
> The sky was good for flying
> Defying the church bells
> And every evil iron
> Siren and what it tells:
> The earth compels,
> We are dying, Egypt, dying
>
> And not expecting pardon,
> Hardened in heart anew,
> But glad to have sat under
> Thunder and rain with you,
> And grateful too
> For sunlight on the garden.

Many of MacNeice's typical images and themes are here:
the sinister ringing of church bells; the noise of sirens,
which may be a reference to air-raid warnings, but almost
certainly is a reminiscence of the foghorns calling from

Belfast Lough; the premonition of political disaster; the savouring of transitory happiness, all the sweeter because it passes so quickly. The ingenuity of the rhyming scheme, the verbal dexterity, the rhythmical assurance, even the allusion to *Antony and Cleopatra*, all play their part in making this poem a memorable expression of MacNeice's complex, ironic view of himself and of the world in the shadow of approaching war.

IV. THE WAR YEARS AND THE LATE FORTIES

The coming of war provided MacNeice with a new range of experiences and deeply affected his emotional development. Although his verse undergoes no spectacular change, it gradually alters its character in a variety of ways, becoming less impressionistic and glittering. MacNeice seems now to be more concerned with the congruence of the images in a poem than with their individual brilliance; in the dedicatory lines 'To Hedli' he says that he has modified the tone and the texture of his verse

> Because the velvet image,
> Because the lilting measure
> No more convey my meaning.

In an article published in 1949, entitled 'Experiences with Images', he attempts to analyse his new method of employing images, and the reasons for the changes in his technique. He explains that he sometimes uses 'a set of basic images which crossfade into each other', and that he has experimented with a 'quasi-musical interlinking of images, with variations on contrasted themes'. He has come to value economy and precision of language, and has a particular fondness for the phrase that concentrates a variety of meanings into a narrow compass:

Thus the lines that I am especially proud of in my last book are such lines as these (of the aftermath of war in England):

> The joker that could have been at any moment death
> Has been withdrawn, the cards are what they say
> And none is wild . . .

or (of a tart):

> Mascara scrawls a gloss on a torn leaf

(a line which it took me a long time to find).

The mood of the poems grows more reflective and sombre, the wit is darker and harsher:

> After the legshows and the brandies
> And all the pick-me-ups for tired
> Men there is a feeling
> Something more is required.
>
> The lights go down and eyes
> Look up across the room;
> Salome comes in, bearing
> The head of God knows whom.
>
> ('Night Club')

In many of the poems MacNeice is haunted by Christian symbols, by the ghost of that Christian morality which he has rejected but not exorcised. The very titles of certain poems—'Didymus' (used for two poems), 'Prayer Before Birth', 'Prayer in Mid-Passage', 'Place of a Skull', 'Whit Monday', 'Carol'—suggest the cast of his mind. Like Clough, a century before, he seems hurt and self-reproachful at his inability to accept the Christian faith. In 'The Springboard', the protagonist stands

> High above London, naked in the night
> Perched on a board.

He is kept there, 'crucified among the budding stars', by his unbelief:

> And yet we know he knows what he must do.
> There above London where the gargoyles grin
> He will dive like a bomber past the broken steeple,
> One man wiping out his own original sin
> And, like ten million others, dying for the people.

The fire-raids on London must have seemed like the
fulfilment of his prophecy in *Out of the Picture*. MacNeice
senses in the scenes of destruction the operation of a principle
that is hostile to human life. In 'Brother Fire', contemplating
the ravages of war, he draws a comfortless moral:

> Thus were we weaned to knowledge of the Will
> That wills the natural world but wills us dead

—an image which recurs in 'Schizophrene', when the child,
hearing an 'ominous relentless noise', recognizes that

> It means a Will that wills all children dead.

Characteristically, the child is terrified by church bells and,
when she hears the cock crow, identifies herself with St.
Peter, for whose denial she wishes to atone:

> But the grey cock still crows and she knows why;
> For she must still deny, deny, deny.

It would be wrong to suppose that all the poems of these
years are obsessed by guilt, forebodings, and despair. There
are poems celebrating the momentary peace which love
may bring when 'Time was away and she was here', or
which may come as an unlooked-for revelation:

> Waking, he found himself in a train, andante,
> With wafers of early sunlight blessing the unknown fields.

'The National Gallery' hymns the 'pentecost in Trafalgar
Square' brought about by the reopening of the Gallery after
the war; in 'Woods', MacNeice depicts his affection for the
gentle English countryside; even in ironical surveys of
human passions and flaws, such 'as Alcohol', 'The Libertine',
'Epitaph for Liberal Poets' and 'Elegy for Minor Poets',

a stoical gaiety and a wry resignation counterbalance the bitterness and the pain. Yet the finest poem of this period is 'Prayer Before Birth', an anguished protest against the impersonal cruelty of the world. For once MacNeice does not take refuge in evasive irony or allusiveness, but speaks out directly against everything that degrades the spirit of man:

> I am not yet born; O hear me,
> Let not the man who is beast or who thinks he is God
>   come near me.
>
> I am not yet born; O fill me
> With strength against those who would freeze my
>   humanity, would dragoon me into a lethal automaton,
>   would make me a cog in a machine, a thing with
>   one face, a thing, and against all those
>   who would dissipate my entirety, would
>   blow me like thistledown hither and
>   thither or hither and thither
>   like water held in the
>   hands would spill me.
>
> Let them not make me a stone and let them not spill me.
> Otherwise kill me.

V. THE MIDDLE STRETCH

MacNeice was always attracted by what he calls 'This whole delightful world of cliché and refrain', and his poems sometimes rely too heavily on his verbal ingenuity, his gift of the poetic gab. Instead of true originality and genuine distinction of language, we are often fobbed off with paradoxes in the style of Oscar Wilde, tags and proverbs slightly twisted, inverted truisms, distorted clichés, ironical borrowings from jazz lyrics, sophisticated parodies of nursery rhymes. Moreover, especially in the longer poems, the moralising tends to become obtrusive, the prevalence of wise saws and modern instances is fatiguing, the sententiousness grows wearisome. MacNeice's vision of the world is civilized and humane, but after reading 'The Kingdom' one is inclined to feel that decency, like patriotism, is not enough. The two worst flaws in his verse, elaborate verbalism and agnostic sermonising, are largely concealed by the vividness and sparkle of his early poems; yet an admirer of his poetry, scrutinising the later work in *Collected Poems 1925-1948*, might well have had doubts about MacNeice's poetic development.

In fact, his verse from about 1949 until the mid-1950's went through a very sticky patch. Even if we were fully acquainted with MacNeice's private life it would be idle to explain this apparent decline in his poetry by reference to his biography. Most artists experience periods of barrenness, akin perhaps to those spells of dryness which are familiar to mystics. The periods sometimes coincide with the onset of middle age; MacNeice himself seems to have been aware that the physiology of a poet is inextricably linked with the development of his art:

> This middle stretch
> Of life is bad for poets; a sombre view
> Where neither works nor days look innocent
> And both seem now too many, now too few.

It is possible that the strain of translating *Faust* left MacNeice temporarily exhausted, and that he was unhappily inspired to emulate Goethe by writing long philosophical poems instead of the short lyrics to which his talents were best suited. Whatever the explanation may be, his first two volumes of original verse after the *Collected Poems* were *Ten Burnt Offerings*, a series of medium-length poems, and *Autumn Sequel*, 'a rhetorical poem' in twenty-six cantos.

The poems in *Ten Burnt Offerings* are, according to MacNeice, 'experiments in dialectical structure'. Despite the interest of their themes, their shrewdness of psychological observation and their skilled craftsmanship, they seldom quicken into poetic vitality: it is disquieting that the liveliest passage in the entire volume is a pastiche—the soliloquy of Lord Byron in Lowland Scots, which begins: 'Bards wha hae for Hellas bled.'

Autumn Sequel, like the translation of *Faust* and *Ten Burnt Offerings*, was broadcast before publication on the Third Programme. It may be unfair to blame its faults on its origin, for it was not commissioned by the B.B.C. although, as G. S. Fraser has remarked, the decision to broadcast it can scarcely have taken MacNeice unawares. Described by its author as an attempt to marry myth to 'actuality', it portrays various friends of the poet, living and dead, including Dylan Thomas, canonized as Gwilym the Maker and depicted according to the conventions of hagiography.

Ezra Pound has drawn superb sketches of his friends and enemies in *The Cantos*, his *vignettes* recapturing their exact lineaments. W. B. Yeats has transformed his contemporaries into heroic myths, forms more real than living men. The figures in *Autumn Sequel* seem to be neither human beings, idiosyncratic and minutely observed, nor successful mythical creations. As for the Parrot, symbol of flux and of negation, the Mountain which has to be climbed because it is there, the Garden and the Quest—these are familiar properties, now grown tatty, from MacNeice's theatrical storehouse.

The metre and the rhyming scheme of the pre-war *Autumn Journal* are admirably suited to the nature of the material with which MacNeice is dealing. The *terza rima* of *Autumn Sequel*, though it lends a semblence of unity to the poem, becomes, long before the last canto, monotonous and wearisome: it is a metre which, though well adapted to produce an effect of weight, conciseness and intensity, does not lend itself to the diffuse, rambling development of loosely associated themes characteristic of *Autumn Sequel*. The poem seldom falls below or rises above a decent competence; it is most satisfying when MacNeice is meditating on his favourite problems or even restating old conclusions, as at the close of Canto XXV, which takes us back to 'An Eclogue for Christmas':

> Meanwhile the Plough
> Ploughs its own stars in deeper while the pails

> Ring with the new day's milk and one still patient cow
> Still stares beyond to where the skies are warning
> That a new sun is rising and that now,

> Take it what way you like, is really Christmas morning.

VI. THE FINAL PHASE

In the mid-1950's there were many who regarded Mac-
Neice as played out, just as the wits of Dublin and the
critical wiseacres had frequently proclaimed between 1900
and 1920 that Yeats was finished. We do not know why a
poet's work declines or why, for some poets, there may be
a renewal of talent after a period of silence or of desiccation.
In his last three volumes, *Visitations* (1957), *Solstices* (1961)
and *The Burning Perch* (1963), MacNeice not only recaptures
his old vitality but also taps more profound sources of
imaginative power than at any time in his career. The poems
of this period are less widely known than those written in
the 1930's, partly because they have not yet found their way
into the anthologies, partly because he was now a somewhat
lonely man in his fifties and no longer a leading member
of a fashionable group. It seems likely, however, that the
work of this last phase will become increasingly admired
as time passes.

MacNeice tells us that he was incapable of writing short
poems while engaged in composing *Ten Burnt Offerings*
and *Autumn Sequel*, and that

when the lyrical impulse did return, this interval of abstention, it
seems to me, had caused certain changes in my lyric-writing . . . I like
to think that my latest short poems are on the whole more concentrated
and better organised than my earlier ones, relying more on syntax and
bony feature than on bloom or frill or the floating image. I should also
like to think that sometimes they achieve a blend of 'classical' and
'romantic', marrying the element of wit to the sensuous-mystical
element.

The poems in *Visitations* were the prelude to another flowering of the lyrical impulse in 1959 and 1960:

In particular, in the spring and early summer of 1960 I underwent one of those rare bursts of creativity when the poet is first astonished and then rather alarmed by the way the mill goes on grinding.

There was a final spurt of imaginative energy in the three years before his death, which resulted in *The Burning Perch*, a posthumous collection of poems.

In these last volumes there is no startling development, no break-through into entirely new territory. Some of the old faults crop up again: the mechanical sprightliness of

> Here come I, old April Fool,
> Between March hare and nuts in May;

the jazzing up of a nursery rhyme—'This is the house that Jack built'—in 'Château Jackson'; a sophisticated juggling with words and concepts which came all too easily to MacNeice. Many of his standard themes recur. There are poems about the British Museum and about childhood, reminiscences of the fire-raids on London, and satirical reflections upon contemporary society in general and metropolitan life in particular. In one of the final poems, 'Memoranda to Horace', he reverts to the image of a mayfly that had attracted him over thirty years before. One section of 'Notes for a Biography' is a virtuoso parody of 'Bonny Dundee', which recalls the episode in *I Crossed the Minch* when MacNeice 'began to sing various scurrilous songs, improvising words to "Bonny Dundee"'.

But although much of this terrain is familiar, MacNeice is exploring it in greater depth than ever before. In 'Beni Hasan' he contemplates himself and his mortality with a fine gravity:

> It came to me on the Nile my passport lied
> Calling me dark who am grey. In the brown cliff
> A row of tombs, of portholes, stared and stared as if
> They were the long dead eyes of beasts inside

> Time's cage, black eyes on eyes that stared away
> Lion-like focused on some different day
> On which, on a long term view, it was I, not they, had died.

The old religious preoccupations are now faced with a quiet dignity, a reverence for

> Poor Tom o'Bethlehem, only a Mary,
> An ox and an ass, a nought and a cross,

and an acceptance of agnosticism that has shed the angry unease of the 1930's:

> Thank God we do not know, we know
> We need the unknown. The unknown is there.

He displays a new awareness of his own nature and, in a harsh, astringent poem, 'The Habits', acknowledges his life-long temptation to surrender to those anodynes which may save us from having to bear the pain of reality. He can review his spiritual life as far back as the age of seven, when he was haunted by fears of damnation, and face the truth of what he has become:

> He was not Tom or Dick or Harry,
> Let alone God, he was merely fifty,
> No one and nowhere else, a walking
> Question but no more cheap than any
> Question or quest is cheap. The sin
> Against the Holy Ghost—What is it?

>   ('The Blasphemies')

In the last two volumes there are many poems about bad dreams, nightmarish journeys and scenes where everything is in flux or the wrong way round. When he assembled the poems in *The Burning Perch*, MacNeice was 'taken aback by the high proportion of sombre pieces, ranging from bleak observation to thumbnail nightmares'. There are, it is true, poems which seem to attain an Horatian resignation:

But my resignation, as I was not brought up a pagan, is more of a fraud than Horace's.

Perhaps the most original achievements in these final volumes are those poems in *The Burning Perch* that convey a sense of desolation, of something gone awry, as though one were walking down a staircase where a step is missing, or had entered a room where everything is in order except for some terrifying absence or reversal of normality. These poems crackle with an eerie vitality, and are shaken by the kind of savage mirth that informs some of Bartok's later music. A few lines from three of these poems may suggest the nature of the spirit which animates them:

> They were introduced in a grave glade
> And she frightened him because she was young
> And thus too late. Crawly crawly
> Went the twigs above their heads . . .
> > Crawly crawly
> Went the string quartet that was tuning up
> In the back of the mind. You two should have met
> Long since, he said, or else not now.
> The string quartet in the back of the mind
> Was all tuned up with nowhere to go.
> They were introduced in a green grave.
> > ('The Introduction')

> In the third taxi he was alone tra-la
> But the tip-up seats were down and there was an extra
> Charge of one-and-sixpence and an odd
> Scent that reminded him of a trip to Cannes.

> As for the fourth taxi, he was alone
> Tra-la when he hailed it but the cabby looked
> Through him and said: 'I can't tra-la well take
> So many people, not to speak of the dog.'
> > ('The Taxis')

> When he came to he knew
> Time must have passed because
> The asphalt was high with hemlock
> Through which he crawled to his crash
> Helmet and found it no more
> Than his wrinkled hand what it was.

Yet life seemed still going on:
He could hear the signals bounce
Back from the moon and the hens
Fire themselves black in the batteries
And the silence of small blind cats
Debating whether to pounce.

('After the Crash')

There is no reason to suppose that MacNeice had any premonition of his death; but it is appropriate that in one of his last poems, 'Charon', he should have described a spectral encounter on the banks of the Thames:

And there was the ferryman just as Virgil
And Dante had seen him. He looked at us coldly
And his eyes were dead and his hands on the oar
Were black with obols and varicose veins
Marbled his calves and he said to us coldly:
If you want to die you will have to pay for it.

VII.   CONCLUSION

MacNeice was an unusually complex individual, whose character was made up of contradictory elements. He was abundantly sociable, yet fundamentally shy, a man in whom Irish high spirits were blended with Celtic melancholy, an extrovert who talked volubly, while retaining an inner reserve and reticence about his griefs and fears. He described himself in youth as one 'whose chief pleasures in life are liking and being liked' and, after remarking that animals are limited because they are specialized, went on:

I shouldn't think it worth it to become even an over-specialized human-being—someone who was only a cricketer, a politician, a storm-trooper, a spritu.list medium, a pianist or a world-authority on any one square inch of subject.

This is why it is pointless to wag a reproving finger at MacNeice for devoting too much of his time to drinking and gossiping with his cronies, and why his faults and virtues, as man and poet, are inseparable. He was, above all, a generous man, who encouraged and helped not only young, up-and-coming writers but those who were elderly and in decline. In 1940 Wyndham Lewis, the old friend and coeval of T. S. Eliot, Ezra Pound and James Joyce, was living in New York, poor and in distress. It was typical of MacNeice that he should have given financial aid to this distinguished writer of an older generation, whose political views and temperament he could scarcely have found congenial.

MacNeice was always keenly responsive to the delights of the world, including those of sexual love. In a fragment of autobiography, written two or three years before his death, he thanked God for the pleasures of life, not forgetting those offered by the Garden of Adonis; and his love poetry is that of a man who has plunged into the turmoil of passion, gladly accepting its joys and its griefs.

During the course of his memorial address, W. H. Auden referred to MacNeice's enjoyment of

those temporal pleasures which he can no longer share with us, his pleasure in language, in country landscapes, in city streets and parks, in birds, beasts and flowers, in nice clothes, good conversation, good food, good drink, and in what he called 'the tangles'.

To which one might add his pleasure in playing and watching games; he frankly admitted that at times he derived more satisfaction from them than from works of art:

> Is it absurd
> To have preferred at times a sport to works of art?
> Where both show craft, at times I have preferred
>
> The greater measure of chance, that thrill which sports impart
> Because they are not foregone, move in more fluid borders.
> Statues and even plays are finished before they start,
>
> But in a game, as in life, we are under Starter's Orders.

Few poets have managed to make poetry out of the enjoyment which they have distilled from the minor pleasures of life. A short list of such poets would include Shakespeare, pre-eminent in this as in so much else, Ben Jonson, Herrick, Burns, Byron, Tennyson and Browning. MacNeice belongs to the select company of those who are able to communicate their delight in the minutiae of daily life, the sense of happiness and well-being that springs from good health, mental alertness and emotional vitality.

During his lifetime MacNeice's poetic reputation had its ups and downs. Even in the 1930's, when he was enthusi-astically praised by many readers of his generation, he was assailed by conservative critics, who denounced him as an angry young iconoclast, and was also viewed with disfavour by the censorious judges on the bench of *Scrutiny*. *The Times Literary Supplement*, reviewing in 1949 his *Collected Poems 1925-1948*, weighed him in the balance and found him wanting, a verdict generally endorsed by critical opinion in the late 1940's and early 1950's. It was not until the last few years of his life that he began once again to command widespread admiration and respect.

In a comment on the obituary notice printed in *The Times*, T. S. Eliot wrote that MacNeice 'had the Irishman's unfailing ear for the music of verse', and spoke of 'the grief one must feel at the death of a poet of genius younger than oneself'. Whatever MacNeice's rank in our literature may be, he deserves to be honoured as a man of letters who practised his craft with devotion, as a pioneer of radio drama, and as a poet whose sardonic gaiety, brooding sadness and integrity of mind are reflected in the few dozen lyrics that are his surest title to remembrance.

LOUIS MACNEICE

A Select Bibliography

(Place of publication London, unless stated otherwise)

Collected Works:

COLLECTED POEMS 1925-1948 (1949)
—the definitive edition of his *Collected Poems* is likely to appear in 1966 or 1967.

Selected Works:

SELECTED POEMS (1940)
EIGHTY-FIVE POEMS (1959)
—selected by MacNeice.
SELECTED POEMS, ed. W. H. Auden (1964)
—a paperback edition, with a brief critical introduction.

Separate Works:

BLIND FIREWORKS (1929). *Verse*
ROUNDABOUT WAY (1932). *Novel*
—written under the pseudonym Louis Malone.
POEMS (1935).
THE AGAMEMNON OF AESCHYLUS (1936). *Verse Translation*
LETTERS FROM ICELAND (1937). *Verse and Prose*
—with W. H. Auden.
OUT OF THE PICTURE (1937). *Verse Drama*
THE EARTH COMPELS (1938). *Verse*
I CROSSED THE MINCH (1938). *Verse and Prose*
—an account of travel in the Outer Hebrides.
MODERN POETRY: A PERSONAL ESSAY (1938). *Criticism*
ZOO (1938). *Prose*
—an account of the London Zoo, with autobiographical digressions.
AUTUMN JOURNAL (1939). *Verse*
—*cf. Autumn Sequel*, 1954.
THE LAST DITCH. Dublin (1940). *Verse*
PLANT AND PHANTOM (1941). *Verse*
THE POETRY OF W. B. YEATS (1941). *Criticism*
—a paperback edition will be published shortly.

MEET THE U.S. ARMY (1943). *Prose*
—prepared for the Board of Education by the Ministry of Information.

SPRINGBOARD (1944). *Verse*

CHRISTOPHER COLUMBUS: A RADIO PLAY (1944). *Verse*
—with an introductory essay on radio drama. New edition, 1963, with a fresh introduction.

THE DARK TOWER AND OTHER RADIO SCRIPTS (1947). *Verse and Prose*
—with an introductory essay on radio drama. The 1964 paperback edition excludes the additional radio scripts.

HOLES IN THE SKY (1948). *Verse*

GOETHE'S FAUST (1951). *Verse Translation*
—an abridged version.

TEN BURNT OFFERINGS (1952). *Verse*

AUTUMN SEQUEL (1954). *Verse*
—a sequel to *Autumn Journal*, 1939.

THE OTHER WING (1954). *Verse*
—a poem, illustrated by Michael Ayrton.

THE SIXPENCE THAT ROLLED AWAY (1956). *Prose*
—a tale for children, illustrated by Edward Bawden.

VISITATIONS (1957). *Verse*

SOLSTICES (1961). *Verse*

THE BURNING PERCH (1963). *Verse*

THE MAD ISLANDS [and] THE ADMINISTRATOR: TWO RADIO PLAYS (1964). *Prose*
—with an introductory essay on radio drama.

ASTROLOGY (1964). *Prose*
—a lavishly illustrated survey.

THE STRINGS ARE FALSE (1965). *Autobiography*

VARIETIES OF PARABLE (1965). *Criticism*

Note

Louis MacNeice wrote a great many book-reviews, articles, and essays, the most important of which are an article on Poetry in *The Arts To-day*, edited by Geoffrey Grigson, 1935; 'Subject in Modern Poetry', *Essays and Studies*, xxii, 1936; 'Traveller's Return', *Horizon*, iii, 14, 1941; 'Poetry, the Public and the Critic', *New Statesman*, 8 October 1949; 'Experiences with Images', *Orpheus*, ii, 1949; 'Lost Generations?' *London Magazine*, iv, 4, April 1957; 'When I Was Twenty-One',

Saturday Book, 1961; and 'Childhood Memories', the *Listener*, 12 December 1963.

There exist manuscripts and typescripts of various unpublished works, including three prose plays, *Traitors in our Way*, *Eureka*, and *One for the Dead: a Modern Morality Play; Another Part of the Sea: a Play for Television*; and a number of radio scripts.

The most important unpublished lectures and articles of which manuscripts and typescripts survive are 'The Unities in Drama', a lecture dated 29 August 1938; 'Broken Windows or Thinking Aloud', an article, undated (c. 1941-2?); and 'Lyric into Drama', the Judith E. Wilson Lecture given at Cambridge on 5 March 1959.

Much of the information contained in this note has been supplied by Professor E. R. Dodds, Mr. Charles Monteith, and Mr. Anthony Thwaite, to whom thanks are due.

Some Biographical and Critical Studies:

A HOPE FOR POETRY, by C. Day Lewis (1934)
—an account of the achievements and hopes of the 'Poets of the Thirties' by one of them.

SOWING THE SPRING, by J. Southworth. Oxford (1940)
—contains a chapter on MacNeice's early poetry.

AUDEN AND AFTER, by F. Scarfe (1942)
—contains a section on MacNeice's early poetry.

'A Poet of our Time', *The Times Literary Supplement*, 28 October 1949
—a long review of *Collected Poems 1925-1948*, which concludes that 'they show a small talent and a limited achievement, with few signs of possible further development'.

ESSAYS ON CONTEMPORARY ENGLISH POETRY, by A. Thwaite. Tokyo (1957)
—contains a section on MacNeice's poetry.

VISION AND RHETORIC, by G. S. Fraser (1959)
—the essay, 'Evasive Honesty: The Poetry of Louis MacNeice', is a generous and perceptive survey of MacNeice's poetry.

LOUIS MACNEICE, by W. H. Auden (1963)
—a memorial address, privately printed. A moving tribute by one of MacNeice's oldest friends.

'Louis MacNeice and the Line of Least Resistance', by S. Wall, the *Review*, 11-12, 1964.
—a severely critical review of MacNeice's achievement as a poet and a writer for radio.

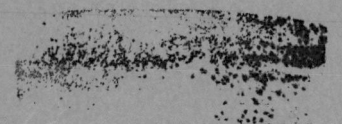